BUSINESS RESEARCH PROJECTS

FOURTH EDITION

Business Research Projects

A. D. Jankowicz, Luton Business School, Luton, UK

SOUTH-WESTERN
CENGAGE Learning

Australia • Brazil • Japan • Korea • Mexico • Singapore • Spain • United Kingdom • United States

SOUTH-WESTERN
CENGAGE Learning

Business Research Projects: Fourth Edition

Publisher: Brendan George
Marketing Manager: Vicky Fielding
Manufacturing Team Lead: Paul Herbert
Editorial Assistant: Jennifer Seth
Production Controller: Eyvett Davis
Typesetter: J&L Composition Ltd, Filey, North Yorkshire

First published in 1991 by Chapman & Hall
Second edition published in 1995 by Chapman & Hall
Third edition published in 2000 by Thomson Learning
Fourth edition published in 2005 by Thomson Learning
Reprinted by Thomson Learning 2006
Reprinted by Thomson Learning 2007

ISBN: 978-1-84480-082-7
British Library Cataloguing-in-Publication Data
A catalogue record for this book is available from the British Library.

Cengage Learning
Cheriton House, North way, Walworth Ind Estate, Andover, Hampshire, SP10 5BE

Cengage Learning is a leading provider of customised learning solutions with office locations around the globe, including Singapore, the United Kingdom, Australia, Mexico, Brazil and Japan. Locate our local office at: **international.cengage.com/region**

Cengage Learning products are represented in Canada by Nelson Education Ltd.

For your lifelong learning solutions, visit
www.cengage.co.uk
Purchase your next print book, e-book or e-chapter at
www.cengagebrain.co.uk

Printed by Zrinski D.D., Croatia
5 6 7 8 9 10 11 – 12 11 10

Contents

Acknowledgements

It is an enormous pleasure to give my first thanks to my students, some of whose stories appear here in the form of instructional vignettes and longer case examples. The details have occasionally been embellished, or simplified, to make the teaching point clearer, but the core of each story is true – it really did happen, once upon a time. In particular, Messrs LinQi Tang, Zhe Liu and Chao Liu gave valuable help with Chinese nomenclature, company details and information on the industrial environment.

Some of the cases required a little research and I am particularly grateful to Ms Kate Pirie of Southern Skies Marketing, a travel marketing company based in Ascot, who helped me with Case Study 4.1; and to Dr Dorota Dobosz-Bourne, whose assistance with materials relating to international knowledge transfer issues was invaluable. Dr Nalita James, late of the British Psychological Society, was a very helpful initial source of bibliographic references relating to e-mail interviewing and e-mail questionnaire work.

Mrs Audrey Stewart, Putteridge Bury Site Librarian at the University of Luton was most helpful with detailed information on information sources and searching and read several drafts of Chapter 7 with enthusiasm and commitment to the improvement of my scholarly judgement. I particularly appreciate her insistence on the value in accessing electronic sources through a library or learning resource centre gateway, rather than seeking them out directly . . . and commend the suggestion to my readers.

Finally, a word of thanks to Ms Geraldine Lyons and Ms Anna Carter, my editors at Thomson Learning, for the care with which they produced this edition and the support they provided as I was learning about the latest developments in textbook production.

With such excellent help, any errors that remain in this book are obviously my own.

Devi Jankowicz
Luton Business School

Thomson Learning would like to thank Gary Akehurst, Julie Haskell, Diana Winstanley and Paula Young for reviewing this book.

A preface and guide

The objective of this book

This book has been written with a single objective in mind: to help you to succeed in the project-based report (sometimes called a 'thesis', or 'dissertation') which you must submit at the end of your management taught course. It focuses on just that one objective. It does not set out to turn you into a professional investigator, an academic, or a business researcher, although those are estimable callings. The only research concepts, principles, and techniques that it provides are the ones you will need to complete your project, on time, and to an acceptable standard.

Its structure

The material has, accordingly, been presented in a very single-minded way. Each chapter consists of:

- basic material (text, tables and figures), with appropriate examples and anecdotes
- links to the supporting *Website*
- case studies, test questions about the cases and feedback notes on your answers
- *Project Guide* material and
- bibliographic references.

Two of these require your special attention.

The project guide

I really mean it about helping you to succeed. But for this to happen, you will need to read this textbook as a working manual and not as a monograph. The Project Guide is a set of instructions, presented chapter by chapter, which you follow in order to progress your research project, and you should aim to work through all of the material presented. You could, if you wished, do some of the exercises and not others, treating this book like any other research methods textbook which offers you worked examples and exercises that teach you the details of some research method or technique. But my aim is different. Rather than teaching you about research methods in principle, I address the actual research topic on which you are working, and guide your work on it, through its various stages, in real time. All of the Project Guide material is designed so that, if you are able to complete every activity I provide, then, by the time you get to the end of this book, your project will be finished, on time, and to the requisite standard. (Actually, you will also have learnt a fair amount about research methods in principle as well but, as I suggest above, that is coincidental!)

The website

This is an integral part of the book. It contains additional examples, further illustrative materials and links to a variety of support resources. Your Organization Behaviour studies will, no doubt, have dealt with the value of feedback in optimizing learning and performance! And so you should make use of *all* of the material on the website, which has a feedback function, to keep track of how well you're progressing.

Using the project guide and the website

Both of these are so important that I have left signposts throughout the text telling you when, and how, you should use them.

Instructions with a star next to them direct you to an exercise in the project guide	

A star with no instructions is a signal that there is related material on the website	

Whenever you see this sign ![star], you know you have to stop reading and do something!

Who the book is aimed at

I don't suppose that this approach will suit everyone; but I certainly hope it suits you. The 'you' I have in mind is really two types of individual. The first is the person without any supervisory or managerial experience. She or he might be an undergraduate, or someone taking their first postgraduate qualification (an MBA or MSC, or perhaps a professional qualification) and, in any event, involved in study on a full-time basis. For want of a better generic, I've used the term 'undergraduate student' to describe you.

The second is the older individual with some supervisory or managerial experience, taking their qualification while still employed, or with close links to employment. She or he may be studying on a part-time basis, by day release, evening study, or through a weekend business school arrangement; or he or she may have taken a year out to pursue an Executive MBA studying full-time. For want of a better word I have described you as a 'post-experience manager'.

The needs of both groups are different, and the kind of business project they do tend to be different. Apart from anything else, the second kind of student almost always does an empirical project in which they collect data of their own, within their own organization; the first kind of student may collect their own data in an organization, but may prefer to do a library-based project, staying mostly within the premises of their university or college.

What it contains

Part 1 (Chapters 1 to 4), is an extended pre-flight checklist. It provides you with guidelines on the reasons for doing project work in the first place and highlights the implications involved. It gives you assistance in choosing a topic and information on the standards to which you'll be expected to work; it handles the practicalities of timetabling and scheduling, the usefulness of writing a proposal document and the minimal equipment that you need for success. These are practical issues – their intellectual content isn't especially deep – yet my experience of 30 years spent in supervising business and management projects suggests that their neglect leads to mediocrity and, all too often, to outright failure. In fact, let that be the first thing you get from this book: a project is not an intellectual assault course, and you don't have to be brilliant to succeed. What you do need is a certain clarity of purpose: an understanding of the fundamentals of your assumptions and approach, as they apply to projects in the business and management field. And that is what I try to provide in Part Two (Chapters 5 to 7). You will find that it pays you to be clear about the nature of research in the first place, so that you can do work which is academically respectable, and, at the same time, practically useful to your organization. Perhaps surprisingly, there are different views of how this can be done, and Chapter 5 is devoted to this issue.

This is partly because the organizational world in which you will be operating is significantly different to the world which the laboratory scientist inhabits. Getting into this world is an issue in the first place, while adopting an appropriate role and becoming attuned to its culture, involve their own issues for you to confront. It's inhabited by people who can hinder you or help you, and how you approach them is critical to success; this is all developed in detail in Chapter 6. Part 2 also provides you with guidelines on scholarship, the importance of which is introduced in Chapter 2 and developed in detail in Chapter 7.

Part 3, (Chapters 8 to 13), deals with the methods and techniques at your disposal. It opens with a consideration of project design, the deliberate arrangement of your data-collection procedures. After considering the distinction between Methods and Techniques and providing some guidelines on which method to adopt (Chapter 9), an account of a number of semi-structured techniques in Chapter 10 is followed by material on the more structured techniques (Chapter 11). Finally,

PART 1 Planning a research project

CHAPTER 1 The purpose and objectives of a project

- The purpose of a project
- The objectives of a project
- The special objectives of professional programmes
- Making the objectives your own

CHAPTER 2 Choosing a topic

- Sourcing ideas
- Basic criteria
- Where do ideas belong? The provenance table
- Specifying research questions
- Starting a project proposal

CHAPTER 3 Standards of assessment

- General guidelines
- The attributes of a successful project
- Assessment criteria
- Format and deadlines
- What the examiner will be looking for

CHAPTER 4 Getting organized for take-off

- Your pre-flight checklist
- Planning and timetabling
- Physical resources

PART 2 Key issues in depth

CHAPTER 5 Basic assumptions about research

- Basic assumptions
- Two ways of making sense to people
- Maintaining credibility

CHAPTER 6 Research roles

- Gaining entry
- Defining your role at home and abroad
- Working under supervision
- Letting go and saying goodbye

CHAPTER 7 Reviewing and using the literature

- Using the literature for review and for referencing
- Literature search: what to look for
- Where to look; how to look
- What to do with it once you have found it: the critical review

PART 3 A guide to empirical work

CHAPTER 8 Planning empirical work

- Planning a design
- Representation and sampling
- The practicalities of design
- In conclusion: timetabling for empirical work

CHAPTER 9 Methods and techniques

- Some definitions
- Choosing and combining methods qualitative and quantitative
- A framework of general guidelines for empirical work
- Your proposal and your pilot study

CHAPTER 10 Semi-structured, open-ended techniques

- Conversations and storytelling
- The individual interview
- The key informant interview
- The focus group
- A note on the validity of what you're doing

CHAPTER 11 Fully structured techniques

- The structured questionnaire
- The structured interview
- Telephone interviews
- Anonymity: procedures and ethics

CHAPTER 12 Further techniques

- The repertory grid
- Attitude scaling
- Observation techniques

CHAPTER 13 Writing it up

- Basic requirements: timing and deadlines
- Format and structure
- The use of language
- On non-discriminatory language and political correctness
- Conclusion

Chapter 12 offers you guidelines on techniques which don't fit comfortably into a structure-based classification and Chapter 13 helps you to write it all up in a rigorous, practical and literate way.

How to approach it

The book is arranged in a structure which anticipates the sequence in which you are likely to address the various stages of your project and the material is organized accordingly. While you should skim the book initially for familiarization, dipping into it in more detail here and there as topics catch your eye, once you get going you will find that a front-to-back perusal in depth is the only way to travel.

Take your time. This isn't a blockbuster, to be read in one gulp from cover to cover; nor is it a textbook, to be dipped into now and again. Steady application, a section at a time, is what's required. Some of the exercises may take a few days to do and others, in which you depend on other people, may have you turning to something else while you await the outcomes of a task I have set you. It's more important to work through all these tasks than to ignore them and just plough on through the text. Work systematically in a measured way. Be gentle on yourself.

I do try to be comprehensive in my coverage and so you will find that some of the material does not apply to you – techniques that you don't need, approaches that you prefer not to take and so on. That is where you can be selective. So first of all, skim-read everything and then work in detail through everything that you have decided applies to you and your circumstances.

Throughout all this, you will discover that the relationship with your dissertation tutor is very important, and I shall be highlighting the occasions when it is essential that you interact with him or her. However, there will be many occasions when your tutor isn't available at just the right time and there may be situations in which you feel your query is a bit trivial and you wish you could just look it up in an appropriate text. Enquire within. (The index is an obvious place in which to look, as well as the contents and the glossary. The glossary provides definitions of key words and ideas. These are printed in **bold brown** the first time they appear in the text.)

This isn't to put the tutor on some kind of pedestal, but to make a rather more subtle point. Tuition seems to work best when you have thought about the matter which troubles you and have developed one or two solutions (or at least a clearly-articulated problem!) to present to the tutor so that a sensible way forward can be hammered out between you. One purpose of this book is to get you to that stage.

⭐ Please turn to the Project Guide below, and address both activities before you begin Chapter 1.

Project guide to the preface

Here is where you begin to use this book as it's intended: as a week-by-week (and sometimes day-by-day!) practical guide to your own project. For the moment, there are just two small, but significant, tasks.

1 Skim-read Part 1 of this book

   a Drift your eyes over the contents, the section and chapter openers and the main tables, to get a feeling for the material to come.

   b Next, just turn the pages of the remainder, looking at the material which suits your own particular circumstances.
     If you bought this book, rather than borrowing it from your library, you might like to mark the main sections you want to come back to with a highlighter pen, or use some 'Post-its' as markers.

2 Obtain a project diary

   a Read the 'Project Diary' part of Section 4.3 in detail.
     It's only one page long. A link with sample materials from a research diary is also provided, on the website.

   b Go out and buy yourself a project diary, ready for use when you begin Chapter 1.

Walk-through tour

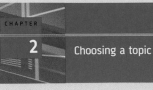

CHAPTER

2 Choosing a topic

Activity Objectives

- To help you to decide on a topic for your project by finding and refining an initial idea
- To initiate a reflective process by which you become more explicit about the provenance of that idea
- To provide you with guidance in turning the initial idea into a usable research question
- To outline the requirements for a written project proposal

At a glance

At this stage, you may have a vague notion about a topic, or you may have no idea whatsoever. The first step is to develop some possibilities you can subsequently work with, and this is achieved by providing you with a number of techniques by which ideas can be generated. Next, you need to choose the most promising of those possibilities, finding the one that you're most comfortable with. That depends on finding the one which interests you most; which you already know something about; and which is pitched at just the right level of difficulty. At this point, your idea is likely to lack focus. You need to become familiar with it and develop a sense of its provenance – where you're coming from with the idea, how it relates to what you know already, and to the subjects you have studied in your course. You also need to examine your rationale for the idea and your basic assumptions about why the idea is important. Once you have a provenance and rationale, the idea will be a lot clearer, and expressible in its final form as a research question which your subsequent work can address. Finally, this work needs to be planned out, thought through in outline and its different stages worked out in a little detail, all in the form of a Project Proposal which will act as a summary, schedule, and aide-memoire as you engage in all of your project activities. Figure 2.1 summarizes the various stages involved. Think of it as a route-map through this chapter.

23

Activity Objectives
Situated at the beginning of each chapter, these outline what stage in your project you should be able to reach after working through the chapter, and the key pieces of information you will need to know to proceed correctly.

BASIC CRITERIA | 31

be readily found? The data may be too difficult to generate, or too expensive. They may take you too long to acquire. Confidentiality, industrial relations climate and the internal politics of the organization from which you are drawing the data, all have a bearing on your choice of topic.

ILLUSTRATION 2.1

Pratima Gupta is a full-time student interested in entrepreneurship, who wants to find some Asian-owned small businesses, to survey their business policy and plans for expansion. Unfortunately, there is no collated database of ethnically-owned businesses in the county, from which she could draw her sample. Some individual boroughs have this information, but some don't. She realizes it will take too long for her to create a directory of businesses which can act as a sampling frame, and so she decides to confine herself to a study of two selected boroughs for which the information is available. Her tutor points out that she may find it difficult to generalize her results more widely, since one of her boroughs is rather atypical of the Asian community in general, and suggests that she thinks again.

Some post-experience students may find that their choice of topic is constrained because people in their organization have a special interest in the kinds of results that are likely to emerge. This may reflect current policy initiatives, political pressures, or budgetary constraints. A topic of this kind will be partially determined by political interests (which you might as well think of as legitimate without taking sides: why make problems for yourself?) and if you find yourself in this situation, a measure of discretion and sensitivity to other people's needs will be required. This may mean that you have to abandon the topic. On the other hand, it may be a sign of its potential usefulness to the organization: one of the signs of practical importance and relevance (criteria your project must address) is that people in your organization are intrigued, engaged and feel strongly about it. This is particularly true of the more strategic, policy-related and corporate issues which make for good topics at MBA level.

Financial outlay

Some otherwise ideal topics are unfeasible because it turns out that to address the issues properly would be too expensive.

ILLUSTRATION 2.2

Alan May, a full-time MSc International Business student, was intending to interview three senior regional development organization managers in Germany, as part of his project on European enterprise development structures. He had to think again when his tutor asked whether he had the personal resources to fund the trip. He shifted the emphasis of his topic from an investigation of the way in which quality standards among small businesses are fostered, to a comparison of how UK and German development agencies support new manufacturing investment, as soon as he realized that the information required for the latter was available from the trade attaché at the German Embassy in London.

46 | CHAPTER 2 · CHOOSING A TOPIC

CASE EXAMPLE 2.3

Choosing and working up a topic: post-experience student

Marco Testa works for an international manufacturing company with factories in the USA, Canada, Denmark and the UK, and is doing an MBA part-time, attending the university on two nights each week. Now that he has to specify a topic for his dissertation, he's quite pleased, as he sees it as an opportunity to work out some answers to a question that's been puzzling him for some time. He has visited the Danish plant and has hosted his Danish colleagues in return; likewise with managers from the other companies in the group. There is something not quite right about the way in which the various companies collaborate. The link with the Canadians is unproblematic, but there seems to be little synergy on issues of production quality between the other factories. The US head office sets global strategy, but the Danes seem to do their own thing a lot of the time. They're good, but they're not as good as they think they are; so why do they have quite so high a reputation for excellence in the company as they do? Some of the processes used in his own UK plant are actually quite good; why do they rate relatively poorly whenever effectiveness is talked about within the company as a whole?

Activity 1

He talks with his line manager, who agrees that an exploration of these issues would be worthwhile. Marco comes up with the notion of 'something to do with the lack of synergy between the companies in our group'.

Activity 2

The topic certainly interests him; and it forms a background to many of his day-to-day activities, so he feels he has the knowledge to handle it. It includes strategic and corporate issues as required in his MBA programme, is not too difficult and can be handled in the time he has available. His boss

has agreed a travel budget which would enable him to talk to key people in two of the locations, and he has to visit one of the others in three months' time in any case, as part of his job.

Activity 3

Filling out the provenance table, Marco remembers that the context in which the different factories operate is different: they're in different countries! He adds the item 'cultural differences' to the Field column, and 'globalisation' in the corresponding Area column. That stimulates the thought that there are other differences too: each is bound by different national and local regulations, commercial lending arrangements, as well as cultural standards. 'Conditions of trade' is entered into the Field column, and 'international business' as an area. He fills out other entries of the provenance table.

Activity 4

He sits down to the final stage: to summarize his topic as a research question. Can you help him?

1 What are the key issues underlying his topic? Look at the list of basic issues shown in Figure 2.1 and identify the one or two that seem most relevant.

2 Having eavesdropped on his conversation with his line manager, you know that his boss confirms that an international comparison would be particularly useful. What sort of research question would be useful, as well as reflecting the issues you identified in step 1?

Answers to Case Example 2.3

1 The first key issue is one of *efficiency* differences. Notice, though, that there is a suggestion that some of them might be more apparent than real. *Beliefs and values* may come in to it.

Illustrations
Helpful examples feature throughout each chapter, providing handy tips and explaining how the techniques explained in the text should be applied.

Case Examples
Case examples are provided at the end of each chapter, demonstrating the theory in practice. Each case example is accompanied by activities or questions, and detailed answers are provided from which you can measure your understanding and revise your learning.

Measures of Progress

Signposted with a star icon and instructions throughout, this feature encourages you to pause and tackle the project guide or case study activities at the end of each chapter.

Glossary Terms

Key terms are highlighted in colour throughout and explained in full in a page-referenced Glossary at the end of the book, enabling you to quickly locate the information you are looking for.

Project Guide

Each chapter ends with a set of activities which, if followed throughout, will result in your project being finished on time and to the required standard.

Website References

Links to the supporting website are located throughout the text and are identified with a star icon. The additional material on the accompanying website supports the theory of the text.

Visit the *Business Research Projects* accompanying website at www.thomsonlearning.co.uk to find further teaching and learning material including:

For Students

- An extended example of a worked research project from start to finish
- A series of weblinks providing helpful supplementary information
- Instructions on the use of the JISCMAIL mailing list system
- A guide to the use of Excel for data analysis
- Links made to the website throughout the text are provided on the open access site

For Lecturers

- A complete set of downloadable PowerPoint slides with accompanying notes
- A detailed teaching plan of the text that refers lecturers to appropriate parts of the text

Planning a research project

The emphasis of this first part is on project work as distinct from research principles (described in depth in Part 2) and empirical work (presented in Part 3). We start with a chapter on your aims, in which the different kinds of projects, each with rather differing objectives, are introduced. You are asked to identify your own circumstances and note the implications for the work that you're going to do and the objectives you'll need to address. The second chapter provides detailed help in identifying and refining the topic you're setting out to research, while Chapter 3 examines the standards which your examiners are likely to apply to your work when it is complete. Finally, Chapter 4 outlines the essential resourcing and timetabling procedures that you'll need to follow in order to complete your research activity by the deadlines which pertain.

1

The purpose and objectives of a project

- To introduce you to the different kinds of management project
- To help you to set objectives that match the requirements of the type of project you're doing
- To help you to think through your *personal* intentions and objectives in doing a project

At a glance

The clearer you are about your purpose and objectives, the better your research will be. This chapter reviews the reasons for doing a project and identifies the more obvious implications from your point of view. It shows how the nature of your audience and its expectations differ, depending on the amount of management experience on which you can draw.

1.1 The purpose of a project

At the most general level, the purpose of a business/management project can be defined as follows:

> To create an opportunity for the application of concepts and techniques acquired during the taught programme, in a management practitioner environment, in order to complete the formal learning experience, and to be of use to the sponsor.

Two basic assumptions underlie this purpose. The first is that action and application, rather than sheer exposition by lecturers and absorption by the student, is what makes for effective learning. People learn by doing! The second assumption is that ideally, some of this learning should take place in the organizational environment. If you are an undergraduate or a young graduate, without any previous management experience, you'll benefit from applying your postgraduate course material in the context of a real-life issue of practical importance in an organization. If you are an experienced manager on an Executive MBA programme, on the other hand, you have a mature learning style and may prefer to learn through activities which take place within the context provided by personal involvement in real management issues as they happen. It's the content of the issue or problem being researched which matters, as much as the principles, underlying theories, or management techniques pertaining to it and while case study and simulation methods may be useful in teaching, the real thing is better (see e.g. Mangham 1986; Ashton 1989). And so, doing an in-company project gives you two kinds of experience: the experience of a time (the placement period) spent in a non-academic, occupational situation, while being faced with a partially academic task to complete; and the experience of a task (doing the project itself) which partially simulates some important aspects of a manager's job. In those circumstances in which it is possible to do a project which includes the implementation of recommendations and a degree of evaluation of the consequences (as in the case of many MBA projects, for example), the simulation of some, but not all, aspects will be fairly close.

Of course, not every student can access, or wants to access, a company in which to do their research; and on occasion, post-experience students find they're unable to do their project work within their own organization (see Figure 1.1). Not every project can take place within an organization and, in this situation, generic

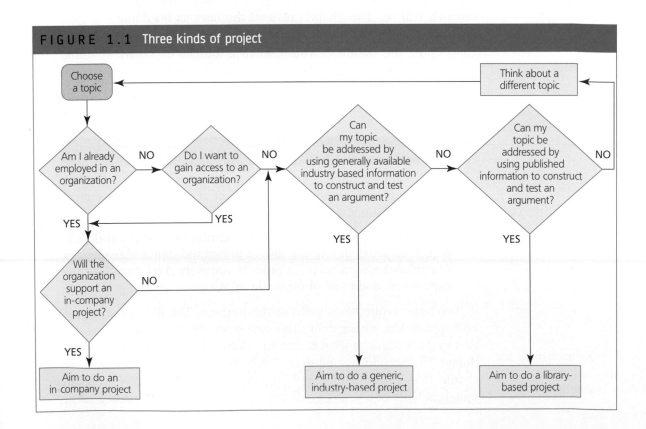

FIGURE 1.1   Three kinds of project

(industry-based) and archival (library-based) projects make viable alternatives. In all three alternatives, though, the aim is to ally practice with theory and to do more than merely describe what's going on. There is more on this in Section 3.2, where the attributes of a successful project are discussed.

Notice that my overall definition of your purpose says nothing about making a contribution to knowledge in the academic sense one associates with Master's programmes 'by research', and with PhD programmes. There is no doubt that if your project is any good at all, someone's knowledge will be enhanced: your own, of course; your tutor's, possibly (perhaps through your provision of a good literature review, new bibliographic citations the tutor hadn't come across, or new case study material, confidentiality arrangements permitting); and your sponsoring organization, most certainly. In the case of specialist Masters programmes (MSc Finance; MA HRM and the like) a conceptual or technical contribution to knowledge in that particular field would be feasible and welcome. But I omit the academic sense of adding to the generally-shared stock of knowledge, or contributing to theory, because I don't believe that successful in-company, practitioner-based projects which form part of a taught management or business programme, necessarily *must* have this intent in the way that a 'degree by research' does.

There is more on this in Chapter 5. For the moment, I want to make a crude distinction in emphasis and to consider the dangers involved in adopting an approach based excessively on the style and intentions of academic research. If you subscribe solely to this academic purpose, you will find yourself handling ideas and concepts in a theory-driven, rather than practitioner, way.

ILLUSTRATION 1.1

In a project on job satisfaction, for example, you might be tempted to identify and report the best fit of a set of non-linear regression equations between organizational variables and some measure of job satisfaction, a topic of great academic interest but unlikely to be sufficiently error free, or generalizable outside your situation, with the sample size at your disposal. Far better to use the same information to identify what the actual factors are, examine them in some detail and discuss the implications for the level of job satisfaction in general.

A second danger is that you'll find yourself adopting methods and techniques based on the research methodology of the social sciences more than you need to. I expect you've noticed how many textbooks on your project reading list concentrate on 'research methods' and how few on 'project methods'! Finally, you'll be tempted to present your project document laid out in a format more appropriate to a research thesis than a project report.

You may have noticed that the statement of purpose is very general. You will need to discover the particular way in which your own teaching institution interprets it and, particularly, which aspects are emphasized by the particular qualification programme that you are following. I would suggest that you do this before giving more than a cursory glance to Chapter 2, which outlines the issues involved in the choice of a project topic.

| 1.2 | The objectives of a project |

A good way of clarifying the purpose of your project is to examine the institutional objectives which it serves. (Here, of course, I am not dealing with the research objectives involved in your particular topic. These are discussed in more detail in Sections 2.3 and 2.5). The institutional objectives should be available, in writing, from your Programme Director. Why do academic programmes require you to do a project? The answer varies, depending on the type of programme which you're studying. A typical example is shown as Table 1.1 and a further selection, taken from the internal publications of several institutions, is given on the website. By and large, objectives of this kind fall into five different kinds, though not every programme will explicitly state them all:

- Acquisition and Practice of Concepts and Techniques.
- The Integration of Material Taught in other Courses of the Programme.
- The Management Environment.
- The Personal Learning Experience.
- The Contribution to the Organization.

Acquisition and practice of concepts and techniques

It's difficult to say much about the particular **concepts** which a project should convey, since they are, by definition, specific to the subject-matter discipline and the organizational issues that you will be handling.

There are, however, some general concepts that apply to all forms of research work. These relate to how evidence is best collected, how analysis and evaluation should be done, and deal with issues of validity, reliability, utility, generality, efficiency and effectiveness. These are rarely spelled out in institutional handouts, (though some reference is made to some of them in some project manuals!) They will be dealt with in Chapter 5 and you should read the relevant section before finalizing your choice of topic.

As for **techniques**, these will also depend on the subject-matter of your project. They could include anything from discounted cash flow in accountancy, negotiation skills in selling on the one hand, or industrial relations on the other, to gap analysis in the definition of service quality shortfalls. And again, this manual does not deal with them, since they are too specific for our purposes. Your tutor will be your best guide here.

There are techniques, however, which are common enough to be relevant to a variety of different projects. These are the data-gathering procedures (observation, interview, questionnaire and the like) associated with the four main research methods: historical review and analysis, case study method, survey method and the field experiment. These are dealt with in Chapters 9 to 12 of this book, together with general material relating to the design of your empirical work.

TABLE 1.1 The objectives of a project: sample listings

Acquisition and practice of concepts and techniques
- To agree a project, negotiating the topic, arguing and defending the analysis and recommendations

The integration of material taught in other courses of the programme
- *not mentioned*

Familiarization with the management environment
- To provide an opportunity for the in-depth analysis of a work-based learning situation

Fostering the personal learning experience
- To provide an experience that links the above to personal and professional development needs

Making a contribution to the organization
- To make recommendations for improvement based on the analysis

Luton Business School (2003). These objectives apply to a Postgraduate Certificate programme in which the emphasis is on the provision of work-based learning for people who have recently completed a first degree. There is a great emphasis on in-company experience as a formative experience and hence an absence of an objective relating to the integration of academic material.

Acquisition and practice of concepts and techniques
- To gain practical experience in selecting and using research techniques
- To learn how to present results appropriately

The integration of material taught in other courses of the programme
- To integrate material across different disciplines

Familiarization with the management environment
- To experience and resolve problems of methodology in practice

Fostering the personal learning experience
- *not mentioned*

Making a contribution to the organization
- To provide analytical arguments leading to practical conclusions

Luton Business School (2002). These objectives apply to all management dissertations done by post-experience Masters students of the business school. A somewhat different emphasis from the aims shown for the other programme.

The integration of material taught in other courses of the programme

The second kind of objective, which underlies the post-experience, Masters statement of objectives in particular, is that you are expected to choose a topic which integrates material across disciplines, rather than confining yourself to a single discipline or business function. This is as it should be: if you have general management experience, you will know that issues and problems do not present themselves neatly wrapped in the cloak of a particular specialism and your choice of topic should reflect this. People who aren't in employment at a middle-to-senior level can, in contrast, afford to choose topics that are more specifically related to a discipline or function and which are, in that sense, more specific.

People who are doing a project as a capstone to a professional postgraduate programme do, of course, need to choose a topic that relates to their business function and that is reflected in the objectives of their kind of project. Nevertheless, the professional bodies are concerned with the strategic status and impact of their profession and so the topic chosen will often reflect the relevant corporate and strategic aspects, and it would seem risky to choose a topic which eschews a significant treatment of the latter. (See Section 1.3 below.)

The management environment

While statements of project objectives refer to a familiarization with the environment, you will rarely find them developed in any great detail in an institutional handout. This is not surprising, since the culture and climate of different organizations vary enormously, between organizations within one country and (for the benefit of those of you who are doing international projects), between countries (see Section 6.2). Nevertheless, some general statements can be made and these are summarized in Table 1.2.

The extent to which your project will provide a simulation of this organizational environment and hence satisfy this objective, depends largely on the level of your course. Undergraduate and most diploma projects expose you to fewer of the pressures associated with the characteristics of Table 1.2 than do most MBA projects. This is one of the factors considered in detail in Chapter 2, when the choice of project topic is discussed. Second, it depends on the basis on which you're doing the course. If you're a part-time student, doing the course on a post-experience basis, you're likely to tackle project topics which involve you more in the issues mentioned in Table 1.2.

If you have not worked as an employee in an organization before, this will be your first exposure to these factors. You may be with the organization to do other work besides your project, or your project may be the only task that you have to complete while you're in place. In either case, what are the implications for your project work?

First, your time is unlikely to be as fragmented as that of the permanent employees. In this sense, the project is only a partial simulation of a manager's job and you should expect to be protected from excessive demands on time that is meant to be devoted to the project. You can satisfy this particular project objective, partly by simply being in the environment and observing how other people operate. If you find that your other, non-project responsibilities impinge on your project time or, in the case of a brief, project-only placement, you're asked to take on other duties, do something about it! Talk to your immediate supervisor in the first instance. (Always deal with your supervisor first, even if you suspect the issue will only be resolved by calling in your next resource, the tutor from your academic institution.)

If all goes well, however, you'll obtain direct experience of some of the other items listed in Table 1.2. Choosing a topic and progressing the project represent tasks and problems which you set for yourself; and the topic, if properly chosen to

---

TABLE 1.2 Characteristics of the management environment

Working on your project is meant to give you an experience of the following:

The content of activities, projects and decisions dealt with by managers
- Events are different to those you encounter in the educational setting
- People's responses to these events are different
- They can't be simulated completely in the educational setting

The ways in which responses are made and decisions taken
- Problems aren't set: they're recognized by an active process
- They're not solved, but resolved: done with, finished with
- Their relative importance must be judged so they can be ignored, postponed, or dealt with as a matter of urgency
- Some of the most important ones have to be anticipated

The uncertainty which managers must handle
- Decisions must be taken on less-than-complete information
- Outcomes may be a long time in appearing
- The standards by which decisions are evaluated may not exist and may themselves involve judgement on the part of the manager about stakeholder views

The fragmentation of experience and activities
- Issues aren't dealt with to completion in a neat sequence: several issues may compete for the manager's attention
- Some of them will have short time-spans; with others, the time between recognition and 'being finished with' will be considerably longer
- Some issues will re-present themselves at a later date; others will be different, but look the same; others will look different, but be the same

The human and interpersonal element
- Managers get work done through other people
- Many of their problems will therefore be human ones
- The manager may be extremely competent at the tasks he or she must deal with, but not as effective in handling the people

be relevant to the organization, will be sufficiently open-ended as a problem to simulate some of the uncertainties handled by full-time employees. You may have to exercise an appreciable amount of social and interpersonal skills in obtaining cooperation from other people. It's very unlikely that you'll have supervisory responsibilities arising directly from your project and so this aspect of organizational life may not be simulated completely.

Finally, you should ensure that one item listed in Table 1.2 definitely does not affect you! Namely, you should be crystal clear about the standards by which your project and the decisions you have made in doing the project, will be evaluated. Chapter 3 deals with this in particular.

 While the best way of satisfying this project objective is simply to be there, in the organization, a useful way of preparing yourself in anticipation is to do a little reading. I've highlighted a number of imaginative and readable texts on the website. They are all easy going – the sort of thing you can enjoy as bedtime reading before your project placement begins.

If you're a part-time student already in employment, a lot of this will seem familiar, with the project as just one more task for you to carry out, one more pressure, among the other responsibilities involved in your fragmented day-to-day job. However, this task is different to your other jobs. It has to satisfy standards of academic, rather than pragmatic, content and rigour. It represents an opportunity to tackle a work-related issue which you might not normally encounter in your day-to-day work. In the case of MBA courses, this has to be an issue in which you stand back from the normal flow of operational events and consider matters of strategic or corporate importance or, indeed, recognize and explore the strategic aspects of the normal flow of events: a much more valuable exercise, some would say.

More subtle, perhaps, is the consideration that the nature of the task and the kind of information which you will need to acquire to complete your project, can be agreed in advance with your tutor and, to some degree with your **sponsor** (the person in an in-company project to whom your report about the project). This has the function of legitimizing what you're doing in a way which isn't always possible with a normal management problem. (In this sense, a project is a technical, rather than management, task, with some fairly firm ground-rules and evaluation criteria.)

So, while your project is 'just one more job to do', it's still worth treating as distinct and somewhat special. You may or may not use a variety of time management techniques in your day-to-day work; you will certainly need to manage your project time deliberately and explicitly. There are a number of techniques for doing so (see Section 4.2); in the meanwhile, it might be worth thinking of the project as sufficiently distinct to merit its own separate weekly day or half-day: a time when you do nothing else.

The personal learning experience

If you're following a programme which assumes that you have had little previous working experience, you'll find that a major emphasis is placed in your project objectives on the acquisition and development of a variety of technical, developmental, interpersonal and persuasive skills required in dealing with the other people on whose goodwill and cooperation the success of your project will depend. Some of these are shown in Table 1.3. By and large, it is assumed that you already possess most of these skills if you're following a post-experience programme and are already a practising manager.

This issue of experience is important, because it will help to determine the scope and difficulty level (see Chapter 2) of the topic which you decide to tackle in your project. If, as an experienced employee, you've acquired some of these skills

---

TABLE 1.3 Characteristics of the personal learning experience

Some technical skills which you will be able to acquire and use
- techniques of time management
- writing letters requesting support
- composing memos and interim reports
- using libraries and information services on-site
- using the Internet as a research medium
- gaining access to respondents
- interviewing respondents
- speaking to an audience

Some social and interpersonal skills you may acquire and practice
- dealing and feeling comfortable with senior managers and chief executives
- persuading people to cooperate
- providing assurances and evidence of confidentiality arrangements
- working with a team of people, usually in a colleague relationship

Some personal pressures which you may encounter	*and the skills you may develop as you overcome them*
- doubts about the credibility of some of your academic concepts and purposes in the organizational environment in which you work	- a more critical perspective on the concepts *and* on your workplace
- dislike of the relatively long periods which you spend in working alone	- relationship building with your mentor; networking skills
- in international programmes, handling the tensions of being a stranger in a strange land	- greater self-suffiency, and a more informed perspective on your home country
- tension arising from the need to reschedule timetables	- improved negotiation and time-management skills
- uncertainty about the data: will they or won't they confirm the arguments you are expressing?	- a tolerance of ambiguity valuable in, and characteristic of, all research work . . .
- uncertainty about the approach which you, as a practitioner not an academic, are taking	- . . . and useful in professional and practitioner decision-making to boot
- a highlighting of your general uncertainties about your capability for successfully completing the qualification programme	- increased self-confidence on completion of the project as you gain your qualification

already, then this is likely to be taken for granted when your project is assessed. If, as someone who hasn't worked in an organization before, you have had little experience in dealing with chief executives, persuading reluctant informants, or working with a team of colleagues, then, while you will be expected to achieve some of these objectives by learning the relevant skills, you won't be judged too harshly if your project shows weaknesses arising from the fact that people have been bloody-minded, from your own insensitivity, or, more likely, from a combination of the two.

ILLUSTRATION 1.2

Peter Watkinson ran into severe difficulties when he was seconded to a different section and omitted to tell his line manager when the head of his new section sent him to a factory 120 miles away to gather some data for his project. He knew everything that classical management theory has to say about unified command, the problems of having two bosses and so on, but wasn't quick enough to make the connection with his own circumstances. The line manager, who came from a production background, didn't give a damn for the theory but knew an unreliable employee when he saw one and as for the head of the new section, he was away on holiday when the student came back to base. The outcomes were upsetting. The line manager refused further cooperation with the project and so the project report had data missing. Fortunately, Peter's tutor made allowances, once she heard the full story.

There is one personal aspect which tends to be underestimated, both in written accounts and in informal dialogue with tutors. Working on a project is a long and somewhat lonely endeavour. Some projects last over a one-term time-span, others last a whole year; and most curricula are arranged in such a way that you're not following any taught courses during this time. A number of tensions may arise and these are included at the bottom of Table 1.3. The first three probably apply more to people without extensive working experience and the last two, to managers currently in employment.

To know a problem is likely to occur and to anticipate it as a typical concomitant of project work, is surely some comfort as and when it might arise. If it's typical, then it's banal, boring, to be lived with in a fairly relaxed way and to be handled with a sense of humour, a trouble to be shared with friends over a pint and not worth troubling over excessively. It just happens, that's all!

If you find that they persist, though, don't do your worrying by yourself. At the very least, share them with someone else in your class. You will find that you're not alone. Try and share them with your tutor. I am not sure how the learning experience involved in handling these issues can be summarized in a neat list of skills to be acquired, which may be why it doesn't appear in a highlighted form among the official lists of objectives given on the website. But I have a feeling that the completion of a project in which these problems have arisen, and been lived through constructively, is a particularly valuable experience in personal development and is surely related to the experience of management for which your programme is preparing you, or in which your programme is providing further development. Some of the favourable outcomes are shown at the bottom of Table 1.3.

A careful reading of the web page at this point reveals another way in which project objectives in programmes aimed at immediate postgraduates differ from those aimed at experienced managers studying part-time. In the first instance, the project can provide an exploratory experience, in which you get the opportunity to try out a variety of tasks in a variety of departmental settings, for the first time, as a way of exploring future career options. In the second, it is assumed that you already have this experience. Nevertheless, the career opportunities, in your case the chance to change direction within your organization, or indeed, to position yourself for a career move outside it, may well be available. This second kind of career objective is just as legitimate as the first and whether you're an immediate postgraduate or an experienced manager, you should keep the future in mind. You might like to choose your research topic very deliberately so that it helps you on your way in your future career.

The contribution to the organization

Somewhat surprisingly, little is written in the general or institutional literature about this fifth factor. I have added it to the general definition of purpose myself because I know it to be implicit in the practice of many academic institutions and because I believe it to be important. It does appear in the guise of a rationale for collaborative research, in-company MBAs and consortium programmes, but it's rarely spelt out among the written objectives for in-company project work in general.

Table 1.4 lists a number of advantages and benefits for the organization in which research-based project work is carried out. A good indication that your project is indeed seen as valuable in this way is given when you're asked to make a

---

TABLE 1.4   The benefits of a project to the sponsoring organization

- The project tackles an issue of relevance to the organization: it should not be a purely academic exercise
- It represents an opportunity to examine an issue of corporate or strategic importance which might be otherwise ignored in the pressure of more immediate, operational demands
- It draws on the backup of the educational institution and if carefully chosen represents an inexpensive form of consultancy expertise
- A carefully chosen project topic will be useful to the immediate company supervisor of the student who is doing the project
- In the case of non-in-company based students and depending on any non-academic components of the work involved, it may release a permanent employee for other responsibilities

presentation of your final report to the organization, in addition to any presentation you have to make to your academic institution.

In the case of university-based projects, it has to be said that the results may not be directly of the same generality as if you were a full-time employee of the organization. This is no reflection on you; sometimes a good topic from the academic point of view may be somewhat limited from the organization's perspective, being seen as more of an exercise, or of only local interest. A lot depends on the support and keenness of your sponsor or direct company supervisor. However, in choosing your topic (Chapter 2), you might give a thought to the needs of your direct boss while you are with the organization and try to choose one which will be of direct personal or departmental use to him or her, even if the wider usefulness within the organization is problematic.

It's very helpful, but not always possible, if your project involves a topic in which your academic tutor's input provides expertise which is otherwise lacking in the organization. The combination of your own efforts (and if you're an employee, you know the company well!) and the tutor (who has relevant subject-related expertise) could well add up to a very powerful form of outside consultancy, which, please note, is free of consultancy fees.

A successful project under this objective is one that has the sponsoring organization crying out for more: expressing a wish to sponsor another undergraduate placement, or wanting to put another of its managers through an MBA, Diploma, or professional programme.

 This is a good point at which to pause, and address Case Example 1.1.

Next, when you have reviewed the answers provided, you need to apply the lessons to your own project idea. Please do so by addressing Project Guide activities 1 and 2, at the end of the chapter.

1.3   The special objectives of professional programmes

Project work done in order to satisfy the requirements of the professional bodies differs sufficiently from the previous types of project to merit a brief section to itself. Such projects take their subject-matter from activities within the business function served by the professional body and do not primarily address issues and topics in general management (though the corporate implications of functional issues may well be considered, as we have seen). Primarily, they serve the purpose of entry into the profession and particularly, of giving you membership of the professional body itself. The other purpose and objectives outlined in Sections 1.1 and 1.2 apply in addition, however.

The most important issue for you to be clear about is the status of the *programme* you are following, as much as the status of the project within the programme. Some professional bodies, like the Chartered Institute of Marketing, (CIM), remain entirely responsible for the content and assessment of the project, which in their case is a report on work done in the past. Others, like the Chartered Institute of Personnel and Development (CIPD), run a dual system in which different regulations for the project apply, depending on whether the responsibility for the programme of which the project forms a part has been devolved onto the educational institution. No doubt you will know which regulations apply to your programme, but you may not be clear initially how these translate into objectives for your project. An example of project objectives for a professional body is among those shown on the website.

Your tutor should have issued you with a handout outlining the intent, objectives, and practical regulations of the project, or possibly a longer, purpose-written project handbook. However, even if there is such a handbook, you might find it useful to do some further personal research by getting in touch with the professional body in question and obtaining a copy of their regulations, to see how your own institution has interpreted them. Have there been any shifts of emphasis? To what degree has the professional body devolved responsibility onto the institution and to what extent does this reflect local or regional knowledge or staff expertise on which you might draw in deciding on a topic for your project or in finding a tutor (to the extent that you have any choice in the latter matter)?

The emphasis in the professional body project objectives is very much on analysis, planning and problem-solving. In this sense, these objectives are similar to the objectives of many MBA programmes. There is also an emphasis on the presentation of recommendations for action, by people who are already in full-time employment and hence able to make meaningful implementation proposals. In contrast, in those programmes following the CIPD general guidelines which have been devolved onto educational institutions as Exemption Programmes (called by names such as 'Diploma in Personnel Management' or 'Masters in Human Resource Management'), the objectives of the project may differ in emphasis, having been set by the institution, albeit approved by CIPD. The students may be part-time or full-time; in the latter case the project would be carried out during a period of industrial placement.

Projects are sometimes used to give entry to the profession to otherwise unqualified post-experience candidates. Thus, the Chartered Institute of Marketing (CIM) uses a Formal Paper as a form of direct entry in the case of mature senior marketing practitioners who do not possess a degree or membership of one of a number of chartered institutes. It differs from those described hitherto, in one major way. Project activity and topic would be historical and at the time of application to the Institute, largely complete; it is the write-up which would be current. Recommendations would have been implemented, the consequences assessed and some interim or final outcomes evaluated. This is fairly unusual: implementation and evaluation of the results is rarely part of project work in general, though it may occur in some MBA programmes.

At this point, glance at Case Example 1.2 and answer the questions posed.

Next, if your programme follows the requirements of a professional body, please go back to Project Guide activity 2, and address activities b) and c) in particular.

1.4   In conclusion: making the objectives your own

All of the foregoing should surely suggest the importance of tailoring your project to the requirements of your particular audience. What you have to do is to prepare a project report which applies programme concepts and techniques in a practitioner environment in a way which completes your learning experience and is of use to someone in the sponsoring organization. The objectives which specify this purpose in greater detail may vary a little according to the level of programme (undergraduate, Diploma, postgraduate MSc, post-experience MBA) which you are following, but vary much more with the extent to which you do or don't have prior management experience.

In all this discussion of institutional purposes, there is one person whose interests may have been forgotten: and that is *yourself*. As well as working to satisfy your tutor and your sponsor in a way which reflects the particular programme which you are following, it is important that you satisfy *your own* wishes and needs. The best way of doing this at this stage is to try to personalize the objectives which you will have to address, in the light of the factors I have outlined above.

So: what is your experience base and what type of programme are you following? Perhaps, while you were reading this chapter, you have been making notes on the purpose and objectives as they apply to you. If you weren't, now is the time to go back over the material and identify the particular emphases and expectations as they apply to your own circumstances. You need to pay particular attention to Activity Checklist 3 (at the end of this chapter) and add to your work after you have read the following chapter, as you finalize your choice of topic. Also, it may be that your final answers will be clearer after you have familiarized yourself with the standards and criteria which will be applied to your project work and so you might return to them again after you have read Chapter 3.

The reason for posing them at this stage and returning to them periodically, should surely be obvious, however. At present, the objectives are someone else's. There they sit, in institutional black and white print. The knack of good project work lies partly in making the objectives your own, that is, in familiarizing yourself with the objectives of your own particular programme and by thinking through your own preferences and circumstances, of expressing the purpose and objectives in ways which are relevant and interesting to you.

 Now, in conclusion, please tackle Project Guide activities 3 and 4.

CASE EXAMPLE 1.1   Choosing a topic

Marvin Ellis is following a part-time post-experience MBA programme on evening release from his employer, Barntree Metals plc. He works as a production manager, in charge of an engineering shop in which heavy bearings are manufactured. There is a variety of product types, but they basically boil down to two: bridge bearings and precision roller bearings. Both go through similar stages (casting, turning, cleaning, surfacing, packing and despatch). A recurrent history of problems with customer returns of certain lines of precision bearings has made Marvin increasingly uneasy and he has obtained the factory manager's agreement to use his project time to 'do something about reorganizing the workflow'.

He feels that because the casting is done in separate locations; because the cleaning involves crude sandblasting and degreasing in the case of the bridge bearings but degreasing and polishing in the case of the precision bearings; and because only the bridge bearings need surfacing (having a composite surface epoxy-glued to the bearing surface) while the issue with the precision bearings is how carefully and securely they are crated for despatch, the two flows of work only coincide in a couple of locations. He decides his project will involve a careful time-and-motion study of alternative arrangements for separating the two kinds of work into two distinct flows through the various work-stations. At the back of his mind is the thought that if the overlap is as small as he thinks it ought to be, he might just propose dividing the engineering shop into two separate departments, located in separate buildings. But the main thing is the study of work-flows.

1   Is he right? Would this make a good topic for his MBA project?

2   Justify it in terms of the kinds of institutional objectives that apply to post-experience MBA dissertations.

3   If you feel that the topic isn't right, can you discern a more appropriate one?

Answers to Case Example 1.1

1   No, he's wrong.

2   Let's look at each kind of objective that a project should seek to achieve.

- Acquisition of concepts and techniques
  It's difficult to see what new concepts and techniques Marvin is likely to acquire through this particular topic that he doesn't have already as an experienced production manager.

- Integration of material taught in other courses of the programme
  The topic seems settled well within an operational engineering setting: a single discipline only.

- The management environment
  Yes, the topic would certainly familiarize someone without production experience very well with this particular environment: but this isn't one of the objectives of a post-experience qualification.

- The personal learning experience
  Again, it is doubtful what personal skills or advantages might come from the topic as initially stated.

- The contribution to the organization
  The topic certainly has the potential to make a contribution to the organization. There are cost-savings to be made!

3   The difficulty, of course, is that the topic is simply far too operational. Now, look at what might be the outcome: there is a possibility that the entire department might be restructured into two separate workshops, with different kinds of employees, under different working conditions, following different procedures and under different supervisory arrangements. Progress chasing, quality assurance, and cost control procedures could well be different as a result. This seems a more

CASE EXAMPLE 1.1   Choosing a topic (cont.)

promising emphasis on which Marvin might concentrate. In other words, what are the managerial, and strategic, implications of the creation of two departments, one specialized for the manufacture of precision bearings? The actual work-flow study is just a small part of the whole project and could well be completed as part of his normal job by an assistant reporting directly to Marvin, with the details excluded from Marvin's project, except as an initial situational factor from which his project takes its departure.

CASE EXAMPLE 1.2   Identifying programme objectives

Joan Rudding works as a senior administrator in a small but growing software business, responsible for accounting and personnel issues. Her first degree was in IT and while she used to regret that she has little time to make a contribution based on those studies, she has developed a keen interest in the business and management side and intends to make her future career as a business manager working for a larger company, most probably still in the IT field. As the software company has grown, she has been careful to foster that interest and hopes shortly to complete her Chartered Institute of Public Finance and Accountancy (CIPFA) Professional 3 programme at her local university.

The first three months of the new year are going to be a particularly busy period at work, which is daunting since it's also the time when she's meant to start on her project. She decides to begin early, starting with a glance at the regulations, to get an impression of the scope of the whole project. She is rather a shy person, and would also like to find out if an oral presentation forms part of the project assessment — she hopes not! Unfortunately, the CIPFA Course Director starts her Christmas vacation as soon as the term's lectures are finished and Joan resigns herself to waiting until she gets back in early January.

1 What might Joan have done instead? If time matters to her, how can she get hold of the information she needs immediately?

2 Is she likely to be able to avoid an oral presentation?

Answers to Case Example 1.2

1 There are several ways that Joan can get hold of the regulations she is looking for if she just puts her mind to it.

   a She could look for the CIPFA Programme Course Manual produced by the university department when she started her programme way back in the Foundation stage. That's quite a long time ago and she's probably lost it! So, instead

   b she could ask another student

   c talk to the departmental administrator and see if she has a copy

   d contact the Institute directly by phone, using the 24-hour support line (0207-543-5678)

   e search the Institute's website http://www.cipfa.org.uk/eandt/prospective/syllabus.ihtml where she will discover that she can download the full Professional 3 syllabus as an MSWord file.

   So there's really no reason for her to wait until January!

2 Unfortunately, no: Joan can't avoid having to give an oral presentation. The downloaded CIPFA syllabus states that candidates are tested on oral communication by making a ten-minute presentation of their project and have to answer questions about it. One of the things that Joan could usefully do when the CIPFA Course Director returns is to see how she might address her communication block before the time comes to present her project under examination conditions.

Project Guide

1 Buy a research diary

If you haven't done so already.

2 Inform yourself

a Get hold of the regulations which apply to project work for your level of course in your department. Examine them with a view to establishing the kind of project that's required.

b If you are studying a professional programme, contact the professional body, ask them to send you the regulations that apply to dissertation work and find out for yourself what the professional body requires and how your department has interpreted them.

c Don't forget to join the professional body as a student member, if you haven't already done so.

3 Think through the objectives as they apply to you

a Work through the project objectives listed in the regulations for your programme. (You will of course have these to hand if you've already done Activity 2a!) Address the following issues in particular.

- What are the concepts and techniques in which you're expected to demonstrate competence?

- To what extent are you likely to be required to integrate material across disciplines, or conversely, emphasize the particular interests and perspectives of a particular academic discipline or professional/business function?

- What kinds of skills it is likely that you will be asked to demonstrate?

- If you are following a competency-based programme, which competencies from your individual learning contract are likely to be demonstrable through the medium of the project?

- If you are an experienced manager doing the programme on a part-time basis, what kinds of past experience might you highlight and draw on during the project period? Have you done any projects on similar topics in any previous courses which you have studied? (But see Section 2.1 on this issue.)

- Depending on your experience base and location, what kind of contribution to your organization is it feasible for you to make, what kind of contribution might you personally like to make and at what organizational level (supervisor, sponsor, departmental, whole-organization)?

4 Personalize your reasons for doing a project

a Think about which of the project objectives described in Section 1.2 interest you most on a personal basis.

b Take 100 points and distribute them among the five kinds of objective: 'acquisition and practice of concepts and techniques'; 'integration of material taught in other courses of the programme'; 'familiarization with the management environment'; 'personal learning experience' (the skills you might acquire); and the 'contribution to the organization'. If you want to give more emphasis to one than another, give it more points: 30–10–10–40–10? 50–0–0–50–0? 20–20–10–40–10? so long as the total across all five adds to 100.

References

Ashton, D. (1989) 'The case for tailor-made MBAs', *Personnel Management,* July, 32–35.

Luton Business School (2003) *Programme Manual to the Postgraduate Certificate in General Professional Practice,* Graduate Business School, University of Luton.

Mangham, I. L. (1986) 'In search of competence', *Journal of General Management,* 12: 2: 5–12.

2

Choosing a topic

- To help you to decide on a topic for your project by finding and refining an initial idea
- To initiate a reflective process by which you become more explicit about the provenance of that idea
- To provide you with guidance in turning the initial idea into a usable research question
- To outline the requirements for a written project proposal

At a glance

At this stage, you may have a vague notion about a topic, or you may have no idea whatsoever. The first step is to develop some possibilities you can subsequently work with, and this is achieved by providing you with a number of techniques by which ideas can be generated. Next, you need to choose the most promising of those possibilities, finding the one that you're most comfortable with. That depends on finding the one which interests you most; which you already know something about; and which is pitched at just the right level of difficulty. At this point, your idea is likely to lack focus. You need to become familiar with it and develop a sense of its provenance – where you're coming from with the idea, how it relates to what you know already, and to the subjects you have studied in your course. You also need to examine your rationale for the idea and your basic assumptions about why the idea is important. Once you have a provenance and rationale, the idea will be a lot clearer, and expressible in its final form as a research question which your subsequent work can address. Finally, this work needs to be planned out, thought through in outline and its different stages worked out in a little detail, all in the form of a Project Proposal which will act as a summary, schedule, and aide-memoire as you engage in all of your project activities. Figure 2.1 summarizes the various stages involved. Think of it as a route-map through this chapter.

FIGURE 2.1 An overview of the process involved in choosing a topic

SOURCING IDEAS

- an idea I've always had at the back of my mind
- an intuition I want to investigate further
- a gap in the literature noted when reading
- suggested by thinking about the day's activities
- found by literature scan/past dissertations
- as discussed with students, lecturers, or boss
- identified through brainstorming
- suggested by a relevance tree
- put together by morphological analysis
- thought about using a decision table

INITIAL IDEAS: EXAMPLES

- Absenteeism in the claims-checking department; rewards, appraisal, motivation
- Is there a market for our roller-bearing repair service in Europe?
- Benchmarking and consequent organizational culture changes
- Something to do with employees as effective team members

APPLY THE BASIC CRITERIA TO THESE IDEAS

Does it interest me?
How much do I know about it already?
How difficult is it likely to be?
- level of qualification
- intrinsic complexity
- availability of expertise
- ease of data access
- financial outlay
- time required for completion

IDENTIFY THE PROVENANCE OF THESE IDEAS

- decide how vague or specific your idea is at present
- assign to an Area, Field or Aspect
- identify the areas, fields and aspects you will need to investigate
- do some initial library work: list some key ideas, concepts, and authors

WHAT'S THE BASIC ISSUE UNDERLYING THESE IDEAS?

To do with
- efficiency? effectiveness?
- appropriateness?
- beliefs, values and culture?
- resource constraints?
- accurate descriptions?
- analysis of causes and outcomes
- identification or implications of change?
- comparisons and benchmarking?
- rational decisions and neutral choices?
- stakeholder preferences?
- structural and design considerations?

FINAL RESEARCH QUESTIONS: RESULTING EXAMPLES

- How can we account for the differences in job satisfaction in Departments A and B, and how does this relate to the way the appraisal system is operated?
- Should we manufacture under licence or export directly into the South American market?
- What are the retraining implications if we reorganize our production procedures to reflect current industry best practice?
- Do people have to be aware of their Belbin team role skills in order to be effective team members?

2.1 Sourcing ideas

Where do ideas come from? And where do they exist before you have them? Most people would answer that they reside in their heads and think of idea generation as a matter of racking one's brains. Well, yes, the idea may be in there somewhere, as an old favourite: an idea which you've had for a long time and can't wait to investigate. It might be just an intuition that needs some more detailed attention when you have time for it. Or it could be a gap in the existing literature which, your general reading suggests, could be filled out with a particular research project that builds on what has gone before. But, as research on knowledge in organizations has shown (see, e.g. Senge 1990; Shaw 1985), ideas also exist out there, in the world and in the community at large – which suggests that sitting and thinking aren't always sufficient. You have to talk and act as well. So, if you don't already have an idea as you sit here reading these words, then try one or more of the following idea generation techniques. Make sure you note down the outcomes in your research diary, for future reference.

- **More thinking!**
  But in a disciplined way. Every night, spend five minutes thinking about the main incidents of the day. What happened that was significant or interesting which you might like to explore further? Make a note.

- **Scanning the published literature**
  Browsing through recent journals, and review articles in particular, may be useful. But if you don't already have an idea as a result of your systematic reading, then at this stage it's more important to scan for ideas than to read in detail. Quickly run through one or more online databases, looking just at the titles initially and then glancing at the abstracts of any that look particularly interesting. Your library should have a convenient way of accessing the ASLIB Index to Theses (a particularly thought-provoking database for your present purposes) through its web site; just enter your university Intranet site and drill down to the particular page you need. There is more on electronic searching in Chapter 7.

- **Scanning previous dissertations**
  Seeing what other students have produced in previous years can trigger ideas. Ask your Course Director if there is a list of past dissertation topics or titles; check with the librarian where the past dissertations are kept and skim through their titles to see what suggests itself. The website provides you with a list of recent project titles offered in my own university.

- **Discussion and negotiation**
  Talk over possible employer projects: something which you, or your boss at work, realize needs doing. Mull over possible topics with your fellow students during a coffee-break. Talk with your lecturer in the subject that you find the most interesting and easy to study and understand. If you're a part-time student, share your ideas with your boss at work. You will probably need to

collaborate with him or her to facilitate your project work, so why not involve them with your project idea from the start?

■ **Brainstorming**

Get together with four to six students following the same programme as yourself. Take turns in:

- stating your interests as clearly as you can
- noting down all the suggestions the others provide, *without making any judgements about their relevance, wisdom, or value to your own project*
- privately identifying the ones which you want to take further
- discussing each of these to clarify what is meant and how you might tackle it
- *here's the place for critical thinking, and not before.*

■ **Relevance trees**

This is a rough-and-ready directed graph which starts with a general title and branches out into three aspects of the general title that may occur to you. Anyone familiar with Buzan (2003) and his graphic, non-hierarchic technique for note-making, will recognize exactly what I mean. You think about each branch and jot down a further three branches to that, at a more specific level. Go through as many iterations as it takes to come up with an idea that looks promising.

■ **Morphological analysis**

Take the broad field that interests you. In three different columns, write down three attributes of the field. Using them as headings, try and list as many different instances of each attribute as you can in the column below each heading. Look at different combinations of one item from each column and see what topic that might suggest. There's an example in Table 2.1, with further examples on the website and you can find further examples of both relevance trees and morphological analysis in Sharp *et al.* (2002).

■ **Decision tables**

This is a technique for reflective analysis suggested by Raimond (1993). Go to the library, find six projects you like and write down your answers to the following questions in a column marked 'yes': what you like about the project; what's good about the project; why you feel it's good. Do the titles and abstracts suggest anything to you? Next, do the same for a different set of six projects that you don't like, putting the answers into a column marked 'no': what you dislike about the project; what's unsatisfactory about it; and why. Now sit back and look for a pattern: what sort of thing do you feel comfortable with?

 Now turn to the Project Guide and complete activity 1.

TABLE 2.1 An example of morphological analysis

Steps:

a Take the broad field that interests you
b In three different columns, write down three attributes of that field
c Using them as headings, write down as many examples of each attribute as you can
d Consider different combinations of the examples, taking one from each column
e What thoughts about the topic suggest themselves with each combination?

a FIELD: Managers as leaders

b *Definitional Problems*	*Behaviour*	*Contingencies*
c Type of manager	Assumption of role	Size of organization
Leader as agent	Task-oriented style	Position power
Leadership as transaction	Person-oriented style	Existing relations
Substitutes for leadership	Personal satisfaction	Nature of task
Effective leadership	Interpersonal skills	National cultures

(The attributes reflects your own reading in and around the subject of leadership. Putting the examples into the columns reflects an association of ideas: one item suggests a second, which leads to a third, and so on.)

d Combination 'Type of manager – Personal satisfaction – Size of organization' may suggest . . .
e . . . that senior managers in small organizations may be more satisfied than senior managers in large organizations.

d Combination 'Effective leadership – Task-oriented style – National cultures' may suggest . . .
e . . . that the definition of what sort of behaviour counts as task – rather than person-oriented style may vary with culture. An interesting issue (see Smith and Peterson 1998; Maczynski 1991) and a good topic at MBA level for someone employed by a multinational.

d Combination 'Leadership as transaction – Interpersonal skills – Nature of task' suggests . . .
e . . . that appraisal systems may be unsuccessful because insufficient training is given to the managers concerned, rather than because inadequate appraisal questionnaires are used. A possible project for CIPD students.

2.2 Basic criteria

Let's assume that you have arrived at a few possibilities as a result of the procedures I've listed above. (Figure 2.1 lists four, under the 'Initial Ideas' heading.) The next step is to find one with which you are comfortable.

Treat the following as a set of guidelines that you apply to each topic idea, regardless of its clarity at the moment. Go through each of these factors systematically, even though you might have considered some of them when generating your ideas in the first place. Make some notes as you read the following section.

Does it interest you?

You will to be living with this topic for quite a long time. If you are considering it because you feel you ought to, because your lecturers said it was important, or because it's currently fashionable in the literature, the chances are that you will be bored with it before you have finished and are likely to do the minimum required to bring the project to completion. Ideally, the topic should be one about which you're curious and one in which you feel you can interest your reader too.

How much do you know about it already?

Clearly, there will be less work to do if you choose a topic which you have encountered and worked on before. Analysis, evaluation, and judgement will come more easily and you'll be more aware of the issues that arise having covered the basic ground already. You'll know what aspects of the topic are likely to repay an in-depth investigation. Any topics which you have already researched, for an essay or assignment, are worth considering for their potential as projects, so long as you feel that they have the depth to carry an extended treatment.

Perhaps the best guide here is provided by the marks you have received for the prior work you have done. Choose something you know well! If your mark for an assignment was poor to average, you are unlikely to be able to expand it into a project successfully, and if you struggled to gain an average mark in a 2000-word essay, you will be unlikely to do well after expanding it into a 20,000-word project.

If the topic looks as though it needs a statistical treatment and you lack the skills, it's best avoided.

Choose a topic within a business function, or discipline, in which you are comfortable. This will tend to happen automatically if you are following a functionally specialist Masters course (MSc Finance; MSc Engineering Management) since the regulations usually require you to do your project within the discipline.

If you are a part-time student following a professional programme, or an in-company-based MBA, your work experience gives you a great advantage, since your topic is likely to deal with your own organization. The danger is that you choose a project which you would have been covering already as part of your day-to-day responsibilities. While your project should be relevant, it should also have a measure of academic content!

This issue is dealt with in greater depth in Chapter 6. For the time being, your best action is to remember that the intent of your course is to add to your personal development as a professional, or as a general manager. Choose a topic which draws on your experience by all means, but also one which helps you to grow in a desirable direction. 'What sort of topic will assist me in my next career move?' is a very helpful and legitimate question in this context and one with which you are familiar in any case, since it is part of the reason for undertaking a period of academic study in the first place. So: which of the topics you listed earlier do you already know most about?

How difficult is it likely to be?

Your previous studies will have given you an idea of which topics you find easy and which ones more difficult. However, you need to bear in mind that some topics are intrinsically more difficult than others and before you tackle them in depth, you may not realize what you've let yourself in for. This is an issue which your tutor will want to address at your first project tutorial. It helps to know what issues he or she will have in mind. 'Difficulty' in this sense breaks down into six issues:

- the level of qualification to which you are working
- the intrinsic complexity of the subject-matter
- the availability of expertise on which you can draw
- the ease with which you can access data
- the financial costs involved
- the time required to complete a project based on the topic in question.

Level of qualification

Some topics lend themselves to an undergraduate project, while others are more appropriate to treatment at Masters level. Some merit a more scholarly treatment and are better suited to a specialist Masters qualification, others are ideal for an in-company based project. Many, I must admit, cross these boundaries! You will also get a better grasp of this issue in the next chapter, which deals with the issue of standards. If in doubt, ask a lecturer.

Intrinsic complexity

Some topics deal in ideas, or require the application of techniques, which are difficult to handle in themselves. There they sit, out on the frontiers of knowledge, making demands on the most experienced researchers. It's easy to recognize them.

- People talk of them as being 'leading-edge' and your common sense suggests that they're not talking about currently fashionable, 'flavour of the month' issues.
- Conversely, they may be out of fashion having been overtaken by alternative approaches and the supportive materials long out of print; either way,
- You notice that there is relatively little material available in your otherwise well-stocked library.
- They are described in language and concepts which belong to your main subject of study, but which you haven't encountered in lectures. Perhaps they rely on statistical, mathematical, or financial techniques which are more advanced than your course expects of you.
- Specialized consultancy services may be the only source of expertise available to you, but are likely to regard their purpose-designed techniques and questionnaires as proprietary commercial products rather than as information freely available in the public domain.

■ Finally, you notice that your basic textbooks make little reference to them, practitioner journals are sketchy and only the most advanced refereed journals provide a thorough coverage, using language that you find difficult to understand.

If you have a topic that you suspect is intrinsically complex in this way, you will find that a lecturer, or your project tutor when appointed, is the best source of guidance on what to do in the circumstances.

 Case Example 2.1 illustrates this sort of difficulty and this would be a good time to pause and tackle the questions posed, before reading on.

Availability of expertise

Very few teaching institutions have expertise in all of the areas within which you might choose your project. Staff have their specialisms in which they can show excellence; their humdrum competencies; and their conceptual black holes, subject-matter which they'd rather you didn't mention with any great enthusiasm. Ideally, you should have been placed with the tutor in whose field of excellence your topic will lie.

A second form of institutional expertise is the library and computing resource on which you might wish to draw. It's worth scanning the library holdings to see if your proposed topic is adequately covered: Section 7.1 will tell you how. If all else fails, ask a librarian!

Similarly, if your topic will depend on specialized software, it's best to explore its availability at the outset. Is the necessary hardware available at convenient times? Check out how the booking system works. How well do you get on with the technician or programmer whose help you may need in due course?

In-company based projects have their own expertise base. You will find two kinds of help particularly important. Firstly, your sponsor, whose role is complementary to your academic tutor: Section 6.3 gives you more details. As with the tutor, it helps if the sponsor is knowledgeable about your topic and, if he or she is more of an administrative appointment, it is useful to cast around for other people who might be expert in the in-company issues which your topic addresses. Also, if your company has already supported people through the qualification you're studying, it's worth making contact with them, especially if they did a broadly similar topic to your own: a **mentor** of this kind can be invaluable.

If you are thinking about an internationally-based topic, it may be that you will have to rely on local expertise in the country in question. How feasible is this? Are communications with the foreign-based manager involved sufficient for your purpose?

Ease of data access

All business and management projects require you to present empirical material (that is to say research evidence of some kind), whether you have originated this yourself, or worked from secondary sources. Is your topic one for which data can be readily found? The data may be too difficult to generate, or too expensive. They may take you too long to acquire. Confidentiality, industrial relations climate and the internal politics of the organization from which you are drawing the data, all have a bearing on your choice of topic.

Pratima Gupta is a full-time student interested in entrepreneurship, who wants to find some Asian-owned small businesses, to survey their business policy and plans for expansion. Unfortunately, there is no collated database of ethnically-owned businesses in the county, from which she could draw her sample. Some individual boroughs have this information, but some don't. She realizes it will take too long for her to create a directory of businesses which can act as a sampling frame, and so she decides to confine herself to a study of two selected boroughs for which the information is available. Her tutor points out that she may find it difficult to generalize her results more widely, since one of her boroughs is rather atypical of the Asian community in general, and suggests that she thinks again.

Some post-experience students may find that their choice of topic is constrained because people in their organization have a special interest in the kinds of results that are likely to emerge. This may reflect current policy initiatives, political pressures, or budgetary constraints. A topic of this kind will be partially determined by political interests (which you might as well think of as legitimate without taking sides: why make problems for yourself?) and if you find yourself in this situation, a measure of discretion and sensitivity to other people's needs will be required. This may mean that you have to abandon the topic. On the other hand, it may be a sign of its potential usefulness to the organization: one of the signs of practical importance and relevance (criteria your project must address) is that people in your organization are intrigued, engaged and feel strongly about it. This is particularly true of the more strategic, policy-related and corporate issues which make for good topics at MBA level.

Financial outlay

Some otherwise ideal topics are unfeasible because it turns out that to address the issues properly would be too expensive.

Alan May, a full-time MSc International Business student, was intending to interview three senior regional development organization managers in Germany, as part of his project on European enterprise development structures. He had to think again when his tutor asked whether he had the personal resources to fund the trip. He shifted the emphasis of his topic from an investigation of the way in which quality standards among small businesses are fostered, to a comparison of how UK and German development agencies support new manufacturing investment, as soon as he realized that the information required for the latter was available from the trade attaché at the German Embassy in London.

Time required for completion

This is associated partly with the difficulty of the topic and partly with the natural timetabling imposed on you by events largely outside your control! Focusing on the latter, if your topic is likely to depend on other people's work, hitherto unpublished research, or the completion by others of personal, in-company, agency, or Government reports, you need to be very careful in estimating timing and feasibility. If you are likely to have to travel to interview respondents, to look up archival data, or to spend time at Head Office or outlying company premises, these need planning for at an early stage. A second opinion by tutor and/or sponsor will be very valuable and your own decision or their advice may lead you to abandon an otherwise promising topic at the early planning stage. Can you form a rough estimate of how long the topic you're considering will take to complete?

In summary

The basic criteria in choosing a topic are, therefore, your interest in it, the state of your prior knowledge and the difficulty of the subject-matter in question. Difficulty is in itself a complicated issue of scope, involving the suitability of the topic to the level of qualification for which you're studying, the intrinsic complexity of the material, the availability of expertise afforded you, the ease of data access during the project, the costs likely to be incurred, and the time required for completion of the particular topic which you might have in mind.

 Now tackle activity 2 in the Project Guide at the end of the chapter.

2.3 Where do ideas belong? The provenance table

The next step is to sharpen up your topic. One way of doing this is to develop a good picture of the **provenance** of your topic: what kind of emphasis it represents, how it fits in among other ideas you might have had and where it lies within the whole body of ideas and knowledge. What you need is a **taxonomy**: a structure which shows you where you're coming from. This will help you to:

- decide how unacceptably vague, or appropriately specific, your initial idea might be, thereby guiding the process by which you change your initial, vague ideas into a developed form
- specify research objectives for your empirical work
- identify the taught courses which are relevant to your topic, offering subject-matter which your literature review will need to describe and concepts which are relevant to the argument you will be building
- identify lecturers who would make an appropriate tutor for your topic once you've worked it up in a final form

■ suggest the types of reading you will need to do in preparing your dissertation – and even provide a pointer to its location in the library!

Imagine that all business and management knowledge can be classified under three headings, Area, Field and Aspect. An **Area** covers the broadest range of scholarly or business endeavour. It can be a basic discipline dealt with in your course, such as 'Behaviour in Organizations'. It might be one of the business functions, like 'Accounting and Finance'. It could be the title of one of the more interdisciplinary course components of your overall taught course, for example, 'International Marketing and Trade'. A **Field** is a component of an Area. It represents a subdiscipline, like Organization Development or 'Employee Motivation'; alternatively it might be a theme within a business function, like 'Cost Accounting' or 'Credit Control'; or, finally, it may be an issue dealt with by an interdisciplinary course, like 'Small Business Marketing' or 'The Exporting Function in Organizations'. An **Aspect** is just that: a more detailed facet of a Field. To complete the running example, it might be 'Introducing an employee participation scheme into Company X: the consequences for staffing policy' or 'Employee Incentive Schemes'; it could be 'Profitability and Efficiency in a Process Firm' or 'Evaluating Consumer Credit Arrangements'; it may be 'Local Businesses as Contractor-Suppliers to the larger Firm' or 'Critical Analysis of Export Marketing Strategy'.

Table 2.2 provides you with further examples of this rough-and-ready classification scheme in use.

TABLE 2.2 Sample of topics by area, field and aspect		
Area	**Field**	**Aspect**
Finance	Cost/management accounting	An analysis of transfer pricing methods
Accounting and Finance	Cost accounting	Cost analysis and cost behaviour in relation to production in Peterson & Sons plc
Finance	Credit control	Evaluating customer credit arrangements
Finance	Management accounting	Development of a ward-based financial information system for Hospital X
e-Business	Service system design	How governmental agencies might learn from the private sector in implementing electronically-based information services
Accounting and e-business	Database and sales ledger management	Transforming the current Smith & Jones' Ltd website into an attractive interactive commercial website
Policy/strategy	Economics	Strategic factors pertaining to primary care groups in the pharmaceutical industry
Policy/strategy	Marketing	The marketing of the University to local students to offset its current dependence on overseas students

TABLE 2.2 Sample of topics by area, field and aspect (cont.)

Area	Field	Aspect
Business policy	Marketing	Development of alternative markets for hand-knitting yarns from a Bangladeshi yarn mill which used to supply a more regionalized trade market
Strategic management	Regional support/ development	The analysis and further development of business support services currently available within the region
Personnel and development	HRM, HRD, training	Opening a new hotel in Dubai: the HRM and HRD implications
Personnel/IR	Recruitment policy, organization culture	Recruitment and retention of uniformed employees in the Fire Service
Personnel/ behavioural	Organization development	Introducing an employee participation scheme into Company X: the consequences for staffing policy
Behavioural	Organization culture	Gaining employee commitment to a 'best-value' regime
Production	New and 'newer' technology	The impact of recent technological changes on manufacturing capacities
Production	Materials handling	Lean materials at TrinCo, including a comparison with the Japanese model
Production	Benchmarking	Benchmarking of the firm's systems capabilities to include glassware/labware; versus current system
Marketing	Market analysis	Marketing of the company's products into new markets in Central Europe, due to the decline in the traditional telecoms and CATV market
Marketing	Marketing strategies	Strategic partnerships between providers and major clients as a move towards globalization
Marketing	Sales & internal communications	The importance of in-store marketing communications in department stores

Building your provenance table

You draw up a provenance table as follows. Treat each of your possible topic ideas separately and do the following for each. Locate your own idea under the appropriate heading, Area, Field or Aspect and then fill out the other columns. Refer to Table 2.3 for some examples: in each case, the original possible idea is shown in bold.

At the outset, it doesn't matter if your ideas are very vague and you find yourself writing them into the Area column ('Something to do with organizational behaviour') or the Field column ('Absenteeism'). As your thinking progresses, however, and you run through each stage of Figure 2.1, you should be able to flesh out the table with an entry at the Aspect level. A good topic is one which has been through this process and your ideas must be progressed through these stages before

TABLE 2.3 Some examples of ideas classified under area, field and aspect

	Area	Field	Aspect	Topic
1a	An idea at a very general level of development I like Organization Behaviour: maybe something in that Area			
1b	The same idea at a more developed level I like Organization Behaviour: maybe something in that Area	Absenteeism, in the claims department: rewards, appraisal, motivation		
2	An idea developed to the level of topic Behaviour in Organizations	Employee motivation	Employee incentive schemes, esp. as they apply to senior staff	A critical evaluation and comparison of employee share participation schemes in two manufacturing companies
3a	A example for a professional programme (CIPD) which combines functional Aspects within the corporate Field			
	Human Resource Development: corporate and strategic aspects	Creating appropriate organizational climates through training	Selling the idea of Action Learning	The transfer of learning from Action Learning Programmes to the organization as a whole
3b	An example probably too operational to be acceptable for IPD			
	Human Resource Development	Creating appropriate organizational climates through training	Job instruction in 'our way of doing things'	A training manual for receptionists and counter staff
4a	An initial idea already specified at the Topic level			
	Corporate Strategy	Strategic Management	Structural and cultural changes affecting nursing training	Changes in training systems after reorganization
4b	Working from the more specific to the more general suggests other relevant Fields and Areas			
	Corporate Strategy Organization Behaviour Department of Health Policy Training & Development policy Professionalization theory (sociology)	Strategic Management Management of Change Clients, providers, and the NHS internal market Nursing 2000 and after Continuing professional development	Structural and cultural changes affecting nursing training	Changes in training systems after reorganization

the bulk of your project work can begin. One problem with weak projects is that, to all intents and purposes, the material is dealt with at the level of Field rather than anything more specific; and a second one, that the Aspect stage was reached too late in the day.

Certainly, by the time you have your second project tutorial, the Aspect stage, together with one further very important task, should be achieved. The Aspect stage is still not the final step. The Aspect needs narrowing down yet again, to focus your idea into the final topic which could well constitute the title of your project report, if you chose to do so. This final step does three things:

- It informs your tutor (and, if the result is a title, the reader) of which issues you have, by implication, *excluded* from your topic and is the result of some initial reading (see Chapter 7 on literature reviewing).

- It demonstrates the way in which your project will be more than a simple description of the subject-matter.

- It completes the process by which your initial ideas get tightened up into a developed form (as in the last section of Figure 2.1).

Take a look at the second example in Table 2.3: Area: 'Behaviour in Organizations' – Field: 'Employee Motivation' – Aspect: 'Employee Incentive Schemes'. A focused topic in this case might be 'A critical evaluation and comparison of employee share participation schemes in two manufacturing companies'. By implication, it *excludes* other forms of incentive scheme (though the literature review would briefly describe the excluded alternatives) and it *focuses* on manufacturing rather than retailing or other forms of privately-owned organizations (e.g. service organizations) where such schemes exist. Secondly, it *avoids pure description* by promising an evaluation and a comparison of specific and, possibly, contrasting practices in two particular companies. (You might like to consider a few additional words and phrases which indicate that your work is doing more than describe. As well as evaluation and comparison, there are 'analysis', 'synthesis', 'assessment', 'the importance of', 'the impact of', 'the influence of', the latter three indicating some exploration of cause and effect and hence some degree of explanation.)

Fleshing out your provenance table

Whether you started off with a vague idea, or a very specific and detailed one, you have one further step to complete. Go to the rightmost column (the specific topic) and *work from right to left*. Here is where you can think through the disciplines on which you will draw; the subjects which are related to your own topic but which haven't yet occurred to you; the concepts and techniques which are generally relevant to the Field, or indeed the Area, within which your topic resides. That's the difference between examples 4a and 4b, in Table 2.3.

Your topic needs to draw on the material which you have encountered during several of the taught elements of your programme and not simply one. Here is your opportunity to flesh out your topic; to identify and draw on the various concepts and techniques dealt with in relevant components of your taught programme; and to be explicit about the provenance of the *various* themes (concepts, ideas, techniques, authors) on which you draw. These rarely reside within the single discipline or business function to which your qualification programme pertains: even the most specialist Masters degrees have an interdisciplinary component to the extent that they deal with management issues. This is especially true of professional qualifications.

ILLUSTRATION 2.3

Hazel Jones is a Senior Nursing Tutor who decides to concentrate on 'Structural and cultural changes affecting nursing training'. She considers this to be an Aspect of the broader Field of 'Health service strategic management', the Field being located within the broad Area of 'Public sector corporate strategy'. However, she realizes that she will have to deal with issues of 'change management' and recognizes that this is a Field within the broader Area of 'organizational behaviour' and includes these in her provenance table. Further items are added under the Area and Field headings as she thinks through the resourcing, costing, and managerial implications of the changes. She adds to the list of key concepts and authors, those that reflect these additional Fields.

Table 2.4 shows Hazel's provenance table in its initial stages.

As you will have noticed from Figure 1.1 and the sample project titles on the website, post-experience students and anyone following their qualification programme while currently employed will most probably choose a topic which is relevant to their organization, while undergraduates and full-time students not in a placement are more likely to choose a general, industry- or sector-wide topic. If as a post-experience student you find with a fairly specific topic from the outset (entering it in the Aspect column), then work from right to left, asking yourself what broader Fields inform the topic; conversely, if as a full-time student, perhaps doing a library-based project, you begin at the very general Area or Field level then spend time in bringing the topic to a focus in the Aspect column, working from left to right, *before* you flesh out the picture from right to left. Get specific before you broaden out.

TABLE 2.4 Hazel Jones' provenance table at an early stage of development

Area	Field	Aspect	Topic
Public sector corporate strategy	Health service strategic management	Structural and cultural changes	The impact of change on nursing training
Organizational behaviour	Change management		
Public sector finance	Health service budgets	Training provision Lead times Virement	
(Health Service) HRM	Staff turnover	Staff recruitment – retention balance: alternatives to training	

The final step in fleshing out your provenance table is to add the particular, specific, and detailed concepts, theories and techniques which you plan to use, to the right most column of the table. Listing the authors on whom you intend to draw is a particularly useful way of doing this, since it helps you to construct a reading list for your project work. Initially, there won't be many items in this column but, as time goes by, it will fill out in a comprehensive manner.

Constructing a provenance table is not an abstract exercise. A knowledge of which course components are relevant to your topic will be an essential aid in marshalling the background reading and specialist tuition and support, which you will need for your project.

 Please give it a try: now is the time to do activity 3 in the Project Guide.

2.4   Specifying your research questions

Glance again at Figure 2.1. You'll notice that each of the ideas in their final form is expressed as a question. Each has been derived by considering two very simple, straightforward and interrelated issues. In the circumstances

- what are you *really* trying to do? And, given what's possible,
- what is it that's *most useful* to do?

The result is the actual question which you will address in order to carry out the research specified in your topic. Everything you do (your methodology, your research design and sampling, the research methods you choose) will revolve round the result: your **research question**.

So, the final task in deciding on your topic for research is to state it: to identify a well-defined question, uncluttered with irrelevant details, which you will seek to address in your project; the one round which you will construct your literature review (see Chapter 7) and for which you will develop a research design (see Chapter 8).

When you first start the process described in Figure 2.1, those two questions, 'What are you really trying to do? and 'What is it that's most useful to do?' may sound like a mystical search for 'right answers'. However, once you have brought your topic to a more focused state by applying the criteria listed earlier and constructing a provenance table, you'll find that there's nothing mysterious about the next step. An appropriate research question can be generated very straightforwardly by addressing both questions directly.

What are you really trying to do?

The answer to this question will depend on what you feel the chief issues are. These depend on the circumstances in which you are doing the research. It may be that the thing which gives your topic its importance is that it offers an improvement in the *efficiency* with which some process is carried out. Alternatively, the key issue about your topic may be that it involves a *choice*: a decision between alternative ways of doing something. Or it may be that the issue isn't one of the best way of doing something, but that people in the know disagree about what 'best' actually means and you realize that what really matters is the different stakeholder positions that underlie the *preferences* that people involved in the decision are expressing.

There are many different angles to a research topic, and Table 2.5 lists some of them. Simply ask yourself which one applies to your topic and you've found the research question to ask. Glancing back at Figure 2.1, you can see that the students whose topics are shown decided that the first topic is really about *descriptions* and analysis of *differences* in two departments; the second about *effectiveness* and

TABLE 2.5 Some issues which commonly underlie performance in organizations	
Is my topic about . . .	**In other words . . .**
■ efficiency	how accurately, quickly, resource-intensively, cheaply can something be done?
■ effectiveness	how well, in comparison to other alternatives, can something be done?
■ appropriateness	how closely matched is something to a set of values, or to some preferred strategy?
■ beliefs, values and culture	are personal attitudes, beliefs, opinions and values primarily involved; to what extent is the real issue to do with broadly shared social norms?
■ resource constraints	what sort of resourcing, optimization, minimization of costs or maximization of outcomes, best value factors are involved?
■ descriptions	what's actually going on?
■ causes and outcomes	does the heart of the issue require a search for one or more causes, mitigating circumstances, contingency factors?
■ change	is the main issue to examine some process of change, or its consequences?
■ comparison and benchmarking	how do other departments, organizations, other circumstances, do something?
■ rational decisions and choices	what options or alternatives exist and how should one of them be selected?
■ stakeholder preferences	are matters resolvable against a single legitimate standard with clear rights and wrongs, or is some balance required between equally legitimate stakeholder positions?
■ structural and design considerations	to what extent does the real issue pertain to differentials between different types of employee; reporting structures, or organizational design arrangements?

choices; the third deals with *implications of change*; and the fourth, about *effectiveness* and *beliefs*.

As you look at this list, perhaps other kinds of issue will occur to you. If you apply each of them to your own topic, one by one, you will be able to answer that question of 'what am I really trying to do?' Some will be clearly irrelevant; some will be of middling importance and leave you rather indifferent and one or two, maybe three, will give you a feeling that *that*, indeed, is the real issue at stake.

What is it that's most useful to do?

There is always more than one issue underlying a topic! You may be interested in the most efficient technique for doing something. However, in the process of researching it, you may realize that there is another technique which may not be as efficient, but which costs much less to apply. So maybe the issue underlying your research question is not one of **efficiency**, but one of overall **effectiveness**?

Choosing between the two, or indeed between any of the other small handful of key issues at which you've arrived, usually depends on circumstances. With in-company projects, that has a lot to do with what other people think is currently important (key individuals like your sponsor, or line manager, or perhaps some director in whose domain your research activities are to take place). In the library-based project, on the other hand, the particular issue to focus on might be determined by the literature: whatever is the most current issue, or the most interesting but not-yet-understood issue, and so on.

And there are times when you decide that you cannot choose between a single main question and just one or two subsidiary ones which cover essential issues that you feel you will need to deal with to do the whole question justice. Asking yourself why these issues are important, and what angle to take towards them, may help you to refine the research question itself, as Andrews (2003: 39–44) suggests. You might like to glance at this brief account if you need further help with the development of your research question.

 At this point, pause, and tackle one of the three Case Examples 2.2, (undergraduates), 2.3 (full- or part-time post-experience programme), or 2.4 (full-time, immediate postgraduate programme). Read over the others if you wish! And now, please look at the Project Guide and complete activity 4.

2.5   Making a dry run: starting a project proposal

Now you have your ideas thought through, to the point at which you can begin reading in depth, developing a research design and engaging in all the other activities described in Parts 2 and 3 of this book. Why not summarize the point that you have reached, in the form of a project proposal? Indeed, your own teaching institution might positively require you to write a project proposal document before you begin work on the project itself.

There are some standard headings to use.

- *The topic*: a brief, one sentence statement of what your project is about, which with suitable rewording and shortening could be used as your dissertation title.

- *The rationale*: a statement of why the topic is worth doing, with sufficient background information about the industry or the company in question to provide a context. A brief overview of the main authors and relevant academic concepts on which you will be drawing can also be placed under this heading.

- *The objective*: a precise statement that refers to your intentions in the form of immediate, observable outcomes. It's important that you distinguish between *immediate outcomes*, *stages* in your research activity and *eventual outcomes*. Only the first of these three counts as a research objective in this sense.

The research question in Sarah Winstanley's professional project (a CIPD management report) concerns the causes of employee turnover. Working on her statement of objectives, she provides the following list:

a to review the indicators and indices for measuring staff turnover

b to measure and cost the level of staff turnover

c to identify and evaluate possible solutions, examining and assessing their corporate implications

d to prepare a report for the Board

e to complete the requirements of my CIPD qualification

The first two of these may be necessary *stages* in her work but aren't the main objective of the project, while the fourth and fifth are eventual *outcomes* of the project once the work has been completed. The third is her *research* objective.

- *The research question*: the precise question that you will be asking when you do your research.

- *The provenance table*: you prepared in activity 3 should be included.

Table 2.6 provides you with an example, following this first set of headings. There are some other headings to use in order to complete a project proposal of this kind and these are taken up again at the end of Chapter 9. They concern:

- methodology, research design, representation and generalization

- methods and techniques to be used and

- a research timetable,

and you will be asked to complete the proposal using those headings once you have worked through the material in the intervening chapters. At this point, you are working on just the first part of the proposal and there will be more to come!

TABLE 2.6 Marco Testa's initial idea and how it appeared as a research proposal. Post-experience Masters level

Initial Idea	Um . . . something to do with the lack of synergy between the companies in our group? The UK company communicates effectively with US head office but the Danish company seems to do its own thing – yet is perceived as getting better results!

The Research Proposal

Topic	A comparison of production efficiencies and quality standards in the US, UK and Danish companies
Rationale	The US headquarters sets competitive strategy with respect to a global marketplace, and determines product differentiation in the local companies (with several manufacturing units within the USA and units in the UK, Denmark, Canada and elsewhere). In-company indicators of labour efficiency, machine utilization, output and rework suggest that the unit which does things its own way with relatively little collaboration with Head Office is apparently the most efficient. This suggests a need for synergy: a better integration of manufacturing systems across all units, bearing cultural factors in mind.
Research Objective and Research Question	To compare the production and quality standards of the US, UK and Danish factories using a range of standard internal indicators, bearing in mind the national differences. What accounts for the differences in their claimed efficiency?

Provenance	Area	Field	Aspect + concepts/reading
	Strategic Management	marketing and distribution	demands made on manufacturing (new products, batch sizes, customer base, quality standards) Denison 'Corporate Culture and Organizational Effectiveness'
	Operations Management and Production Technology	support functions (planning, quality, engineering); reliability of equipment and processes	Edwards 'Managing the Factory'
	HRM	policy and procedures	selection, training and motivation
	Globalization	cultural differences: national culture; NB Hofstede, and Trompenaars	Tayeb 'Management of a Multicultural Workforce'
	International business	conditions of trade	
	OB and HRD	group dynamics and sociotechnical systems considerations leadership theory, especially communication, participation, performance management	Jaques 'Changing Culture of a Factory' Bion 'Experiences in Groups' Neale 'Performance Management' Vroom and Yetton 'Leadership and Decision Making'
	Finance	cost/management accounting	Identical transfer pricing policies? Innes and Mitchell on Activity-based costing Investment decision/return on capital

★ Now, in conclusion, please go to the Project Guide and complete activity 5.

Two years ago, Andrea Mathews became interested in the concept of tacit knowledge when her boss told her about the company's new initiatives in knowledge management. He mentioned that the speaker at a recent seminar he had attended advised companies to spend more time on ways of capturing knowledge rather than simply developing IT networks for its dissemination, and her own reading in her MSc (BIT) course suggested that it's the understated, informal, often inarticulate expertise that was particularly beneficial to identify. She wanted to choose this topic for her project but ran into a conceptual problem: there seemed to be no strong theory of knowledge which incorporated a sufficiently robust tacit knowledge elicitation technique. Her tutor had suggested she look at Personal Construct Theory with its associated Repertory Grid Technique, but to her frustration all the technical manuals (Bannister and Mair 1968; Fransella and Bannister 1977; Stewart and Stewart 1982) were long out of print, and she wasn't sure she could find an appropriate account of the theory.

Is there any point in persisting with this topic? Does she have to give up, or are there ways round the difficulty?

Answers to Case Example 2.1

Andrea's problem, caused by a topic which is too difficult because the sources she needed weren't available, is, firstly, one of timing. Her access to texts on the Repertory Grid Technique, which is clearly useful for eliciting tacit knowledge, was hampered by the fact that relevant texts were out of print. As it happens, a new publication (Jankowicz 2003), has become available more recently, which provides exactly the kind of information she was looking for. Sometimes a topic which can't be attempted in one year becomes feasible a year or so later for another student.

Another difficulty she faces is that, until a research field reaches a certain point of development, relevant materials are too obscure to be easily obtainable. Hunt has done useful work on the definition of knowledge and the implications for knowledge elicitation, but for some years this was available only as an internal research report of Stockholm University (Hunt and Hassmen 1997). The ideas are more readily obtainable now, in their application to managerial decisions and to knowledge management: see Hunt (2003).

Whenever you suspect that the subject is intrinsically too difficult, talk again with your tutor and look for feedback on the material you *have* been able to find. Tutors' knowledge is more extensive than your own, but it is also more up-to-date, since at the early stages of research, you will be working from textbooks and perhaps one or two journals (see Chapter 7), while they are working from current issues of journals and from conferences at which the most recent material has been presented. The tutor would certainly have pointed Andrea towards several accounts of the underlying theory: Kelly (1991) or Burr and Butt (1992) for example.

If you are fortunate enough to be in full-time employment and have access to a budget, you might consider paying a consultancy firm for techniques that you lack. This is how Andrea resolved her problem. She found a consultant to teach her the Repertory Grid technique and her boss was able to meet the fees out of his current budget. But this solution is uncommon.

CASE EXAMPLE 2.2   Choosing and working up a topic: undergraduate

Martha Gowling wants to work in personnel. Highly focused by the time she starts her third year, she is doing a BA (Business Studies) degree, specialising in HR by taking a number of elective modules which she hopes will ease her subsequent CIPD professional studies in personnel management. She is casting around for a topic for her dissertation and decides to work systematically through activities 1 to 4 of the Project Guide.

Activity 1

She looks at the idea-generation techniques listed in Section 2.1 with great enthusiasm, and starts by simply discussing her interests with three of her class-mates during the morning coffee-break between lectures, scribbling down ideas as they occur. This is useful but a little frustrating, because she ends up with plenty of different ideas – but every one is rather vague. 'Something to do with stress', 'Women in management', 'Managers as leaders', ' Something to do with the management of diversity', 'Job satisfaction among small business employees' are just some of the ideas she writes into page 1 of her research diary later that evening. Her HR lecturer, when consulted, suggests that she looks through some of the textbooks on her reading list, scanning the sections which deal with these topics and paying particular attention to the titles of journal articles in the bibliography of each book, to see what other researchers have done with topics like these. She comes across a reference to an old article by Rosabeth Moss Kanter in which it was asserted that once any category of employees falls below a certain proportion of the total number of people in an organization, they tend to be seen as 'token' representatives of their group rather than as individual people. This sounds promising: Aren't women in the minority in many occupations? What about this as a topic? It's grim to be viewed merely as a token. What is their job satisfaction like compared to men?

Activity 2

She finds this step easy. She has read a lot on job satisfaction and on women in management, and finds the concepts used in this field unproblematic. Her lecturer shares some of these interests and would probably agree to act as her tutor. Accessing respondents may not be too difficult since she has an uncle in the Fire Service and a neighbour who works as a nursing tutor in a local NHS Trust, both of whom have said they might be able to provide support. Her lecturer confirms that on this basis, a topic along these lines would be feasible, but that it still needs working on to identify a precise research question.

Activity 3

As she does a first draft of her provenance table, it strikes Martha that while the item 'Job satisfaction' fits well in the Field column, what she is really interested in is job *dis*satisfaction – and so she puts 'stress' into the Aspect column. Among the other Fields she thinks she should draw on, she lists 'labour force composition', with 'male-female balance' as an important Aspect.

Activity 4

1 Advise Martha. Using Figure 2.1, identify the kinds of issues which pertain to her topic.

2 It looks as though she is going to survey a number of respondents, male and female; in this case example, access to people willing to be surveyed is important and, in particular, the types of respondent available to her. In these circumstances, and given what you know from the way she has addressed the previous three activities, what kinds of research question would make sense?

Choosing and working up a topic: undergraduate (cont.)

Answers to Case Example 2.2

1 One obvious issue relates to *comparison* and another to *organisational culture*. Martha suspects that the pressures on women are different to those on men: that the experience of work differs and in particular, that the level of stress is different. However, there are *structural* issues too. Not all organizations are dominated by males; in fact, in some occupations, females predominate.

2 One possible comparison she might make is to ask simply whether females are more stressed than males. A more specific variant, likely to show a strong effect, is to ask whether this is particularly true for managerial grades of employee, where there are fewer females than males in most occupations. Looking at the nature of the respondents potentially available (the Fire Service, preponderantly staffed by males, and the Nursing Service, with a strong history of female job occupancy), the following research question might also be asked. Do women in traditionally masculine occupations encounter greater stress than women in traditionally female occupations? (And is the same true for men in like circumstances?) (You might care to look at Gardiner and Tiggeman (1999) where a slightly more complex variant of this last question was asked.)

CASE EXAMPLE 2.3

Choosing and working up a topic: post-experience student

Marco Testa works for an international manufacturing company with factories in the USA, Canada, Denmark and the UK, and is doing an MBA part-time, attending the university on two nights each week. Now that he has to specify a topic for his dissertation, he's quite pleased, as he sees it as an opportunity to work out some answers to a question that's been puzzling him for some time. He has visited the Danish plant and has hosted his Danish colleagues in return; likewise with managers from the other companies in the group. There is something not quite right about the way in which the various companies collaborate. The link with the Canadians is unproblematic, but there seems to be little synergy on issues of production quality between the other factories. The US head office sets global strategy, but the Danes seem to do their own thing a lot of the time. They're good, but they're not as good as they think they are; so why do they have quite so high a reputation for excellence in the company as they do? Some of the processes used in his own UK plant are actually quite good; why do they rate relatively poorly whenever effectiveness is talked about within the company as a whole?

Activity 1

He talks with his line manager, who agrees that an exploration of these issues would be worthwhile. Marco comes up with the notion of 'something to do with the lack of synergy between the companies in our group'.

Activity 2

The topic certainly interests him; and it forms a background to many of his day-to-day activities, so he feels he has the knowledge to handle it. It includes strategic and corporate issues as required in his MBA programme, is not too difficult and can be handled in the time he has available. His boss has agreed a travel budget which would enable him to talk to key people in two of the locations, and he has to visit one of the others in three months' time in any case, as part of his job.

Activity 3

Filling out the provenance table, Marco remembers that the context in which the different factories operate is different: they're in different countries! He adds the item 'cultural differences' to the Field column, and 'globalisation' in the corresponding Area column. That stimulates the thought that there are other differences too: each is bound by different national and local regulations, commercial lending arrangements, as well as cultural standards. 'Conditions of trade' is entered into the Field column, and 'international business' as an area. He fills out other entries of the provenance table.

Activity 4

He sits down to the final stage: to summarize his topic as a research question. Can you help him?

1 What are the key issues underlying his topic? Look at the list of basic issues shown in Figure 2.1 and identify the one or two that seem most relevant.

2 Having eavesdropped on his conversation with his line manager, you know that his boss confirms that an international comparison would be particularly useful. What sort of research question would be useful, as well as reflecting the issues you identified in step 1?

Answers to Case Example 2.3

1 The first key issue is one of *efficiency* differences. Notice, though, that there is a suggestion that some of them they might be more apparent than real. *Beliefs and values* may come in to it.

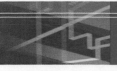

CASE EXAMPLE 2.3   Choosing and working up a topic: post-experience student (cont.)

Also, notice that question 'why?': there seems to be a search for *causes*.

2 Something along the lines of 'Are the different companies as good as they claim, and why?' would seem to meet the requirement.

However, a little more specificity would be helpful. What do you mean by 'good'? And does Marco really need to cover the Canadians? He feels he understands them already. So, in conclusion, a research question along the lines of 'Comparing the production and quality standards of the US, UK and Danish factories: what accounts for the differences in their claimed efficiency?' would seem to be appropriate.

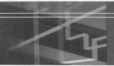

CASE EXAMPLE 2.4 Choosing and working up a topic: full-time postgraduate student

Xie Yanshao (known as Johnny Xie to his fellow students) is a Chinese exchange student who is about to start on his full-time MSc (e-business) dissertation. The topic he has in mind reflects his family background, as both his parents work for a consumer goods wholesaler and his uncle in retailing. 'Something to do with online shopping', is his initial idea.

E-business is a relatively new development in China and the experience of the two largest retail chains is that, while a growing number of people use their sites for product information and comparative pricing, few are ready to use this medium for online purchasing. Not everyone has a bank account or credit card, for example, to be drawn on in an online purchase. Nevertheless, a couple of companies are reporting successes. How might the customer best be approached? If he can address this and related issues successfully, he sees an opportunity to consult in this field when he returns home after finishing his degree, working for one of the international consultancies that are setting up in China.

Activity 1

Yanshao already has the idea at the back of his head, but what particular angle should he take? He talks with his lecturer, who suggests that he and the other ten students registered for the Masters degree organize a brain-storming session in which they will write down a range of specific ideas. As it turns out, the most popular direction proposed is the investigation of various aspects of 'pure-play' e-retailing (that is, companies that trade solely though the internet without a conventional presence in the market) but because of his family connections, Yanshao prefers to examine how *existing* retailers might make greater use of the business potential of the Internet.

Activity 2

He prefers this because he sees greater potential for independent consultancy, outside the state framework, helping existing retailers develop internet-based services. He is knowledgeable in the field and has excellent grades in the most relevant modules of his course; the mixture of specialist operational, and organizationally-strategic, issues is exactly what the MSc (e-business) project requires; and, provided he manages his efforts carefully, the project can be done on time. He is planning to return home during the summer vacation and will easily be able to access his respondents; his parents and uncle have promised to help him find suitable interviewees. He will need to arrange to use his UK university library for his reading, both before the vacation and after his return.

Activity 3

As soon as he sits down to sketch out his provenance table, he realizes there are three main Areas of involvement: those that reflect the *market*, the *service provider*, and the *technical issues*. He notes down as Areas 'traditional marketing' (with the Fields of 'buyer behaviour', 'marketing strategy', and 'branding' being particularly important); 'e-commerce' (subdivided into the Fields of 'online promotion', 'e-retailing development', and 'service quality'); and 'internet marketing' (comprising the Fields of 'web design and development' and 'automated payment systems'. There is more to come, he feels, but this will do for the moment.

Activity 4

What kind of research question might suit his situation?

1 What are the key issues underlying his topic? Look at the list of basic issues shown in Figure 2.1 and identify the one or two that seem most relevant.

2 Yanshao's lecturer listens to his account of his initial idea and why he is interested (the material provided in the first paragraph above). Put yourself in the lecturer's shoes. If you had this information, what sort of research question would you encourage Yanshao to address?

Answers to Case Example 2.4

1 Since there are a couple of companies that seem to be making a success against the general trend, some sort of *comparison* between them and the other companies would seem to be indicated. What are they doing that works for them? Which, in turn, suggests issues of *effec-tiveness* rather than simple technical *efficiency* are important.

2 You might, if you were Yanshao's lecturer, point out that there is another issue involved, that of *change*: consumers are happy to use a company website in one way (online information), but not another (on-line purchasing). How can people be moved from the first to the second?

Putting all this together, a suitable research question might be 'What is it that the two successful companies have done with their websites, in getting people moving from information to sales, that is different to what the less successful companies have been doing?'

Project Guide

By the time you finish these activities, you should have arrived at a research question, and be capable of writing the first section of your research proposal.

1 Identify a topic.

Use one of the approaches listed in Section 2.1 to identify five different topics. If you find this difficult:

- try some of the other techniques in that section
- look again at Table 2.2 and the sample project topics on the website and see what the list of topics might suggest for you (without reproducing any of those shown there!)

Record the results in your research diary.

2 Apply the criteria

Take each of the possible topics that resulted from exercise 1 and run them through the criteria outlined in Section 2.2:

- what is there about each one that interests you?
- what is it that you know most about each one?
- what might the difficulties be with each, in terms of suitability to the type of programme you're studying, the intrinsic difficulty of the topic, the availability of a tutor for the topic and the amount of interest your boss might have in it?
- which aspects of the topic might you best be able to obtain data about, bearing in mind the costs of time and money that might pertain?
- use your research diary throughout.

3 Make a provenance table

- Take a fresh page in your research diary, rule it into three columns headed by 'Area', 'Field' and 'Aspect' and fill out as much as you can.
- Flesh it out by working from right to left, identifying the different subjects on which you will need to draw. You will need to do some thinking and some library searching to complete this step; at the very least, read over your lecture notes on the material you have in mind.
- If you find that you don't get very far with your first topic, repeat the exercise with another from your list of five.

Try to construct a provenance table for at least two of your five topics.

4 Specify your research question

- Now that you have provided a research question for the case example, write one for your own project.

5 Start your research proposal

- using Section 2.5 and Table 2.6 as your model, prepare a table like it and fill it out with as much detail as you can. Your deadline is four weeks after you have started on your project, or three weeks after you have started on any taught course in research methods associated with your project, or the date on which you are meant to hand in a formal research proposal if that forms part of your assessment, *whichever is the earliest*.
- Continue this activity after reading Chapters 5 and 9.

References

Andrews, R. (2003) *Research Questions,* London: Continuum.

Bannister, D. and Mair, J. (1968). *The Evaluation of Personal Constructs,* London: Academic Press.

Burr, V. and Butt, T. (1992) *An Invitation to Personal Construct Psychology,* London: Whurr.

Buzan, T. (2003) *The Mind Map Book,* London: BBC Consumer Publishing.

Fransella, F. and Bannister, D. (1977) *A Manual of Repertory Grid Technique,* London: Academic Press.

Gardiner, M. and Tiggeman, M. (1999) 'Gender differences in leadership style, job stress and mental health in male- and female-dominated industries', *Journal of Occupational and Organisational Psychology,* 72: 3: 301–315.

Hunt, D. P. (2003) 'The concept of knowledge and how to measure it', *Journal of Intellectual Capital,* 4: 1: 100–113.

Hunt, D. P. and Hassmen, P. (1997) *What it means to know something,* Report no. 835, Department of Psychology, Stockholm University.

Jankowicz, A. D. (2003) *The Easy Guide to the Repertory Grid,* Chichester: Wiley.

Kanter, R. M. (1977) 'Some effects of proportions on group life: skewed sex ratios and responses to token women', *American Journal of Sociology,* 82: 965–990.

Kelly, G. A. (1991) *The Psychology of Personal Constructs,* London: Routledge.

Maczynski, J. (1991) *A Cross-cultural Comparison of Decision Participation Based on the Vroom–Yetton Model of Leadership,* Institute of Management, Technical University of Wroclaw.

Raimond, P. (1993) *Management Projects,* London: Chapman and Hall.

Senge, P. M. (1990) *The Fifth Discipline: the Art and Practice of the Learning Organization,* London: Random House.

Sharp, J. A., Peters, J. and Howard, K. (2002) *The Management of a Student Research Project,* Aldershot: Gower Publishing.

Shaw, M. L. G. (1985) 'Communities of knowledge' in *Anticipating Personal Construct Psychology,* Epting, F. and Landfield, A. W., (eds.) Lincoln, Nebraska: University of Nebraska Press: 25–35.

Smith, P. B. and Peterson, M. F. (1988) *Leadership, Organisations and Culture: an Event Management Model,* London: Sage.

Stewart, V. and Stewart, A. (1982) *Business Applications of Repertory Grid,* London: McGraw-Hill.

3

Standards of assessment

Activity Objectives

- To provide you with information on the standard expected of your completed dissertation and to list the attributes of a successful project
- To identify the kind of evidence required in the three broad kinds of project work (in-company based, generic, and library-based)
- To introduce the ethical considerations which apply when you engage in project work
- To outline the kind of criteria applied when your examiner grades you

At a glance

Standards of difficulty vary across the range of projects you might undertake. After presenting a simple model which you can use to recognize the standard which applies in your own case, the attributes of a successful project are outlined. Next, we look at some of the marking schemes used by tutors when they assess project work, and peer inside their heads to see what they're thinking as they mark a typical project. Different types of project are structured differently and two of the most common structures are described.

3.1 General guidelines

Your project is going to be examined when it's finished. Someone is going to be assessing the standard which you have reached. Your tutor will do it formally, in order to assign a grade, while your boss, assuming you're in employment, may also pass judgement – less formally, but, potentially, with an equivalent impact on your future. If you can get some idea of the level of excellence which they will expect from you, it will enable you to anticipate their judgements, monitor your progress towards the standard and do something about it if you get the feeling that your work is unsatisfactory. In effect, you become one of the examiners, which is a good thing to be, if only because you have greater control when you're self-assessing than when you're being assessed.

We start with the banal assertion that standards are related to level of study: in some sense, less is expected of the undergraduate projects, more of the postgraduate Diploma and more again of the Masters-level project. But less and more of what? Focusing on academic standard in general and leaving aside, for the moment, the issues arising from the involvement with in-company relevance which characterizes a business or management project, one way of defining the level is as follows.

Putting it very crudely, there are three types of information which you will be supplying for assessment:

- Theories, concepts, rational argument, the use of existing ideas and literature, and the links you establish between these existing ideas and your own.

- The methods and techniques which you use to obtain your evidence.

- The evidence itself: data derived from your empirical investigations, together with inferences leading to conclusions and recommendations.

Now, 'information' is defined as anything which removes uncertainty – anything which is new to its recipient. So one way of thinking about standards is to ask what is new about your work.

A PhD student (bear with me), who is conventionally required to make 'a significant contribution to knowledge', will do well if he or she develops new concepts (developing an existing or new theory, for example); develops new methods or techniques; or comes up with new findings – and preferably two of these, the first and second, or the first and third. In addition, the student's technical expertise (the rigour with which the methods are used, whether existing methods or newly developed) must be perfect.

Why talk about the PhD student? Simply because this level of work offers you a useful rule of thumb. You are expected to do less and specifically:

- At Master's level: one of the above (new concepts, new methods, or new findings) and the technical expertise must be competent, without major blunders in the methodology.

- At the postgraduate Diploma level: one of the above, perhaps at a lower standard of difficulty, with some tolerance for the odd mistake or incompleteness in method.

- At undergraduate level: almost always the last one (new findings), with some tolerance for mistakes and greater tolerance still for incompleteness, in your use of methods and techniques.

This rule of thumb describes the average expectation at any one level of study. It's a crude statement of the standard which ought to put you in the 55 per cent to

60 per cent bracket at each level. Aim to do more; go deeper if you can and take your tutor's advice on the feasibility of this intention, given the topic you choose.

Is there a corresponding non-academic, in-company based rule of thumb for specifying the standard which you must reach? Indeed there is, and it focuses on the issue of *relevance*. You will be judged on the extent to which your work illuminates an issue which concerns your sponsor and on the extent to which you provide findings which are important to the organization involved. When you apply the rule of thumb outlined above, do two things. Add the word 'relevant' to the wording. Second, notice the emphasis on results: in general, your sponsor would much rather you offered new data and conclusions, than new concepts or new methods and techniques. (There may be an exception in the case of some professional projects: a new application of a technique, or indeed an amendment to a technique, would be most acceptable.)

3.2 The attributes of a successful project

We saw in the previous chapter how to turn an initial project idea into a precisely stated and well-focused research question. The nature of this research question will determine your scope for success – your chances of doing the kind of work which gets good grades. There are six attributes of a successful project and these should shape the development of your research question.

Originality

There are two senses in which this word is used, each interrelated. I introduced the idea of **novelty** when I outlined the rule of thumb in the previous Section: the fresher your use of concepts, methods and findings, the more informative the project will be. Tutors grow old and grey in direct proportion to the number of retreads they read; indeed, it's quite common and on balance justifiable, for a tutor to steer you away from a project which you have in mind because something very similar was offered by a student last year, even though the topic is exciting to you. Aim, if you can, to write something which excites them; which gives them an insight; which has them saying 'aha'!

You do so for a very good reason. As well as being named individuals with whom you have a relationship, your tutor and your sponsor stand for the wider community of readers implied in the very notion of standards of assessment. To satisfy these readers and give them an experience of something new, you will have to discover what's old: what has gone before, what has already been done and covered in the academic literature, and the things that are taken for granted in the organizational setting.

In seeking originality, it's useful if you can avoid the merely faddish: topics which are 'flavour-of-the-month' without sufficient depth to bear an extended investigation. This can, at times, be a difficult judgement to make. There are good arguments (see Abrahamson 1996; Meyer 1996) which state that the processes by which fashions emerge and develop in organizations can be a valuable force for the renewal of organizing ideas that stimulate innovation and renewal. If you can research the topic thoroughly so that you can provide recommendations of genuine, rather than spurious, worth were the organization to adopt them, you will have made a very valuable contribution.

You can tell that your work is original and valuable when both your sponsor and your tutor get excited about it and want others to learn from it. Your sponsor wants you to circulate the executive summary of your project to other people in the organization. You are asked to give an oral presentation. It gets written up in the company magazine. Perhaps your tutor encourages you to present a selection from the project report as a paper at an in-college seminar, or external conference. You have achieved something you never expected: your ideas have arrived in the wider arena, beyond the confines of the assessment process!

The second sense in which your work must be original is that it has to be your own. It mustn't be plagiarized. **Plagiarism**, 'copying' from someone else's work, is a matter of degree and can arise unintentionally if you are unaware of the rules for reporting, acknowledging and referencing direct quotations. The rules are outlined in Section 7.1 and Table 7.3. Very occasionally, tutors encounter deliberate plagiarism, where an entire project report, or a significant section, is taken from another person's work. If they can prove it, the consequences are ruinous and terminal for the student concerned. Asking students to submit their dissertation on disk as well as in hard copy, so that it can be checked with specialist plagiarism checking software, is increasingly common.

Generality

In research-driven projects, it is comparatively simple to ensure that project work has generality, that is, a relevance beyond the situation and setting in which the data were gathered. Research projects identify the issues to be investigated by referring to a theory, concepts, or group of ideas and make their contribution by extending or adding to that theory in some way. Since theories are general by nature and the purpose of research is to make general statements, then the projects achieve generality when they draw out the implications of the data for the theory.

Business and management projects aren't quite the same. They don't relate to a theory in quite the same way (see Chapter 5), but the issue of **generality** still matters. If your conclusions apply only to this year's accounts; if your recommendations about employee participation address just one office or one part of a department; if your marketing plan ignores a closely related group of products to the product on which your findings are focused; then your project is unlikely to be successful. It will be acceptable to the extent that its recommendations can be extended to different times, locations, markets, departments and so forth.

More subtly, perhaps, they'll only be useful if they state or imply the circumstances which constrain this extension.

ILLUSTRATION 3.1

For example, in a Personnel Management project on Communicable Diseases which examines the practices and hazards of night-shift workers, a recommendation which advises a Local Authority Cleansing Department to provide plastic gloves to sewer workers on the night shift is weaker than one which advises the Authority to provide them to all sewer workers – unless there is evidence that the day shift is not exposed to the hazards which require the use of gloves in the first place and this evidence has been highlighted.

Many in-company projects base themselves on a case study of an organization, usually your own. The issue of generality is particularly important here and you will need to check that your conclusions apply in some wider sense to your organization and possibly organizations like it, rather than simply to the department or section in which you gathered your case study data. Section 8.2 has further information on this theme and shows how you can make appropriate arrangements through sampling or replication techniques.

Pragmatism/applicability

A good project should be applicable. That is, the answers to its research question should lead to recommendations that can be put into effect. This is partly a matter of practicality, and partly of what is possible on both technical and common-sense grounds.

ILLUSTRATION 3.2

A project on 'competitive advantage' which recommended organization-wide downsizing would be *impractical* if it arose from work carried out in a large multinational organization and took no account of the local companies' individual human resource strategies. It would be *unsuccessful on technical grounds* if it didn't consider the number, experience and age of employees in each company; the activities which incurred costs and of these, those which are and aren't offset on the other side of the balance sheet; and the costs of the associated restructuring or, where it occurs, replacement by contract staff. I call this a 'technical' issue since the evidence which would qualify the recommendation is known and easily available in the literature: see, for example, Pfeffer (1996); Swain (1999).

Finally, there is the matter of common sense: a project may be poor because the recommendations fly in the face of more general information which a few moments' thought, or a discussion with the sponsor or tutor, would have identified as a constraint on the actions being recommended.

This sometimes happens with undergraduates and immediate postgraduate dissertations, where recommendations are strongly urged without taking constraints into account. ('Vital' is a greatly overused word – do you really mean that the issue is a matter of life or death?) Where statements of this kind are problematic is in situations:

■ where qualifying evidence has not been considered

■ where it is assumed, without looking for evidence, that the organization has not considered the issue before

■ where the organization is believed to be perfectly free to act on the recommendation.

You can ensure that your project is sufficiently pragmatic if you are clear about the distinction between efficiency and effectiveness. You may recall this from Section 2.4, where we looked at the factors to be considered in deciding on the research question. Efficiency has to do with technical possibility and feasibility and answers the question '*Can* it be done?' If your recommendations are supported by evidence, and follow logically from the evidence, then they are efficient. Effectiveness, on the other hand, has to do with the constraints on the applicability of technically acceptable recommendations. It answers the question '*Ought* it be done?' given the wider implications. The main implications are usually financial (what will it cost?), temporal (is the timing right?), resource-based (have we the skills or the equipment to do it; can we do it in another and better way?), political (what interest-groups will be affected?), and policy-related (does it fit with the way we wish to do things?). Research projects can sometimes ignore the issue of pragmatism; in-company projects can never ignore it.

Balance

This is my own word for an issue which you will recognize if you've ever done an academic, research-based project before, or if you have a background in a scientific discipline which conducts its research by the formal testing of hypotheses. You would recognize it under the name of 'symmetry of potential outcomes' and a good account in these terms is provided by Gill and Johnson (1997: 14–15).

The issue addresses your project objectives and research question and how your expectations are confirmed by the data you gather. To talk of 'expectations' is not to say that you ever know the results of project work in advance (or that you're going to bend the evidence to fit your preconceptions). What's meant here is an expectation that if you have done your background reading properly, then you should know what kinds of outcomes are possible in answer to your research question. A balanced project is one in which the outcomes will be equally valuable whether your expectations are confirmed, or negated; an unbalanced project is one in which evidence which agrees with your expectations will leave you helpless, or, equally, one in which evidence which disagrees with your expectations will have no value.

ILLUSTRATION 3.3

Jane Selby, who is studying full-time, is doing a library-based project on corporate strategy in the water supply business, looking at their annual reports and related press coverage. She is exploring the idea that companies which have diversified into new products and services (manufacture and retailing of domestic garden hoses and fittings, for example) are more resistant to takeover than those which have not. A positive finding would be very interesting and would permit some fairly powerful recommendations. A negative finding would be equally interesting and would suggest that diversification is a poor strategic option. The topic of this project is balanced.

Pete Saunders, also a full-time student doing a library-based project, soon forms an impressions from his early reading that venture capital firms prefer to invest in business startups where a market niche is likely to be created, rather than in startups in which a commodity product is being sold. His lecturer advises him against making this the centre of his project work, however. As he puts it, 'Evidence that confirmed your expectation would be banal, given what we known about this topic already: remember Gorman and Sahlman (1986). It is exactly what you would expect! Venture capitalists invest in technical advances, niche products and highly focused activities. Of course, evidence which negated your expectation would be extremely exciting . . . but highly unlikely.' The topic in this instance is very unbalanced.

Balance is a matter of what is known already; of the potential value of positive and negative findings; and of the likelihood of either kind of finding. A topic in which your expectations and hunches are unbalanced is a risky one in which to engage. A good way of checking the balance of a project topic is to ask yourself whether your recommendations following *either* kind of outcome are likely to make a difference to the decisions made by a manager in the kind of company to which those findings might apply.

The nature of evidence used

One issue in which your examiners will be very interested is the nature of the evidence you provide. This depends largely on the extent to which you are dependent on primary data as opposed to secondary data. **Primary data** – (*data* is a plural word, by the way, whose singular is *datum*) consist of material that you have gathered *yourself*: systematic observations, information from archives, the results of questionnaires and interviews, case studies which you have compiled. **Secondary data** include everything else, being the results of *other people's* primary data collection as reported in a wide variety of formats: company annual reports, technical manuals, government and trade body publications, books and journals.

You might find the distinction between primary and secondary difficult to draw at times. After all, if you are compiling a case study (primary) you may wish to include financial reports drawn up by the company's accountant (secondary). If you take the line that there's nothing new under the sun, why should you bother with the distinction?

There is one very good reason. Data are primary if they have been gathered according to your own rationale and interpreted by yourself, to make a point which is important to your own argument: in other words, if they are relatively original. Data are secondary if they come to you with someone else's rationale and assumptions about what is important. That is, if they carry the possible risk of constraining your own freedom to interpret findings because of the author's emphasis or selectivity. Goldstein and Goldstein (1978: 258) deal with this issue well, in the context of the broader issue of the originality of evidence.

You can see why the distinction is important. You will be assessed on the clarity of thinking which you have shown in gathering and interpreting your own data, and you will have to satisfy the examiners on the expertise you show in recognizing and demonstrating the relevance of secondary data to your own argument. The ground-rules for primary data are outlined in Part 3, in quite some detail. The standards which will be applied in the case of secondary data may not be quite so obvious however.

Basically, don't believe everything you read! The information in secondary data may have been derived by eminent people (by definition, you might argue, since their work has been published and yours has not), but unless the source is widely known to be idiosyncratic but essential, it is you who will be held responsible for the accuracy and interpretations which you reproduce from the source. Your project reaches a high standard when:

■ you summarize their argument or their evidence in your own words, quoting their own words only sparsely and always with a full reference to the source so that there is no impression that you are trying to pass off the work as your own

■ you state the assumptions under which the information was compiled, as well as presenting it, and show that these assumptions are relevant to your own situation

■ you identify the obvious biases in the information (as, for example, the sampling limitations of a particular set of survey evidence, or the known political constraints or public-relations intentions under which company handouts and reports were compiled)

■ you qualify or evaluate other authors' inferences or conclusions, in the light of other information known to you.

The balance of primary and secondary data can make the difference between a good and a poor project. It would be very unusual to find a good project with no reference to other people's writings, whether the references are presented as a formal separate literature review, or are interspersed among your own material. Similarly, a project with no empirical content that you had originated yourself, would be unlikely to be successful.

However, your personal circumstances may make a difference to the kind of project you do and the proportion of primary to secondary data, as follows. (You may recall that I defined these three alternative approaches in Section 1.1, and suggested a strategy for choosing among these approaches in Figure 1.1.)

In-company focused projects

Many projects are done within a single company or organization: your employer, a sponsoring company with whom you spend an industrial placement, or a sponsoring company with which you have built links in order to carry out your project. Chapter 6 develops this theme and most of my comments hitherto have made this assumption. As you will have gathered, your aim in these circumstances is to address an issue of importance to that particular organization.

Generic, industry-based projects

You may want to carry out a generic project right from the start; more commonly, though, people choose this sort of project as an alternative to the in-company project because they can't gain access to a company, or if employed, because their employer is uncomfortable with the close inspection of people, policy, practices and procedures which the completion of a such project would demand. So you carry out a project that takes an issue that is generic to an industry or industry sector as a whole, and builds a case using published evidence. You are probably more dependent on secondary data here, although if you were able to organize the resources required, you could still gather primary data using one or other variant of survey method (see Section 9.1) – for example, by developing a postal questionnaire which you sent to a sample of companies in the industry.

Library projects

The inability to find a sponsoring organization, or resource limitations, or, sometimes, personal choice, may lead you to focus on a conceptual or theoretical issue in which your main resource is the library and your main data are secondary. As well as reporting other people's data, of course, you would be able to present your own slant by compilation from various secondary sources and by appropriate selection, collation and organization of material. If you did this carefully, developing a reasoned, structured argument, the result would be almost equivalent to primary data in its strength of support for the position you are building, as you

- develop
- contrast and
- evaluate

contending ideas and practices, while

- assessing their practical implications.

Your department should have detailed guidelines on the kinds of projects which it accepts, and what to do if you are unable to gain access to a company to carry out an in-company project. It would be wise to consult these before deciding on whether to do a generic project, or a library project, if an in-company project is not an option for you.

This is a good point at which to pause, and tackle activity 1 in the Project Guide at the end of this chapter.

Ethical issues

Managers are people, managing through people. Businesses run on people and their knowledge as much as they do on money or on information or raw materials. You will need to cooperate with other people in many ways, as collaborators (see Chapter 6) and as respondents (see Section 3) and you may encounter problematic situations in which special rules apply precisely *because* you're dealing with people rather than money, information, or raw material.

The development of formally stated ethical guidelines for the conduct of project work is relatively neglected and, until 1998 or thereabouts, ethical guidance for dissertation work was somewhat overlooked. This reflects the general neglect, albeit growing appreciation, of the value of formal ethical codes in business. It was only in 1997 that the number of companies with formal ethical codes reached a majority, in samples surveyed over the preceding ten years (IBE 1998), although this may change in time, as evidence accumulates that there is an association between the existence of an ethical code in a company and a variety of measures of business success (Webley and More 2003).

In business schools hitherto, ethical guidance for research activities has been available less formally within the tutorial relationship when an issue arose. In consequence, the formal statements that may be currently available to you are based fairly directly on guidelines published for medical researchers or people working in psychology laboratories or in sociology, rather than in business and management. One such set is referenced in Table 5.1 of Saunders *et al.* (2003: 129), and if you were to use them, you would certainly need to adjust them to your own circumstances. Nevertheless, if you are doing your studies within a UK academic department, the onus will be on you to show that you have thought through the ethical implications of your empirical work, possibly signing a document to prove it. How?

First, you need to *inform yourself* by obtaining a copy of some appropriate ethical guidelines. These may be available through your course manager at departmental level; or through the Dean of Research or equivalent at university level. Failing either of these, you could scarcely do better than to adopt the guidelines published by the Association for Human Resource Development (Russ-Eft *et al.* 1999). They are comprehensive and aimed directly at research and project work done within the context of a business school, being a development on the other psychological, sociological and medical compilations referred to above. As Donaldson (1989: 129–131) points out, ethical codes represent values that have been deliberately adopted, *after comparison with other alternatives*, as the 'right' way of doing things, not merely the 'best', and in my view, these are the appropriate ones for your circumstances.

Next, *apply the guidelines* to your own project activities. Think through the implications for what you can and cannot do (Table 3.1 provides a few guidelines, based on the AHRD code). Consult with your tutor and, where you feel it may be

TABLE 3.1 Ethical standards for business and management research

Your work should . . .	. . . that is . . .	Who is responsible?
. . . be Professional and Responsible	■ informed about, and consistent with, the standards of your theoretical and methodological perspective (passing off an impressionistic interview record as a reliable and objective record isn't just sloppy, it's unprofessional; reporting it following the guidelines pertaining to constructivist work, e.g. triangulation against other sources, would be entirely appropriate);	You; your tutor as guide
	■ be based on information and techniques sufficient to provide appropriate substantiation of findings;	You; NB, literature review
	■ be based on a research plan which protects rights and welfare of the people researched;	You; your sponsor
	■ be limited to tasks in which you have competence or, as trainees, under appropriate supervision;	Your tutor; your sponsor
	■ conform to professional and legal standards, and the standards of your institution.	Your tutor
. . . use appropriate means of data collection	■ draw conclusions from techniques which reflect current professional knowledge about e.g. design, standardization, validation, reduction of bias;	You; your tutor as guide
	■ taking care to make appropriate adjustments as required, to reflect factors such as gender, age, race, ethnicity, culture, sexual orientation, disability, language and socio-economic status;	You; your sponsor
	■ taking care to store data securely and confidentially (NB UK Data Protection Act 1998).	You; your tutor
. . . involve informed consent	■ inform participants of the nature of the research in language they understand, documenting this;	You
	■ participation being voluntary, informed of the factors involved (e.g. risks, discomfort adverse effects, limitations on confidentiality), the foreseeable consequences of declining being conveyed;	You
	■ provides protection from adverse consequences of declining, where you are in an authority relationship to respondents (e.g. personal subordinates, students of yours);	You

TABLE 3.1 Ethical standards for business and management research (cont.)

Your work should . . .	. . . that is . . .	Who is responsible?
	obtained in advance where recording (e.g. taping, filming) is done, unless the observation uses only naturalistic observation in a public place and the record cannot cause personal identification or harm;	You; your sponsor
	provides an opportunity to examine the nature, results and conclusions; correcting misconceptions;	You
	describes who will see any results which might be personally identifiable, offering anonymization if requested (this may make a real difference to the structure of your data tables) and pointing out any limitations on total anonymization, if any, that may remain;	You
	describes who will see the final report or dissertation, offering an embargo if requested;	You; your tutor
	avoids excessive or inappropriate incentives; where these involve a professional service in kind, its full nature, risks, obligations and limitations must be made clear.	You
. . . carefully control deception	avoid techniques dependent on deception unless justified by the research, educational or applied value AND no equally effective non-deceptive alternatives are feasible;	You; your tutor; but should you have chosen this topic?
	avoid all deception which could affect voluntary consent (unpleasant emotional experiences, discomfort, physical risk);	You
	explain any otherwise legitimate deception as early as possible, preferably immediately after participation and no later than the conclusion of data-gathering.	You
. . . be carefully interpreted	taking into account factors which reduce accuracy of interpretation, providing evidence of reliability indicating any significant reservations about accuracy or limitations on interpretation;	You
	preferably giving access to personal results together with an appropriate explanation of their meaning and inferences drawn;	You
	avoid conclusions from data that are out-of-date or obsolete for the current purpose.	You

After Russ-Eft et al. (1999) section 2, "Research and Evaluation"; rewordings and minor additions by the present author.

appropriate, with your in-company sponsor. Write up the result as a brief document which you put in your research diary.

Some academic institutions require you to complete a form which shows how you have thought out the ethical implications of your proposed project. The document may have to be signed off by your tutor or go before an Ethics Committee (NHS-related projects, for example). Where you have to prepare a research proposal (either as part of your research methods course assessment, or as the first stage of your project work), such a declaration is often required as part of the proposal document. Circumstances sometimes change, so you need to be prepared to review this part of the proposal document periodically and amend it if required.

> And the time to start is now! Please do activity 2 before reading on.

Probably the most common ethical issue that you are likely to encounter concerns other people's expectations. Project work which examines opinions, attitudes and preferences (especially, but not limited to, matters of job satisfaction) raises hopes that 'something will be done about' situations, practices and circumstances which might not be to employees' taste. A moment's thought suggests that these expectations will be most energetic (but not necessarily most optimistic) in organizations where practices are perceived as onerous; the climate is one of low morale; and yours is the first occasion in which people have been asked what they think. You need to be careful in handling the situation. Section 6.2 offers you some specific guidelines about the stance to adopt and later chapters offer you some procedures which preserve anonymity and confidentiality.

Notice from Table 3.1 that in most cases, the personal responsibility for getting things right is mostly yours, though your tutor and your sponsor share your responsibility in others and certainly as regards this matter of increased expectations. You are not the fully trained researcher at whom many of the ethical codes of practice are aimed and there are issues which it is your tutor's (or sponsor's) responsibility to resolve. You may not have the experience to have the foresight to anticipate certain kinds of consequences that follow, even when you're clear on the ethical issue itself. Be guided by your tutor.

This is certainly true when circumstances change during your period of data-gathering. If you plan to collect data by open observation of employees and permission is refused at the outset, the ethical procedure is *not* to press ahead regardless using covert observation, but to change your topic, or rely on secondary sources. But it may be difficult to decide what's best if some of your respondents change their minds about their inclusion in your sample after your data collection has started (for example, after they have talked to people from whom you have already collected data). The ethical answer is still clear – you cannot try to pressurize them into continuing – but the implications for your research design, your sample and how to reconstitute it, may need a discussion with your tutor to resolve.

As you can see, this last attribute of a successful project is a little different from the previous ones. Though your work will be more valuable in absolute terms, you are unlikely to achieve a higher mark by following the ethical guidelines – but you will certainly be marked down if you deliberately ignore them. The issue is outlined here, at the outset – while you're beginning your thinking about standards – to emphasize its importance to everything you do. You will find more detailed examples throughout the remainder of this book, as the particular circumstances emerge.

 Before you go on, please address Case Example 3.1 and answer the questions posed there.

One of the ethical requirements that is easily overlooked, often unwittingly, is your responsibility under European data protection legislation. (Assuming that you are currently resident or working within the European Union, of course.) But even if you aren't, following the spirit of the regulations, Directive 95/46/EC, is a good idea; see URL http://www.dataprivacy.ie/6aii.htm. Within the UK, the relevant legislation is the Data Protection Act 1998. Table 3.2 summarizes the main provisions; if you are in doubt, contact the Data Protection Officer designated within your university for further advice.

TABLE 3.2 The principles of data protection
If you are processing personal data, you have to comply with the following eight principles. Data must be: ■ fairly and lawfully processed; ■ processed for limited purposes; ■ adequate, relevant and not excessive; ■ accurate; ■ not kept longer than necessary; ■ processed in accordance with the data subject's rights; ■ secure; ■ not transferred to countries without adequate protection.
By and large, an individual about whom data are held and processed has the right to know the nature of the data, and to see a copy.
Where the data are used for research, then, so long as the research does not support decisions about particular individuals, is not incompatible with the original reasons for gathering the data, and is processed in a way that doesn't cause damage or distress to those individuals: ■ the data can be kept indefinitely; ■ the individual's right to see the data is qualified, so long as the results of the research or any resulting statistics are not made available in a form which identifies any of the individuals concerned.
These notes summarize the main provisions of the UK Data Protection Act 1998; other equivalent legislation exists for each Member State of the European Union and is compliant with European Union Directive 95/46/EC. The full text of the UK Data Protection Act 1998 is available at: http://www.legislation.hmso.gov.uk/acts/acts1998/19980029.htm

 Finally, please tackle activity 3 in the Project Guide.

3.3 Assessment criteria

Most teaching institutions have their own project standards, published in the form of a handout which is distributed to students when they begin their project work. Some will incorporate guidelines published by professional bodies where these apply. All of them vary substantially, from a single page which identifies the main headings under which projects are evaluated, to detailed manuals of up to 50 pages which give reasons for the standards and a mass of useful information on project work besides. If anything I say in what follows conflicts with your local standards, then ignore what I say and stick to the local version, since it is that which will apply!

Some of these handouts are criterion-referenced; that is, they specify the level of your performance against each criterion, as well as describing the criterion itself. These are offered to the staff who will act as your tutors and examiners, who use them as they think fit in marking your work. (Your tutor may automatically be one of your examiners, or may be excluded from this function; practice varies between universities.) Some staff find such criteria very helpful and stick to them fairly closely when assessing your project; if you know that this is true in your own institution or of your own tutor, you should make a particular effort to get hold of them. Table 3.3 provides an example, at Masters level.

You may notice that word 'scholarship'. All institutions at all levels expect this of you and, though they don't necessarily think about it in the same words, so do all employers involved in project work. It's a word of the finest pedigree: but what does it mean? The primary meaning is quite clear:

- detailed attention to the development of research resources to be used by yourself and the researchers who will come after
- careful and accurate use of evidence
- care in the discovery and attribution of sources
- thoroughness in the coverage of subject-matter
- respect for truth and the validity of data and assertions.

There is also a connotation to the word 'scholarship', a connotation which conveys a value. Namely, that in a fallible and fragmented world, in which fashion, the 'easy way out', charisma, prejudice and bigotry contaminate our understanding of what's happening around us, there is some merit in struggling to achieve the attributes listed above. To ignore scholarship is to make you prey to the charlatan and the demagogue: to the proponent of the latest management fad. So if you are aiming at a moderate to excellent assessment for your project assessment, I feel that you need to subscribe to the value I have expressed. That applies to in-company based projects as much as it does to generic, or library-based, projects.

The remaining tables provide examples of assessment criteria at other levels. Table 3.4 is an example of a professional programme project assessment, which reflects the requirements of the Chartered Institute of Personnel and Development

TABLE 3.3 Assessment criteria, Masters dissertations: generic example, after Luton Business School (2000)

Univ. Scale	A+	A	A−	B+	B	B−	C+	C	C−	D+	D	D−	E	F	G
Grade points	16	15	14	13	12	11	10	9	8	7	6	5	4	2	0
Verbal equiv.	Excellent			Above average			Average			Satisfactory			Refer	Fail	N.Att.
Introduction and/or Theoretical Background	Objectives crystal clear; strategic importance demonstrated, all issues (and thesis, if any) entirely appropriate; the approach clearly described, appropriate and rigorous; organizational background interesting and relevantly stated.			Objectives clear; strategically relevant; most of the issues (and thesis) appropriate; approach generally appropriate with some argument possible over its rigour; organizational background well stated.			Occasional lack of clarity in objectives; strategic relevance discernible with some assumptions; approach not entirely clear and/or justified; organizational background is a description.			Objectives in some doubt; uncertainty over strategic relevance; some arbitrariness in approach discernible; some aspects of the organizational background missing.			Objectives missing or unclear; little or no strategic relevance seen; approach unstated, confused or arbitrary; organizational background, trivial or irrelevant where provided.		
Conceptual Analysis and Lit. Review	Material selected from all appropriate sources; scholarly and practitioner detail consistently high, with good evidence of originality; argument is logical, systematic and persuasive with direct relevance to objectives.			Almost all sources consulted; scholarly and practitioner detail high with small omissions with respect to the argument; generally systematic and persuasive presentation; generally relevant to objectives.			Some sources omitted; reasonable grasp of those consulted and with relevance to argument; no particular originality; some unevenness in presentation; occasional doubt as to relevance to the objectives.			Obvious omissions of relevant sources; some misunderstanding; argument not following a particularly clear thread, or not particularly convincing; objectives rarely referred to.			Key sources omitted, much misunderstanding; little if any argument; lack of a critical stance just an incomplete list of authors, taken mainly from basic texts.		
Methodology	Crystal clear and entirely justifiable, awareness of limitations; research design, method and techniques shown to be exactly appropriate to objectives and/or thesis; sampling appropriate and as complete as possible.			Methodology generally sound, limitations mentioned, research design dealt with as an issue and appropriate to objectives; method and techniques appropriate; sampling complete enough for the purpose.			Methodology discussed though with incomplete awareness of limitations; research design and method considered, techniques fine but not conclusively shown to be relevant; sampling occasionally incomplete or unconsidered.			Methodology confused with description of methods and techniques; unaware of or confused about research design; methods and techniques taken for granted; errors in sampling, which may be incomplete.			Insufficient discussion of methodology, little awareness of its importance; unaware of research design; methods and techniques inappropriate or incomplete; sampling unconsidered as an issue.		

TABLE 3.3 Assessment criteria, Masters dissertations: generic example, after Luton Business School, (2000) (cont.)

Univ. Scale	A+	A	A–	B+	B	B–	C+	C	C–	D+	D	D–	E	F	G
Grade points	16	15	14	13	12	11	10	9	8	7	6	5	4	2	0
Verbal equiv.	Excellent			Above average			Average			Satisfactory			Refer	Fail	N.Att.
Results	Triangulated results drive the argument onwards, completely and fairly; contrary findings used to illuminate or extend the argument. Library-based projects provide crystal-clear rationale using published sources to support the argument seamlessly.			Results substantiate the argument, some triangulation attempted, occasional unawareness of scope and/or limitations. Library-based projects provide an explicit rationale for the approach taken, draw well on published sources with exceptions appropriately handled.			Results related to the argument, but without deep awareness of limitations; triangulation not attempted; a one-source set of evidence. Library-based projects draw on some published sources as evidence in support of the argument; occasional lapses or gaps in the evidence.			Results patchy, presented without progressing the argument: assertions sometimes presented as evidence; little critical awareness; no triangulation. Library-based projects draw on a few published sources as evidence but with gaps in the evidence; the argument just holds water.			Results scrappily presented, little clear argument; many unwarranted assertions rather than evidence; illogical, with appreciable non-sequiturs; no critical awareness. Library-based projects provide weak evidence and do not sustain the argument.		
Discussion Conclusions, Recommend	Well-organized, logical, fully supported by evidence, alternatives dealt with fully, conclusions clear and irrevitable, strategic implications critically considered; recommendations driven by conclusions; practical, feasible, costings provided			Logical and generally supported; evidence of organization; some alternatives discussed; reference to utility, scope and relevance, strategic consequences considered; recommendations arise from the conclusions; reasonably practical and feasible.			Supported by evidence; some discussion of alternatives; gaps in issues concerning utility, scope and relevance; reference made to strategic issues but perhaps not explicitly or fully competently; some consideration of practicalities.			Gaps in reasoning; some obvious conclusions omitted from the list; other conclusions not especially driven by the findings but from 'common sense'. Alternatives little considered; strategic relevance little understood; scarcely any consideration of practicalities.			Assertions little related to evidence, frequently illogical or arbitrary; conclusions disorganized; alternatives not considered; strategic relevance unmentioned or merely asserted; recommendations weak and little based on discussion.		
Presentation	Fully documented and styled according to the brief; written in attractive, engaging and compelling language; specialist terms defined; tables and illustrations beautifully prepared; excellent allocation of material to main body of text, and appendices.			Well documented and styled according to the brief; text free from spelling and grammatical solecisms; vocabulary appropriate; illustrations and tables well prepared; data generally integrated into discussion.			Documentation, e.g. appendices, bibliographic items, generally complete; occasional carelessness in spelling and grammar; vocabulary and style lacking polish but understandable; illustrations and tables adequate.			Some incompletenesses of documentation, e.g. appendices; bibliography incomplete; carelessness in spelling and grammar; vocabulary and style uncomfortable but on balance acceptably conveying meaning; some data, illustrations and tables missing or incompletely presented.			Documentation seriously at fault: missing, misplaced, difficult to find one's way around; persistent errors in spelling and grammar, solecisms or occasional failure in conveying meaning; typescript messy with uncorrected errors and missing or incomplete illustrations.		

TABLE 3.4 Assessment criteria, CIPD Management Report (TBS 1999)

To Pass	To achieve Merit/Distinction Grade
Identifying the problem ■ Clear problem statement. ■ Sufficient detail to understand the organizational context. ■ Aims and objectives clearly stated.	■ Student impresses on the reader why the report is important to the organization. ■ Aims and objectives appropriate for dealing with the issue/problem. ■ Organizational background is interesting to the reader.
Methodology ■ Clear description of methods used, with the reason made clear. ■ Method should be appropriate to aims and objectives. An analytical stance required.	■ Comprehensive methodology, looking outside the organization where possible. ■ Alternatives discussed and reasons for rejection outlined. ■ A critical evaluation of the methods used.
Academic content ■ Reference to academic literature and concepts.	■ Literature well used by the student, informing the report. ■ Concepts are developed/put to use.
Findings ■ Clearly stated and presented.	■ Findings analysed, not merely described. ■ Good use of charts and tables. ■ Thorough analysis of data.
Conclusions ■ Must follow logically from the body of the report, addressing the particular aims and objectives and being clearly presented.	■ Require support with evidence or reference to the evidence. ■ Alternatives acknowledged and discussed.
Recommendations ■ Should follow logically from the conclusions. ■ Should be specific and clear, leaving the organization in no doubt as to what needs to be undertaken.	■ Should be practical and feasible. ■ Clear resource implications required, together with a timetabled implementation plan.
Presentation ■ Appropriate length and format.	■ Well structured and well written; few or no typographical errors. ■ Good use of tables, charts, illustrations. ■ Appropriate use of appendices. ■ Correct referencing.

Pass: 50–59	Merit: 60–69	Distinction: 70+

(CIPD) and highlights some of the specific comments made in Section 3.2 above – for example the need to show relevance to the organizational context and a concern for implementation, in addition to achieving a high academic standard.

3.4 | Format and deadlines

Most institutions specify the format in which the dissertation is to be presented: everything from the length of the document to the colour of the binding. This is sometimes listed explicitly in the assessment criteria and sometimes in a separate document which you should use as your guide. Some general points about format follow below, to give you an early indication of the kind of requirements these institutional documents provide. Also, when the time comes to begin writing, you will need to look at Chapter 13 in detail.

Length

This is usually the first question that occurs to people. It's certainly the first thing you should clarify with your tutor, since the requirements vary very widely, from a minimum of around 5000 words in the case of some professional bodies (e.g. Chartered Institute of Marketing give a benchmark of 5000 words, and CIPFA look for 6 to 8000 words plus appendices), to a maximum of some 40,000 words, depending on the level and nature of qualification. At a rough 300 words to the page, that's a range of between 17 and 140 pages; at the lower level, statements of length usually exclude appendices, title and content pages and the like. For example, the CIPD Management Report regulations (which require no more than 7000 words excluding appendices) explicitly require you to place details of methodology and organizational context in an appendix. You will soon discover that the problem isn't finding enough to say to match the minimum requirement, but rather, one of trying to fit your material within any maximum that might be specified.

Layout and makeup

You are aiming to produced a typed, bound document. The print should be double-spaced, with a 1.5" margin at the left and a 1" margin elsewhere, except in the case of direct quotations and highlighted material, which can be single or one-and-a-half spaced and indented from the left margin by a half-inch or so. The document should be word-processed and, eventually, professionally bound, although many institutions allow you to submit it in a ring- or comb-binding until it has been confirmed that no changes are required.

Timing

While the factors of length and layout and makeup can make a difference between an adequate and a somewhat more than adequate project, there is one factor which can make a difference between complete success and abject failure: and that is the matter of deadlines. If your project document has to be submitted by a certain date, then you simply must comply, if you are to succeed.

 Please pause for a moment and do activity 4 in the Project Guide. It won't take long.

Structure

The minimum requirements for a project report are as follows:

- A title page
- A summary, which can be of two kinds: sequential (otherwise known as an Abstract); or an Executive Summary
- Contents pages
- Acknowledgements
- A general introduction, which states the topic, defines the scope, provides a rationale, lists related objectives, and describes the organization: usually in that order
- The main body of your dissertation, in which you make your argument. This comprises material which describes other people's relevant work (the literature review), your own conceptual material, your methods and results, your discussion and conclusions, possibly followed by recommendations
- Bibliography
- Appendices

in that order. If you are clear on this sequence and aware of the additions which you are required to make to suit your institution's special requirements, you'll go a long way towards satisfying the presentation requirements.

Your project document is more of a management report than a research dissertation, so the summary is particularly important. It gives your reader the first inkling of the structure you will adopt, as well as specifying the content of your project. The 'sequential summary' is rather like the abstract of a journal article: it states the topic, gives the background and rationale for what was done, briefly mentions how it was done, lists the main conclusions and highlights the recommendations. In contrast, in an 'executive summary', this sequence is more or less reversed: topic; recommendations; evidence for recommendations; the methods only if the recommendations depend on them (in the sense that they lead to different and better recommendations than the use of some other method); the background which led to the project; and the importance of taking action, given this background.

Make sure which kind of summary is required in your case.

3.5   What the examiner will be looking for

The structure of the dissertation

The way in which your project document hangs together is particularly important to how it is assessed. The bulk of the content begins with the Introduction, the purpose of which is threefold. First, it provides your reader with everything needed to understand your objectives, your topic, the organizational background and hence your rationale for choosing the topic. Second, it attempts to create interest in what you have to say. Third, it provides an overview of your thinking on the issues covered by the topic and is never assessed in isolation, but in context with the Findings, Discussion and Recommendations which you will present at the end of your project document. The problem with many weak projects is that the author never made this connection and left the reader to flounder within the structure, not quite sure whether everything which the author intended to achieve was in fact achieved.

In-company based projects

In the case of the in-company based dissertation, there are, very broadly, two different kinds of structure to follow for the remaining material. The first kind deals with a single theme or issue (often a research hypothesis) which is identified and clarified in the Literature Review, empirically researched and discussed. Figure 3.1 provides an example.

The figure is more or less goblet-shaped, since the literature review begins with a wide scope and narrows down to a more detailed consideration of the theme that relates directly to the topic of the project. The bowl rests firmly on the stem, in the sense that the research questions which you ask and report results on in the stem, should follow logically as the obvious questions to ask given your discussion which leads up to that point.

One of the most common problems with this kind of dissertation is that it's 'broken-stemmed'. In other words, there is no link between the presentation of the literature review and your own empirical work. The writer says all he or she knows about the background, describes what he or she did and shows no awareness that the two are related. Another (and this is often the case with undergraduate projects) is the absence of a sufficiently broad base. If the Discussion and Recommendations are missing, or if the Recommendations are based on an inadequate Discussion, the project document will be top-heavy and fall over. If the material which should be in the Appendices is put into the empirical section, the same will occur. The first is self-evident; as for the second, you might care to note that the empirical section is the place for evidence directly relevant to the expression and evaluation of each of your results and no more; and the Appendix is the place for the background material essential in supporting your argument. (More detailed guidelines are provided as part of my description of each empirical technique in Chapters 10 to 12, with a brief summary in Chapter 13.)

The second kind of structure is more suited to a situation in which there are several issues to be investigated, often in an in-company setting. This is characteristic of the more multifaceted topics chosen by post-experience students (particularly at MBA level) as they seek to address some live issue within their organization. You might find the candle-and-holder image offered in Figure 3.2

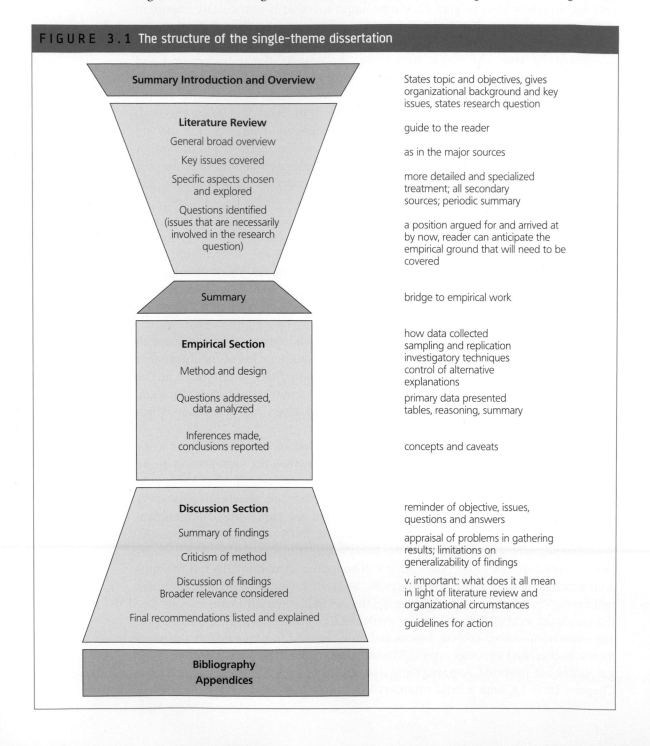

FIGURE 3.1 The structure of the single-theme dissertation

Summary Introduction and Overview

States topic and objectives, gives organizational background and key issues, states research question

Literature Review

General broad overview

Key issues covered

Specific aspects chosen and explored

Questions identified (issues that are necessarily involved in the research question)

guide to the reader

as in the major sources

more detailed and specialized treatment; all secondary sources; periodic summary

a position argued for and arrived at by now, reader can anticipate the empirical ground that will need to be covered

Summary

bridge to empirical work

Empirical Section

Method and design

Questions addressed, data analyzed

Inferences made, conclusions reported

how data collected sampling and replication investigatory techniques control of alternative explanations

primary data presented tables, reasoning, summary

concepts and caveats

Discussion Section

Summary of findings

Criticism of method

Discussion of findings Broader relevance considered

Final recommendations listed and explained

reminder of objective, issues, questions and answers

appraisal of problems in gathering results; limitations on generalizability of findings

v. important: what does it all mean in light of literature review and organizational circumstances

guidelines for action

Bibliography
Appendices

FIGURE 3.2 The structure of the multi-issue dissertation

Executive Summary Main Issues Related Issues	States topic, objectives and research question, states key issues, gives recommendations
Corporate Aspects / General Literature	guide to the reader; significance of each issue addressed. General background literature surveyed for the broad class of problem being dealt with

Issue A presented	Issue B presented		
Literature adduced	Literature adduced	etc.	each issue dealt with in its own chapter or section (the vertical threads)
Question(s) identified	Question(s) identified		for each issue, a position argued for and arrived at; at end, reader can anticipate the empirical ground that will need to be covered
Summary	Summary		how data collected; sampling and replication; investigatory techniques; control of alternative explanations

Empirical Section Method and design	bridge to empirical work

Questions addressed data analyzed	Questions addressed data analyzed		
		etc.	primary data presented; tables, reasoning, summary; again, each issue dealt with in its own chapter or section
			concepts and caveats
Inferences made, conclusions reported	Inferences made, conclusions reported		substantial complexity of inference since the various issues are drawn together

Discussion Section Summary of findings Criticism of method Corporate implications considered Final recommendations and action plan	reminder or objective, issues, questions
	appraisal of problems in gathering results; limitations on generalizability of findings
	what it all means... ...translated into action

Bibliography Appendices	

more helpful. The project starts with a particular issue of significance to you, your department, or your organization. Its company-wide and/or strategic implications and a survey of relevant general literature lead you into a consideration of a variety of related issues or problems. This candle, you recognize, sits within a body of knowledge which your study suggests is relevant and which you outline and draw on: a candleholder which will guide you in narrowing down to some specific research question for each issue. Given the complexity of the issues you are considering, the lower (empirical) part of the candleholder is quite broad and you will find yourself combining conceptual argument and empirical data in several distinct sections or segments – before arriving at a set of conclusions. Finally, the same kind of broadening occurs as in the single-issue model, in which conclusions, recommendations and the rest follow.

A common problem with this kind of dissertation is that the reader gets lost in the details. With this sort of structure, you need to signpost the argument periodically. You do this by providing summaries, bulleted lists of points that have been made, and points that will need to be made next. One way of providing a structured account is to start with an Introduction as outlined above and then *present each separate issue in its own chapter*, with the relevant literature and method being outlined, and the results presented and discussed, in that chapter; issue by issue, chapter by chapter. You would then need an overall discussion and conclusions at the end.

Dissertations of this kind should be preceded by an Executive Summary. This should be on one page, with recommendations placed at the start. I'm not sure of the image to offer: a candle-flame, perhaps, which results from and illuminates the contraption below.

Generic, industry-based projects

Here, you will not be reporting your own research findings, but instead working with information available in, or ordered through, the library, and by means of the various media that you can access through the internet. The model to follow is the one shown in Figure 3.1. There will be an introduction as before, followed by an account of the literature; you will have to present a methodology and a research design as before; and you will present data likewise. However, you will be working from sources which have already been published, selecting, reorganizing, putting them together to present a case.

Library-based projects

A variant of the above, in which the literature is reviewed to present a conceptual argument, rather than one which is dependent on empirical data. I am tempted to call it 'a literature review' and so it is, but a review of a particular kind. The aim is not necessarily to be comprehensive and the purpose is certainly not to summarize everything published that is relevant to the topic. Rather, the intention of this kind of project is to marshal evidence, available in the published literature, to state a case. 'Having considered the various issues, weighed the arguments and counter-arguments, here is what the relevant literature on the issue boils down to'. This

ILLUSTRATION 3.4

Jane Selby, you will recall from the discussion of *balance* in Section 3.2, is doing a library-based project about diversification strategies in the water supply business. A project which defines corporate strategy, gives an overview of the water supply business, states the main performance issues facing companies and lists the various diversification strategies open to them, going on to evaluate each, is the sort of thing one would expect of any dissertation, including the in-company based ones. Jane can't get access to a company to do any empirical work that establishes a hypothesis or fits a model; somehow, she has to make an argument and justify her assertions, from the published literature itself. She decides to adopt an industry-based project strategy and sends off for the last 10 years' annual reports of 12 different water companies. She divides the companies into those which were taken over during that period and those which weren't. She scours the Chair's Statement and the information provided about the product range, to see if she can justify her argument that companies which diversified were better able to retain control than those which did not.

may end up as a state-of-the-art statement, or, depending on the topic and your ability to be original, it may present and argue a fresh interpretation of what has been written.

Projects of this kind will sometimes draw on empirical results presented in an organized way, where the structure of Figure 3.1 applies; at other times, they may be entirely conceptual. In the latter case, the structure of the project will look more like Figure 3.3. The 'General Approach' section here is the equivalent to the Summary or 'bridge' of Figure 3.1: in providing the reader with a summary of the argument to be presented, it allows him or her to anticipate what is to come and approach it in a critical way.

The main difficulty with this kind of dissertation occurs if it does not progress beyond the kind of literature review which 'states everything you know about' the topic; in other words, when it is uncritical and when it does not succeed in arguing a case.

There are detailed guidelines on how to make an argument, how to be critical and how to go beyond simple description, in Chapter 7; with related material in Chapters 4 and 13.

Before continuing, please complete activity 5. ★

FIGURE 3.3 The structure for a library-based dissertation

Summary Introduction and Overview	states topic and objectives, gives organizational background and key issues, states research question
Background Literature Broad overview of background literature Main theme announced	guide to the reader; general background literature surveyed for the broad class of problem being dealt with
General Approach to be Taken Overview of argument Issues identified	a rationale is given for the approach; the argument is expressed in a nutshell; 'here is what I will argue for each issue'

Issue A Presented	Issue B Presented		each issue dealt with in its own chapter or section (the vertical threads)
Literature presented to argue a case	Literature presented to argue a case	etc.	for each issue, a position argued for and arrived at using the literature only; (there is no empirical work to follow)
Summary	Summary		positions arrived at; by now, the reader is as convinced as he or she ever will be

Discussion Section
Implications arising from the arguments
Critical approach taken
Broader relevance considered
Final recommendations listed and explained

reminder of objectives, issues, questions

substantial complexity of inference since the various issues are drawn together

appraisal of problems in making the argument; recommendations; limitations on generalizability of findings

Bibliography
Appendices

The examiner's thoughts

The examiner is looking at a project on the introduction of psychological tests into an existing employee selection procedure.

'Well, here we go again. Um. Interesting title; I wonder what that means? Let's see the Abstract'. She or he skims the Contents and might glance at the Bibliography to see whether key authors are present – an impression of what might be involved is being formed – and looks for a context of company background as provided by the Introduction. 'Seems okay; now, what exactly is the intention? Ok, now why did the student feel these were useful objectives to choose . . . and is there any indication of how they're to be achieved?'

The examiner continues to read, looking for information relevant to the criteria which she or he has in mind (depending on the nature of the course involved) and hoping that this information will be readily available in the form of a coherent, readable and interesting argument. For much of the time, he or she is concerned with the structure of the argument being presented.

Inadequate structure

'Well, in this project about employee selection methods, he's told me every-thing he knows about selection methods in the lit. review. Not a lot, but that matters less than the fact that I can't see the relevance of much of it. And on the next page here's a set of results; that's a bit sudden. How did he obtain them? Oh, I see, he says he prefers interviews to questionnaires but doesn't say why, and in any case it looks as though he ran out of time to do the question-naire properly. Here's some answers to questions on the way in which the company trains its staff to use psychological tests, and there's some more in the appendix which looks very relevant to the main discussion. Why did he decide to ask those questions in the first place, I wonder? And finally, here's a list of conclusions. Well, I don't think much of them: he could have arrived at these kinds of conclusions without all the data-gathering. Now, hang on, what did he say the objectives were?'

And the examiner will leaf back to the first chapter, hoping that objectives are there, reminding him- or herself of what they were (often necessary at the end of a woolly account), and trying to decide if they have been achieved.

An adequately structured account

This is one in which in clarity of thinking is revealed by the structure. The exam-iner is more likely to be thinking something like the following

'Ok, here are the generalities that apply to the selection process as a whole, and they're followed by the more specific issues that relate to some commonly used selection methods. She's considered the issues relating to the use of psychological tests for employee selection, and highlighted ones relevant to her company circumstances which relate to training in the use of tests; she summarizes the argument by listing a number of interesting and important questions. I wonder if there's anything on validity and meta-analysis? Aha, yes; good so far.'

If you look at Figure 3.1, you can see that the examiner has reached the bottom of the 'bowl' at this point.

'Now, how is she going to answer the questions she raises, and what's her rationale for the methods she uses? Given the constraints on her time, and the technical arguments and rationale she's provided, it's not a bad methodology; can't wait to see the answers she obtained.' We've reached the stem. 'If I'd got answers like these . . . hang on, what exactly were her objectives? Well, well, I don't have to turn to Chapter 1, she's restated them here for me, excellent . . . if I'd got answers like these, I'd be coming to conclusions X, Y and Z. What are hers?'

The examiner reads them, and is ready for a clear discussion in which the conclusions are interpreted in the light of relevant wider information about selection, and related issues in the company in question.

'Ok, if that's as it is, what recommendations make sense? Good . . . yes . . . plausible given her previous argument, oho, and some costings too, excellent.'

The examiner has reached the base and is in the mood for a suitably generous mark.

As you can see, it's the existence of an argument and the way that it's structured, that makes a big difference between success and failure. There is more on this in Chapters 4, 7 and 13.

 Just one more thing to do: please turn to activity 6 in the Project Guide.

CASE EXAMPLE 3.1   Ethical issues

Mahmoud El-Baradie is a newly-qualified psychology graduate who stayed on for another year to take a full-time MSc in Management. He had no success in getting into a company to do the data-gathering for his dissertation so he decided to change his approach, and do a library-based project instead. Reviewing the literature he came across some work on competency development (Pedler *et al.* 2001) and became intrigued by the thought that it might be possible for him to measure change in analytical and critical thinking skills. Forty students in the year 1 student group were about to take a popular elective module on personal decision-making skills, and he realized (being a qualified level A psychometric tester) that he could apply the Watson-Glaser Critical Thinking Test on a before-after basis and see if their module had made any measurable difference to their test scores. He also gave the test to the 50 students who didn't take the course, ending up with a good control group and a classic 'before-after-with-control' research design. Having explained what he was doing and provided assurances of anonymity and confidentiality, he went ahead and collected the data at the start and end of the semester in which the module was available.

The results are very interesting, with a statistically significant difference for the students who took the module, but no difference for the students who didn't, on two of five the sub-scales of the test: Evaluation of Arguments, and Deduction. So he decides to write the study up as a research note in the practitioner's journal, *The Occupational Psychologist*. While he's at it, since he has the test scores he decides to combine the 90 'before' scores into one sample and report the frequency distribution of all these scores in the form of test norms.

1 Two months later he gets a phonecall out of the blue from one of the students who provided the data, who accuses him of unethical behaviour in breaking the assurances of anonymity given before the study. Is that student right to complain?

2 Are there potentially any other ethical issues?

Answers to Case Example 3.1

1 There are no problems of anonymity arising from Mahmoud's publication of the norms, since a frequency distribution does not identify the people who contributed the data on an individual, named basis.

2 Just because data are anonymous does not necessarily mean that there can't be a problem with *confidentiality*. (For example, publishing an account externally of unprofessional practices within a department breaks confidentiality and might conceivably, e.g. if it affected the promotion prospects of staff in that department who were not involved in the practices in question, be unethical, even though no names were named.) In this instance, though, the nature of the information published would not seem to raise any confidentiality issues.

Is there an issue regarding *informed consent* to the publication of the data? Well, how long is a piece of string: how much of one's research design and developments over time, should one share with one's respondents? At the outset, what was planned was a before-after study and Mahmoud told everyone about this in advance and obtained consent. What he didn't anticipate then was that he would have a sufficiently large sample to publish the results as a set of test norms. There is no problem from the fact of publication in itself since all the results preserve anonymity; and one cannot anticipate all of the results one is going to wish to publish, so there is really no basis for complaint because consent was not obtained to the publication. This would only arise if someone was placed in a disadvantageous position as a direct result of the publication of the results and if this could have reasonably been anticipated in advance such that informed consent had to be obtained.

Project Guide

Once you have finished this chapter, you should have completed the following activities.

1 Establish the nature of the evidence you will be using in your project

- Depending on your circumstances, decide whether it is likely to be In-company Focused, Generic, or Library-based.

- If you decide on an in-company based project and are in employment, make an appointment to talk to your boss, in some detail, about it; if you're not, then you will need to start making plans to access one or more relevant organizations. If you anticipate difficulties in arranging access, talk to your lecturer or tutor about alternatives.

- If necessary, revise the provenance table and the Project Proposal Document (see Section 2.5) accordingly.

2 Address the ethical issues

- Inform yourself.
  Obtain a copy of some appropriate ethical guidelines.

- Apply the guidelines to your own project activities.
  Next, think through the implications for what you can and cannot do, and make some notes in your project diary.

- Complete any ethics declaration that may be required by your department drawing on the notes you have just made; submit it to the Ethics Committee, if there is one, in good time.

- Be prepared to review and revise your declaration as necessary, as you continue to think through your methodology in Part 3.

3 Reassess the research question

Match yourself against the remaining specific attributes of a successful project. In your research diary, write a one-sentence statement of your topic, enter the following as headings and then complete the sentence in each case:

- 'The research question is *original* in the sense that . . .'
- 'It has *generality* because . . .'
- 'It is likely to be *pragmatic* provided I remember to . . .'
- 'It is *balanced* since, if my expectations are fulfilled then . . ./ and if my expectations are not fulfilled then . . .'.

4 Note the following down in your research diary

The deadline for submission of your completed project report and the maximum length it should be. Just for future reference.

5 Decide on the broad structure of your dissertation

- Does the research question deal with a single issue, so that the structure will look more like the conventional shape of Figure 3.1? Or is this more of an in-company project with several intertwined issues to be teased out and presented in separate chapters, as in Figure 3.2?

- Are you likely to be emphasizing straightforward conclusions arrived at from the data you present, or, will you additionally have to make recommendations which you have to implement and evaluate?

6 Obtain a copy of the marking criteria, if available

- Contact your tutor or lecturer and ask for any general statement of the standard to be

▶

achieved and any marking schemes (they'll look like Tables 3.3 or 3.4) which are available. They may be printed in the main programme document written when the academic programme you are following was first designed; as a one-off handout; or as part of a student guide which collates all the information you need about your project work.

■ Familiarize yourself with the standard required to obtain an average mark. Look particularly carefully at the differences between a just-passing and a just-failing grade.

■ Check to see if there is any specification of the format of the dissertation. If not, you'll need to ask for a separate document that covers dissertation format, length and layout details.

References

Abrahamson, E. (1996) 'Technical and aesthetic fashion', in *Translating Organizational Change*, Czarniawska, B and Sevón, G., (eds.) New York: Walter de Gruyter: 117–137.

Donaldson, J. (1989) *Key Issues in Business Ethics*, London: Academic Press.

Gill, J. and Johnson, P. (1997) *Research Methods for Managers*, London: Paul Chapman Publishing.

Goldstein, M. and Goldstein, F. (1978) *How We Know*, London: Plenum Press.

Gorman, M. and Sahlman, W. A. (1986) *What do venture capitalists do?*, Paper given at the 1986 Babson Congress, University of Calgary, Alberta.

IBE (1998) *Report on Business Ethics*, London: Institute of Business Ethics.

Luton Business School (2000) *Assessment Criteria, Masters Dissertations*, Luton Business School, University of Luton.

Meyer, J. W. (1996) 'Otherhood: the promulgation and transmission of ideas in the modern organizational environment', in *Translating Organizational Change*, Czarniawska, B. and Sevón, G., (eds.) New York: Walter de Gruyter: 241–252.

Pedler, M., Burgoyne, J. and Boydell, T.

(2001) *Manager's Guide to Self Development*, London: McGraw-Hill.

Pfeffer, J. (1996) *Competitive Advantage through People: Unleashing the Power of the Workforce*, Boston, MA: Harvard Business School Press.

Russ-Eft, D., Burns, J. Z., Dean, P. J., Hatcher, T., Otte, F. L. and Preskill, H. (1999) *Standards on Ethics and Integrity*, Baton Rouge: Academy of Human Resource Development.

Saunders, M., Lewis, P. and Thornhill, A. (2003) *Research Methods for Business Students*, London: Prentice Hall.

Swain, P. (1999) 'Organisational learning: developing leaders to deal with continuous change – a strategic human resource perspective', *The Learning Organization*, 6: 1: 30–37.

Teesside Business School. (1999) *Dip/MA HRM Management Report Assessment Criteria and Schedule, Post-Experience Professional Programme*, Internal mimeo, Teesside Business School, University of Teesside.

Webley, S. and More, E. (2003) *Does Business Ethics Pay?* London: Institute of Business Ethics.

Getting organized for take-off

- To assist you in the development of a project timetable
- To encourage you to assemble the relevant physical resources

At a glance

This chapter is relatively short. First, it helps you to concentrate your mind on what is to come, by addressing the issue of planning and timetabling, based on information on how long various project-related activities take to complete. Second, it discusses a number of physical resources which you will need to organize for yourself as you begin work, including the most useful kinds of computer software.

4.1 Your pre-flight checklist

By the time you read this chapter, your project should be well under way. That statement assumes that you have carried out all the activities outlined in the project guides for the first three chapters. Table 4.1 summarizes them. Have you tackled them all? Remember the approach adopted in this book! The purpose is not to teach you research methods in the abstract, but to take you, step-by-step and in real time, through your complete project.

 Please glance at Table 4.1 and do activity 1 in this chapter's Project Guide.

4.2 Planning and timetabling

A little time spent in drawing up a timetable at the outset may save you much bitter regret at the end. This is common sense, yet so few students seem to do so in appropriate detail.

The first step is to be clear about the various stages of your project, and to order them sequentially. What counts as a 'stage' depends very much on the topic you choose, but it seems sensible to regard the main headings shown in Table 4.2 as major, and applicable to all topics. The table makes no distinction between primary and secondary data at this stage. Remember, though, that if your project is a library-based one, then the bulk of your data collection will be done there, or through the library by post and using e-mail to various sources of secondary data.

TABLE 4.1 Getting started on your project: a checklist	
Chapter 1	
■ Buy a research diary	A single location for materials and project planning.
■ Obtain a copy of the regulations applying to your project	Check that your topic matches the Aims and Objectives in broad terms.
■ Get hold of any statements of special requirements	e.g. the professional guidelines, in the case of projects done in a professional programme.
■ Identify your own personal objectives for the project	What would you like it to achieve for *you*? What concepts, skills, competencies do you seek?
Chapter 2	
■ Find a topic you like and know about	Using any of the techniques mentioned. Make sure it's not too difficult and that appropriate support structures and resources are available.
■ Develop it by means of a provenance table	Get to the Aspect stage; form an idea of how the topic is more than a description; find two or three key authors. All to the level of detail shown in Table 2.5
■ Specify a research question	Or perhaps two different research questions, to give you some scope for choice.
■ Write a draft research proposal	Stating the topic, rationale, research objectives and research question; and adding the provenance table.
Chapter 3	
■ Decide whether this is an in-company project, a generic project, or a library project	Double-check your level of access to in-company data and adjust your plans accordingly.
■ Start thinking about any ethical issues that may pertain	Make a list of issues to discuss with tutor and/or sponsor; complete any documentation the university requires.
■ Reassess the research question	Identify the anticipated level of originality, generality, pragmatism and balance implied; adjust the question as necessary.
■ Map out an initial structure for the eventual project report	This will become clearer as you progress; for the moment, what relative emphasis is to be placed on data and recommendations as opposed to implementation and evaluation?
■ Obtain a copy of the marking criteria	Form an initial impression of the standard to aim at;
■ Check deadlines	and the regulations pertaining to length.

TABLE 4.2 The major stages of a project which require timetabling

Preflight checklist activities
- Familiarization with regulations
- Choice and development of topic: including preparatory reading
- Application of criteria to topic; checking ethical issues
- Completing the project proposal document

Basic familiarization
- Library work and literature review
- Organizing in-company written information
- Meetings with initial informants; confidentiality arrangements
- Writing and major note-making begins

Identifying main thrust of arguments and their critical features
- Expectations: hunches and hypotheses, models and theories
- Thinking through the implications for data collection
- Deciding on the details of methods and techniques for data collection
- Deciding on the analytic techniques to be used, quantitative and qualitative
- Reading and talking to people continue; writing and note-making continue

Data collection and analysis
- Initial pilot work
- Revision/fine-tuning of expectations and techniques
- Main data collection
- Scanning the data, 'eyeball' testing, thinking
- Further data collection
- More systematic analysis, tentative conclusions
- Checking the plausibility, reliability and robustness of these conclusions
- Further data collection with cross-checks; perhaps different technique or method
- Possibility of implementation and evaluation of some recommendations
- Reading and talking to people continue; writing and note-making continue

Writing-up
- Systematic and organized writing
- Checking that objectives as stated at the outset have been achieved
- Checking of drafts with tutor, sponsor and other relevant people
- Reading continues; final update of literature review elements

Production
- Typing or word-processing
- Frequent revisions
- Last minute panics over bibliographic references
- Further typing or word-processing
- Binding

Delivery
- Distribution of project document
- Presentations

The idea is to divide the stages into the total time available to you, allocating time to each. Then, as you begin work and develop a better idea of the details involved in each stage, allocating smaller amounts of time to each activity within each stage.

The items provided within each stage are there to give you a flavour of the kind of activities involved. What you put in their place will depend on your topic. The time-demands of some of the activities will be easy to estimate; of others, more difficult. I have suggested some standard times in Table 4.3. Some are taken directly from, or are based on, Berger and Patchner (1988) and Sharp *et al.* (2002). Many are my own estimates, based on recent personal activities; the rationale for these is occasionally obscure, but they seem to work and will do as a rough guide. (For example, on cross-checking a respondent's assertions, has it ever struck you that you can find out any non-classified piece of information by asking and refining your question in a sequence of phonecalls? The first call will refer you to someone more likely to know, the second to someone much more likely to know and so on. There is more on this in the context of electronic searches in Chapter 7.)

Some activities are particularly vulnerable to neglect and it is worth discussing these in more detail. In what follows, we work *backwards* through the main sequence, since this is a good way of designing a project timetable and since, in an unplanned project, the problems always seem to come home to roost at the end.

Delivery

Deadlines matter! And because no-one cares quite as much about your project as yourself, it's safest if you deliver the document, by hand, yourself. Allow time for any travel that may be involved; allow time to prepare yourself for any oral presentation that is required. If yours is a group project, this activity in itself may take up to a fortnight.

Production

Often neglected, because it comes at the end. Estimate the time it will take to type up your manuscript. Two weeks in which you do nothing else is a fair estimate for typing, proofing, reconsidering, adjusting, and so on, a typical project of around 20,000 words. Hopefully, you have been typing earlier drafts as you go along and all you are doing at the moment is preparing the final draft and pulling it all together. The bibliography, particularly, takes time, preparing all the references which you thought you had filed safely but seem to have lost. Then add another fortnight, part-time, to be on the safe side, for more editing, last-minute retyping, and collating and binding.

This assumes that you will be doing all the word-processing yourself. The evidence is that the process of writing electronically is different to the pen-and-ink procedure and there are some pitfalls peculiar to the medium; have a look at Turk and Kirkman (1989): 119 for the details.

Make sure you make a regular backup disk (a set of floppies or a single CD) and take the trouble to keep it in a different physical location from your computer. A portable hard drive with automatic backup software is a good idea if you can afford it; this works by backing up all, or a significant proportion, of your whole computer hard drive and need cost no more than £130 for 20GB. Alternatively, the small

TABLE 4.3 Estimates of standard times for some project activities	
Locating and accessing archival, secondary data	up to 3 weeks
Locating and web-based www and ftp data	1 minute–1 day
Accessing Usenet-based mailing list: with time to lurk before joining	up to 5 days
Reading an empirically-based journal article thoroughly	3 hours
Reading a book thoroughly	10 hours
Absorbing and using a statistically-based technique based on five texts	50 hours
(with a total elapsed time of . . .	6 weeks)
Preparing a ten-question interview schedule	1 day
Pretesting the schedule on two interviewees and amending the result	1 day
Destroying a relationship through lack of pretesting an inept interview schedule	1 minute
Conducting an interview	1 hour
Conducting four interviews in the same location (five possible but very tiring)	1 day
Transcribing one hour of taperecorded interview	7 hours
Cross-checking an interviewee's assertion: up to . . .	4 phone-calls
Content analysis of 300 one-sentence written items already typed onto cards	7 hours
Reliability cross-checking of the result	6 hours
Final version: add another . . .	2 hours
Informal pretesting of a questionnaire by five respondents located on one site	1 day
Piloting a larger questionnaire more formally: up to . . .	4 weeks
Pretesting a single summated rating scale for internal consistency	2 days
Reaching postal questionnaire sample by first-class mail	1 week
Time for respondent completion	2 weeks
Time for postal return	1 week
Add lag time since many respondents peak at two weeks, but some take longer	2 weeks
Time to post, complete, return chase-up letter and questionnaire	3 weeks
The 'psychological week' (at the end of which period, an inquiry to a respondent made at the beginning of the time will be forgotten)	5 days +weekend +5 days
Creating a six-field (mixed numeric and textual) database ready for printout	4 hours
Filling the database with 50 records each of 400 characters across 6 fields	5 hours
The sample size below which it probably pays to hand-analyse a simple 15-question questionnaire with no appreciable cross-tabulations	100 people
The sample size above which it usually pays to use a computer, even though you aren't familiar with the software in question	200 people
It all depends	100–200 people
Time taken to absorb SPSS manual sufficient to do one analysis, assuming you understand the basic statistical procedures involved but don't know SPSS	3 days

'flash' drive dongles that slip into your USB port and store 64MB for around £30 are very affordable, if somewhat poorer value byte for byte. Finally, if you have a computer at home, e-mailing files to yourself from your institution is another backup solution. Of course, if you don't have a computer and printer of your own, you will need to make arrangements well in advance to book the facilities required.

Writing-up

As you can see from Table 4.2, writing is something you do throughout. Many people find it relatively easy to get the Introduction out of the way early on, to write up their Methods while they're collecting their data and to write up their Data during the main Analysis stage. Time estimates for these, as well as for the major stage in which you pull the various sections together, should be made well in advance. There is more information on the writing process itself in Chapter 13.

It shouldn't be forgotten that writing also involves talking: with your tutor and sponsor. If you can allow time for either or both of these people to read your project report in a draft form, chapter by chapter or the manuscript as a whole, you will find that their comments can make a substantial difference to the grade you finally receive, provided of course that you note them and act on them. This is true regardless of the amount of tutorial contact you have had while carrying out your project. Allow additional time for the necessary rewrites.

Data collection and analysis

Time requirements vary enormously, depending on the method you choose. This is the stage at which you are most dependent on other people. Contacting your respondents always involves a lead time: they don't just sit there in suspended animation waiting for your call and your visit! The same applies to the various librarians who look after archival data in other organizations. Before you can use a research method and its associated techniques you need to know how to do so, which may mean setting aside some time to learn it in practical terms, as well as knowing it in principle from previous lectures on the subject.

Questionnaire-based surveys always involve chasing up non-respondents, which increases your initial estimate of how long to allow for postage and questionnaire completion. Information obtained from interviews, especially if they are carried out to write case studies, needs cross-checking with other interviews; content analysis of interview data requires twice as much time as you initially assign, since someone else has to carry out the basic procedure (described in Section 10.2), as well as yourself, to ensure reliability. Postal questionnaires, you will notice in Table 4.3, can take nine weeks from the time of despatch to the moment you close your books on the sample and begin analysis. This is based round a unit of one week for delivery of first-class mail (which irritated one of my MBA students, a senior employee of the Post Office, enormously a couple of years ago!). However, it's best to allow yourself plenty of leeway and not imagine that transmission is instantaneous.

Identifying main thrust of arguments

This stage is the most difficult for which to plan ahead. It often runs contemporaneously with the preceding and the succeeding stages, since, in many in-company projects, ideas are developed, critical analyses undertaken and hypotheses generated in parallel with the collection of information and data which test them out. (This important contrast with the main model used in scientific research work is developed in detail in Chapter 5.) It also involves selecting, and learning about, the main method and techniques which you will be using, in Section 3 of this book: include the time required to read it in your time estimates!

For his MBA dissertation, Inspector David Bates is planning a study of the civilianization of administrative tasks within his police force. His initial reading has suggested that some constabularies have made substantial savings by civilianizing the preparation and maintenance of documentation for cases that are to appear in court, so he decides he will need to collect information on the workload in his own constabulary, and develop a way of costing the work. Talking this over in his first interview, with the Superintendent who heads administration, he learns that a proper accounting and evaluation would require him to broaden his researches substantially. There is little training for these kinds of jobs, yet, as the number of civilian employees increases, some form of systematic training will be required and, soon, a properly organized career structure in place of the present ad-hoc arrangements. All this will cost money, the Superintendent says: shouldn't David take the costs of civilianization, as well as the cost savings, into account? Realizing that there are no training cost figures available internally, he decides to plan to hold some interviews in a nearby constabulary which has recently introduced a civilian training scheme and can provide the actual figures he needs. What started as a straightforward internal study based on documentary evidence is turning into a comparative case study dependent on face-to-face interviews, so he will need to allow additional time for the work in question.

Basic familiarization

The problem here is often one of locating information. You need to allow time for internet searches and for personal visits to various information centres, commercial and academic libraries and interviews with key informants. Chapter 7 provides you with guidelines for bibliographic searching; for the moment, it's a useful rule of thumb to see this process as one involving three stages:

- stage 1, in which you refer to immediately accessible sources already known to you
- stage 2, in which you draw up, and read and interview a list of sources somewhat more systematically (e.g. the formal literature search)

■ stage 3, in which you read and interview a list of sources to which your stage 2 reading and interviews have referred you and read material in the light of your empirical findings.

There is an appreciable time-lag between stage 2 and stage 3. For example, it takes ten days to three weeks for items to arrive via inter-library loan; it may take two to four weeks for yourself and your planned informant to find a mutually convenient time in your diaries.

Of course, many of these activities can take place at roughly the same time. Many are critical, in the sense that your subsequent work depends on their prior completion. The way to handle these issues and produce a very clear timetable for your whole project, is to use some form of critical path analysis. Although micro-computer-based software exists, you would probably be better to carry out a simple version by hand. The rules involve listing the activities in time, putting simulta-neous activities in parallel, associating time estimates with each activity, and taking care to identify the activities which are critical in the sense I meant above. A brief and useful description of a simple form of critical path analysis and Gantt charting is provided in Sharp *et al.* (2002) and an example is shown in Figure 4.1. Note how some activities are ongoing and how others can be done simultaneously as you wait for respondents to reply; note, also, how it's useful to include planned meetings with your tutor (the symbols in dark brown) into the programme.

This kind of planning can be very useful so long as it's not over-elaborate, getting in the way of the actual work! This point is emphasized by Wield (2002): 65 who is talking in the context of the much longer and more complex research activities associated with three-year PhD programmes. All the more reason to keep it simple in your own case!

 Now read and complete Case Example 4.1, to see a second example of project planning.

 Then, when you have looked at the case study feedback, please prepare a Gantt chart for your own project. This is activity 2 in the Project Guide.

4.3   Physical resources

You will already have seen and taken action on the first, and arguably the most important, bit of equipment you need:

The project diary

A simple hard-backed notebook will do, or a loose-leaf ring binder. An A4 accounts ledger gives plenty of space. You've already seen examples of the various uses to which it can be put in the previous chapters; its purpose is to:

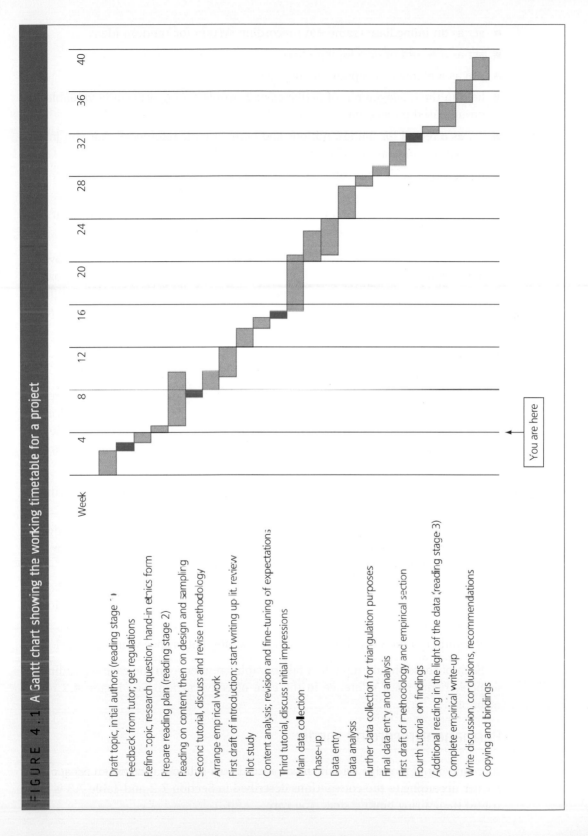

FIGURE 4.1 A Gantt chart showing the working timetable for a project

- act as an immediate (same-day) recording system for random ideas
- act as a record of developing ideas
- use as a planner for appointments and schedules
- help in the management of activities and people (being especially valuable in group-based project work)
- act as a record for names, notions and bibliographic references that you just happen to come across when doing something else
- provide you with a personal briefing in preparation for meetings with tutor and sponsor
- form the basic store of data for any intermediate reports which you might be required to provide in the course of your project work.

 See the website for some samples from a research diary. It's up to you how you organize it and use it. My only thought is that it shouldn't be a diary with pre-printed dates, since you will have varying amounts of material to record in it on different days. Use it just for your project work, keeping it separate from any other, personal diary you might keep.

Instant note-taking media

You may want to keep a small stock of 3″ × 5″ record cards for making notes on. (Some people prefer to use an electronic organizer like the Palm Pilot for this purpose, others find it difficult to write extended notes comfortably unless they use cards!) Regardless of the medium, though, it's good to get into the habit of carrying one or other in your pocket. Use them for the following:

- **Précis**: a note which summarizes an argument in briefer form while staying faithful to the source's assumptions and mode of expression.
- **Paraphrase**: a note which reproduces an argument in about the same length while reflecting your own emphases and expression (most usefully cast in a form which links the material to other ideas which you plan to use).
- **Synopsis**: a note which summarizes briefly, but in your own words; unlike the previous forms of note taking, it needs substantial reworking and expansion before using the material in your project document.
- Quotation: a note which reproduces the source's utterance word-for-word.

Each of these should include a bibliographic reference in the case of reading, or a speaker-date-place reference in the case of conversation. See Figure 4.2 for an example.

Permanent recording media

A second set of filecards on which you record your bibliographic references, one to a card, according to the conventions described in Section 7.2 and Table 7.3 is more useful than a ring binder, since you can:

FIGURE 4.2 The use of filecards for note-making

Schön's original text

In management as in other fields, 'art' has a two-fold meaning. It may mean intuitive judgement and skill, the feeling for phenomena and for action that I have called knowing-in-practice. But it may also designate a manager's reflection, in a context of action, on phenomena which he perceives as incongruent with his intuitive understandings.

Managers do reflect-in-action. Sometimes, when reflection is triggered by uncertainty, the manager says in effect 'This is puzzling: how can I understand it?' Sometimes, when a sense of opportunity provokes reflection, the manager asks. 'What can I make of this?' And sometimes, when a manager is surprised by the success of his intuitive knowing, he asks himself 'What have I really been doing?'

Filecard used for Paraphrase

The term 'Art' carries the same connotations in management as in other disciplines. It can stand for the way in which experience and gut feelings give rise to competent performance, as a form of 'knowing' in itself. Additionally, the term can be used to express the manager's attempt to make sense of events which his/her intuitions didn't anticipate, a private effort to 'know about'. This attempt at deliberation and explicit explanation is made whenever the manager acts as a scientist, to comprehend unexpected events; or when s/he behaves as an entrepreneur, to exploit opportunities, or when s/he acts as a psychologist, trying to understand the ways in which his/her intuition works.

Schön D.A. *The Reflective Practitioner* London. Temple Smith 1983: 241

Filecard used for Précis

'Art' has the same two meanings when used in management, as elsewhere: the exercise of subjective judgement ('knowing-in-practice') or a reflection on events which seem counter-intuitive ('reflection-in-action'). Managers reflect-in-action when they're uncertain, when they mull over possible opportunities, and when they seek to understand a successful situation.

Schön D.A. *The Reflective Practitioner* London. Temple Smith 1983: 241

'Knowing-in-practice': way in which competent performance is itself a form of knowing.
'Reflection-in-action': deliberate problem-solving (solving a puzzle or seizing opportunities): trying to understand processes of own intuition.

Schön D.A. *The Reflective Practitioner* London. Temple Smith 1983: 241

Filecard used for Synopsis

'Art'
'may mean intuitive judgement and skill, the feeling for phenomena and action...'
or
'reflection in a context of action, on phenomena which the manager sees as incongruent with his intuitive understandings'.

Schön D.A. *The Reflective Practitioner* London. Temple Smith 1983: 241

Filecard used for Quotation

■ treat them as a simple database, conveniently grouping and reordering them for analysis purposes if you are doing an industry- or library-based library project

■ ungroup and reorder them alphabetically when you are ready to type up your bibliography.

These could be transferred to a computer database at any time (see below).

Voice recorders

Whether in magnetic tape, mini-disc, or digital format, these are useful in some kinds of systematic interview-based survey work, for recording conversations with key informants and for collecting verbatim comments in case study preparation.

You might argue that the pocket Dictaphone kind is a useful way of recording ideas as they occur to you, in addition. The decision to voice-record interview data is a major one. On the one hand, it increases the completeness of the data you record; on the other hand, it only results in useful information if you transcribe the data accurately and you can see from Table 4.3 that this is a very time-consuming process. This is a decision best discussed with your tutor.

A note on computing resources

Most undergraduates work with a combination of filecards, ring binders and the departmental machines they book to use when their department, or library, is open. Many people, whether undergraduate or post-graduate, will probably have a computer at home or at work. The laptop variety is probably the most convenient, since you can take it out into the field with you, whether for note-making, or formal data collection. Table 4.4 lists some software which you may find useful. You can do a lot with a simple word-processing package and spreadsheet, catering for all of your project report requirements (since most spreadsheet packages have good facilities for producing figures, and the tables can be done conveniently with a word-processing package). There is just one additional piece of software I would strongly advocate and that is ENDNOTE, with which you can maintain and utilize a set of references, using it to search out and compile your bibliography, automatically presenting it in the format required by your university (see Section 7.1 for a description of the formatting options).

However, you may well require one or other of the specialized analysis packages shown in Table 4.4, and these are most conveniently run on your departmental computers, with the results being saved to disk in .pdf format using ACROBAT for reference, or in .doc format using MSWORD on your home machine if you have one. (You can get free ACROBAT *reader* software from the CD-ROMs issued with the popular computer magazines and your departmental machines should have the more expensive ACROBAT *writer* software already installed. Unless you have the writer software at home, the file is not editable and so ACROBAT is more of an archiving solution. Use MSWORD files for editable material.)

Another way of transferring data if you have a machine of your own at home is to save it in the appropriate format and send it as an attachment to an e-mail addressed to yourself. A further alternative is to use the USB 'flash' drive dongle described earlier when the value of making frequent backups was advocated.

If you plan to use largely qualitative rather than quantitative analysis techniques (see Chapters 5, 8 and 9) and are in a position to choose specialized software, you will find that Weitzman and Miles (1995) gives detailed reviews and provides practical guidance on the use of 25 different packages under the following headings: text retrieval, text management, coding and retrieval for content analysis, code-based theory building, and cognitive mapping. This review is helpful but dated; once you have read the details of the software in which you are interested, do a Google search to discover the supplier's website and scan it for details of the latest edition or up-date.

TABLE 4.4 Some suggested software resources and uses

Resource	Uses
Generic	
Word-processing	Find a favourite (maybe part of an integrated package) and stick to it. Save files in .rtf format for transfer between different platforms (you'll never be sure of whom you'll be sending to).
Drawing software, for figures	Likewise, save in a portable format: original format encoded to .jpg for transfer over the Internet is a useful combination.
Safari, Internet Explorer	Latest versions combine e-mail with web browsing and ftp facilities, and can give Usenet access through DejaNews.
Specialized	
EndNote	Outstanding bolt-on to MS Word, which simplifies bibliographic record-keeping, compilation and printout. Available from Adept Scientific www.adeptstore.co.uk
e-mail	If you are working from home and don't wish to incur the connection charges involved in web reader use for this purpose.
Fetch, Gopher	Specialized ftp software for transferring files from remote sites without the graphics offered by web readers.
Analysis	
Spreadsheet package: Excel or similar	For data management (and simple analysis via a database); statistical analysis.
Statistical package: Minitab, SPSS, Statview, GB-Stat and similar	For a more convenient and wider range of statistical analysis. Links to an Excel guide on the website of this book.
General qualitative analysis packages: Atlas, Nud.ist	Provide a variety of categorization and content analysis facilities, together with useful data structure visualization facilities for hypothesis building and testing.
Specialized qualitative analysis packages: RepGrid, Decision Explorer	Provide facilities for describing respondents' personal cognitive structures (RepGrid) and researcher cognitive structures via a form of directed graph technique (Decision Explorer).
All-in-One	
Methodologist's Toolchest	Somewhat procrustean but useful in forcing you to think through your planning, research design and sampling, statistical analysis, and ethical stance.

Please address activity 3 in the Project Guide.

And that brings us to the end of part 1 of this book, with your project well under way.

CASE EXAMPLE 4.1   Devising a research timetable

Harold Ramotswe from Botswana is in the second semester of his MBA Marketing degree, specializing in the leisure and tourism sector. He plans to start his dissertation as soon as he has finished the taught element of his course, in early July. Before beginning his Masters studies, he worked for two years as an assistant hotel manager for a hotel chain in South Africa; once his studies are complete, he intends to return to his home town, Gabarone, in Botswana, to continue his career in hotel management. Prospects in this field for a bright young man like Harold are very good: the hotel field is booming, based on leisure and tourism (game-viewing in the wild-life reserves from June–October, with August being the peak period) and (something he knows lots about from his father, a bank manager) a revived economy that encourages inward investment and infrastructure development.

His dissertation topic is service quality and he intends to apply the 'Servqual' model (Zeithaml *et al.* 1990) to customers and staff in several of the hotels there for the empirical stage of his project. He knows that this model offers a neat way of identifying service quality gaps by means of a couple of standard questionnaires and he is sure it will make for a well-structured dissertation, building his expertise in a topic that will look very well on his CV when he looks for his next post as a hotel manager. The deadline for submitting his dissertation and terminating his studies is 28 November.

He has been promised help in arranging his research samples by a friend in the Marriott hotel in Bulawayo, where he last worked. The friend says he knows several of the Gabarone hotel managers and can provide Harold with an introduction so that he obtains a large sample of respondents. All looks

FIGURE CASE 4.1 Gantt chart for the Harold Ramotswe case

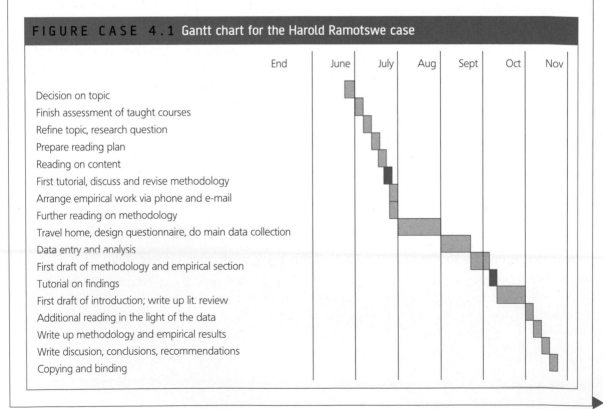

CASE EXAMPLE 4.1   Devising a research timetable (cont.)

well and just before getting down to work on his taught course assignments, Harold sits down and works out a Gantt chart to show his intended timetable (see Figure Case 4.1)

It's all very straightforward, really: he will use one-week blocks for various activities and set aside a solid month for his survey questionnaire, which he will deliver by hand to the various hotels (for postal return to his Gabarone address) since he is planning to go home for a working holiday for the month of August. He will then return to the UK to complete his write up as shown in the chart.

1 Imagine you are Harold's dissertation tutor. What sort of comments might you make about the intended plan of work when you see it at Harold's first tutorial? Are there any major problems with it?

2 You might like to comment on Harold's plans for writing up the dissertation.

Answers to Case Example 4.1

1 There is one obvious problem and that is *time*.

- Four and a half months from start to finish is a rather short time for a survey-based project. You really wish Harold had come to see you earlier than in late July, so you could point this out and suggest he take a case-study-based approach to the Servqual model. And from this one problem, several others follow.

- It's always a good idea to do some prepara-tory work on the dissertation during the second semester of a one-year course, juggling activities between the project and the taught course requirements. (If two of the

courses in question were service marketing and research methods, it would be all the more important to think of the dissertation as starting in February with the start of the second semester and not June!)

- The final arrangements for the empirical work have, likewise, been left rather late: the last week in July, just before Harold flies home.

- A month in which to design and send out a questionnaire (even the standard format in which the Servqual model is couched), for return by post, is cutting things a little fine.

- Particularly since August lies in the busiest period in Botswana's annual tourism cycle. Harold's friend's introductions are likely to fall on deaf ears. For an empirical dissertation, that's very serious. (*)

2 It might be useful to write up the Introduction and Literature Review a lot earlier, at least sketching out a draft of each before the empir-ical work begins. Literature reviewing, as we've already mentioned, is a matter of constructing an argument, and the effort involved in writing it down engenders fruitful ideas about research methods and techniques, which need time to be digested before empirical work begins.

(*) You might recall that Harold's father is a banker. In circumstances like these, using family and friend-ship contacts, while not the ideal way of going about things, can save the planned research project from collapse. His father may be able to call in a few favours, especially if he has clients among the hotel managers in the city, or colleagues with influence among the business community. There again, these things take time. The arrangements should have been tested and confirmed or repaired, a lot earlier!

Project Guide

Once you have finished this chapter, you should have completed the following activities.

1 Complete the project checklist

- Run through Table 4.1 and make sure you that you have completed all the activities to date.

- They all involve action. You will need to collect information, make phonecalls, visit websites, go to the library to put together an initial reading list. They all take time. Please spend that time now, before returning to Section 4.2 and reading on.

- It is particularly important to complete this stage if you are doing a very short project (some professional projects on full-time programmes are just three months long from start to finish, if you want to graduate as planned. Miss the deadline and you may have to wait a whole year!).

2 Prepare a Gantt chart

- Working with the information in Tables 4.2 and 4.3 and your own knowledge of your final deadline, prepare a chart showing the main stages of your project activity from start to finish. This is just a simple draft at this stage. Be prepared to amend this as you go on, but be cautious if you find yourself extending deadlines!

- Indicate the occasions on which you plan to meet with your tutor (see also Section 6.3 for further particulars).

- Very important: if you've done activity 1, then you should already have started and completed some of the activities which you are charting. Note how the 'You are here' arrow in Figure 4.1 is already a month into the whole project . . .

3 Assemble your physical resources

- At least the filecards!

- Create a new file on your hard disk, subdividing it into whatever seems most appropriate.

- If you have already started noting down references and making research notes, transfer them onto whatever permanent form you will be using from now on.

References

Berger, R. M. and Patchner, M. A. (1988) *Implementing the Research Plan*, London: Sage.

Schön, D. A. (1983) *The Reflective Practitioner*, London: Temple Smith.

Sharp, J. A., Peters, J. and Howard, K. (2002) *The Management of a Student Research Project*, Aldershot: Gower Publishing.

Turk, C. and Kirkman, J. (1989) *Effective Writing*, London: E & FN Spon.

Weitzman, E. A. and Miles, M. B. (1995) *Computer Programs for Qualitative Data Analysis*, London: Sage.

Wield, D. (2002) 'Planning and organising a research project', in Potter, S., (ed.) *Doing Postgraduate Research*, London: Sage Publications.

Zeithaml, V. A., Berry, L. L. and Parasuraman, A. (1990) *Delivering Quality Service: Balancing Customer Perceptions and Expectations*, New York: Free Press.

Key issues in depth

In this section, we concentrate on scholarship, and examine three of its aspects in detail. The first chapter examines research principles, and provides guidelines for critical analysis and a structured way of approaching it. Two distinct approaches to research are outlined and one in particular, the interpretivist approach, is advocated as particularly relevant to business and management. The second chapter is, perhaps, unexpected. In examining the roles of researcher, tutor, sponsor and mentor we articulate a set of relationships which have as much to do with the success of your project as any of the methods and techniques dealt with subsequently, though these roles may not appear to have anything to do with scholarship at first glance. Lastly, Chapter 7 provides you with one of the main tools which you will be using to state, justify and examine the case you're making: the literature review.

5

Basic assumptions about research

- To provide you with a rationale for what you're doing, together with a set of basic assumptions
- To help you to progress your research plan
- To define the process of critical analysis and to provide you with a structure by means of which an appropriately critical approach can be achieved

At a glance

You may be surprised to learn that there are different kinds of research, each kind reflecting different assumptions about what it is to carry out a systematic investigation and increase knowledge about the topic in question. These assumptions are, in some cases, mutually incompatible. You need to be aware of them, so that you can make a reasoned choice of the approach which you will adopt. This will make a difference to the kinds of question you ask and to the kinds of answer which you're prepared to take seriously. We start by examining the assumptions and their philosophical underpinnings.

Next, we provide some guidelines for choosing between the different approaches and an argument is made for the value of adopting an interpretivist approach, rather than a positivist approach, to most research questions of the kind you will be posing when you work on your project. Business and management situations are rarely simple enough to be investigated as if you were in a laboratory and positivist definitions of what you're doing can often miss the point and lead to trivial and over-simplified conclusions.

Finally, we review some important concepts which relate to the credibility of your work. You are setting out to build an argument which rests on three foundations: your literature review (see Chapter 7); your own empirical work (see Part 3); and your presentation, which is a mixture of clear reasoning, critical analysis, and a dash of sensitive intuition, all of which is examined herein. The reliability of this process and its stance with respect to truth ('validity'? or 'understanding'?), complete the account and bring us full circle, confronting us with the philosophical assumptions that underlie all research.

5.1 Basic assumptions

If a colleague asked you what you were currently doing, at this stage in the process you would, I am sure, be able to provide them with a concise statement of your topic, and a fairly precise list of objectives. They might press you further and ask, 'But why are you bothering with that? Why do you think it's important? You're making some big assumptions there! Is that really worth it? What are you really doing?'

Ontology, epistemology and values

Though it's not obvious at first, an interrogation of this kind is very valuable, since it prompts you to think harder about where you are heading and how you intend to get there. It actually involves an examination of three fundamentals: your ontology, your epistemology, and your underlying values.

Ontology

Ontology is a branch of metaphysics which deals with the nature of existence. That sounds rather abstract, but it is in fact very practical. As a manager you encounter ontological dilemmas all the time and, without seeing it in quite these terms, will have worked out your ontological position quite a while ago! In your daily round, what do you notice and what do you ignore, because it's less important? The same issues apply to your project. What, in your view, is your topic basically about? What should be looked at and what is irrelevant? Different people looking at the same topic might, depending on their role, their stakeholding and their background, think very differently about it.

Of course, there isn't a 'right' answer to the questions raised in Illustration 5.1 in absolute terms. It is a matter of matching the basic beliefs to your research question in a productive way. The answer you adopt will define your **ontological position**: your fundamental belief about the nature of being, or at least, that small part of it which you are currently researching. For your purposes, is it most useful to see the world as consisting of people, or processes, or effectiveness, or guiding principles, or actions, or language communications, or rules and belief systems, or motives and constraints? It can't be all of these. The events you decide to notice and the events you decide to ignore; the evidence which you will collect and the evidence which you will set aside in building your argument – indeed, the very decision on what counts as an event or as evidence, and what doesn't – all depend on your ontological position.

'Events' don't exist 'out there' waiting to be recognized, and evidence doesn't lie around like so many nuggets of gold, waiting to be picked up and used. This may

ILLUSTRATION 5.1

Let's eavesdrop in the staff dining room as the MD and her directors finish off their Monday morning meeting over a cup of tea. They've agreed the week's priorities, but sitting back and ruminating for a moment, what's the current difficulty with the plastic extrusion line really about? Peter, from HRM, used to be a trainer. Now that he thinks about it in detail, it makes sense to think of it 'really' as being about people and their collaboration on producing the product. Arnold's the factory manager responsible for the product in question and to him it's patently obvious that life is all about the processes which lead to a better, more efficient and cost-effective product, and the difficulty is a series of small manufacturing hitches. Marie is the accountant and sees the same issues in terms of numbers, accounts and the bottom line. Nonsense, says Steve, the marketing manager. All of that is mere detail, that any competent technician ought to handle; 'what really matters is the integration of customer demand, strategic stance, product development, delivery and distribution which makes up the "marketing philosophy", and here we're running off-track in living up to our commitments as part of our main customer's supply chain.' Arnold understands the jargon and even respects it but, in the end, believes that actions speak louder than words. Only up to a point, says Steve (who spent time as a very successful sales rep); it's the words people use and the stories they tell which provide the best understanding of what they're up to. Alison, the MD, sits, listens and asks herself whether it's the operating procedures which her team collaborate to develop which are most important, or whether it's the motives and constraints with which they work in their position as stakeholders which really, really matter. Which should she try to facilitate: team action or resource provision? What's it really about?

seem like a radical statement, but how else can you explain why different stakeholders seek different priorities, different witnesses report different things and different people express different priorities about what they are doing?

The world out there is simply a 'humming, buzzing confusion', to paraphrase James (1897/1958) and rather than talking about 'events', it is best to stay neutral for a moment. Something is going on, which we can refer to as the 'phenomenal flow'. Your background, your experience and education, your training and professional membership and your current concerns, all predispose you to a particular stance towards it. What happens next? You take a pair of perceptual scissors, as it were, and cutting the flow in two places, call the result an 'event'. Where you make the cuts, what you decide is worth noticing as an event and what isn't, depend on your ontological position. Other people may disagree with you.

So: what kinds of things are worth noticing? That was the issue you addressed in Section 2.4. That is how you turned your topic idea into a research question (see also Figure 2.1) and it will make a difference to the research method you choose and to the data-gathering techniques which you adopt, as we will see in Chapter 8.

At this point you might care to address activity 1 in the Project Guide for this chapter. ★

Epistemology

This is to do with your personal theory of knowing. Epistemology deals with knowledge. It provides ways of deciding what counts as knowledge and what doesn't and, related to this, what counts as evidence and proof, and what doesn't.

In your topic as you identified it, is the technically best solution the one to follow, or do you feel that the technical criteria are subordinated to policy considerations? If you believe that, as a rule in life, policy disputes are usually resolved in favour of the most powerful stakeholder, do you suspect that your main task will be to find out what that person's preferences are, rather than focusing on technical details?

Which poses the question of whether preferences and beliefs count as knowledge, worthy of being reported in your dissertation. Now, suppose you discover that the main stakeholders' views are idiosyncratic and no other stakeholder agrees. How useful is it to regard personal viewpoints, preferences and prejudices as legitimate knowledge? Is a study of the rumours and hearsay going round the Board as valid as an opinion survey of all the Board members?

If you feel that entrepreneurs' intuitions about worthwhile new products are as important as the latest survey of the market for these new products and you set out to do a study of entrepreneurs' intuitions, are you, by the same token, justified in accepting your *own* gut feelings that an informant is, basically, correct when his evidence clashes with the story told by other informants?

Further, what counts as evidence? It is worth addressing your research question from this point of view and activity 2 in the project guide asks you to do just that. Mason (1996: 22–23) provides some interesting examples of the process, taken from a project on family inheritance.

ILLUSTRATION 5.2

Her research question was 'What is the interface between families and the law on matters related to inheritance?' She justified one data source, 'Probated Wills' by arguing that these provide data on the formal expression of testators' wishes while demonstrating the way in which the law constrains such wishes. She justified the data source 'interviews with family members' in terms of their use in demonstrating laypersons' knowledge of, and experience with, the law, and the impact of professional guidance on this form of knowledge. Finally, she justified the use of interviews with solicitors by pointing to their value in revealing something of the negotiations which take place between testators and lawyers and the role of the lawyer in these negotiations. Thus two techniques, archived documentary evidence and two different rounds of face-to-face interviews were justified, because they gave access to three different modes of information, each of which she decided was an acceptable kind of evidence: legally legitimized statements of personal intention; lay understandings of the law and how it operates; and statements of professional judgement and practice respectively.

Marshall and Rossman (1995) give further examples.

You may recognize that you already addressed these questions in Section 2.4, when you fleshed out your research question by asking 'what am I really trying to

According to the positivist approach it is assumed that when you do research, the best way of arriving at the truth is to use scientific method, which is otherwise known as the **hypothetico-deductive method**. This is made up of the following minimal components:

- a formally expressed general statement which has the potential to explain things: the **theory**
- a deduction that if the theory is true, then you would expect to find a relationship between at least two variables, A and B: the **hypothesis**
- a careful definition of exactly what you need to measure, in order to observe A and B varying: the **operational definition**
- the making of the observations: **measurement**
- the drawing of conclusions about the hypothesis: **testing**
- the drawing of implications back to the theory: **verification**.

The ground-rules for the making of observations are very well developed, possibly because measurement is the stage over which the researcher has most control. Measurements must be **valid**, that is, they should be accurate, reflecting the information present in the data in an unbiased way. This is often established by seeing whether the information is consistent with other measurement methods, or with what is known and recorded already. They must also be **reliable**, that is,

TABLE 5.1 The basic assumptions of positivism and interpretivism	
Positivism	**Interpretivism**
■ Phenomena can be analyzed in terms of variables	■ Phenomena can be analyzed in terms of issues
■ Data can be collected by a dispassionate outside observer	■ Data are collected by participants and by observers, all of whom have varying degrees of involvement and detachment
■ Given evidence, we are always capable of distinguishing what is true from what is untrue, and are therefore enabled to agree on the real reasons for things if we wish to do so	■ Truth can't be determined in any absolute way; we are capable of using evidence to work towards a consensus, but must sometimes agree to differ, and sometimes conclude that the truth is undecidable
■ The purpose of enquiry is to build theories; these are general statements which validly explain phenomena	■ The purpose of enquiry is to gain sufficient understanding to predict future outcomes
■ Once such theories have been developed sufficiently, we should seek to apply them for productive purposes	■ There is no need to seek to apply theories; understanding and prediction are already theory-in-action, being theories-from-action

precise: the same answer should be obtained on remeasurement with the same measurement method, assuming the situation has not changed, of course. See Collis and Hussey (2003: 57–58) for a good summary, Brindberg and McGrath (1985) for a comprehensive approach at Masters level and Giere (1979) for further details of the thinking which underlies the method itself.

The last component, verification, is always seen as provisional, in the sense that, while you can cast doubt on, or even overturn, a theory by disproving the hypothesis, you can never verify a theory as true by proving the hypothesis. All you can do with a proven hypothesis is to say that the theory remains intact for today. However, if it remains intact for a long time, despite repeated testing of various related hypotheses, your belief that the theory is true will certainly increase.

Hypothetico-deductive method has a variety of techniques appropriate to various situations. The most powerful of these is the formal **experiment**, in which the hypothesis is stated as an association between A and B (the variable A is correlated with the variable B), or as a causal relationship between A and B (variable A is seen as independent, causing changes in variable B, which is seen as dependent). In the former case, the influence of other variables which might contribute to the association is controlled by careful design of the experiment and by a statistical technique called 'partialling out'; in the latter case, experimental design is the main method of control and statistics is used mainly for analysis. There are other techniques, used in the analysis of survey questionnaires, which model themselves on the experiment and also look for the influence of one variable on another (see Section 11.1).

There is also a major variant to the positivist approach, which relies less on hypothetico-deductive method and more on the development and testing of models, that is particularly suited to the analysis of business systems. If your topic is in this field, you might find the account given by Arbnor and Bjerke (1997) very useful. It provides an excellent practical description in the context of a review of the major epistemologies which apply to knowledge creation in business.

When scepticism fails

Approaches based on positivism have been highly successful during the last 250 years; so successful, indeed, that they are normally thought of as the only way of conducting research, largely because most people base their understanding of 'research' on the model of the physical and biological sciences in which (the inductive creation of classificatory schemes apart) the hypothetico-deductive method is the only one used.

However, I believe that the kinds of issues which are important in organizational work are essentially different to those in the physical and biological fields, because different ontological and epistemological assumptions apply. I'm not alone in this view (see below) and so, before considering the alternative approach which I advocate as the way of making sense to others in your research, a review of that organizational world is required.

First of all, we take a step back and consider the activity of research in general (see Figure 5.1). We begin with the thought that research in business organizations

FIGURE 5.1 Thinking about research: Case A, pure research; Case B, consultancy; Case C, project work as applied research

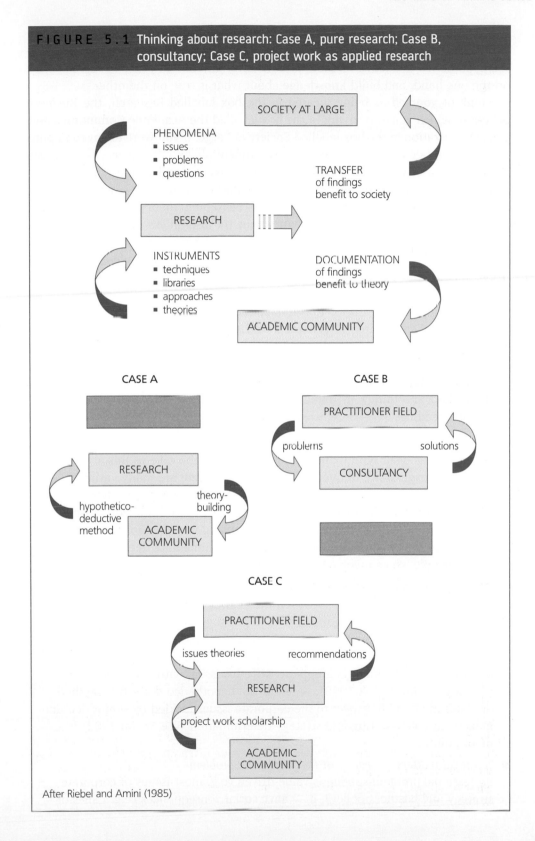

After Riebel and Amini (1985)

is essentially *applied* research. All research, pure or applied, is seen as an activity which draws on the instruments available in the academic community – including the hypothetico-deductive method, and the alternatives – in order to serve society on the one hand, and build knowledge about what is true on the other.

Think of yourself as being located in the box labelled Research, the Business School in which you're studying in the box labelled the Academic Community, and your Organization in the box labelled Society at Large. If you were engaged in pure research, particularly in a classical, experimentally-based subject like physics (Figure 5.1 case A), then the hypothetico-deductive method would make eminent sense. If you were a management consultant doing consultancy work (Figure 5.1 case B), clearly, it wouldn't: your job wouldn't be to build theory but to help resolve problems. There is considerable debate about the usefulness of the hypothetico-deductive method in applied research (Figure 5.1 case C): the issues presented by the Practitioner Field don't readily lend themselves to it. Finally, when the applied research takes the form of a project in business or management, I would argue that there is rarely a place for the method at all.

Many people involved with the problems of consulting, professional practice, social and applied research in general would agree with me. Some useful sources here are May (1993) among the social researchers, and Marshall and Rossman (1995) and Mason (1996) among the qualitative researchers. Reason and Rowan (1981) argue that all research is, at root, non-positivist. The difficulties which positivist method encounters in handling the practitioner field can be summarized under five headings.

- *The problems are inherently complex*
  The problems dealt with by professionals (and for the sake of this argument, I include managers) are frequently very complex: there are many variables, some modifying the relationships between others. To say, as positivists frequently do, that the theory incorporating these variables needs further development to handle the full complexity arising in professional practice is of little use to the practitioner, who needs to take immediate decisions. For more on the people issues involved, see Allport (1981).

- *Problems cross discipline boundaries*
  Practitioner problems don't sit within the neat boundaries of academic knowledge, or within categories which might suggest an appropriate technique to apply; they're frequently 'messy' (Eden *et al*. 1983). Different knowledge bases, methods, and assumptions, must be used. The developing field of knowledge management is grappling with this issue, with some difficulty (Davenport and Prusak 1998). Whether the hypothetico-deductive method operates at all, with respect to the corporate issues tackled by senior decision-makers, in policy-setting and strategy determination (see Schön 1983) is a moot point.

- *Technical matters are rarely at the root of the problem*
  Professional problem-solving is value-driven (e.g. most issues of corporate strategy and business policy), may have social consequences (e.g. issues of

quality in manufacturing and service management), and is frequently intertwined in contradictory assumptions about social policy (as in e.g. Health, the Social, and Emergency Services). Technical questions scarcely feature among the larger problems dealt with. Yet management, in this sense, is pre-eminently a professional, and not a technical activity.

■ *Problems don't have an independent life of their own*
Professionals don't think in ways which are easily analyzed by the hypothetico-deductive method, which assumes a dispassionate 'observer', the existence of problems and truth 'out there', and a situation which sits still enough for the effects of scientific interventions to be noticed. Intuition, gut feeling, and flair are involved in management decision-making, and this is true at senior corporate level (Eden *et al.* 1979); and at middle management level (Isenberg 1984). Much of the manager's time consists, not of testing out the truth of questions, but of framing the questions in the first place. Where are the variables that hypothetico-deductive method requires? The manager has to determine what counts as evidence by recognizing it as it goes by in the flow of events, and this is an active process of construction and judgement, rather than a dispassionate assessment of what is objectively 'out there'.

■ *Problems are culturally relative*
The manager is a product of his or her own culture with its particular history and operates within a language which slices up phenomena in a culturally idiosyncratic way. If he or she is operating in a foreign market, he or she rapidly discovers that what counts as evidence to the foreign business partners may radically differ (Hampden-Turner and Trompenaars 2002), and require special attention (Baumgarten 1995).

Of course, you could argue that I am confusing the difficulties which exist in the subject-matter being researched, with the activity of research in itself. You may grant me that the field to be researched is unreasonably complicated in the ways I have described above, but that this should not prevent the application of scientific method. After all, even insanity – unreason itself – can be studied using the hypothetico-deductive method!

But the difficulty with this is that in order to carry out this sort of 'scientific' research in management, you have to distort the issues so much to get them to fit into the language of hypothesis, variables, and theory; you have to elide the intuitive and the judgemental; you have to ignore so much of what makes the issue worth researching in the first place – that the result of your labours may turn out to be largely irrelevant. With some exceptions such as quantum mechanics (see e.g. Feinberg 1997) the positivist approach works in the physical sciences because the phenomena it investigates can be understood and predicted accurately enough by believing that there are events out there, that the status of the data is unarguable, that truth exists independently of the people who seek it, and that the researcher can in principle remain separate from, and uninvolved in, the phenomena being investigated. Unfortunately, this doesn't work as well with organizational phenomena.

Interpretivism

In contrast to positivism, **interpretivism** (sometimes presented under the rubric of 'phenomenology'; see, e.g., Maykut and Morehouse 1994: 7–24), the approach I would advocate for your work in business and management, eschews scepticism and works with the alternative. In its strong form, **constructivism**, it works with conviction directly, and adopts an ontology and epistemology which do three things:

a Legitimize the value and weight of individual belief and conviction (after all, it is the individual who decides on what constitutes an event, who makes measurements, who interprets, and who accepts or disputes observations and explanations made by others).

b Avoid any search for *truth*, and focus instead on a socially agreed *understanding*. There is no ultimate proof of what is true, and the best we can do is to accept whatever the community of researchers and theorists finds useful for the time being, in understanding and predicting the events we have agreed on as worthy of study. The individual researcher needs to convince this community of the accuracy and value of his or her own understanding, pointing to the evidence available, and knowledge proceeds by consensus, a consensus which is always open to revision.

c Facilitate the constant, conscientious, and careful monitoring of the personal, social, and situational factors which, experience in the field under study suggests, may lead to a consensus which is likely to turn out to be unhelpful: biased, unreliable, or tendentious.

Table 5.1 summarizes the main assumptions in the interpretivist approach in contrast to those of the positivist approach. Notice two things. First, that the managers and employees whose role in a positivist approach would be as 'subjects' or 'people being studied' – are usefully thought of as *collaborators* in constructivist research. Interpetivism makes no distinction between the investigator and the person doing the investigation; epistemologically, their views and understandings are of equal status (Kelly 1955/1991). Chapter 6 explores the practical implications.

Second, notice the care taken that individual beliefs have evidence in their support, that observations are reliable so that the grounds for consensus are available, and that monitoring is possible. If we are to drop our adherence to positivism and hypothetico-deductive method with its search for the truth 'out there', we must still retain a rigorous approach to ensure that our understanding is complete enough to permit workable prediction (note the difference in emphasis: not 'truth', but 'understanding'). The necessary rigour is supplied in the form of a number of procedures advocated by interpretivists, which address the problems identified in the previous section. These are shown in Table 5.2.

In short, we are making the following assumptions.

■ If there is no easily identifiable absolute 'reality' or 'truth', as the hypothetico-deductive method would assert, we try to identify how the people involved understand what's going on, and what they see as the evidence involved.

- Knowledge does not come from the application of theory to practice, but rather by identifying the differing theories that different stakeholders embody as they go about their daily business. Behaviour is in itself a theory. This is not as mysterious as it may appear. When you set your alarm clock to get to work on Monday and walk to the bus-stop for a particular bus, the time you set, and the speed at which you walk, express an implicit theory about bus frequencies on a Monday morning. Your actions *are* the theory.

- If theories are embodied in practice, then it is essential for you to involve practitioners in shaping your project and designing the questions to ask, not merely in answering your questions. Research should be collaborative, rather

---

TABLE 5.2 The interpretivist approach and the five problems of the practitioner field

The complexity of the problems addressed
- Accept the messiness of the real managerial environment (Eden *et al.* 1983).
- Think in terms of issues, not variables, discovering them through a period of detailed familiarization.
- What are they, who says so, what significance have they, what is their context, which academic theories might apply?
- Which are the important ones, what evidence do you have for that judgement?
- Don't just import a theory from outside, but a theory from these practices. (See e.g. Parlett 1981).

Problems cross discipline boundaries
- Don't force incompatible academic disciplines together; accept the messiness and build a framework relevant to the practitioner field, working by collaboration with the people involved.
- Who sees themselves as 'owning' the problem, who else might be involved without realizing it, what personal theories do they hold and what stories do they tell about what's happening (Mair 1990; Read *et al.* 1989)?
- How will they be affected by your findings; how can you preserve the integrity of your viewpoint while recognizing the differing stakeholdings?

Technical matters are rarely at the root of the problem
- Is the real issue dependent on the situation?
- In which case, a series of comparative case studies (Section 9.2), each exploring the issues and their situational determinants, make a good research method.
- Do the differences arise because of different stakeholder positions?
- Then try the key informant interview technique, Section 10.3.
- Is the real issue due to the divergent views of different pressure groups and political stances taken?
- Use conversational techniques (Section 10.1) to identify them and then seek to cross-tabulate the different views with more structured techniques (Sections 10.2 and 11.1)
- Is the issue messy because views change over time?
- Try historical review and analysis method (Section 9.2). See Miles and Huberman (1994: 143–148), for further particulars.

TABLE 5.2   The interpretivist approach and the five problems of the practitioner field (cont.)

Problems don't have an independent life of their own
- They may depend on the personal values, biases, and stances of the individuals involved, who construct a set of interlocking personal realities around them.
- So make these stances explicit; identify who has good evidence in support of their views and who hasn't; see if there are any systematic biases operating (see Table 5.3, and Gilovich 1991); see who agrees with whom, and who disagrees and for what reason.
- How are conflicts resolved?
- To what extent are intuitions involved, are these well based in evidence, and do they change or stay constant?

Problems are culturally relative
- The effective ways of handling the issues are likely to be culture-dependent; so, what is the local reality, and what are the particular customs, habits and constraints which account for the local view, and with which any effective solution will need to be compatible?
- How do people from outside the culture handle these issues, and what scope do they have for adapting flexibly to local constructions?
- Can a common way of construing the issues and resolving the problem be worked out between the individuals involved?

than something which you bring in from outside. (Clearly, the project you will submit has to be your own work, and you will be responsible for its shape and its outcomes. But 'your own work' consists of making the project come about by asking the questions listed in Table 5.2). To quote Stewart and Stewart (1982: 6), 'Many managers are fed up with experts offering them ready-made solutions', and Hunt (1987: 109), 'Unless theories come from practice, they will not apply to practice'.

- If there is no epistemological difference between your own understanding and the understanding of the people you are studying – if your attempts to make sense of the world are of equal status – then it is important to be aware of the kinds of errors in reasoning that we are all liable to make, and as researchers, to design the research so as to minimize them. Table 5.3 lists them.

- You are not looking for 'a right answer'; you are seeking to bring understanding by providing a description of a state of events and the situation which enfolds them – for meaning arises from the situation. You will choose a relevant theory from the literature, or construct your own by means of the Grounded Theory method (see Section 12.3 for the details) and adopt a method and techniques for data collection to suit, as listed in Table 5.2. (See Morse 1994 for more on this.)

 Collect your thoughts by addressing activity 3 in the Project Guide. This would also be a good point at which to tackle Case Example 5.1

TABLE 5.3 Some common biases in constructing explanations
In their task of making sense of the information available to them in making decisions, it is assumed that people – whether managers or researchers – make judgements; that is, that they use their experience to: a draw on pre-existing mental frameworks or personal theories b apply these in order to interpret the significance of the information c develop a plan for action which makes use of the information. In doing so, they may be led astray by the information available to them, into choosing an inappropriate mental framework or elaborating it in inappropriate ways.
Input Biases: Biases in what is attended to, triggered off by: ■ *Availability of information*: how easily certain data can be obtained, regardless of their relevance to the situation involved: personal preferences or values are often responsible. ■ *Salience of information*: perceived relevance of data to the issue at hand, due to the vividness of the data, regardless of relevance. ■ *Anchoring effects*: misinterpretation of the meaning of data, due to the impact of previous data; insufficient search for further data. ■ *Perseverance effects*: adherence to initial view regardless of further data.
Output Biases: Biases in the kinds of responses which are preferred, triggered off by: ■ *Functional fixedness*: pre-existing orientation towards a category of responses found to be helpful in achieving the manager's goals. ■ *Social desirability*: responses reflecting colleagues', or the organization's, preferred way of doing things; an insidious form of political correctness. ■ *Reasoning by analogy*: responses chosen due to apparent similarity of present situation to other situations
Operational Biases: Biases due to inaccurate inferences in making decisions, set off by: ■ *Inappropriate sampling*: use of data which don't represent the situation adequately. ■ *Absence of information*: missing out data that are essential to the type of decision being taken. ■ *Attribution errors*: confusion between personal and situational influences on behaviour. ■ *Illusory correlation*: seeing patterns and links in different kinds of data where no such association exists.
There is some evidence that personality may predispose a manager to particular idiosyncratic biases: Haley and Stumpf (1989). The main reference is Tversky and Kahneman (1982).

5.3   Maintaining credibility

As you can see, effective project work depends on making an appropriate match between your methods, and the issues which you are researching. Most of the time, the nature of the practitioner problems which you address will require an interpretivist approach while, less frequently, positivist assumptions and methods will pertain.

In either case, though, the quality of your work is an issue. You either believe that there is a truth out there which you ascertain through scepticism, disbelieving your convictions until they survive the mangle of disinterested, objective proof; or you believe that useful understanding can be derived by developing and establishing your convictions, and that, if knowledge is socially defined by means of consensus, you had better provide evidence towards that consensus as robustly as you can.

Critical analysis

All business dissertations, regardless of the level of the programme you're following, need to go beyond mere description and be based on a **critical analysis** which ensures that your understanding, the story you have created, convinces the tutor and examiners who are your readers. It's helpful to think of critical analysis as involving two components: conceptual analysis, and evidence and argument.

Conceptual analysis

This involves you in making a relevant selection of appropriate theoretical, conceptual and/or empirical findings, which you review to express your understanding of the issues with which your project deals. Your literature review leads you to choose a particular **analytic framework** (a coherent set of ideas, model, or theory) by which to do so, and Chapter 7 describes the mechanics involved.

The framework may be a concept, model, or approach commonly used by other researchers. Such analytic frameworks as:

- the value chain
- strategic drivers
- the Ansoff matrix
- portfolio analysis
- the Dunphy-Stace organizational change matrix (Dunphy and Stace 1988),

are just some of the many conceptual models available in projects on strategic management and change, for example. All would involve you in describing the model, exemplifying its uses in similar situations in the literature, and identifying it onto your organization: in other words, in showing how the issues with which you are dealing fit the model and justifying this assertion. In each case, you would need to recognize the limitations of the conceptual framework (no model is perfect in itself, or in its application to a particular situation); you'd need to make an argument for any extra factors which you decided to take into account; and you would review alternative conceptual frameworks which other workers in the same field have used, justifying your own choice.

This is what turns a literature review from a bare descriptive account of relevant authors, to an argument, in which you state your case for the particular approach you are adopting, and for the empirical work that you will shortly describe in the empirical section of your dissertation.

ILLUSTRATION 5.3

Towards the end of his literature review on service quality, David Carter decides to use the Zeithaml approach (Zeithaml *et al*. 1990) as his analytic framework to describe and evaluate the relationship between what his organization (the local police constabulary) provides by way of service to two client groups: the general public; and a variety of groups internal to the criminal justice service. He justifies this particular model for quality, rather than alternatives he has reviewed, because the Zeithaml approach defines 'quality of service' in terms of the mismatch between client wants and provider capability, rather than in absolute terms, and expressions of what the public wants are particularly important in setting policing policy in any constabulary. He has altered some of the provider–client relationships in the model to reflect the two different client groups involved, justifying the alterations by looking at what other authors had done in related circumstances, and by means of a review of recent shifts in strategic orientation within his constabulary which he has conducted collaboratively with some of his colleagues in provider and client departments.

In all cases, the end-point of a conceptual analysis is a working model, identified onto your own organization and expressed in just those terms that the empirical questions which you will address in your own data-gathering will be obvious to the reader. It is an argument, with justifications, which results in questions to be asked and, often, proposes a single strong thesis to be justified. In this regard, you might find the following useful. There was a forum on theory building in the October 1989 issue of the *Academy of Management Review* (14:4), while the special issue of *Management Education and Development* (21:3) was devoted to postmodern approaches to management.

With some topics, it is possible to adopt an approach which provides you with a formal scheme for combining both the constructivist and hypothetico-deductive approaches. This is called **grounded theory**, and, technically, involves a process of analytic induction (Burgess 1982). The approach merits longer discussion than I want to give it here (it doesn't entirely resolve the criticisms I have levelled at the hypothetico-deductive method, for example, as Burgess (1982: 211) points out. But you may find it useful if you have the time for it, so the following thumbnail sketch may be helpful.

It works by collecting data, generalizing findings into statements about the possible relationships involved and checking out these statements by further data-collection to a point at which you can categorize types of result. Further data are collected to check the plausibility of these categories, to enable you to posit variables which may be involved, and the relationships between them. At this point, your conceptual analysis results in a small theory, which you proceed to extend with further data-collection, until you have the beginnings of an explanation for whatever is going on in the situation which you have been investigating. As you can see, the theory is said to emerge by induction from the realities of the situation, rather than being 'brought in from outside' in the way, illustrated in Figure 5.1, which is claimed for hypothetico-deductive approaches.

First described by Glaser and Strauss (1967), Strauss and Corbin (1998) is the main text to look at. There are some brief comments on this approach as applied to the development of a scheme for structured observation in Section 12.3.

Evidence and argument

This is the part of your project which is most your own, in which you report on the empirical data which you have collected, developing your account in a way that provides convincing support for your point of view and compels acceptance by your reader. Part 3 will provide you with the techniques to use; for the moment, it is sufficient to summarize the procedure involved.

Your argument will include a methodological discussion justifying the approach you took to the data you gathered; it will also present the data themselves, analyzed and digested, presented in an informative way to illuminate the conceptual analysis, to give evidence concerning any thesis or theses which you are seeking to establish, to justify your assertions, and to move your whole argument forward. It will involve you in discussing the significance of the findings you have obtained, for your organization and organizations like it in the case of an in-company project, and for the selected organizations you have chosen in the case of a generic, industry-based project. It may also lead to recommendations for action, especially in the case of a post-experience project done inside your own organization.

If you have the opportunity to implement and evaluate recommendations as well as simply making them, your project will be particularly valuable. While this is rarely possible, since you may not have sufficient time to take action and follow the results through in order to evaluate them prior to your graduation, a partial implementation of interim recommendations is sometimes possible within a one-year final year project framework. The name for this approach is 'action research'. There is an excellent overview in Marsick and O'Neil (1999), while Whitehead (1994) provides an excellent example of the ways in which management research and management action go hand in hand.

Qualitative versus quantitative approaches

Much of my argument in this chapter, making the case for interpretivist epistemology in business research, draws on authors who advocate qualitative, rather than quantitative methods. Marshall and Rossman (1995), Mason (1996) and Maykut and Morehouse (1994) all referred to earlier, are texts with 'Qualitative Research' in the title, largely because qualitative research draws on interpretivist, rather than positivist, ontology and epistemology. Similarly, many of the procedural guides you will be using for data collection and analysis in your empirical work emphasize that term 'qualitative': see, for example, Miles and Huberman (1994), or Symon and Cassell (1998).

It is very important not to confuse the two distinctions: that between positivist versus interpretivist ontology and epistemology on the one hand and between qualitative versus quantitative data and analysis on the other. Even the most experienced of researchers (see e.g. Morgan 1998) make this mistake. It's true that, historically, positivist approaches have given primacy to the quantitative – to the need to measure using numbers, with qualitative approaches being relegated to the initial exploratory stages of research. Interpretivist approaches do argue for the primacy of qualitative methods and techniques. But in point of fact, depending on the precise technique you adopt, you can of course use both qualitative and quantitative techniques in your research, even when it is based on a purely interpretivist rationale.

Clearly, to the qualitative researcher it is the nature and content of what is said – its meaning – rather than the number of people who are saying it, or the frequency with which it is said, which matters; but there are many (granted, not all), qualitative techniques in which meanings are identified, categorized, and their relative importance or impact listed, enumerated . . . and counted, in one way or another. The issue is *not* one of numbers versus meanings, but of the basic metaphysical assumptions (ontology and epistemology) on which the research method and techniques are based. There will be circumstances in which you use numbers in your dissertation and, equally, many in which you don't.

So the arguments which I outlined in Section 5.2, in other words, don't apply simply to qualitative problems in management research or social research. In case it isn't clear by now, they reflect an ontology and epistemology for *all* management and social science research, with no special status being granted to the quantitative approach: Henwood and Pidgeon (1992). As Gill and Johnson (1997) point out, this is a radical view (especially to people trained in physics, science and engineering prior to their study of management!) and I can only refer you to the authors cited above, who reflect what is currently known as the post-modern paradigm of research.

Now, please complete your planning by attending to activity 4 in the Project Guide.

The ethical implications: confidentiality in particular

Regardless of your approach, you will of course need to be careful about the confidentiality of information which you receive from your respondents. Confidentiality has a peculiar importance in the interpretivist approach, however, since you no longer believe you're gathering 'objective', hence supposedly neutral, evidence on the 'reality out there'. You have adopted the approach of conviction, come to terms with the messiness of phenomena and events, and are aware that you are dealing, as rigorously as you can, with a fallible world in which truth is developed, or, if you will, created, by fallible human beings – and that includes yourself and the people whom you are studying. You deal in information which is value-laden, personal, judgemental, and frequently, politically sensitive. The ethical issues are, consequently, a very important aspect of the quality of your work, as outlined in Section 3.2.

Whether your approach is positivist or interpretivist, you will need to:

- obtain permission to quote
- conceal the provenance of particular viewpoints when you are particularly requested to do so. (This basic issue of anonymity is discussed further in Section 11.4.)
- keep data in a secure place and
- (where projects involve commercially sensitive data), make special arrangements for restricting the circulation of your project report. Your tutor is your guide here.

However, you are likely to find that these usual arrangements are insufficient. In involving your informants in the design of your investigation, in asking them to share their intuitions and judgements, and in involving them in helping you evaluate the validity of statements other people have made, you are already encountering situations in which confidentiality is an issue, well before the need to preserve confidentiality in writing your project report presents itself.

You will find that you make very little progress at all, unless you confront the issue early on; and the way to do this is by negotiation. It is your special responsibility to draw the four issues to the attention of your informants and, in creating a situation in which your collaborators can take a part in your project in the various ways I defined in Section 5.3, create a 'safe space' in which you can all fruitfully work together. The details are developed in the next chapter.

Janne Jarvinen runs a small business in Finland, which produces a new form of disposable face-mask for people suffering from cold and flu symptoms. Based on the kinds of light mask worn as a matter of course in Japan, it is impregnated with a herbal compound that has a mild antibacterial effect. Happy with sales but wishing to expand them and grow the business, he decides to take an action research approach to the issue, devoting his MBA dissertation at Helsinki University to an examination of ways of doing so.

He is aware of the ways in which the more effective initially 'alternative' products are adopted by the mainstream pharmaceutical companies and has a gut feeling that now would be a good time to try and move in that direction, providing a stronger antisepsis based on pharmaceutically refined products, and obtaining the necessary approval from Laakelaitos Lakemedelsverket, the Finnish National Agency for Medicines and a range of international bodies such as the UK Medical Control Agency and the US Food and Drug Administration. He decides to carry out a series of interviews with representatives of several large pharmaceutical companies to see how this might be done and identify the different strategies involved. He would need to approach them carefully and work out a collaborative agreement. While the larger firms are intensely competitive outside their range of ethical drugs (which are effectively protected by patent) there is a lively collaboration between them and the smaller companies. He is well-connected and knows that knowledge is freely negotiated between them and the clinical researchers.

Perhaps he can do a couple of case studies, interviewing the owners of other entrepreneurial companies to see how they succeeded in obtaining health and safety approval and how they approached the public bodies involved. Antti Forsström, his business partner, disagrees. He feels strongly that this will get them nowhere. If they wish to maintain their independence they cannot afford to get into bed with the large companies.

Janne responds that this is, in practice, the only way they can cut short the long and expensive process of certification, but concedes that it might be difficult to find other entrepreneurs who are willing or able to share experience. Perhaps they should stay within the 'alternative medicine' market after all. But in that case, how can they grow?

Antti says he as a better idea. He has been reading a book about the 1985 Manchester air disaster, in which passengers trapped inside a stationary plane died through smoke inhalation. Forget intuition and gut feelings. Why don't they expand their product range and develop a light face hood with a smoke filter built in, to be distributed though the airlines, who would make them available as part of their safety procedures, handing them out to passengers as they boarded the aircraft, and giving instructions on how to use them as part of their cabin safety talk prior to take-off? The manufacturing technology was similar to their present face-mask, although there would have to be some retooling. He suggests that if Janne wants to research a new product, his time would be far better spent talking to potential suppliers about different kinds of charcoal filter technology, and transparent plastic sheet materials, after which he should do some systematic costings. They would also need to speak to the company that supplied their specialized assembly equipment (gluing and sewing machines) to see what adjustments might be required in the assembly process. If he is to do some interviews as part of his project, why not talk to some companies already in the field about their distribution arrangements? Selling the product directly to the airlines, perhaps, as Saf-T-Glo had done with their cabin floor illumination systems? (*Business Weekly*, 2003). What options did they consider and what kinds of deals did they arrive at? In arriving at a sales agreement that worked, why did it work? What didn't, and why?

Janne responds that even if they went this route, what is being proposed is radically different: expansion by expanding the range rather than by a

steady product improvement. Besides, he's not sure about Antti's distribution strategy. As someone for whom intuitions matter, he feel that passengers make decisions in a similar, impressionistic manner. The airlines are very careful about how they deal with issues of safety with their passengers, not wishing to draw passengers' attention to the risks associated with flying. Issuing smoke-masks as a matter of course? Seat sales would plummet! No, the face hood should be designed to be light and flat, packaged so that it folded into an outer enve-lope and sold directly to passengers in the airport shopping areas. To the extent they think about it, people like to feel in control of their own safety. If the airline is the provider they are forced to think about it rationally, sitting there in the flight cabin and take it more seriously – rather than simply making an impulse purchase in the customer-friendly environment of the shopping concourse prior to going to the departure lounge. People don't actually think in terms of actuarial risks involved in flying; it is impressions that matter to them.

1 How would you compare Janne's and Antti's ontological positions?

2 And their epistemologies?

Business Weekly (2003) '$6m Boeing boost for Norfolk air safety firm'
WWW.   http://www.businessweekly.co.uk/news/view_article.asp?article_id=4580
accessed 15 September 2003.

Answers to Case Example 5.1

This case includes two different viewpoints about business growth. There are a variety of fundamental assumptions involved, and (though it is more obvious in the case of action research), it is, typically, difficult to disentangle the assumptions about busi-ness from the assumptions about research. You might deal with the former by drawing on your studies of small business expansion and business

growth strategies; the following points can be made about the research assumptions.

1 Janne's ontology is based on *negotiation*. He sees relationships between larger and smaller companies as negotiative in nature, and manageable using an approached based on mutual self-interest. He believes that it should be possible to come to an agreement whereby a large pharmaceutical company will share its certification procedures and expertise. Notice how he applies this to is own empirical research. He proposes to talk to other companies like his own, to learn from their experience (though he has not, perhaps quite worked out why it would be in their interest to talk to him).

Antti's ontological position, in contrast, emphasizes technology and *technical compe-tence*. Basing his strategy on an expansion of their product range, he construes the growth problem in terms of tooling changes, materials technology, production and distribution pro-cedures. His suggestions about research reflect this stance. If life is about *effective procedures*, what better than to systematically review the various distribution arrangements that other companies have found feasible?

2 For Janne, knowledge is based on *consensus* and *intuition*. He is comfortable to talk to other companies to extend his knowledge of custom and practice in the trade, and he is prepared to follow his gut feelings that the times are appro-priate for the growth strategy he is proposing. His argument against Antti's distribution proposal is also intuitive, based on an appraisal of how airline passengers feel as they prepare to take off.

Antti's epistemology matches his ontology. He mistrusts intuition, and deals in *operational-ized evidence*; quite simply, what accounts for the difference between a successful deal and an unsuccessful one? The proof is in the sales or lack of sales, not in the climate of opinion among experienced small business owners.

Project Guide

Much of this chapter has been conceptual. However, there are several practical tasks which you could beneficially address at this point, in order to crystallize this material in a form which is directly relevant to your own project work.

1 Identify your ontological position

- Reread Section 2.4.
- Thinking back over the last two years, make a list of the organizational *events* which you feel are particularly significant to your topic, on a second sheet of paper. What kinds of thing, for you, count as 'an event'?
- Categorize the events by looking at Table 2.5. Do most of them relate to any particular kind of issue listed in the table?
- Use this information to flesh out your research question, jotting down the results in your research diary.

2 Identify your epistemological assumptions

- Take a sheet of paper and divide it into two columns; label the left-hand one 'Positivist Approach?' and the right-hand one 'Interpretivist Approach?' Now make a list of beliefs you have about your topic, allocating them either to the left-hand column or the right-hand column as follows. If these beliefs feel to you like hypotheses which you can establish, by gathering data to test them, put them down on the left; if, however, they feel more like interesting hunches and gut feelings which you, or the people involved in your topic (colleagues in the organization you're studying), use to make sense of the situation, put them down on the right.

- Take a second sheet of paper, this time with the two headings, 'Variables' and 'Issues'. Referring to the lists you produced in the first two parts of this exercise, identify the variables involved, and the issues involved, respectively. Next to each variable, try and think through how you would operationalize it: what would you actually need to measure? Next to each issue, specify the kind of thing that would count as evidence about it.
- If the two right-hand columns of each sheet of paper have more items; or if the significance, to you, of the items in the right-hand columns is greater, it does look as though a interpretivist approach is going to be more appropriate, doesn't it?
- Now check your conclusions with your tutor and your sponsor at work. Write the agreed position into your research diary.

3 Amend your project proposal

Go back to the project proposal you prepared in the Project Guide for Chapter 2, exercise 5, and amend your research proposal in the light of what you have learnt about positivism, interpretivism, and ontological stance – particularly the section entitled 'Design' (see the example given as Table 2.6).

4 Think though the implications for the structure of your project document

- Glance once more at Figures 3.1 and 3.2. Are you dealing with a single hypothesis or main issue, or will you need to do empirical work on several related and intertwined issues? Make a provisional decision about which structure is likely to suit you best.
- Add a new section to the research proposal: make an initial list of the chapter headings into which you anticipate you will have to divide your dissertation as a result of the first part of the present exercise.

References

Allport, G. W. (1981) 'The general and the unique in psychological science', in Reason, P. and Rowan, J., (eds.) *Human Inquiry: a Sourcebook of New Paradigm Research*, Chichester: Wiley.

Arbnor, I. and Bjerke, B. (1997) *Methodology for Creating Business Knowledge*, London: Sage Publications.

Baumgarten, K. (1995) 'Training and development of international staff' in Harzing, A. and Ruysseveldt, J., (eds.) *International Human Resource Management*, London: Sage.

Brindberg, D. and McGrath, J. E. (1985) *Validity and the Research Process*, London: Sage.

Burgess, R. G. (1982) 'The role of theory in field research', in Burgess, R. G., (ed.) *Field Research: a Sourcebook and Field Manual*, London: George Allen & Unwin.

Collis, J. and Hussey, R. (2003) *Business Research: a Practical Guide for Undergraduate and Postgraduate Students*, London: Palgrave Macmillan.

Davenport, T. H. and Prusak, L. (1998) *Working Knowledge: How Organizations Manage what they Know*, Harvard Business School Press.

Dunphy, D. and Stace, D. (1988) 'Transformational and coercive strategies for planned organisational change: beyond the O.D. model', *Organization Studies*, 9: 3: 317–334.

Eden, C., Jones, S. and Sims, D. (1979) *Thinking in Organisations*, London: Macmillan.

Eden, C., Jones, S. and Sims, D. (1983) *Messing about in Problems*, Oxford: Pergamon Press.

Feinberg, G., (ed.) (1997) *Quantum Mechanics*, *The Academic American Encyclopedia* (The 1997 Grolier Multimedia Encyclopedia version), Danbury, CT: Grolier, Inc.

Giere, R. N. (1979) *Understanding Scientific Reasoning*, London: Holt, Rinehart & Winston.

Gill, J. and Johnson, P. (1997) *Research Methods for Managers*, London: Paul Chapman Publishing.

Gilovich, T. (1991) *How we Know what Isn't so: the Fallibility of Human Reason in Everyday Life*, New York: Free Press.

Glaser, B. G. and Strauss, A. L. (1967) *The Discovery of Grounded Theory: Strategies for Qualitative Research*, Chicago: Aldine.

Haley, U. C. V. and Stumpf, S. A. (1989) 'Cognitive trails in strategic decision-making: linking theories of personalities and decisions', *Journal of Management Studies*, 26: 5: 477–497.

Hampden-Turner, C. and Trompenaars, F. (2002) *Building Cross-Cultural Competence: How to Create Wealth from Conflicting Values*, Chichester: Wiley.

Henwood, K. L. and Pidgeon, N. F. (1992) 'Qualitative research and psychological theorising', *British Journal of Psychology*, 83: 1: 97–111.

Hunt, D. E. (1987) *Beginning with Ourselves: in Practice, Theory, and Human Affairs*, Cambridge, MA: Brookline Books.

Isenberg, D. J. (1984) 'How senior managers think', *Harvard Business Review*, 62: 6: 81–90.

James, W. (1897/1958) *A Pluralistic Universe*, New York: Longmans, Green.

Kelly, G. A. (1955/1991) *The Psychology of Personal Constructs*, New York: Norton, and London: Routledge.

Mair, M. (1990) 'Telling psychological tales', *International Journal of Personal Construct Psychology*, 3: 1: 121–135.

Marshall, C. and Rossman, G. B. (1995) *Designing Qualitative Research*, London: Sage.

Marsick, V. J. and O'Neil, J. (1999) 'The many faces of action learning', *Management Learning*, 30: 2: 159–176.

Mason, J. (1996) *Qualitative Researching*, London: Sage.

May, T. (1993) *Social Research: Issues, Methods and Process*, Buckingham: Open University Press.

Maykut, P. and Morehouse, R. (1994). *Beginning Qualitative Research: a Philosophic and Practical Guide*, London: The Falmer Press.

Miles, M. B. and Huberman, A. M. (1994) *Qualitative Data Analysis: an Expanded Sourcebook*, London: Sage.

Morgan, M. (1998) 'Qualitative research ... Science or pseudo-science?', *The Psychologist*, 11: 10: 481–483.

Morse, J. M. (1994) '"Emerging from the data": the cognitive process of analysis in qualitative inquiry', in Morse, J. M., (ed.) *Critical Issues in Qualitative Research*, London: Sage.

Parlett, M. (1981) 'Illuminating evaluation', in Reason, P. and Rowan, J. (eds.), *Human Enquiry: a Sourcebook of New Paradigm Research*, Chichester: John Wiley & Sons.

Read, S. J., Druian, P. R. and Miller, R. C. (1989) The role of causal sequence in the meaning of actions, *British Journal of Social Psychology*, 28: 341–351

Reason, P. and Rowan, J., (eds.) (1981) *Human Inquiry: a Sourcebook of New Paradigm Research*, Chichester: Wiley.

Remenyi, D., Williams, B., Money, A. and Swartz, E. (1998) *Doing Research in Business and Management: an Introduction to Process and Method*, London: Sage.

Riebel, F. H. and Amini, S. (1985) 'Research and teaching', *Der Tropelandwirt*, Special Issue 24: 9–23.

Schön, D. A. (1983) *The Reflective Practitioner*, London: Temple Smith.

Stewart, V. and Stewart, A. (1982) *Business Applications in Repertory Grid*, London: McGraw-Hill.

Strauss, A. and Corbin, J. (1998) *Basics of Qualitative Research: Techniques and Procedures for Developing Grounded Theory*, Newbury Park: Sage.

Symon, G. and Cassell, C. (1998) *Qualitative Methods and Analysis in Organizations: a Practical Guide*, London: Sage.

Tversky, A. and Kahneman, D. (1982) 'Judgement under uncertainty: heuristics and biases', in Kahneman, D., Slovic, P. and Tversky, A., (eds.) *Judgement under Uncertainty: Heuristics and Biases*, New York: Cambridge University Press.

Whitehead, J. (1994) 'How do I improve the quality of my management? A participatory action research approach', *Management Learning*, 25: 1: 137–153.

Zeithaml, V. A., Berry, Leonard, L. and Parasuraman, A. (1990) *Delivering quality service: balancing customer perceptions and expectations*, New York: Free Press.

6

Research roles

■ To help you to find an in-company placement in support of your project, and to establish yourself and your project within an organization. Particular help is given to students who have no pre-existing relationship with the organization in which they seek to do project work

■ To continue discussion of the ethical issues involved when you study people within an organization

■ To examine the different kinds of role available to you

■ To review the mutual expectations involved in relationships with your tutor, your sponsor and your mentor

At a glance

How do you wish to be seen? When you engage in project work, a variety of roles is open to you, whether you are working within an organization, doing a generic industry-wide project, or relying on published work available in your library. This is particularly important for people who have no prior connections but wish to do their empirical work in a particular organization and that is the first issue to be addressed.

Next, we examine the issue of role in some detail. A role is defined less in terms of what you do ('role-playing'), and more as a set of *expectations* of what you ought to be doing as you engage in your project. This is an important matter, because how you are seen will make a difference to how you are treated. Furthermore, how *you* see yourself will make a difference to how you treat with other people.

If you are doing an in-company project, there are several different kinds of people who can help you: your tutor; your sponsor; and your mentor. We review what they might have to offer and see how you can obtain equivalent help if you are on your own doing a generic, industry-based project, or a project which is library based.

Finally, we look at how you might end the relationship with your helpers and move on, either literally or metaphorically. All investigative work involves four main stages: gaining entry to the field, defining your role, doing work under some form of supervision and leaving the field of work. These stages form the main sections of this chapter.

6.1   Gaining entry

The phrase actually has two meanings. Taken literally, it concerns the ways in which your arrival in the project organization comes about, whether this is arranged for you, or contrived by yourself. There are specific procedures (particularly useful for undergraduates and people not in employment following full-time programmes) which are described below. There is also a metaphorical meaning, and this is probably more important, relating to the ways in which you establish yourself, and gain access to data, through the development of appropriate relationships with people who can help you. The latter is a matter of role, and is dealt within Section 6.2.

Arranging a project placement with a local company

In most projects, the placement with a company will either be automatic, because you are employed there already, or it will be arranged for you by your teaching institution. Occasionally, however, this doesn't happen, or you may choose to make an arrangement for yourself despite the existence of an arranged scheme. Some guidelines are provided in Table 6.1.

Your efforts in the latter case will be appreciated by your course tutors, provided – and this is an important proviso – that you go about it the right way. The main steps and issues in arranging a project placement for yourself are as follows:

- *Talk to your tutor first.* Discuss the placement you have in mind, in detail, with your course tutor or project tutor, take his or her suggestions regarding which organizations are approachable, and remain in contact while you're making the arrangements. Don't ever proceed independently, since your attempts at entry may clash with other people's and organizations dislike dealing with several people from a single academic institution who appear to be unaware of each other's existence. Identify the ground-rules regarding salary, if any, with your tutor.

- *Contact the right person.* Telephone the organization in the first instance, to establish the appropriate person to approach. If your entry is by personal acquaintance, establish with that person whether you shouldn't also be dealing with someone else and particularly, someone in the organization's personnel department.

■ *Begin on the arrangements, allowing plenty of time.* Your next step is to write, even if you have a good contact and a firm verbal promise. Provide a clear account of what you intend to do while you are with the employer (Robson 2002). Your course tutor or project tutor should be able to advise you on a pro-forma, or a letter of their own which explains the programme and backs up your approach, and may supply you with background brochures about your institution's work placement policy and sandwich course arrangements. If there isn't a brochure, you might consider putting the basic details (advantages to the employer; what they're committing themselves to; what you're committing yourself to; how the scheme works) on a single sheet of paper to be enclosed with your letter. Provide a stamped, self-addressed envelope; allow plenty of lead-time, and if you like, approach several organizations at the same time to maximize your chances of a favourable early reply.

T A B L E 6.1 Gaining entry into an organization

■ Be opportunistic
Base your approach on doing what's possible, feasible and relevant to the organization, rather than something excessively wedded to a particular academic approach; be wary about work that can only be done using hypothetico-deductive approaches.

■ Allow plenty of time
Arranging a project usually takes longer than you expected. Start working on it well before you need access to data.

■ Use existing contacts
Be shameless in the use of friends, relatives, or previous acquaintances to assist you in gaining entry.

■ Use non-threatening language
Plan your approach carefully: words like 'research', 'investigation', 'publishing results', may carry unacceptable connotations, in contrast to words like 'learning from your experience', 'discussion', and 'writing it up'.

■ Be positive about practicalities
Worries about the time demands of employee involvement can be countered by showing your flexibility; worries about confidentiality, by discussing a general approach in advance, and specific mechanisms after entry.

■ Offer a report of the outcomes
This would be specially written in a form most useful to the organization; a good project report, especially when written in 'management report' style (see Section 3.4, Structure), is good, while a synopsis of a quarter the length is better.

After Buchanan *et al.* (1988)

■ *Show how your work will be useful to the employer, using appropriate language.* Most students are good at asking for help, and stating how the employer might be able to help them by giving them a placement . . . but what about telling the potential employer how your work on the project might help the employer instead? Put yourself in the shoes of the person who reads your letter – which sort of statement would you rather read? Which one irritates you through the use of inappropriate language? Which of the two, Arnold Wilson or Anna Delaney's, provides you with evidence that the applicant is the sort of person to be taken seriously? Establish your credibility!

ILLUSTRATION 6.1

To whoever it may concern,
Rayrol Collins plc.

Dear Sir,

I am writing to you to ask about the possibilities of a placement in your organization. I am currently studying a Bachelor's degree in Business Studies at Alcaster University and in my third year of studies have taken the option of undertaking a practical work placement, during which I have to carry out a piece of research, in place of some additional theory-based modules in my specialism, which is personnel management.

I am very interested in the development of training manuals and particularly, the best approach to task analysis, comparing top-down (hierarchic) and sequentially-based task description techniques. I need to write a dissertation which describes your approach to task analysis in some detail, making a comparison with the procedures followed by training departments in similar companies in your industry, most probably using a comparative case-study design.

I feel that having this practical placement behind me will increase my employment prospects immensely after my graduation next year. It would be nice to be paid a salary while I am with you and I would like to discuss this with you.

I would be enormously grateful for your help in this matter and look forward to hearing from you.

Yours faithfully,

Arnold Wilson

ILLUSTRATION 6.2

Mr Alan O'Keefe,

Training Manager,

Rayroll Collins plc.

Dear Mr O'Keefe,

I am writing to you at the suggestion of Mrs Walker of your HR department, who thought you might be interested in the possibilities offered by the Alcaster University cooperative education scheme. Under the scheme, students are placed for a six-month period with local employers to carry out a mutually agreed project on a topic which the employer wants to address. I enclose some information describing the scheme and the advantages to sponsoring employers.

There are two outcomes. You receive a written report with comments and recommendations; I write a more detailed account for my tutor, under the conditions of strict confidentiality described in the attached, and subject to a library embargo should you request one.

My own expertise includes the development of training manuals based on various task analysis and presentation techniques which can result in time and cost savings when assembly jobs in companies like your own are redesigned. I would of course be delighted to discuss alternative topics in the broad field of training and development which may be of more pressing interest to you.

I gather from Mrs Walker that the basic decision is yours, but anticipate that she will be involved in discussing the terms and conditions which Rayroll Collins would wish to apply to a placement. I am available for a visit in w.b. 15 May if that is convenient, to talk over the possibilities, and look forward very much to hearing from you.

Yours sincerely,

Anna Delaney

■ *Negotiate the topic in detail.* Liaise with your tutor and then attend whatever interviews may be involved, following the usual procedures for preparation and self-presentation. One of your purposes will be to discuss the topic (ideally, involving the organization in the initial stages of choice and definition), to clarify how it can best be useful and relevant to them, and to identify the balance of project-related and other work which you will be doing for them. The organization may wish to state the terms of reference to which you will be working: payment if any; completion dates; and the objectives and scope of additional work you do for them, as distinct from the work you do on your project. There may be a formal document which both parties need to sign; if so, you may need to discuss the details with your tutor.

- *Await a response in writing*. When it arrives, confirm your acceptance of the offer in writing, confirm the arrangements for starting, and report the details to your course tutor. If you received offers from more than one organization, make sure the tutor knows: he or she will be delighted, as it may increase the pool of employers for future projects. Make sure you reply personally to the organization whose offer you turn down, regardless of the action your tutor takes.

- *Establish yourself appropriately*. On arrival, confirm who is going to be your line manager (direct boss) and who is going to be your sponsor, if more than one person is involved.

How do you establish a pool of potential organizations to approach? I would be surprised if you were entirely on your own, but if this is the case, try the Chamber of Commerce and ask for their list of local companies. Failing that, the County Council's Economic Development Unit should be able to provide you with details of local employer networks or perhaps a directory of local companies which they publish themselves. Your local TEC publish booklets listing training opportunities for unemployed people; while you would be ineligible for the schemes in question, you could still build up a list of local companies whom you could approach with your own query. Employers' associations and trades unions are suggested by Saunders *et al*. (2003) as appropriate people to approach. The same authors also suggest that the local branch of the professional body for whose examinations you are preparing may have lists of suitable organizations through their membership list, and may be willing to put you in touch with those members.

You might find it useful to adopt some of the rules of thumb used by your tutors and other qualified academic researchers, when they seek entry into an organization with their own research questions in mind. Table 6.1 presents some guidelines. I have dealt with many of these in detail already; so, for example, if you follow the suggestions of Chapter 5, your work should be feasible and relevant and if you plan to write your project in the style I have suggested in Section 3.4, it should be easy to derive a brief synopsis to offer your putative employer. The table is based on Buchanan *et al*. (1988) a reference which is well worth reading in full. Another reference from the same book (Beynon 1988), is a sobering account of the defensiveness of, and pressures on, employers when they're approached with requests for project involvement, together with the ways (only some of which apply to you) for coping with the ensuing situation.

Arranging a project placement with an overseas company

It is highly unlikely that you would have to make your own arrangements. Where they exist, projects based overseas are almost exclusively an integral part of a taught course and formal arrangements will be made for you. However, if you aren't on that kind of programme and your institution gives you the freedom to try and make your own arrangements overseas, your first step, as before, would be to obtain addresses.

Your academic library should have a copy of *Kompass Europe,* which lists companies by country; alternatively, try the commercial section of your public library. The latter should also stock *Chambers of Commerce Worldwide,* which lists Chambers of Commerce by country. The commercial section of the information service of the Embassy for the country in question is another source. Finally, if you're interested in central and eastern Europe, and your university is involved in one of the EU or British Council sponsored programmes in this part of the world, you might care to explore the possibilities with the lecturer in charge. His or her budget will probably be too tight to take on an extra student, but he or she may be able to provide you with company details or other contacts in the country in question. You would then develop your contacts with the overseas company following the steps that apply to local companies, given above.

Activity 1 in the Project Guide has been devised to help you to get started. If you want to do an in-company project and need to find an employer, please tackle the activity now.

6.2   Defining your role, at home and abroad

Regardless of its location and basis, your project will demand that you define your role. There are six reasons for doing so:

- to build trust and a series of working relationships
- to gain access to informants and information
- to help define each other's stance on what is important and significant
- to gain support in approaching other people
- possibly, to gain support for implementation proposals
- to gain permission to report the findings externally.

In some cases, as Table 6.2 suggests, you will step into a predefined role. In others, you find yourself having to develop your role from scratch, overcoming, at times, some strange preconceptions on the part of your sponsor in doing so. It helps if you see yourself as engaged in a negotiation in the development of a contract. That is, you can't pre-empt the other person, or insist on your own point of view regardless of the other person's views; but, at the same time, you have a job to do which involves rules and constraints, which the other person must be persuaded to respect. You have to be prepared to meet halfway or thereabouts; and you may have to examine your own preconceptions about the organizational setting, being prepared to alter some and defend others, through a two-way process in which both yourself and your sponsor, are engaged.

TABLE 6.2 Project entry arrangements		
Type of project	**Example**	**The main issues facing you**
Integrated	Teaching Company Scheme Competency-based In-company taught	Interpreting your role within guidelines already laid down; handling the development of a relationship with a sponsor who may also be your line manager; often, working with a series of linked assignments rather than a single project, hence, a series of people.
Part-time	Diploma, MBA, professional programmes in which the project is done for your employer, but academic input is by and in the teaching institution	Developing your role, usually within expectations on the part of the teaching institution, but with underspecified expectations on the part of your employer; occasionally, employer expectations have been set, for good or ill, by previous projects done in the company; finding a mentor anywhere that's appropriate.
Full-time, entry arranged (also some distance-learning programmes)	Any programme in which a course or Project Tutor works from a list of previously participating companies, to which he or she keeps adding new companies	Developing your role in a situation where support and goodwill exist in principle, but where the previous projects done will have a strong bearing on how you're received; making your line manager into a sponsor; improving links with the in-company contact person for the scheme; building new project opportunities for the future.
Part-time, entry not arranged	Some distance-learning programmes; some Diploma-level programmes	Arranging a project in the first place; mustering teaching institution support.
Any group-based project	Some Diploma programmes; some integrated programmes	Add to the relevant items above, the development of group working relationships, and careful reporting/liaison arrangements with tutor and sponsor.

Ethical issues

You will recall from Section 3.1 (see also Table 3.1) that the existence of expectations which your presence as a researcher engenders among employees of your sponsoring organization raises a number of issues which have serious ethical implications. The principle of informed consent means that your collaborators need to know that they are involved, why they are involved, and to what extent they are involved. Outline what you intend to do in advance; do not harass people into participation; emphasize the right to withdraw; and clarify the arrangements which you have made to ensure the confidentiality and anonymity of the information they give you, to the degree that these attributes pertain. (Of course, a research project does not *have* to be confidential or anonymous. This depends on the exact circumstances and the sort of agreement which you have negotiated during entry.) In practice though, some degree of both confidentiality and anonymity will be involved and so your presence, with all its ramifications, needs to be thought through in detail. Use Table 3.1 as a guide in doing so and then clarify your thinking by extending the Chapter 3 Project Guide, activity 2, in the Project Guide for the present chapter: see below.

There are two issues with ethical implications which are particularly troublesome to people doing their first research project: the first being one which will probably occur to you as you go through the exercise and the second you are unlikely to anticipate in advance.

Deception

Your research design may require you to limit the degree of detail in which you describe your purposes. Covert participant observation, for example, is a familiar technique in anthropological research method in which you make observations of your co-workers as a co-worker, without explaining your research role or informing the co-workers that you are there to make observations; and, while the right to privacy operates in the sense that you would never intrude on private or intimate aspects of your co-workers' lives, the data that you gather are, in a sense, obtained under false pretences, because informed consent was not obtained.

Opinion varies on this matter, with much talk of ends which are benign and which thereby justify the means (see e.g. Saunders *et al.* 2003: 138). My own suggestion is that you look very suspiciously indeed at arguments of this kind and, more radically, that you avoid this kind of covert role. As Saunders *et al.* point out, people habituate: if they know you are observing them, they soon get used to you. Your presence, openly announced, may not be as intrusive as you originally thought. So, if your research design requires covert observation, try and alter the research design, or seek a topic which does not require covert techniques. Apart from anything else, there is value in collaborative research, as described earlier in Chapter 5, and 'collaboration' includes the people being studied!

On balance, I personally feel it is best to avoid covert participative observation as a technique. If you feel you have to engage in it, then Gummesson (2000) reviews the issues well in the general context of qualitatively-based research.

Unanticipated changes

Unless you are sensitive to the ethical dimension of your work, it is easy to overlook the need to renegotiate your role when you find yourself having to make changes in the middle of an extended project programme. Time passes, the research topic develops and grows as you examine initial findings and it is natural to flesh out your initial plans beyond the level of detail specified in the project proposal. The danger is that you might forget some of the early details, with their procedural and ethical arrangements.

ILLUSTRATION 6.3

I once carried out some research for the Benefits Agency, the purpose of which was to identify the personal values and beliefs of job centre counter staff on the subject of internal and external fraud and security breaches (Jankowicz 1996). One way of achieving this objective could have been to collaborate only with the Agency's security department in conducting an observational study as a covert participant observer, being employed by the Agency for the period required and gathering data from day-to-day conversation from which personal values could be inferred. Personal values are always subject to 'social desirability bias' (see Table 11.2), by which people tell you what they think you want to hear if they know the purpose of your research. So the technique of covert participant observation was, potentially, a way of minimizing this effect. However, the sheer practicalities of becoming trained sufficiently well to pass muster in the role precluded this approach, quite apart from my personal distaste at the deception required by the role. In the event, a combination of Repertory Grid Technique carried out by myself (see Section 12.1) and the use, by a separate team of investigators, of focus groups as a means of triangulating the findings (see Section 10.4) provided solid results and allowed powerful conclusions to be drawn. Both of these techniques depend fundamentally on involving people in a collaborative mode and take what they have to say seriously, as I have advocated in Chapter 5.

ILLUSTRATION 6.4

Michael Mambwe, who has a qualification in employee selection testing, is at a private college in South Africa where he is taking an MBA through a collaborative arrangement with an English university. At the start of his project, he collected aptitude test results in a local company, in order to construct new test norms. ('Norms' are a collection of test results, expressed as a frequency distribution of scores gained by a sample of respondents.) He did the work under the condition that no-one but he would have access to the original, 'raw' test scores in a way which identified the original respondents. Six months later, the company's training officer happened to mention that he had some trade test results obtained at the end of a training course from the same sample of respondents, and the two of them collaborated to put the two sets of results together, to see whether the aptitude test could be used to predict training outcomes. One of the sample of respondents complained in writing to the English partner university, pointing out in no uncertain terms that if Michael had wished to extend the original terms of reference of the agreement, he should have carried out the comparison of the two sets of scores by himself, working alone. He always thought that Michael was the sole researcher, and had not been told that other staff in the company would be involved in the research. How well did the English university monitor its courses at the South African college in any case? In the end, Michael's apology was accepted by the respondent in question, but what particularly concerned his South African tutor was the involvement of the English partner university, since the issue could easily have been resolved at a local level.

Some universities ask you to collaborate with your tutor to devise and sign a formal Ethical Agreement document before you begin your project work. All projects done for the UK National Health Service require formal approval from an ethics committee. If neither your organization nor your university require it, it is still a good practice to go over your plans using Table 3.1 as a checklist, identify the ethical issues as we did in activity 2 of the Project Guide of Chapter 3, discuss them with your tutor and keep a record of the outcomes of this discussion in your research diary.

> This might be a good point at which to address activity 2 in the Project Guide for the present chapter!

Arranging time for your project

One of the earliest things which you will have to establish with your sponsor is the nature and amount of other work, unrelated to your project, which you are expected to do for your host organization. If your project is 'Integrated', as I've described it in Table 6.2, the expectation will be that you do little else; although there may be occasions, when there's a 'panic' on in your department, that you help out to the extent that you're qualified to do so.

Undergraduate students will almost certainly be placed as full-time employees for the duration of their project and will be given additional work to do. Hopefully, the work will be in the broad area or field of your topic, at a level suited to your abilities and skills and you find that you learn a lot from your general work that is useful to your project. Even if it is not directly relevant, the level of work you are asked to do is unlikely to be too difficult for you (see Saxton and Ashworth 1990), and you may learn a lot from it even though it does not contribute massively to your project.

ILLUSTRATION 6.5

Peter Williams, an undergraduate interested in computer-assisted learning and training, was very despondent with the work he was asked to do during his project placement. He was being asked to do labouring and semi-skilled work, focused round the operation of a 10-ton press on the shop-floor of a heavy manufacturing company, and was given little time in the company's training offices. He spoke with his tutor, who contacted the sponsor in the company and expressed his concern. The employer pointed out that Peter was a wage-earner who had to pay his way, but agreed to provide one day off in five in the second half of the placement period, during which Peter could progress his project. Five years later, as a Training Officer himself, Peter remarked on the invaluable insights his shop-floor experience had given him into informal norms, unofficial leadership, and the sheer power of shop-floor culture. He had learnt all about these conceptually during his academic course in Behavioural Studies, but that was no substitute for the lived experience. As someone in a formal managerial position in his present organization, he could no longer be a party to it and he felt sorry for his colleagues who had never spent time 'at the coal-face' and had a very narrow perspective on organizational culture.

If you find you are being overstretched, however, and have insufficient time for your project work, then two things are important. First, keep track of how much time you have been able to devote to your project (your Project Diary is a useful aide-memoire in this respect) week by week. Second, make sure that you talk to your sponsor and/or your line manager, if you feel that the time is insufficient. You may wish to involve your tutor as an advocate in talking to the sponsor as part of this process.

If as a post-experience student you are already an employee of the organization in which you are doing your project, it's particularly important to sort this issue out quickly. The temptation to do little else but 'think about' the project, for weeks that turn into months, will be severe, given the day-to-day work which creates pressures on your time. Much will depend on the amount of support which exists for your involvement in the programme in the first place. At one extreme, you may be forced into doing all your project work at home, at weekends; at the other, you may be lucky and find yourself with a project topic which is an integral part of your normal work. All you have to do in this case is to negotiate additional time off for any data-gathering and analysis which need to occur outside company premises.

Managing perceptions

At home

The process of negotiation does not end when you come to an early agreement on the time you will have available for your project. Your role in the organization depends on perceptions and impressions which are formed and developed throughout the whole period in which you're doing project work, and, while first impressions are important, so are enduring perceptions of yourself in the job. This is important if you're an undergraduate, since it will affect the degree of cooperation you get for the project. It is even more important if you're in-company based, since you will not be walking away from the firm when your project is complete. Not immediately, at any rate. On the other hand, as Holliday (2002: 26–27) indicates, you have the enormous advantage over the undergraduate/placement student of knowing the ropes, and having an established role already. In your case, the question becomes whether your new role as a researcher fits compatibly with your pre-existing one, or whether some redefinition will be required.

It helps to anticipate some of the roles which are open to you, and some of the expectations and responses which these might engender. Table 6.3 presents a number of possible combinations. Some of these are viable and would be likely to lead to fruitful cooperation, others will result in a dissipation of energies and, if persevered in, can be terminal to the success of your project. Admittedly, parts of the table are a little burlesqued and I am not quoting a reference to an empirical study; but I have encountered all these combinations as a project tutor and would suggest that there are some obvious kamikaze roles which it would be wise to avoid.

The roles of 'informed assistant' and 'intelligent apprentice', would seem to fit best if you're an undergraduate; coming across as a 'self-and-company-improver', handled with due modesty, should work if you're in-company based; and 'professional aspirant' ought to increase your support if you're in a professionalized department and are following a professional programme. In all cases, the notion of negotiated contract is helpful. Once agreed, a contract is a bargain from which both parties expect to gain: so, the better your contract, the more people will help you because in doing so, they also help themselves. This is the role of 'someone doing a project for mutual benefit'.

While on the subject of burlesques, if you want some light relief from your project work, you may enjoy reading Lodge (1988). It's a novel which illustrates how not to go about building in-company relationships. The descriptions of attitudes

TABLE 6.3 The project student's role: stances and responses		
Project type	Your role as you intend to be perceived	The response it engenders
Undergraduate full-time	A subject matter expert	Someone with many corners to be knocked off
	A supplicant who needs help	A nuisance
	An enquiring mind	A bit exhausting, but bright-eyed and bushy-tailed
	An informed assistant	Someone potentially useful
	An intelligent apprentice	Good: give him/her something useful to do, help as much as there's time for
Diploma MBA, in-company	An academic employee	A curiosity, possibly resented
	Someone who's learning all the answers	A bit of an irrelevance, or even a threat
	An employee who's making him/herself more marketable	A potential competitor or deserter
	An employee improving him/herself for the good of the firm	A useful source of ideas and techniques; we admire the energy involved
Professional	A technical expert	Boss: Fine if I can use the expertise, otherwise I'm a bit indifferent
		Colleague already in profession: join the club
		Colleague not in profession: I feel a bit guilty
	A person working hard at joining the profession	Deserving of sympathy, respect and help
All	A scientist engaged in research	A wild-eyed idealist
	A person who knows more than they	A pointy-headed intellectual
	Someone doing a project for mutual benefit	A realist, to be assisted and helped to the extent that mutual self-interests are served

in the manufacturing environment, at both shop-floor and management level are a little stereotyped and, at times, awkwardly expressed, but quite informative if you have never been in a 'metal-bashing' industrial environment before.

Overseas

Much of what you take for granted about working relationships will be different when you do your project outside your home country; of course, you know this, since the resulting personal development challenges are probably part of your reason for seeking an overseas placement. This is an argument for greater sensitivity and more tentative exploration of the role expected of you. If you have management experience as a member of a part-time DMS or MBA programme, you might be regarded as a foreign 'expert' in some cultures; if an undergraduate, you may be construed according to the norms which apply to students, rather than employees, in the country in question.

Norms vary dramatically, and you should take advice on how to prepare yourself for the culture before you leave. The student role in much of central and eastern Europe is that of 'consumer of the academic expert's wisdom', and the role of in-company management trainee involves somewhat more passive exposure to an authoritative trainer or supervisory style (Holden *et al.* 1998; Jankowicz 1999), than is the case in the UK. Your own reading of such texts as Hofstede (1991) or Smith *et al.* (1989) will prepare you in general terms for the interactions involved in being supervised by an overseas manager in his or her own culture. However, if you have not already encountered them as part of your lectures in the behavioural subjects and are preparing from scratch, you would probably be better served by the Butterworth-Heinemann *Cultural Guides* series, choosing the book which covers your country of interest, and perhaps reading Moran and Johnson (1992) for Europe or Gesteland (1999) as a text with a global scope. Boisot (1994) is particularly good on issues in the post-command economies and will give you useful information on China, should your journey be in that direction.

The basis of your expertise

Even your most expert activity depends on negotiation. Your project may involve you in gathering data using techniques which nobody else in your organization understands. But, to the extent that the outcomes of your project will inform the decisions which people in the organization make, this expertise should be shared through negotiation. People who take decisions operate in idiosyncratic personal worlds for much of the time (Eden *et al.* 1979); intuition and judgement are very personal things (Isenberg 1984), as you'll remember from Section 5.2. To be useful, your use of expertise will be most effective if you've negotiated the questions and approach with the people involved.

You may find a succinct statement of Eden's ideas helpful in this respect. He talks about three possible roles: those of Expert; Empathizer; and Negotiator (Eden and Sims, 1979). The **Expert** has *coercive power,* a power that comes from the techniques he or she deploys.

'If the peddler of science and reason suggests a formulation for a problem and a solution to it, the client who ignores such advice and help may be seen by himself and his colleagues as a backwoodsman, kicking in the face of rationality.' (Eden and Sims 1979: 123)

The **Empathizer** operates by offering his or her services as a *sympathetic problem-solver* to the individual who's closest to the project (your sponsor, in most cases). The **Negotiator** focuses on the perceptions of the issues and problems being investigated in the project and handles the task of problem definition and resolution cooperatively (since, as I've said above, the definition is often part of the problem being researched in your project). In their account, which deals with the roles available to Operational Research consultants, Eden and Sims argue in favour of the role of Negotiator and I'm inclined to agree.

As someone rather different, not a consultant but a person who's working on a project, the role of 'technical expert' isn't available to you (unless you're in certain foreign companies, and even then excessive reliance would be undesirable). If you remember the definition of role, you will recall that it involves the way that other people see you and whether you're an undergraduate, or an in-company colleague, the people you work with will not view you in the same as an outside consultant, as a person with substantial power and expertise.

You could conceivably be seen as an Empathizer, but there are dangers. To empathize is to share in the concerns of the last person who's spoken to you and to get tangled up in potential conflicts of loyalty. Though personal involvement is an integral part of the research process (the argument expressed in Section 5.2), excessive empathy would remove whatever basis you have for ensuring the validity of your findings, which (you will recall from Section 5.3) requires you to work with many views, without subscribing blindly to one.

You're left with the role of Negotiator as a basis for your expertise. What is involved? Briefly, the definition and redefinition of issues and problems with the people involved in and affected by, the issues which your project explores. In more detail, the adherence to the mode of operation outlined in Section 5.3, which I wrote with this role especially in mind. Moreover, this is exactly the role to adopt if you are in a placement overseas.

In the role of Negotiator, your work becomes explicit, because others have shared in its planning. Many of your assumptions are shared by other people; and your goals have been discussed and argued over in detail. The kind of debate on the legitimacy of secrecy and concealment of objectives which characterizes accounts of sociological and anthropological field projects (Burgess 1982) and which we saw earlier has its ethical problems, should not be required in management project work. In discussing overt participant observation methods, Burgess provides you with two additional role descriptions. If you're a post-experience student working on your project in your own organization, you might consider the implications of considering yourself as a 'participant as observer'; whereas, if you're an undergraduate in a placement, what about the role of 'observer-as-participant'?

Burgess also has some interesting findings to report on the matter of sex-roles, specifically, on the degree of cooperation which male and female researchers get from the people with whom they are working. There is also a good article on role problems for female researchers by Easterday *et al.* (1982).

 Now spend some time preparing your role by working through activity 3 in the Project Guide.

6.3   Working under supervision

All investigative work is done under some form of supervision. Academics working with grant aid will have a person in the funding agency to whom they report periodically, while those without grants will occasionally be asked how things are going by their Heads of Department. So the fact that you have to report to someone else isn't unusual. What is different about project work is that the people you report to will have an involvement in your assessment – your tutor, almost invariably, and your sponsor, frequently. There is also a mentor, the third in the network of helpers you have available to you. The obvious implication is that the relationship you have with them is an important one and needs to be maintained in good repair.

Your tutor

With one exception, the worst project I've ever seen was one in which the student never met me and ignored all attempts to make contact. Somewhat more satisfactory, but still leading to very weak work, were the projects in which the student met me once, at the start, and never appeared again. Thinking back on where the weaknesses arose, it would seem particularly necessary to make contact with your tutor at the following points in time:

■ When you first start and are considering possible topics; indeed, you may be talking to several potential tutors at this stage. At this point, you are looking for general guidance, judging the kind of relationship you are likely to have, and estimating the interest each tutor has for your topic ideas. You should expect some initial suggestions on the reading which would help you confirm the topic. Think of yourself as choosing the tutor, as much as of the tutor choosing you, and consider changing topic or tutor diplomatically if you are uncomfortable.

■ When you confirm your choice of topic, the terms of reference which your sponsor has offered you, and the approach you plan to adopt. Some help with the structuring of your project, advice on the terms of reference, and an initial, fairly focused reading list are the things to expect.

■ When you have done some substantial reading, and are looking for feedback on your early ideas. You might wish to combine this with advice on your theme, discussion of the issues you intend to investigate, and guidance on the project methods and analysis techniques which you are aiming to use. If you have begun writing at this stage, you might like to send it all, or a sample, to the tutor in advance of your meeting. (Make sure you check that he or she is happy to work in this way.) You might be referred to more specialist texts at this stage. This is also probably the latest time for a discussion of the form which your project document should take.

■ When you have the results of your pilot study, or the findings on the first issues you investigated, and are looking for a friendly and informed brain with which to mull over the results, and fine-tune the main empirical stage. Have something on each of these in writing, and send it in advance if you can. This might be a useful time to offer any further material which you have written, for the tutor's comments.

■ When the main data on most of the main issues are in, and analyzed, and you have some conclusions to discuss. This may be an opportunity to discuss the need for further investigation or implementation and evaluation; or for additional reading.

■ When the bulk of your project document is ready, and you're looking for the results of an informal assessment.

If you have been showing your tutor your written work as you produce it, there may be no need for this last stage. Indeed, some tutors would be unwilling to read a complete draft in this way, but if you can get their help, it could make a difference to the assessment you finally receive. Provided, of course, that you act on the tutor's advice.

Six contact occasions works out at one every month or six weeks in a long project, and one every week in a short, professional project. Many students combine some of the stages, and see their tutor face-to-face on just three occasions. It is important to establish at the outset how your tutor would like to organize the relationship. Some tutors prefer a written draft of material in advance, with sufficient time to read it before meeting in their office. Others dislike working with hard copy, and prefer to receive material by e-mail, which they annotate and send back to you prior to, or instead of, one or more of the face-to-face meetings. Of course if you are engaged in a distance-learning or e-learning qualification, this is the way you will proceed in any case.

Your tutor can also be helpful on an unscheduled basis. Tutors are particularly useful in backing you up when you need to approach informants outside your organization, and in helping you negotiate special equipment, expenses and the like. Make sure that you have discussed this kind of issue with your sponsor first.

The undergraduate placement visit

Undergraduates who have been placed in an organization as part of a formal scheme by their university can normally expect at least one visit from one of their lecturers. Not every placement requires you to do a research project, of course (see Section 7.1); but if you are using a placement to gather data for your project then you should certainly seize on the visit as a major opportunity to deal with one or more of the stages outlined above. Much will depend on the timing of the visit with respect to the stage you have reached in your project work, and this is likely to be beyond your control, as your tutor may have a number of students to visit. Occasionally, a single placement tutor does all the visits to all the students following a particular programme, and you may not meet with your own project tutor. Nevertheless, you will find that the placement tutor is interested and helpful, and at the very least he or she will be willing to act as a messenger on your behalf. This is a particularly essential service if your placement happens to be overseas.

Table 6.4 shows some research findings on role relationships. The Phillips and Pugh (2000) item is taken from their work on the PhD process, but the comments made certainly apply to your own level of work.

Your sponsor

Your sponsor plays an important part in your project quite apart from any role he or she might have in assessment (though the latter is usually rare).

In principle, your sponsor should have a well-defined and formal relationship with you, having agreed to act in the sponsoring role. In some kinds of project (e.g. those associated with Work-Based Learning placements), the role might be part of a formal written agreement. In day-to-day terms, this relationship may not be quite so straightforward. If the agreement has been made directly between the two of you (in the case of in-company-based projects), or between the sponsor and your institution, many issues will have been ironed out in advance. In other cases, the arrangement may have been made by someone else in the organization, and your sponsor only becomes involved on the day you arrive in the Department. It's wise to establish which case pertains, in advance of your arrival.

The sponsor's primary and overriding concern will be to manage your presence, your work, and its outcomes, as a contribution to the work of his or her department. Any concern with your training and personal development may, in this case, be secondary from the sponsor's point of view and you should expect any early negotiations which establish your role and the entire period under supervision to be conducted on this basis. Having said that, the help which sponsors give is rarely negligible and often contributes substantially to the success of your work, both as a mentor and a friend.

Undergraduates sometime forget that the sponsor has other management responsibilities as well as looking after a student. You should determine what kind of assistance and involvement your sponsor is prepared to provide, as early as possible. Quite apart from the informal contacts which you may have on a day-to-day basis, it will be useful for you to arrange a regular progress meeting with him or her, every week or fortnight. You will find that this is best negotiated a week or so after your arrival, rather than immediately. Give yourselves time to get used to each other.

One of the first things you will need to do is to discuss the arrangements for confidentiality which your organization requires.

TABLE 6.4 Roles and relationships between student, tutor and sponsor

In the tutor–student relationship:[1]

Tutors expect their students to:

1 be more independent than the students expect
2 produce regular written work, ideally, typewritten
3 attend meetings regularly, organized at their own initiative without needing to be chased
4 report their progress honestly
5 follow the advice they're given
6 be enthusiastic about their projects
7 surprise them: come up with findings, ideas etc. that hadn't occurred to them
8 be part of a mutually enjoyable relationship.

This is reciprocal.

Students can expect their tutors to:

1 actively supervise them, being available when needed
2 read and understand written project extracts submitted by them
3 be accessible, friendly, open and supportive
4 be constructively critical
5 have a good knowledge of the topic of the project
6 make arrangements so they can give their full attention to the student during tutorials
7 add to the information available to them by recommending appropriate reading
8 be part of a mutually enjoyable relationship.

In the sponsor–student relationship:[2]

Your Sponsor may adopt one or more of the following roles towards you:

1 Negotiator
2 Mother
3 Pressuriser and reminder
4 Colleague and equal
5 Protector
6 Confidence builder
7 Laissez-faire neglector, leaving you to just get on with it.

Your Sponsor's style may be one of two kinds:[3]

1 Empowering	Holds back with the answers
	Frames questions in ways which forces you to think through the issues
	Transfers ownership to you
	Acts as a resource, removing obstacles.
2 Facilitating	Creates and promotes a learning environment
	Gets you to see things differently
	Uses analogies, scenarios, examples
	Sets communication expectations in light of the organizational 'big picture'
	Talks things through
	Provides and solicits feedback

1 Based on Phillips and Pugh (2000)
2 Saxton and Ashworth (1990)
3 Ellinger et al. (1999)

Arranging confidentiality

This is an issue which matters very much at the end of your project, but which should be thought through, raised with your sponsor, and agreed, well in advance. Who is to see your project report? Three people at least will be involved:

- your sponsor

- your tutor, especially in the role of internal examiner

- the external examiner should he or she choose to do so.

An employer who objects to the latter two people is simply not a viable project proposition, and you should establish this from the very start.

But you may have a rather wider audience. You may have to make a presentation in your teaching institution to more than one internal examiner, or to an audience of students and staff. You will certainly be expected to deposit a copy of the project report in the library.

Where your report contains sensitive information, the concern of employers is usually to ensure that what you have to say is accurate, regardless of whether it is favourable or unfavourable to the organization or some interest group within it. My impression is that in the overwhelming majority of cases you don't have to worry about any form of 'censorship'. If you have followed the negotiating strategy outlined in Sections 5.2 and 6.2, and have engaged in a process of cross-checking as an inherent part of your approach to the research process (see Section 5.3), you should already have ensured the accuracy of your report, and tackled the issues arising from conflicting perspectives on the interpretation of your work, well before the time comes for you to submit your report.

Occasionally, however, your project will have involved you in commercially sensitive issues, and your company may wish to prevent their competitors from learning the details of your findings. While this event would be unlikely, their concern for the possibility must be respected, and you will find that your institution has arrangements for putting your report under an embargo for a number of years, preventing access to library copies. You should contact your tutor, explore the arrangements with your librarian, and make sure that your sponsor receives details of the arrangements in writing from your institution.

Working with your sponsor

Sponsors differ in the styles they adopt towards their placement students. Saxton and Ashworth (1990) suggest that different sponsors adopt different roles, and the really good ones vary the role according to your needs. The roles they encountered in their research on this topic are shown in Table 6.4. Clearly, someone who adopts the 'negotiating' style is, as my comments in previous sections suggest, most likely to respond to the particular needs arising from your project work, and to your own adoption of the negotiating style which I advocate.

The sponsor can be very helpful in:

- providing information about the organization

- advising you on the politics of the organization, and suggesting the likely stance people might take on the issues with which you plan to approach them
- arranging access to other people
- acting as a sounding-board for your ideas
- informing you of the ways in which the concepts, procedures and techniques, which you have learnt in your programme, translate into practice
- advising on the realism of your developing project ideas
- informally evaluating your results and conclusions
- advising on the feasibility of implementation of any of your recommendations.

The sponsor of an overseas project should, if approached appropriately, be a particularly helpful source of information about local customs and mores.

Undergraduates in particular will find that the sponsor's role of sounding-board, evaluator, and 'reality-monitor' is especially helpful when they are analyzing their early results. Your concern at that stage, very properly, is with the accurate extraction of information from data, and that is the time when you are so close to the figures that the implications may escape you! But there is an interplay between the technical meaning of data, and their practical implications, so that the meaning of the former is determined by the latter, as we noted in Section 5.3. Your sponsor is well placed to ask apparently naïve 'non-academic' questions, which will contribute to technical accuracy while suggesting practical implications.

As a student doing my first project, I remember collecting data on the ways in which managers made forecasts, and showing the results to my sponsor. I had expected him to be interested in the issue of the managers' accuracy, but his question was somewhat different. 'This is all too technical for me, and I don't really follow the details. Never mind, I don't need to. In any case, what they're doing is actually quite difficult, so I wouldn't expect them to be very accurate. But tell me: is this a way of identifying who's more of a risk-taker, and who isn't?'

He was interested in their style and their personalities, as people he knew very well. For me, the question served to focus my attention on the extremity of managers' forecasts, irrespective of their accuracy, and forced me to establish something which I should have addressed anyway, namely, to discover what counts as a non-extreme forecast or, in statistical jargon, the 'expected value of scores'. I had to know this before I could get much further with my own, technical question, which concerned the development of a method for measuring forecasting accuracy, but the issue simply hadn't occurred to me.

Finally, there's a form of help which is often under-utilized, but which is particularly important because it helps to determine the practical scope, relevance, and applicability of your ideas. You will find that it helps to view your sponsor as a repository of the current practices and conventional wisdoms of the overall industry, product range, or market in which the organization operates. The way in which this knowledge is expressed is often implicit in the advice he or she gives you, and it will be up to you to make it explicit, by asking the question 'why?' and by making inferences for yourself.

If you are an employee of the organization, and your topic is one which deals with strategic issues, or one in which you are working on an issue directly related to the work of your department, your sponsor will show keen interest in your activities, and may have a role as the member of a team of supporters with whom you meet regularly. A recent project with which I was connected concerned the review and development of various forms of strategic partnership between the student's company and some of its overseas clients, with a view to the development of the company's strategy on a global scale. As you can imagine, the sponsor showed keen interest and was particularly involved in supporting the work, as he would have the responsibility for managing and monitoring the eventual implementation!

It is important to form a good relationship with the sponsor, and use him or her as a coach (see the next section on coaching style), ally and friend. Not every manager has the skills required, but an increasing number of organizations have recognized the importance of this role in boss–subordinate relations within those enterprises which see themselves as learning organizations (see, for example, Ellinger *et al.* 1999). Their style may vary from empowering to facilitating; but whatever it is, you will find this person a powerful resource if you can negotiate this relationship to suit you from the outset.

Your mentor

Sometimes, a sponsor remains fairly distant from your project, simply being there as a line manager to whom you report. In this case, many of the activities which I have outlined above will fall to someone else: a person you've chosen as mentor. A mentor can offer most of what your sponsor can do, as I've described it above, and is a key figure among your network of helpers. The difference is that you will have chosen the individual concerned yourself; he or she won't have line management responsibility for you, may be a colleague, and is more likely to help you purely as a friend. After all, mentoring is becoming increasingly popular for management development in general, whether as part of personal development, for assistance in non-college based project work (Smith 1990) or management action research in general (Whitehead 1994). Take advantage of this trend, and look for a mentor for yourself! As you'll recall from Section 2.2, the most useful mentor you can have is someone who has already completed a project, having been a student registered on the same kind of programme as yourself, if you can find such a person. He or she will be particularly helpful in the role of a coach.

Coaching is a skill in which tasks are set in such a way that two things are achieved: the task itself is completed, and the person carrying out the task learns something new in the process of task completion. How much care and attention your mentor will give you, and whether their interest in your work will stretch to an explicit setting of tasks which have this effect, will depend very much on the relationship you develop, and on the insight which your mentor developed into his or her own project activities.

Some tasks he or she will set you are no more than questions, reflected back at you to encourage you to think the answers through for yourself, and followed by appropriate feedback: the style which Ellinger *et al.* (1999) calls 'empowering'. If you think your own queries through in this way, you may find that you can act as your own mentor for much of the time! Certainly, this form of coaching is an acquired skill. Many tutors have it, and some sponsors. In setting up your network of helpers, you might like to look for people who are useful because they have this knack of helping you to think things through, without simply 'giving you the answers'.

Other members of your network

In-company students will find that a project is a good time for extending their existing network. You might wish to consider:

- Your own department head if he or she is not already involved.
- Heads of departments in which you plan to collect information.
- Someone in Training or Personnel, because the project is part of your own development as a senior employee.
- Colleagues with whom you meet socially, on a Friday night after work or at other times.
- The 'keeper of the organizational history', if there is such a person in your organization. This is a person, usually with long service, who has been in a variety of roles and survived reorganizations and mergers by keeping their head down, staying in a quiet backwater and learning how things work.
- The network of secretarial staff. Think about it: they know what's going on across the organization, because they often transfer from one boss to another, retaining personal contacts as they do so. They know where the bodies are buried, as it were. They can predict how their boss will respond to your approaches, and can usually be relied on to indicate the best time for an approach. They may be quite powerful gatekeepers. They will give an administrator's perspective on the managerial implications of your project ideas and proposals. You'll never join their network, but you might tap into it to a degree.

Before going on, please address activity 4 in the Project Guide.

6.4   Letting go and saying goodbye

It may seem strange to be considering this issue so soon after starting. However, there is a good reason for doing so. In one sense, project work (like research work in general) never finishes. Initial findings expand the scope of your interests, your investigation raises issues which demand further exploration and (especially if your topic wasn't thought through sufficiently at the outset) you arrive at the realization that you're only getting to grips with the real issues when your initially planned data-gathering and analysis are nearing completion. There is every temptation to go on for too long. But the deadline for submission is rapidly approaching and the process of writing up and submitting your project report will, as I've described in Section 4.2, take longer than you initially estimated. If you decide on a firm date for completion well in advance and stick to it, you will find that you are able to structure and progress your work effectively throughout.

Sticking to the completion date is only a part of the disengagement process: a number of other activities should be anticipated and planned for.

The employer's report

Your sponsor may be interested in reading your project report (the dissertation or thesis document you have to produce for your institution). He or she will certainly appreciate a briefer, practitioner-oriented summary. (If you promised a synopsis as a condition of entry, then of course it's mandatory that you produce this in any case.)

A good way for an undergraduate to bring a project placement to an end is to ask the sponsor for the form this summary should take. One useful form is to provide a brief, non-academic, non-critical account of the main points which you wish to bring to the organization's attention. For example, the five major conclusions arising from your work which you feel will be most helpful to the organization, together with your supporting evidence for them (Buchanan *et al*. 1988: 64). An oral presentation to your sponsor and a small group of colleagues will act as a demonstration of your sincere interest in the organization which has given you a placement, will thank them for their efforts, and may provide you with the opportunity of influencing the organization in a small way prior to departure. So many undergraduate projects end with the quiet disappearance of the student; with a whimper rather than a bang.

In-company students may wish to treat the report as a basis for the future implementation of their findings. This may influence the scope of your own job for the next few months. In the case of topics of major corporate importance, it may affect the nature of your job and its responsibilities, especially if you are the person who is asked to be responsible for implementation. Viewed from this perspective, a successful in-company project may be the means by which you reposition yourself within the organization and, in effect, rewrite your job description. This is worth thinking through in advance!

As a final, pre-departure activity, implement the various confidentiality arrangements which you discussed and agreed with your sponsor at the outset, as outlined in Section 6.3 above.

The impression you create

Whether you're an undergraduate or an in-company employee, the impression you create when you depart will affect the chances of other people doing projects of this kind with the organization in the future.

CASE EXAMPLE 6.1   Arranging a project placement

Aidan Collins is a full-time student in an Irish university which runs a US-style Cooperative Education scheme, a form of 'sandwich' course in which undergraduates spend two periods of six months in work placements with employers during the course of their four-year degree programme. Some of the placements are with employers in Ireland and some in the UK, taken from a register the university has built up over the years. However, the university also encourages students to obtain placements for themselves if they wish, either locally, or with organizations outside these islands.

Aidan has some savings from holiday work, and a small grant on which to support studies in his final year, but these resources won't be quite enough, and so he decides to use his second Co-op placement period to improve his finances, seeking the most lucrative employment opportunity available. He e-mails Ayesha, his girlfriend, an Asian who has just graduated from his own university and started a rewarding job back in her home town in Kenya. Does she know of any opportunities for him? The response is extremely encouraging. She is certain she can arrange a placement for him with her employer in Nairobi. She encloses an attachment showing an extract from her company's brochure, about the many short-contract opportunities available. Excellent! He will be able to make some savings, as well as seeing his girlfriend over the next six months. Aidan spends his grant on an air-ticket to Kenya, and takes his savings to use for initial living expenses. And so, with everything arranged, he flies out to Nairobi.

Ayesha is of course delighted to see him, but says she has some awkward news for him. Her employer is being rather difficult. It would appear that the government has recently re-emphasized the regulations which specify that jobs should not be given to foreigners if there are Kenyan citizens with appropriate qualifications available to do the work. There may in fact be no job for Aidan.

He gets an appointment with Mr Mthethwa, the company's personnel officer, the following Monday. Mr Mthethwa expresses regret, but points out that his initially favourable stance when Ayesha asked was, to be honest, a matter of politeness. And how was he to know that the 'citizens first' regulation would return to the political agenda in any case? He says he will see what he can do – come back next week – indeed he would like to see Aidan's CV if he has it with him, and make a photocopy – but he strongly suggests that Aidan might want to make some backup arrangements. 'By the way', says Mr Mthethwa, 'what is this "Co-op scheme" you've just mentioned?'

It's obvious that things have gone badly wrong for Aidan. List the mistakes he has made. Beside each, state what he should have done.

Answers to Case Example 6.1

- Did Aidan discuss the placement with his tutor? We don't know, but he certainly didn't obtain any written materials which he could make available to the potential employer.

- Aidan was *too* opportunistic. He relied on his girl-friend's best judgement, which is fine, but he did not make any direct contact with the potential employer. Such contacts should be in writing, and should provide appropriate briefing information. This should include personal biographical details in the form of a CV, quite apart from any institutional materials that the tutor might provide. Waiting until he arrived in Nairobi to tell Mr Mthethwa about the Cooperative Education scheme was not a wise move!

- In the circumstances, an interview prior to arrival was not feasible. So it was all the more important that Aidan communicate formally, in advance, in writing, and make no serious commitment until he had heard back from the employer, also in writing. Hard copy for preference, and not just an exchange of e-mails.

CASE EXAMPLE 6.1 Arranging a project placement (cont.)

- He didn't allow sufficient time for this exchange. Remember, in this context 'the employer' means someone from the company's personnel department, rather than the personal contact through whom the initial approach was made.

- Aidan put all his eggs in one basket. He had no alternative arrangement even partly organized, and he committed all his available funds to the single arrangement.

Looking back over the case, it sounds as though there may be some hope. However, if he gets the post he was looking for, he will be extremely lucky. Mr Mthethwa would be entirely justified in showing Aidan politely but firmly to the door!

Project Guide

1 Create a list of potential employers and use it

a Review Section 6.1 and make a list divided into the following columns:

- information sources: organizations and people who themselves have lists of enterprises that might provide you with a placement

- their phone number

- the outcome of your call.

b Glance ahead at Section 11.3 on telephone interviewing, and note the comments about the need to log the outcomes of every phone call you make. You will be making a lot of phone calls and some people will be out, some will promise to call back, others will ask you to call again on a specific day; yet others will be represented by secretaries, or engaged, and so forth, and you will be likely to forget the details unless you log them.

c When you have collated three or four possibilities, go through the subsequent steps described in Section 6.1.

2 Ethical issues

a If your university or department uses a formal Ethical Agreement document (see Section 6.2 above) you may need to add to it after discussing the details of your role with the company in which you will be doing your research. Consider the following points, all of which relate to your role:

- To whom will you be reporting on a daily basis who might want to examine and discuss your results?

- Will anyone be assisting you in your data collection or analysis and what is their relationship to you and to the organization?

- Who, apart from your tutor, your examiner and any external examiner that might be involved, will wish to see your dissertation?

- Who in the organization will receive your final report?

b If there is no formal document, take the private list which you compiled in activity 2 of Project Guide 3 and amend it as necessary

c Paste a copy of the Ethical Agreement, or your private version of it, into the back cover of your research diary where they are available for instant access and periodic review.

3 Your role

Once you know when and where you will be doing your project, spend some time thinking through your role, and how you might be most usefully perceived.

a Glance again at Table 6.3 and identify the kinds of roles which are available to a person in your circumstances. Think about Eden and Sims' three role types. Which of all of these seem the most appropriate?

b If you are an in-company student, working in your own organization,

- talk about your research with one or two of your closer colleagues who you feel might be involved, and ask for their help during the time of the project

- check with them how they feel your project might be helpful to them, how if at all, the project might be a hindrance to them, and how you might avoid the latter

- who in the organization is likely to care about the research or see their interests affected; who, in their view, are the stakeholders?

c If you are an undergraduate in a work placement, this discussion will need to wait until you have joined it.

- in the meanwhile, ask your tutor if he or she knows what to expect in that particular organization, and how any previous students fared there

▶

- if the students are still in your institution, go and talk to them about their experience, what went well, what went badly, who is likely to be helpful and who less so

- once you have arrived, talk to your sponsor along the same lines you discussed with your tutor, and compare the two sets of impressions.

d Finally, what are the implications? How might you best present the role you identified in Table 6.3 in step **a** above? How might you handle any conflicts which you might anticipate?

4 Relationships with your sponsor

As soon as it is feasible, arrange to meet with your sponsor and:

a If you haven't done so already, agree the amount of time which will be available to you for your project. Be flexible! Two afternoons per week is as good as a whole day free. (But two mornings isn't, particularly for in-company people doing the project in their own organization: you're tempted to rush through the project work in order to get on with your regular job.)

b Ask his or her advice on any early issues that are puzzling you. At this stage, their view on your research method or intended techniques is very valuable, and will alert you to any problems of access, confidentiality, and anonymity that may pertain. Make a checklist under these headings and discuss them in detail.

c A second, and very important, reason for this exercise is for you to form a judgement on the style they are likely to adopt as a sponsor. You may care to review Table 6.4, and read the Ellinger *et al.* (1999) paper.

References

Beynon, H. (1988) 'Regulating research' in Bryman, A., (ed.) *Doing Research in Organisations*, London: Routledge.

Boisot, M. (1994) *East-West Business Collaboration: the Challenge of Governance in Post-Socialist Enterprises*, London: Routledge.

Buchanan, D., Boddy, D. and McCalman, J. (1988) 'Getting in, getting on, getting out, and getting back' in Bryman, A., (ed.), *Doing Research in Organisations*, London: Routledge.

Burgess, R. G. (1982) 'Some role problems in field research', in Burgess, R. G., (ed.) *Field Research: a Sourcebook and Field Manual*, London: George Allen & Unwin.

Easterday, L., Papademas, D., Schorr, L. and Valentine, C. (1982) 'The making of a female researcher: role problems in fieldwork', in Burgess, R. G., (ed.) *Field Research: a Sourcebook and Field Manual*, London: George Allen & Unwin.

Eden, C., Jones, S. and Sims, D. (1979) *Thinking in Organisations*, London: Macmillan.

Eden, C. and Sims, D. (1979) 'On the nature of problems in consulting practice', *International Journal of Management Science*, 7: 2: 119–127.

Ellinger, A. D., Watkins, K. E. and Bostrom, R. P. (1999) 'Managers as facilitators of learning in learning organizations', *Human Resource Development Quarterly*, 10: 2: 105–125.

Gesteland, R. (1999) *Cross-Cultural Business Behavior: Marketing, Negotiating and Managing across Cultures*, Copenhagen: Copenhagen Business School Press.

Gummesson, E. (2000) *Qualitative Methods in Management Research*, London: Sage.

Hofstede, G. (1991) *Cultures and Organisations: Software of the Mind*, London: McGraw-Hill.

Holden, N., Cooper, C. and Carr, J. (1998) *Dealing with the New Russia: Management Cultures in Collision*, London: Wiley.

Holliday, A. (2002) *Doing and Writing Qualitative Research*, London: Sage.

Isenberg, D. J. (1984) 'How senior managers think', *Harvard Business Review*, 62: 6: 81–90.

Jankowicz, A. D. (1996) *Personal values among public sector employees: a methodological study*, 3rd Conference of the European Personal Construct Association, Reading, UK, April.

Jankowicz, A. D. (1999) 'Planting a paradigm in Central Europe: do we graft, or must we breed the rootstock anew?', *Management Learning*, 30: 3: 281–299.

Lodge, D. (1988) *Nice Work*, Harmondsworth: Penguin.

Moran, R. T. and Johnson, M. (1992) *Cultural Guide to Doing Business in Europe*, London: Butterworth-Heinemann.

Phillips, E. M. and Pugh, D. S. (2000) *How to Get a PhD*, Milton Keynes: The Open University Press, 3rd edn.

Robson, C. (2002) *Real World Research: a Resource for Social Scientists and Practitioner-Researchers*, Oxford: Blackwell.

Saunders, M., Lewis, P. and Thornhill, A. (2003) *Research Methods for Business Students*, London: Prentice Hall.

Saxton, J. and Ashworth, P. (1990) 'The workplace supervision of sandwich degree placement students', *Management Education and Development*, 21: 2: 133–149.

Smith, B. (1990) 'Mutual mentoring on projects: a proposal to combine the advantages of several established management development methods', *Journal of Management Development*, 9: 1: 51–57.

Smith, P. B., Misumi, J., Tayeb, M., Peterson, M. and Bond, M. (1989) 'On the generality of leadership style measures across cultures', *Journal of Occupational Psychology*, 62: 2: 97–109.

Whitehead, J. (1994) 'How do I improve the quality of my management? A participatory action research approach', *Management Learning*, 25: 1: 137–153.

Reviewing and using the literature

- To encourage you to begin reading for, and writing, your project, by outlining the function of a literature review, and describing the techniques used in documenting your sources
- To describe a variety of sources available to you, through electronic media in particular
- To outline a variety of strategies for searching the literature, with particular emphasis on electronic search
- To encourage you to make a start on reading, and on writing the literature review, in a draft form, in a suitably critical way
- To emphasize the importance of social support as you familiarize yourself with your research field

At a glance

There is little point in reinventing the wheel. Whatever your epistemology, the work that you do is not done in a vacuum, but builds on the ideas of other people who have studied the field before you. This requires you to describe what has been published, and to marshal the information in a relevant and critical way. We start by examining the function and structure of a literature review, and the referencing systems available for documenting the assertions you make as you write the review. With all the world's scholarly literature available to you through the paper and electronic media accessible in your institution's library, and at home through your computer terminal, it is important to know what sort of material to look for, where to look for it, and how, if you are to use your time economically and wisely. When you have found it, how best to make use of it? Exactly how should you present the information you have found? These are the main themes addressed in this chapter.

7.1   Using the literature for review and for referencing

Review

The techniques and procedures reviewed in this chapter are described from the point of view of the student who is doing a project and preparing a dissertation, whether this is done on an in-company or a library basis. However, it is worth pointing out that not all students who are placed with an organization are there to collect material for a dissertation. Undergraduates in particular may be there to satisfy their degree requirements through a placement, simply working in the organization as a temporary employee and gaining work experience relevant to the subject of their degree. Nevertheless, they will find the material in this chapter helpful if they have to produce reports for their employer while placed with the company. The need to substantiate assertions by referring to other people's work is just as important in an internal report as it is in a dissertation!

If you are doing a project, you will need to review the literature at the outset, when you choose a topic for your project; and throughout your work, when you present other writings more thoroughly and systematically to your readers as you build your conceptual analysis (see Section 5.3). The former activity is self-evident, being one of the methods open to you in choosing and identifying a topic, as outlined in Chapter 3. The latter – the need for some detailed library time, in order to brief yourself and familiarize yourself with the literature rather more thoroughly – is perhaps less obvious. Knowledge does not exist in a vacuum, and your work only has value in relation to other people's. Your work and your findings will be significant only to the extent that they are the same as, or different from, other people's work and findings.

The result of this more detailed reading is twofold. You become more informed; and you put yourself in a position to inform other people, your readers, by means of a literature review presented in your project document. This is more than a simple description. It is a critical analysis of what other authors have said on material relating to your topic. It is usual to subdivide this material into different subjects, starting with the more general statements of broad scope, and going on to consider the different subjects in more detail, so that you end up narrowing down to a consideration of a small number of authors whose ideas and results are directly relevant to the precise subject-matter of your topic. (Glance back at the discussion in Section 3.5, and Figures 3.1 to 3.3, on this issue.)

Many undergraduate project documents handle the literature review as a single, connected account presented shortly after the Introduction, and before the empirical section begins. This is particularly appropriate where a single, fairly technical issue forms the basis of the project, as shown in Figure 3.1. This is less likely in other kinds of project. You may be dealing with a number of related themes, and it may be more convenient to present the literature in different stages (perhaps in different sections or chapters) as you tackle various aspects and issues throughout the project document: see Figure 3.2, building your argument issue by issue. If your project is entirely library-based, your literature will be your entire resource, and you will want to present it theme by theme after a general, broader introduction, as shown in Figure 3.3.

In all three cases, you would also expect to return to the literature during the discussion and conclusions sections of your project report. You will want to present the significance of your empirical findings in the light of other people's work, and you will want to draw on other authors in arguing for the recommendations which you wish to make in the light of your findings. This is the 'broadening out' stage of the project document.

An example of literature reviewing is shown in Table 7.1. It is a very brief outline, to show what I mean by presenting other people's work, and to demonstrate the way in which you progress from the general to the more specific in the course of the review. The ellipses (. . .) indicate positions in the review where you would wish to expand the preceding point in more detail than I have. I am limited to just a page, whereas literature reviews in business and management projects tend to be between 4 and 20 or so pages in total! It's difficult to be more precise than that, but my impression is that projects based in the more numerate subjects (finance, accounting, quantitative methods) would tend to have briefer reviews, or to concentrate in greater detail on a smaller number of authors than my example.

However you present and structure your review, you have to reference it. That is, you have to identify who said what, and where the ideas you have cited come from. Not to do so would in effect be plagiarism which, intentional or otherwise, is as you will recall from Section 3.2, unacceptable.

Referencing

A reference consists of three parts: the text being referenced, the reference itself, and the corresponding bibliographic entry. The first two, text and reference, will appear in the main body of your project report, while the third appears in a bibliography presented at the end of your project report.

You should find yourself using references throughout your project, for a number of different purposes outlined in Table 7.2. What you are doing is, essentially, twofold. You are justifying the statements you make, in a way which demonstrates your knowledge; and you are referring the reader to the original secondary source, specifically enough so that he or she could, in principle, look up the original author for him- or herself.

A number of conventions govern the form taken by the reference itself. There are in fact two main conventions for referencing paper-based media and a separate convention for electronic media.

Referencing conventions for paper-based media

You have a choice of two conventions: the name-date referencing convention (known generically as the 'Harvard' system) and the numbered referencing convention (known generically as the 'Vancouver' system). You should not mix the two: decide on one kind and stick to it throughout. The first, the name-date system, is shown in Table 7.3. This itself has a number of variations, and you should check to

TABLE 7.1 The literature review as a critical argument

In an MBA project dealing with negotiation and sense-making skills training for leadership, the main thrust of the argument might run as follows:

The early work on leadership in management can be divided into three phases. At first, leadership was viewed as a property of the person , the 'trait theories' being reviewed by Stogdill (1948) and Mann (1959).	Starting at a general level
The main findings were that [. . .]	A few sentences
However, the main difficulty from the manager's point of view was that none of these theories indicated what he or she should do in order to be effective. It might be more helpful to ask what skills were involved in leadership: skills which anyone might learn to become a more effective manager. The emphasis shifted to a focus on behaviour, largely as a result of the Ohio studies (Stogdill and Coons 1957) on [. . .],	Brief summary
and the Michigan studies of supervisors (Likert 1961) [. . .].	Brief summary
Bales' work on leaderless groups (Parsons *et al.* 1953) was also influential, since it demonstrated that [. . .]	Brief summary
The general thrust was that [. . .].	Brief overview
However, the difficulty was, as Fiedler first indicated, that the behavioural style which a manager adopts is unlikely to be effective in all situations: (Fiedler 1967) [. . .].	Brief summary
Indeed, style is contingent on situation, and various aspects of this view have been presented in recent years, e.g. [. . .]	Examples most relevant to project
Most recently, however, there has been a shift of emphasis, away from the behaviourally explicit, to an exploration of the ways in which managers perceive, interpret and understand the situations in which they exercise leadership. Smith and Peterson (1988) presented an early exposition, in which their observation that leadership involves the management of events is particularly important to the work reported in this project [. . .]	More detailed account
Specifically, events must be recognized as significant in the organizational culture (Misumi 1985) [. . .]; Weick's work on organizational sense-making is clearly relevant (Weick 1995).	Brief summary Brief summary
Leadership arises as the supervisor actively manages the understandings and meanings of his or her subordinates (Pfeffer 1981) [. . .]; and this involves a process of negotiation with others (Hosking and Morley 1988) [. . .].	More detailed account of both
Current interest in the 'Learning Organization' (Edmondson and Moingeon 1998) reflects these authors on leadership, together with an interest in the design arrangements for employee involvement at all levels in functions previously reserved for senior managers in leadership roles (Garratt 2001) [. . .]	. . . much fine detail, with many authors: the issues to be explored in the empirical section will shortly be presented and must follow on seamlessly as a continuation of the argument.

see whether your tutor or your librarian recommend a particular variation before proceeding with the form that I have provided. If you use the name-date convention, one very useful bit of fine-tuning is to include the number of the page where you obtained the quotation, immediately after the name and date in the body of your text, as I have done in the first example in Table 7.2.

Numbered references take much the same form in the bibliography as the name-date reference; however, instead of providing a name and date in the body of the text, all that appears is a number, which refers the reader to the full name and date details given in the bibliography. These are listed sequentially in the order in which they occur in the main body of the text.

TABLE 7.2 Using the literature: for purposes of referencing

- **To attribute a quotation**
  You may be making the point that senior executives often hold very firm ideas, being people who believe strongly in what they are doing. You might wish to include the following quotation: 'A rude awakening, such as when Iacocca was fired by Ford, may be required for the leader to make a meaningful change in personal and corporate direction' (London 1988: 53). Quotations are always enclosed within inverted commas, and must always have a reference; a page reference is valuable too.

- **To provide justification for a strong statement**
  For example, your text might be making the firm statement that 'a single event may have an enormous impact on national policymaking'. You might continue with the example of the impact which the Soviet launch of the Sputnik satellite had on US Government policy on science, technology, and the professions, ending your text with '(Schön 1983)', where just this point is made.

- **To tell your reader where an idea comes from**
  Take the idea that Japanese chief executives avoid stating corporate objectives very explicitly, because, unlike their American counterparts, they prefer to assume that their managers understand corporate philosophy and organizational environment sufficiently well that their intuitions will tell them the precise objective to set in any particular situation. If your text made this assertion, the reference would be Ouchi (1981). He said it first.

- **To argue for the reasonableness of your methods, since they are as used by other people working in the field**
  You might justify your use of semi-structured interviews with some departmental managers to check the results of interviews with other managers, by pointing out that this is an example of 'historical' or 'anthropological' technique, commonly used in such situations. You would quote a number of authors who advocate it, thus: (Barzun and Graff 1985; Parlett 1981); or who have used it in similar circumstances to your own.

And also:

- **To help interpret your results**
  You would quote any similar findings obtained by other people (and also any contradictory ones).

- **To help you to build your argument**
  Who agrees with you, who disagrees with you, who suggests that under certain circumstances, things might look this way, whereas, (according to someone else), if other issues were taken into consideration, the opposite might follow. 'Therefore, on balance, the following seems sensible . . .'

TABLE 7.3   The name–date referencing convention for paper media

In the body of the text

- Just after the material which you want to reference:

  Open bracket, author surname, year of publication, close bracket

  In the case of two authors, give both surnames separated by 'and'. In the case of more than two, give the first surname followed by 'et al.'

In the bibliography

- Where the item is a book:

  Author surname, initials (of each author involved, the last one, if more than one, being preceded by 'and', all but the last separated by commas); open brackets, year of publication, close brackets, full stop; title of book, each word beginning with a capital letter, the whole title italicized, full stop; place of publication, colon, name of publisher, comma, edition number if not the first, followed by the word 'edition'.

  Fransella F., Bell R. and Bannister D. (2004). *A Manual for Repertory Grid Technique.* London: Wiley, 2nd edition.

- Where the item is a journal article:

  Author surname, initials (of each author involved, the last one, if more than one, being preceded by 'and', all but the last separated by commas); open brackets, year of publication, close brackets, full stop; open inverted commas; title of the article, only the first word beginning with a capital letter, close inverted commas; title of the journal italicised, each word beginning with a capital letter; volume number, comma, issue number, comma, inclusive page numbers.

  Clark I. (1999). 'Corporate human resources and "bottom line" financial performance' *Personnel Review* 28, 4, 290–306.

- Where the item is in a collection of items with an editor:

  Author surname, initials (of each author involved, the last one, if more than one, being preceded by 'and', all but the last separated by commas); open brackets, year of publication, close brackets, full stop; open inverted commas; title of the item, only the first word beginning with a capital letter; close inverted commas, comma; the word 'in', editor's surname, initials (of each editor involved, the last one, if more than one, being preceded by 'and', all but the last separated by commas); open brackets, the abbreviation 'ed.', or 'eds.' if several editors are involved, close brackets; title of the book, each word beginning with a capital letter, the whole title italicized, full stop; place of publication, colon, name of publisher.

  Brown L. D. and Kaplan R. E. (1981). 'Participative research in a factory' in Reason P. and Rowan J. (eds.) *Human Inquiry: a Sourcebook of New Paradigm Research* Chichester: John Wiley & Sons.

Note that:

After the first line, the left-hand margin of a reference running over more than one line is indented by a few characters to help the reader pick out each separate reference.

The numbered reference convention is useful because it allows the inclusion of marginal comments and 'footnotes' in the numbered sequence, as well as references themselves. These involve a few additional conventions as follows.

- When you find yourself referring to the same item as one referred to earlier, you don't repeat the full details in the bibliography each time, but simply write the abbreviation '*op. cit.*' (*opere citato*: 'in the work quoted'), together with the page number if you wish, after the sequence number and author name.

- If this repetition is of an item on the same page as before, you write '*loc. cit.*' (*loco citato*: 'in the place cited') instead of '*op. cit.*' and you must then provide the page number.

- However, if you refer to the same item as before *in immediate succession*, just use the abbreviation '*ibid.*' (*ibidem*: 'in the same place') instead, with a page number if required.

Finally, if you are using this convention and plan to include footnotes as well as bibliographic entries, the list of items at the end of your project report should be headed 'References' rather than 'Bibliography'.

Referencing conventions for electronic media

Different electronic media have slightly different requirements, and a universal convention for each medium is yet to emerge, but you will find the guidelines provided in Table 7.4 will be acceptable to your tutor. As with the conventions for paper-based media, the level of detail should be enough to enable your reader to find the item referred to should he or she wish. There is, however, one difference. Electronic media are evanescent. Websites occasionally change their URLs (addresses), while items posted to Usenet Newsgroups are only held at the service providers' sites for a few days before being archived. To cope with this situation, the reference to an item in any of the electronic media (e-mail, e-mail mailing lists, ftp sites, websites, and Usenet Newsgroups) must always include the precise date on which you yourself obtained the material which you are referencing in the case of e-mails, and the date on which you accessed the material in the case of newsgroups, web pages, and data files.

A review referenced in these ways looks quite impressive as, for example, the extract shown in Table 7.1. So it should: it represents the knowledge which you will have developed by the end of your project, and the scholarly skills which you will have learnt. But how do you get to this point? How do you find all this out in the first place?

TABLE 7.4 The name–date referencing convention for electronic media

In the body of the text

- Just after the material which you want to reference:

  Open bracket, author surname, year of publication, close bracket

  In the case of two authors, give both surnames separated by 'and'; In the case of more than two authors, give the first surname followed by 'et al.'

In the bibliography

In all the following specifications, the words between < > signs should appear exactly as they are given below. Do not reproduce the punctuation signs but do use the named punctuation (e.g. where I say 'comma', use a comma!)

- Where the item is a personal e-mail:

  Author surname, initials; open bracket, year of publication, close brackets, full stop, subject line from the header of the e-mail only the initial letter being capitalized, full stop, <E-mail>; type of e-mail, <to>, name of recipient, comma, date of posting (day and month), full stop.

  | Bell R. (1998). Measuring personal values. E-mail personal communication to A. D. Jankowicz, 15 January.

- Where the item is an e-mail item sent to a mailing list

  Author surname, initials; open bracket, year of publication, close brackets, full stop, subject line from the header of the e-mail only the initial letter being capitalized, full stop; <E-mail on>, name of mailing list, comma, address of server hosting that mailing list, comma, date of posting (day and month), full stop.

  | Fransella F. (2003). Re.: in search of source for Kelly quote. E-mail on PCP, jiscmail@jiscmail.ac.uk, 28 November.

- Where the item is in a Usenet newsgroup

  Author surname, initials; open bracket, year of publication, close brackets, full stop, title of the thread (i.e. subject line form the header of the item) with capitalization as in the original, full stop, <In>, address of newsgroup, comma, <Usenet>, comma, date of access (day and month), full stop.

  | Heslop P. (2003). Re.: Angel at Night. In uk.local.geordie, Usenet, 12 December.

- Where the item is from a website, i.e. obtained using a web reader)

  Author surname, initials; open bracket, year of publication or last amendment if available, close brackets, full stop, title of the page (i.e. the name that appears at the top of the window), comma, command path details being careful to include the embedded dots <WWW>, comma, command path details being careful to include the embedded dots and slashes, date of access (day, month and year).

  | Greenaway R. (2003). Experiential learning cycles, WWW, http://reviewing.co.uk/research/learning. cycles.htm, 17 December 2003.

NOTE: In the case of e-mails, NEVER include the writer's e-mail address in the reference.

7.2 The literature search: what to look for

Knowing what to look for is the chief problem if you have not researched the topic in any great detail before. You know that there's information out there somewhere, which will help you choose a particular topic for your project in the first place, or allow you to present the work of other people in a systematic way once you get going, but – what work? in which fields? done by which authors? Moreover, you know something about the literature already, from your taught courses and from your reading, but – this isn't sufficient, is it? how much more is needed? what kind of material is lacking?

Searching the literature is based on a three-stage process:

- identifying subject-matter relevant to your topic. You will be using a mixture of concepts and ideas; topic names (keywords or key terms); and author names, to

- develop a systematic list of references to authors who have published on these subjects, constructing a relevance tree (see Section 2.1); going on to

- use this information, in the form of key terms, to access the publications themselves, looking particularly for the core texts of your subject-matter.

Your actual search for literature is an iterative process which cycles through these three steps several times over as you familiarize yourself with the field.

Identifying subject-matter: initial steps

If you know what subject-matter is relevant to your topic, all is well. You use keywords to look for references to authors who have covered precisely this subject. If you don't, you will need to discover the subject-matter and the keywords, starting with some feeling or hunch that certain types of material may be involved. How do you develop this hunch?

Ask your tutor

At the beginning of your project, as soon as you are clear enough about your *aspect* (see Section 2.3) and topic to discuss them with your tutor, you can expect to be given an initial reading list at the end of the tutorial. This is likely to consist of enough items to give you a breadth of coverage, involving subject-matter which the tutor anticipates will be directly relevant to your topic as it develops, but also related material. The items will most likely be mixture of concepts and ideas; topic names and keywords; and author names known to the tutor. If he or she does not offer you such a list, you should ask for one. Needless to say, you must then get hold of all the items on the list! Scan all of them, and read some of them in detail, immediately.

Review your lecture notes

A second source of ideas is your set of lecture notes on the field in question. Jot down a list of the subjects which occur to you as you read over the notes most relevant to your topic and research question and copy out the names of any authors who sound relevant.

Read with attention to authorship

As you begin your reading, take in the content of what is said and make notes of the key points. Section 7.5 and Table 7.7 provide you with some guidelines on academic reading. Notice the importance of noting author names, of the piece you are reading, and the other authors the present one mentions. As time goes on you will recognize that some authors are central to your research question; add them, and their particular articles or books which appear to be relevant, to your list.

Prepare your introductory chapter

A very good way of pulling these thoughts and sources together is to write a first draft of the introduction of your project document. This should include a statement of your overall aim, your research question, and why you arrived at it. The latter always involves a description of why the topic is important, either:

- to the company in which you're located, which requires a brief description of the company and in what way the topic is relevant and important to them; or

- to the industry or sector in which you're working, in the case of a generic project; or

- in conceptual terms, in the case of a library project.

 You may find it helpful to tackle activity 1 in the Project Guide at this point.

Develop a systematic list

Your list will soon grow. Web searches, in particular, develop your thinking about what's relevant in ways which you may not have anticipated initially. You will shortly discover that the list begins to get messy: to sprawl out over many fields, sub-fields, people, dates and places. You need to bring some structure to it, in order to guide your literature searching and reading more systematically, and so that you can work out, for each subject, where and when to stop reading.

Construct a relevance tree

You may remember this from Section 2.1, where the relevance tree was introduced as one of the techniques to use in choosing a topic. A tree for systematizing your reading is very similar, being a directed graph of headings and sub-headings standing for the different subjects, and their subordinate aspects, which you feel you should read. An example is given as Figure 7.1. The advantage of the tree is that it helps you to make judgements on relevance, timing and importance. If in doubt, check your judgements with your tutor.

- *Relevance*: which subjects are directly relevant to your topic, as opposed to those which are less relevant and therefore probably not worth spending further time in locating, reading and writing up in your literature review.

- *Timing*: which subjects you will locate and read now, as opposed to those which you will need to locate later on in your project work.

- *Importance*: which subject is more important, and which is less important. While your own judgement is involved here, you do have some direct clues from the shape taken by the tree as it develops. You will notice, for example, that the more important subjects tend to have more branches 'pointing to' them in the tree.

FIGURE 7.1 A sample relevance tree for literature searching. The student has chosen the topic of 'Funding entrepreneurial startups'.

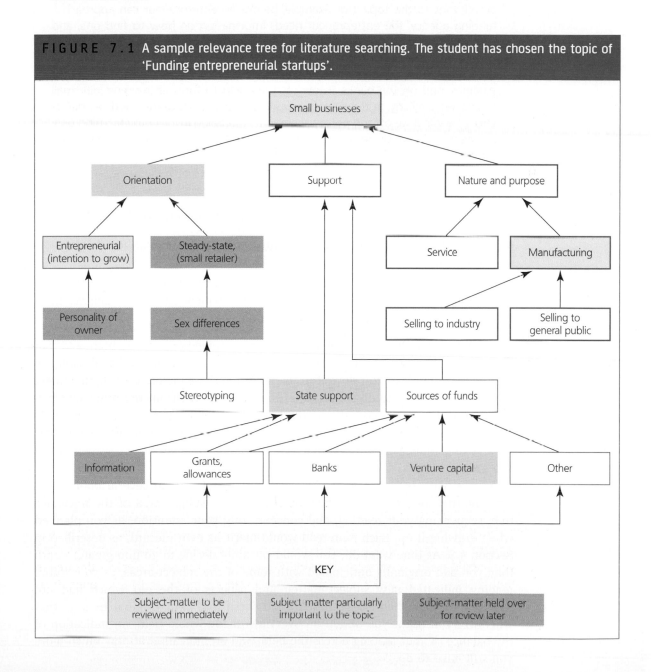

ILLUSTRATION 7.1

The relevance tree shown in Figure 7.1 has been devised by John Bartlett, whose interest lies in the second-stage (i.e. post-start-up) funding of small businesses. He has decided to focus his initial reading in three subject-areas: support for small businesses; those with an entrepreneurial orientation; and particularly those in the manufacturing supply chain. He is particularly interested in the funding available from venture capitalists. He recognizes that the literature on non-entrepreneurial small businesses, and on State-funded information services, may be relevant to the topic (for example, before an entrepreneur can approach a funding agency, the entrepreneur needs information on how to find one, and State information services can be particularly useful here). However, John chooses to leave his reading in these subject-areas till later. While intending to read all there is to know about venture capitalists, he will only focus on state allowance schemes, and on the banks, insofar as they help to fund entrepreneurial small businesses. Similarly, in the subject-areas of personality of owner, and sex differences, he will close off the potential amount of reading involved by focusing only on the ways in which personality, and sex stereotypes, affect the decision by the funding agent to lend money to the entrepreneur.

The decision to close off a branch of the tree depends on two things:

- the chances of not spotting relevant subject-matter if you stop here (a question of how much material is left to be found)
- the costs, in terms of important subject-matter ignored, of stopping at this point (a question of the standard of excellence which you wish to achieve in demonstrating your knowledge of the field).

If you feel that the chances of missing relevant subject-matter are high, and that the costs of ignoring important subject-matter are high, then you should split up that item of subject-matter down further. If both of these factors are low, then there is probably no need to do so. If one of the factors is high but the other low, you have a judgement to make! Although there is no absolute answer to either of these questions, as your reading progresses and you become familiar with the literature around your topic, you will find that your confidence in answering these questions will grow.

As you will see from Section 7.3, you can expect to read several books, articles, internet locations, and other sources for each subject-area of the relevance tree, sequencing your reading, and concentrating your attention, as you planned when drawing it up. Each item read would merit its own filecard, as described in Section 4.3. As time went on, you would certainly decide to go into greater depth than you had originally anticipated with some of the subject-areas, as your initial reading indicated new subject-matter, and aspects of the old which had not occurred to you. It would be best to add these into your original tree, so that whenever you use it you obtain an overview of the whole field, an indication of the balance of your reading across the field, and an indication of how much more you still have to do.

Start off the relevance tree on a double-page spread of your project diary, write small using an erasable pen or pencil, and spread the items out with sufficient space between them so that you can add more items as your reading progresses.

> Before continuing, now is a good time to get organized for your review. Start your own relevance tree by tackling activity 2 in the Project Guide.

As the chief popularizers of this technique Sharp *et al.* (2002: 85) suggest, apart from helping you to manage the reading list systematically as we have seen above, there are two other outcomes of relevance tree technique. It helps you to identify core texts; and it is useful in generating key terms, which you can use subsequently in a more exhaustive search.

Core texts are those which are frequently quoted: books which embody the key ideas of a subject, and journals in which the main work in a given field tends to be published. As your familiarity with the various branches of the relevance tree grows, you will recognize them as they re-occur in the various authors you consult.

Key terms or keywords, on the other hand, are the words which you use in conducting your search. Their use is described in Section 7.4 below.

But before seeing how the search is conducted, it is helpful to examine the kinds of sources you have available.

7.3   The literature search: where to look

Table 7.5 summarizes the variety of sources which you have at your disposal. The items are organized in descending order of detail and ascending order of organization, from top to bottom in the table. By which I mean that, lower down in the table are those data sources in which someone else has attempted to provide you with a guideline, or summary, of the data generated or presented by other people before them. Generally speaking, if you know exactly what you are looking for, you would approach a data source higher up the table; if, on the other hand, you're not quite sure but you wish to obtain an overview of the data that are available, you would approach a data source towards the bottom of the table.

As a general rule, when turning subject-matter into author references, try to enter Table 7.5 at as specific a level as possible: higher up rather than lower down. A list of the more important tertiary sources held by any academic library is shown in Table 7.6. Using them is quite straightforward.

■ Normally, if you want to identify the different aspects of a broad subject, the chapter headings, section subheadings, and index of a secondary source like a standard textbook, or book of readings, will provide you with an overview. If you want subject-matter at a less specific level than this, work within Segment A of Table 7.6. In other words, use the subject search facility in library catalogue, looking on the shelves for items under the classification numbers

TABLE 7.5   Sources of information

Data generated by individuals and organizations
- Government bodies
- Private companies
- Trade associations
- Chambers of commerce
- Local employer networks
- Trade unions and employers organizations
- Research organizations and professional bodies
- Patent Office
- Consumer organizations

Data recorded in primary sources
- Monographs (books on a single topic)
- Academic journal articles
- Conference papers
- Unpublished research reports (available from author)
- Newspapers and magazines (some features and news items)
- Company annual reports
- Company price-lists
- Company internal 'house magazines'

Data organized, collated and indexed in secondary sources
- Books of readings (collations of journal articles)
- Textbooks
- Encyclopaedias
- Bibliographies
- Dictionaries
- Academic journal review articles
- Academic journal annual index pages
- Annual Review books (of topics in academic disciplines)
- Abstracts (periodic issues in many academic disciplines)
- *Current Contents* (a collation of journal contents pages)
- Web of Knowledge (a major resource published by the Institute for Scientific Information)

These are summarized and signposted in tertiary sources
- Subject guides
- Library catalogues (OPAC, COPAC)
- CD-ROMs
- On-line databases
- Information services
- Librarians
- Your tutor

You turn these data into information by asking the right questions

After Hunter Brown and Faulkner (1998), and Sharp *et al.* (2002).

TABLE 7.6 Tertiary sources: general catalogues and indexes

A Start off with

■ *The library catalogue*, known as the *OPAC* (On-Line Public Access Catalogue): a database containing all the resources held by an academic library. It normally holds details of a range of resources, including books, journals, videos and projects. You would access this through course support software like Blackboard or WebTC; directly via the main university network, or by accessing your university's library web pages over the Internet.

■ The OPAC allows you to search for items from a variety of access points. How you search will depend on what information you already have available:

by subject: this lists all the resources.
by author
by title
by keyword

B If it's not in your own library, try

■ *Another university's library*, directly through HERO.ac.uk, or via the Endnote bibliographic software add-on to Microsoft Word if you own this very useful software; otherwise, via the SCONUL scheme (http://www.sconul.ac.uk/use_lib/, an essential source which includes a vacation access service)

■ *COPAC* (Common On-Line Public Access Catalogue): this Website provides a unified access to the catalogues of some of the largest university research libraries in the UK and Ireland.
See http://www.copac.ac.uk

■ *British Library Catalogue, National Union Catalogue (Library of Congress)*: paper media which list all the books held in stock, since the fifteenth century to the present, by these two libraries (which are copyright libraries: that is, they receive a copy of every book published). These are now on-line. Most items are referenced by author, not by title. The most important information is the classification number, Dewey or Library of Congress, and the ISBN number, a unique identifying code for the book in question. Use these to order older books via inter-library loan, if not held by your own library.
The British Library website offers direct access to the catalogue, its journals, manuscripts, and microfiched material catalogues: see http://www.bl.uk/catalogues/listings.html
The Library of Congress website also offers direct access to its catalogue and, as a major US gateway, gives immediate access to the library catalogues of US university libraries: see http://lcweb.loc.gov/z3950/

■ *British National Bibliography, British Books in Print, Cumulative Book Index, Books in Print*:
These paper media list all the books published and in print in the UK and USA respectively, from 1950 onwards. Use these for your general needs. Subject, Author and Title sequences are included.

C Some of the above don't cover theses, so try in addition

■ ASLIB Index to Theses: a paper medium, bi-annual publication listing MPhil and PhD theses prepared for higher degrees by students in British universities and polytechnics. An electronic version, not quite as comprehensible as the paper version but very easy to use, is now available at:
http://www.theses.com

■ Dissertation Abstracts: Provides a brief paragraph summarizing the content of each thesis prepared by PhD students in the UK and USA.

■ CRIB (Current Research in British Universities and Colleges): Lists all research currently being carried out in the UK: useful for making direct contact with people in your field.

TABLE 7.6   Tertiary sources: general catalogues and indexes (cont.)

D But few of the above include journals, so look at

- Business Periodicals Index: Alphabetic list of authors, titles and subjects of business journals: see http://www.hwwilson.com/newdds/wp.htm and use the free trial.
- ANBAR: Lists management books and journals by author and subject. Electronic access is at http://www.anbar.co.uk/management/index.html via EMERALD
- Ulrich's Guide to International Periodicals: offers a professional access point to a wide range of periodicals for a fee; check if your library subscribes: servicehttp://www.ulrichsweb.com/ulrichsweb/
- Journal Catalogues: you can find out if your library holds a copy of a particular journal title by Searching the OPAC via the journals sub-catalogue or by using the printed guide to the journals list.

There are very many resources in this last category. Talk to a librarian. Go to the orientation and skills courses offered by your library. Once you have established the titles you are interested in, start looking for online full-text articles: EMERALD is just one such collection; more complete listings are via the EBSCOhost electronic journal service.

the catalogue suggests are relevant. Authors' names will be among the results you obtain. Other books by the same author held by your library can then be found through a search by author in the catalogue.

- If you already have an author's name and the publication is not held in your library, then move to Segment B of Table 7.6: the full reference can be obtained from one of the tertiary sources listed here. The publication can then be ordered through inter-library loan. (Note: many supplying libraries charge for this service, a charge which will often be passed on to you, so you need to budget carefully.)

- While working at this broad level, you might wish to consult sources in Segments C and D of Table 7.6: research-oriented items, and journals respectively.

- Some tertiary sources are shown in Table 7.8.

As you become more knowledgeable about your field you might want to work at a very specific level indeed, contacting data sources directly, because you know the information isn't available in the library, or because you think you can find what you want faster if you make a direct contact. Individual companies already known to you, Chambers of Commerce, and Information Services are often helpful in helping you contact firms and individuals directly. Some other individualized sources are shown in Table 7.5.

Finally, there is a tremendously useful tertiary source which enables you to get a feel for the development of ideas over time: a **citation index**. You will notice, when you chase up the subjects in your relevance tree and read the authors whose work you have discovered, that they refer to other authors in their bibliographies, and you may need to find some of those items and read them in their turn. This allows you to go backwards in time from the author in question. However, on occasion you will need to find out what happened to the ideas which that author presented, and ask yourself 'I wonder who ever referenced this author in turn, subsequently to this particular publication?' working forward in time, as it were.

A citation index allows you to do just that. You will probably find that the Social Sciences Citation Index is the most useful to you. It is available in three forms: in print; as a CD-ROM; or online, as one of the three databases within the Web of Science section of the ISI Web of Knowledge (see Table 7.8). The index provides a list of their publications for any author you name. For each publication, it gives the abstract; the bibliography; and a listing of other authors who have referred to this publication since it appeared.

The items mentioned in these tables represent a much wider range of sources, too numerous and specific to individual libraries to be listed here. You can glance on the website for more detailed information still.

7.4   The literature search: how to look

All of these possibilities can be rather confusing. Quite apart from the sheer variety of sources, there is also the problem that what you find by looking at those sources is data, as opposed to information. **Data** (a plural word by the way, the singular of which is *datum*) are specific findings and assertions, which may or may not be meaningful to you. **Information**, in contrast, is made up of data expressed in such a way that they remove your uncertainty. Information *informs*, that is, it provides an answer to a query you posed.

The obvious query relates to content: 'who has said what in relation to' one of the issues involved in your research question.

- At the outset, you will search using the obvious terms that are suggested by the entries in your relevance tree. So, for example, in the tree shown in Figure 7.1, John Bartlett would start off with terms such as 'venture capital' and 'entrepreneurial' in his search of sources under a more general heading of 'small business'.

- As you find journal articles which are clearly relevant to your research question, you will notice a set of key terms which the author has provided for you, in the knowledge that the various abstracting services in which the journal is cited will use those terms to help you locate the article. Similar articles will tend to have similar key terms and thus you go from the article in hand, to new ones, which are related.

There is however, a second kind of query to pose when you seek to turn data into information; in fact, there are several. Preparing a critical literature review (see Section 7.5 for further particulars) always involves the use of a set of **reading questions**: questions with which you will interrogate the data available to you, not just to find content relevant to your research, but to make sure that the content really is informative, and can be presented as part of a critical argument, rather than as sheer, messy, unorganized data. Before you start to read, scribble down some answers to the following. These will be the particular issues you are addressing as you read.

- What do I need to know?' The items in your relevance tree, and the point you have reached in building your argument, will guide you in deciding what you are looking for, and the more specific items in the tree will be particularly helpful.

- 'How will I know when I've found it?' Summarize what you know about the subject already, and be prepared to look for information which is consistent, complementary, or relevant. Does it make sense, taken with what you know?

- 'How precise an answer do I require?' You are likely to need greater precision towards the end of your project, and less precision early on. Don't worry if, at the start, you can only think in generalities. As you read more, the specificity will come!

- 'How much effort should be devoted to related data that could be relevant, but might not be?' This is particularly problematic when you are working with online material rather than with library-shelf sources, and there's no easy answer to it. However, after a while you will learn which Internet search engine gives you the material most relevant to your topic, and which gateway or database lead to the most appropriate sources. The alternative search strategies, listed below, also have a bearing on this question.

- 'How important is it that I should find the answer?' There is little point in spending a long time on something which is trivial, or which represents a 'fine-tuning' of your existing information. Therefore, decide on:
  - 'How long will I spend in looking for the answer?
  - 'How recent should the answer be? Knowledge in some subject areas changes very rapidly (e.g. economic statistics, or information on the performance of a particular company), while knowledge in other areas is slower to change (e.g. theories about employee motivation). In the former case, you must look for recent publications. You have more freedom of choice in the latter case. Is your purpose to record the broad thrust of the ideas, or to summarize current thinking?

- And, finally:
  - 'Is there anything I really *must* know?' This is a catch-all question, probably more important at the beginning of your reading, which refers to the existence of core texts. As mentioned earlier, these are statements about your topic which are important, either because they contain the best wisdom available about some aspect of your topic which anyone working in the field is required to know, or because they're written by someone who was either wise or controversial in the past, or is currently being quoted by other people working in your field. At the outset, your tutor's initial reading list should be your best source.

Table 7.7 suggests ways of reading a book or a journal article with these questions in mind.

TABLE 7.7 Reading critically for research purposes
Reading a journal article
■ Look at the *title* first. It will tell you the field, aspect or topic to which the author feels a contribution is being made. ■ Next, glance at the *abstract*, where the author summarizes the issue, why it is important, the approach adopted, and the main finding or conclusion. Don't necessarily take his or her word for it, but be informed about what it is.
Next, a variety of approaches can be adopted by way of orientation. ■ Some people like to glance at the *bibliography* next, to get an impression of the provenance of the article and the kind of approach being taken. Are there any surprising omissions? Does the list reveal an orientation to one particular approach? ■ A comparison of the objectives as outlined in the *introduction* and the main points of the *discussion* or *conclusions* section(s) will allow you to form an impression of the extent to which the author's objectives have been achieved. ■ A second glance at the abstract will allow you to check whether this impression is correct or, at least, in line with the author's. ■ When reading an empirical paper, many people would look at the *results* next. What are the main empirical findings? ■ At this point, they may need to glance at the methodology section, to help make sense of the data and information presented in the tables. The design, the sample size and the main ways in which the sample has been stratified are particularly important.
Once this orientation phase is complete, ■ If you know the field very well, are familiar with the line the article is likely to take, and are confident that the orientation has enabled you to address fully the issues you identified with your reading questions, then you may not need to do any more. Check that your notes are complete and move on! ■ If you are new to the field or topic, or if the orientation has left you unsure about anything, you need to settle down to reading the whole article thoroughly from the introduction onwards in sequence, making notes as you go.
Reading a book
The same rationale applies, but even more so, to a book. Many people orientate themselves by glancing at the *contents*, the *section headings* if any, the *bibliography*, and, more rarely, the *index*. A glance at the *first and last paragraph* of each chapter may serve to give a flavour of the argument overall. Reading the *preface* and the *introduction* enables you to check that impression.
There may or may not be any need to read the whole book. A careful reading of one or two chapters, reading sequentially within each chapter and making notes, may be sufficient to address the issues you identified in the reading questions.
And finally . . .
Don't put the item away until you have recorded the full reference for use in your own bibliography. Do this immediately, using the conventions stated in the text and in Tables 7.3 and 7.4. (It is highly likely that if you rely on returning to the original articles, books, URLs etc. to obtain the full reference when you are actually completing the writing of your dissertation, you will be unable to locate some of them.)

So, quite apart from the content questions which you wish to pose, to obtain information from the data available, literature searching requires you to do some preparatory work to think through how best to identify this information. This is particularly so with electronic information sources.

Search strategies for electronic sources

The main search strategy of the late 1980s and early 1990s, which consisted of an experienced librarian acting as a professional guide to your searches of CD-ROM and JANET online-based facilities, has almost entirely been replaced by the online versions of the same facilities accessed via the Internet. While some of the search techniques remain the same, the strategies are of a more do-it-yourself nature, and break down into four broad types.

a *Simple surfing*, in which you search for information by going to a web page known already, and follow the URL links (normally highlighted in blue) provided to other pages and sites which look relevant. This can be fun, and lead you to discover sources which would never have otherwise occurred to you, but is likely to waste your time enormously. It would be rather better to . . .

b *Use a search engine*: a web page which allows you to enter a Boolean search phrase. This is a string of words separated by spaces, logical AND, OR, and NOT terms or their equivalents in the form of single characters. For example, a '+' between two words will ensure that the search will be for those two words as a pair, rather than for either of the two words, thus cutting down the number of hits to a more practicable number. The problem here lies in the sheer volume of possible hits obtainable, and you would be well advised to read the 'advanced instructions' section of the search engine you are using. Common ones which you are likely to have encountered already, possibly because they may be already provided in your web reader software, are *Altavista, Google,* and *Ask Jeeves* (see Table 7.8). These are useful:

1 for the location of initial items
2 for finding Usenet newsgroup items by author once they have been dropped from your service provider's server (*Google* in particular)
3 for finding non-current items posted to e-mail-based mailing lists.

A more focused strategy, however, is to:

c *Access a research database* which you know to be relevant to your topic, Field or Area of work. Table 7.7 lists those which are particularly useful for research in business and management topics.

And, further, familiarize yourself with just one or two. . .

d *Subject Directories or Gateways* Think of these as organized collections of the kinds of databases mentioned above: someone has done the surfing for you and compiled lists of useful databases and other resources!

Scholarship began, it is said, when collections of written materials grew too large for the casual user to find the scroll he or she was looking for. Only the person who

TABLE 7.8 Some useful Internet sites for electronic search and retrieval

Search Engines

Altavista	http://www.altavista.com/
Google: go straight to 'advanced search' option	http://www.google.co.uk/advanced_search
Ask Jeeves	http://www.ask.com/

Note:

The URLs at the right, below, are given for orientation purposes only. It is always best to access the sites through your own university library system, since this ensures free access. When you do so, you will notice that the URLs may differ, being slightly longer though usually with the same root details. Once you have found a site or search engine which is particularly useful, you may want to set your web reader to point directly to it, using the long address. On return, you will be asked to re-enter your ATHENS details.

Research Databases and Online Journals

BIDS
Among its facilities offers the contents of journals (some abstracts, some full text), through the Ingenta service. — http://www.bids.ac.uk

Emerald
Full text versions of around 100 journals in the management, HR and marketing fields. — http://fioriliji.emeraldinsight.com

Some Gateways

biz/ed
a business-specific gateway. Their Internet Catalogue is a useful way of focusing your surfing of hundreds of potential topics; a useful Company Information service too. — http://www.bizednet.bris.ac.uk:8080/

BUBL Information Service
Particularly useful for accessing marketing journals. — http://www.bubl.ac.uk

Department of Trade & Industry
General gateway for the DTI. The 'Select a site' and 'Select an industry' search menus are particularly useful for identifying useful contacts. — http://www.dti.gov.uk

ISI Web of Knowledge
Your best entry point to the Social Science Citation Index (SSCI). Select 'Change Products to Search' to confine your search to SSCI, unless you want to search two other citation indices and some additional resources at the same time. — http://portalt.wok.mimas.ac.uk

UK National Department of Statistics
Entry to an enormously wide collection of databases; the 'Browse by Theme' menu is particularly important. — http://www.statistics.gov.uk

OCLC First Search
One of several resource guides.
Offers access to 85 online databases and the text of 5 million online articles on a per-item fee basis. — http://oclc.org/firstsearch/

TABLE 7.8   Some useful Internet sites for electronic search and retrieval (cont.)

Social Science Information Gateway
A gateway for social science and business resources; 'Editors Choice Recommendations' offer useful free resources.　　http://sosig.ac.uk

The JISCMAIL System
A collection of mailing lists on over 4700 topics; the Business Management group alone has over 80 active lists, inc. Finance 23, Marketing 8. Has over half a million subscribers. Start with the Category Pages menu.　　http://www.jiscmail.ac.uk

looked after the collection knew exactly where everything was, being able to make connections between the *ideas* contained in the different scrolls precisely because he knew in which pigeonholes the physical *documents* could be found. Every now and again he would give a talk about the contents of scrolls which covered similar material and, in this sense, the librarian's role precedes the lecturer's.

Something similar is happening today: the vast collection of data out there is being organized into information by the staff of the university libraries. Some of the organization is deliberate, as the specialist librarians write tertiary literature subject guides to databases and gateways which are particularly relevant to their specialist disciplines; and some is *de facto*, the result of resourcing pressures whereby one library will subscribe to one set of databases and gateway services, and another library, to another. You will soon discover, if you conduct your literature searches from a home-based machine over the Internet, that a particular database may be available through several gateways, and that its address may differ one year from the next, so that it may be difficult to find the items in lists such as Table 7.7 when you look for the first time. Other sites contacted directly may simply refuse you access.

So the best way to find what you're looking for, is, always, to enter the Internet *through your own university library website*. You can do this in three ways:

a internally, through the university network

b internally or externally, through a course support website such as Blackboard or WebTC connected to your university library directly through the network, or indirectly from home via the Internet

c externally, via an ATHENS account. This authenticates that you are indeed a student of your university and provides access to those resources to which your university subscribes, over the Internet from wherever you are located. Ask for an account (it's free) in the library, if you don't already have one.

Once you have located a site, web page, file, or indeed any other information by electronic means, it is useful to make a note of its address by using the 'bookmark' or 'favourites' facility of your web reader, learning how to file and manage the long list of URLs which you will gradually accumulate. You may need these for subsequent access, and you will certainly need them when you compile your bibliography.

Winship and McNab (2000) is written with your needs directly in mind. Quite apart from these issues of Internet-based information search and retrieval, this book offers excellent guidance in the essential communications skills involved, and offers lots of tips on how to use the Internet in a student research environment.

I take it for granted that you will attend all the workshops and training sessions which your university library will have made available to you; and not just at your induction into the taught programme, but any subsequent training offered in support of your project work in particular. This is essential if you want to conduct your literature review searches efficiently.

Time to try your first research-related literature search. Firstly, glance at Case Example 7.1 to see what to do and what not to do!

Next, please glance at activity 3 in the Project Guide, and develop your own literature search by following the suggestions provided therein.

7.5 What to do with it once you have found it: writing a critical review

You are doing all this searching and writing in order to provide a critical review of other people's ideas, concepts, research findings, models and theories. This is done so that you can select, or develop, a framework with which you will be able to address your research question. The process is illustrated in Figure 7.2. A literature review is anything but a parade through hopefully relevant material; it is the result of a critical search for an analytic framework, or frameworks, which you can put to work to test a hypothesis (if you have adopted a positivist approach) or to systematically investigate a set of issues. Section 5.3 has presented the process in some detail. Chapter 8 will provide you with information on the next step, the choice of a research design through which you can conduct your test or your investigations.

In what ways is your review a critical one? The quality of your thinking

Achieving a suitably critical stance in your literature review involves familiarizing yourself with what has been said by the authors you are covering, and forming an informed opinion of the extent to which what they have said makes good sense. This requires you to:

■ know which are the key texts, as mentioned above; and then, for each key text, to understand the chief points which the particular author is making

■ recognize where and how he or she differs from other authors on the topic, being able to say so, with evidence from the authors in question, in the review

FIGURE 7.2 Elements of the research design process: A

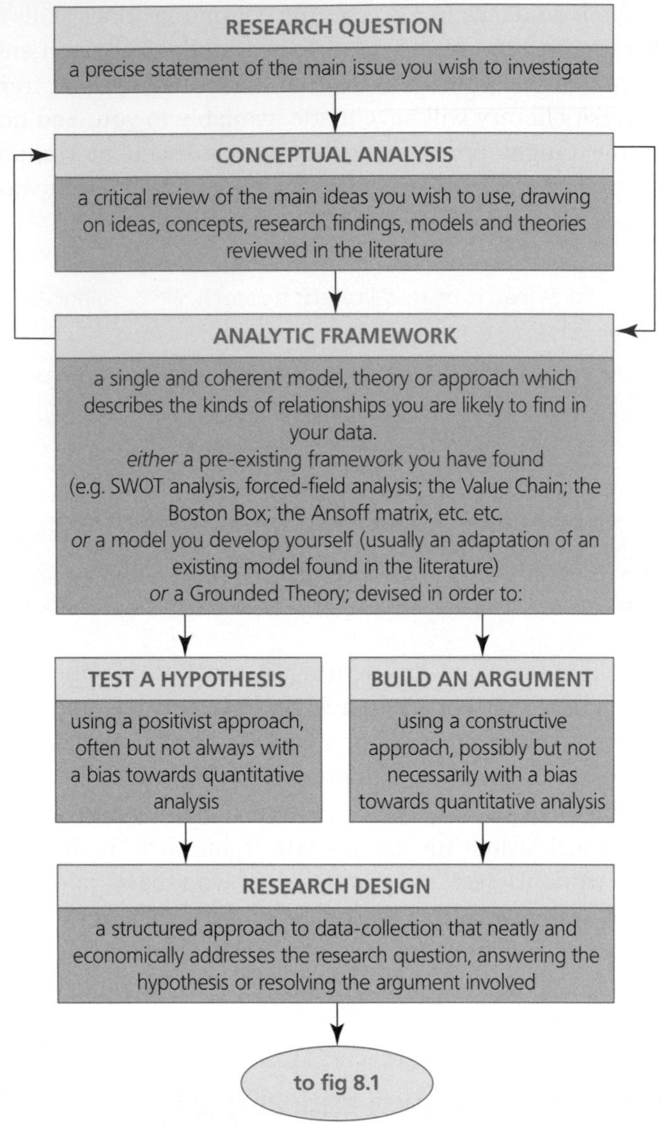

RESEARCH QUESTION

a precise statement of the main issue you wish to investigate

CONCEPTUAL ANALYSIS

a critical review of the main ideas you wish to use, drawing on ideas, concepts, research findings, models and theories reviewed in the literature

ANALYTIC FRAMEWORK

a single and coherent model, theory or approach which describes the kinds of relationships you are likely to find in your data.
either a pre-existing framework you have found
(e.g. SWOT analysis, forced-field analysis; the Value Chain; the Boston Box; the Ansoff matrix, etc. etc.
or a model you develop yourself (usually an adaptation of an existing model found in the literature)
or a Grounded Theory; devised in order to:

TEST A HYPOTHESIS

using a positivist approach, often but not always with a bias towards quantitative analysis

BUILD AN ARGUMENT

using a constructive approach, possibly but not necessarily with a bias towards quantitative analysis

RESEARCH DESIGN

a structured approach to data-collection that neatly and economically addresses the research question, answering the hypothesis or resolving the argument involved

to fig 8.1

- this requires you to understand their purposes and objectives and, as your familiarity with the literature grows, to form and express judgements, quoting appropriate evidence, about how well different authors have argued their case
- demonstrate their relationship to your own work – who supports you, who doesn't and, where you differ from others, what the significance of that might be for the argument you are building.

Finally, all your efforts to familiarize yourself with the literature, and all your hard work in referencing your presentation in an appropriately scholarly way, may be irrelevant if your knowledge is not presented in a sensible form. While your tutor and sponsor don't look for the fundamental wisdoms that redefine the boundaries of knowledge in your subject area, nevertheless they would like you to express yourself in a clear, logical, and self-consistent manner.

This comment applies as much to primary data as it does to the secondary data which you describe and analyze in your literature review. In the former case, the rules governing your use of the methods and techniques with which your data are gathered will provide you with safeguards (see Part 3); in the latter, you need to be clear on the forms in which secondary data can be presented and are aware of some pitfalls of thinking and presentation. This is especially important if you are doing a library-based project (see Section 3.2), since you will not be gathering any empirical data yourself, but simply compiling data available in other people's published work.

To speak of critical analysis as a review of ideas, concepts, models and theories is to use terms which sound familiar, but which are often used interchangeably and inaccurately. They suggest that the process is logical, searching, and rational. These terms are defined in Table 7.9. This summarizes some of the most common forms of discourse which you are likely to encounter in your reading, and utilize yourself in your written project report. Perhaps the best way of using the table would be to acknowledge that your report will be a mixture of all of these forms; to understand each of them well enough so that you know when you're using each; and to refer to the table while you are writing.

It helps if you work to a pre-existing model you have encountered in the literature, or construct a model to guide your work, as outlined in Section 5.3): and especially, if you are explicitly aware that you are doing so. Indeed, your research question (see Section 2.4) is itself the beginnings of a model, and you may want to flesh out this model a little more as you work within the terms of your research objective. If your project report comprises conceptual analyses, evidence and critical argument as outlined earlier, it has be leavened by reference to principles, and will include an element of explanation for some of the issues which you have explored. Most regulations insist on some form of empirical content; clearly, if you're gathering and presenting data, you can do so only with some prior principles in mind, as an outcome of some theory which states that it's just these data which you should gather to justify the assertions which you wish to make.

At some stage or other, then, you will be using each and every one of the forms of argument shown in Table 7.9. Make sure that you know which is which. Weak projects are often unsuccessful because the student thought he or she was explaining, when all that was presented was a description.

 This would be a good point at which to address activity 4. You might like to devote just a day or so to it in the first instance.

TABLE 7.9 Forms of argument and presentation

- **An assertion:** An utterance written down by yourself: a simple statement.
- **A description:** An account of whatever you see to be the case: a series of assertions which define something or some state of affairs. These assertions may or may not be accurate, detailed, or exact. Descriptions are always made from some point of view, or to some purpose; so alternative descriptions are always possible. The case studies which you're given in your lectures (especially at MBA level) are neither explanations, models, nor theories: they're descriptions.
- **A model:** Sometimes used loosely to stand for a relatively inaccurate or underspecified theory, the word is properly used to stand for a systematic description which maps or represents some state of affairs. Another way of saying this is that it's a statement of what the state of affairs would look like if your description mapped them accurately or exactly. You design models as a starting-point, to enable yourself to experiment with, and understand, the state of affairs.
- **A principle:** A statement about the relationships between variables, issues or events, which has been previously researched and found to be accurate in general as well as in specific instances.
- **A theory:** A set of statements incorporating principles, using which it is possible to explain a particular occurrence as an instance of a wider set of affairs.
- **An explanation:** A description which provides reasons and thereby removes uncertainty or increases understanding, by means of assertions which say something about the relationships between two or more variables, issues or events, and which draw on previously established principles. You cannot claim to have explained something if all you've done is describe it. A very detailed description is almost an explanation, except for one characteristic: an explanation provides sufficient understanding of principles for you to envisage an alternative, or improved state of affairs; a description need not. Explanations are expressed by means of theories, and a theory is more than description.
- **An analysis:** A critical account of the component parts or factors involved in some state of affairs: the variables, issues, or events making up the state of affairs. However carefully the parts are described, an analysis doesn't explain the state of affairs, just as a description doesn't explain: you require some reference to principles in order to explain.
- **So, for example –** A *description* of the lighting system in your room can be provided by a series of assertions about switches, light bulbs, wiring, and power sources, enough for your reader to be able to put on the light. A *model* of the lighting system would be provided by an electrical circuit diagram, and an *analysis* provided by means of a list of electrical components involved. An *explanation* of the lighting system would be sufficiently detailed, and refer to just those *principles*, for your reader to be able to fix the lighting system if it went wrong, or to be able to envisage a better system. The principles would be taken from a theory of electricity and, conceivably, materials.

Sharing your thinking with others

An excellent way to develop the quality of your thinking is to debate your work with other people. The value of collaboration with people in the organization you're studying was discussed in Section 5.2; now is the time to collaborate with other researchers. The world is a small place, and someone, somewhere, whom you can easily contact through the Internet, is likely to be doing a research study in the same Field (or possibly, on the same topic), as yourself. The way to get in touch is to join an e-mail-based *mailing list*. The JISCMAIL gateway is the obvious place in which to search: see Table 7.7. A mailing list works by providing you with a single e-mail address to which you send a message, which is then e-mailed to all the other members of the mailing list; you, in turn, receive a copy of every e-mail the other members have sent to the list. Any one list will be populated by people who share similar academic and research interests, from the most distinguished authorities in the field, to the newest and freshest beginners; indeed, one of the most frequent types of message is the one which asks, 'I'm researching topic A for my dissertation; how do I do X, Y or Z'? The help available to you is enormous, and is always freely given, so you should not feel shy about joining a list or two, lurking for a while, and then posing your own queries and joining in discussion.

You join a mailing list by:

a pointing your web reader at: http://www.jiscmail.ac.uk/ finding a list that interests you under 'Find Lists' and either

b clicking on its name to get to its web page, choosing the simple 'join or leave the list' option or

c sending an e-mail to jiscmail@jiscmail.ac.uk with the message 'join <name of mailbase> <your own name>. Thus, if John Harrison wanted to join the KNOW-ORG list (a list devoted to organizational learning and knowledge management), he would send 'join know-org John Harrison'.

A confirmation is sent once you have joined.

Research can be a lonely business, especially if you are doing a library-based project and are not meeting people in individual organizations (since you're not out there collecting empirical data). Membership of one or two research mailing lists provides you with an excellent opportunity to share your experience, your troubles and your triumphs.

And this is something to arrange right now, as outlined in activity 5.

CASE EXAMPLE 7.1   Starting an internet search

Michael Ormston is engaged in a project on public attitudes to the arts as part of his MSc in Marketing. His research question addresses the issue of how museums and art galleries might learn from popular cultural forms (e.g. street theatre, karaoke) how to attract a younger clientele, and he has started to compile an author list drawing on his main tertiary source, Kotler and Kotler (1998) and to collect key words, in order to build a useful reading list.

He begins his searches by addressing the 'ISI Web of Knowledge' gateway, http://isiknowledge.com/ which he has seen highly recommended in several research methods textbooks. Unfortunately, he cannot gain access to it. Every attempt ends with the message 'Sorry, you need a subscription to an ISI Web of Knowledge product in order to follow this link'. He decides to try again later after talking to a librarian, and in the meantime, use his time productively by using a generic search engine.

The first key word that comes to mind on re-reading some of his marketing lecture notes is 'marketing of services'. An initial search using *Google Advanced Search* reveals over 8000 possible items relating to this phrase. A swift glance at some of these shows that the proportion of useful journal articles and research reports among all these items is likely to be small.

So he tries narrowing the possibilities by using 'Marketing of museums and art galleries' as his key words. The outcome is negative: no web pages meet this description. 'Marketing of art galleries' likewise provides no hits. He tries the other term, using 'Marketing of museums'. Success! He finds 81 items, a small enough number to be handleable. He scans each of the relevant eight *Google* pages systematically and views the more plausible items in detail, one by one.

There are very few journal articles here, though. A researcher's name comes up several times, branding is mentioned, one or two university courses in related subjects (e.g. the University of Sheffield MA in Arts and Heritage Management)

are listed. Not a satisfactory outcome! For the most part, most pages he has looked at provide only passing mentions of museum marketing; there's lots about library services, a few keynote speeches and policy statements about museum management, but nothing very relevant to his topic.

How might Michael make further progress towards the more specific literature that his topic requires?

Answers to Case Example 7.1

There are four things Michael could do.

a First, having got to these sites, he should spend just a little additional time digging deeper. Any University listed in an initial search for a topic will have staff who conduct research in that field; it may also provide a list of research students' topics, and possibly a list of completed dissertations in the field. For example, the University of Sheffield site that Michael accessed provides the following more detailed pages.

■ http://www.shef.ac.uk/management/research/interests.shtml a listing of staff research interests and publications in this department, though these seem to deal more with Sport and Leisure Management than with Arts and Heritage, despite the degree title

■ a glance at the list of student dissertations given at http://www.shef.ac.uk/management/msc/ahm/diss.shtml is much more useful, throwing up several dissertation titles related to his own topic. For example,

'An evaluation of the marketing strategy used by the West Yorkshire Playhouse to attract young audiences'

'Education through entertainment? A study of motivation and attitudes towards battle re-enactments in Britain'

'An assessment of the potential for the development of community arts at the Burton Street Project'

'A study of community education and outreach in museums'

'"Not for such as us": Attitudes to art on an inner city estate'

are just some of the titles listed. Obtaining a copy of each dissertation and simply cross-referencing the relevant items from the bibliographies would give Michael a start on an immediate reading list. Have any of these titles been placed in an on line facility? He can contact the library to find out.

b Second, he should remain alert to key words which appear in his searches which relate to concepts from his taught course, which he will be able to put to work in his dissertation:

■ 'branding' is the obvious concept found in his original search. Even a brief Google search using 'branding of museums' provides four hits, one of which, http://www.colum. edu/mediarelations/Category.htm leads him to the name and publications of another author who might usefully be added to the author list and her address noted for a subsequent e-mail request for an offprint of the paper itself.

c He should consider alternative ways of addressing his original intention. Using a general search engine like *Google* is *not* a very efficient process.

The reason Michael wasn't able to access the ISI Web of Knowledge through http://isiknowledge. com/ is because he did not look for it through his own university's Learning Resources (library) gateway, which is specially set up to provide ease of access to sites like this and provides a more appropriate access address. The details differ for different libraries, but the generic procedure is a simple matter of just three easy steps.

■ enter 'ISI Web of Knowledge' into the search box provided on the library's home page, gateways list, or digital library page

■ provide an Athens account name and password when requested

■ select one of the indexes offered by 'ISI Web of Knowledge'.

Michael enters these details into the General Search facility of the ISI Web of Knowledge, using 'Branding' as his key word, and receives 319 hits. He combines 'Branding' with 'Art Galleries' with no result; and with 'Museums', obtaining just 1 result. 'Branding' and 'Services' provides 16 hits. Extending the ISI Web of Knowledge search to include the associated ISI Proceedings and Current Contents databases does not make an appreciable difference.

At this point, he decides to broaden his search further to include other gateways and databases, but to exclude web search engines like *Google* and *Alatvista*. He returns to his library *'Metafind'* facility, selects all 12 sites that are offered, and receives a list of the number of hits each might provide for the keywords 'marketing and museum'. This indicates that eight sites will provide access to over 600 items between them, of which the Business Source Premier and Academic Search Elite sites appear the most promising, with 399 and 141 hits respectively. The keywords 'branding and museum' provide 23 hits, with Business Source Premier promising 18. He is ready to access the full bibliographic reference of each (in the format described in Section 7.1 above), to add to his author list. In some cases what he gets is a detailed abstract, and in a few cases, the item accessed is the full article, available in online form.

It is often more efficient to start a search with paper sources. If Michael were to obtain the initial items he identified in the bibliography to Kotler and Kotler (1998), use their bibliographies for a scan backward in time, and access the Social Science Citation Index (through ISI Web of Knowledge) for a search forward in time, he would soon have a substantial, well-focused reading list.

Project Guide

1 Progress your introductory chapter

Literature reviewing works best if you already have a clear picture of your objectives and research question, while the preparation of a first draft of your first chapter will help you to address the literature in terms of its relevance to both objectives and research objectives. So, firstly:

a take the provenance table you prepared as activity 3 of Chapter 2; the research proposal you began in activity 5 of the Project Guide of Chapter 2, and completed in activity 3 in Chapter 5; and your research question (activity 4 of Chapter 5). By now, you should also have tackled the checklist activities given in Table 4.1. The outcomes of all these activities should be in your Research Diary.

b Write a draft of the first chapter of your dissertation – your introduction – if you haven't already begun it, taking feedback on it from your tutor.

2 Start your literature search

a Working with your provenance table to hand, prepare your first relevance tree or equivalent reading plan (see Section 7.2).

b Begin your reading in detail, locating items easily available in your university library, and collating references using the filecards you prepared in activity 3 of the Chapter 4 Project Guide.

c Begin making notes of the further references, mentioned in the bibliographies of the items you read, which you know you will want to locate and read next.

3 Begin your searches of electronic sources

a Assuming you have tried out some of the websites and other resources mentioned in Section 7.3, organize yourself for a more systematic approach. Clear the irrelevant bookmarks/favourites from your web reader and start recording the useful sites you visit, ignoring the rest.

b Consider setting your web reader, to open as its home page, a search engine which you have found particularly helpful, so that it's to hand as soon as you begin a work session.

c If you haven't done so already, you might like to get hold of a copy of Winship and McNab 2000 and dip into it as required.

4 Put pen to paper: start writing your review!

a Draft the main headings of your review, following the guidelines about structure given in Section 3.5, and the suggestions made in Section 7.1 above.

b Begin writing. This will be an ongoing activity as you continue reading the subsequent chapters.

c Nevertheless, try and plan to have around half of the review finished by the time you next see your tutor; make an appointment with him or her as appropriate, bearing in mind the timetable you specified in the research proposal, and the Gantt chart you constructed in activity 2 of Chapter 4.

5 Join a research community

Spend a little time exploring the possibilities offered by JISCMAIL as listed in Table 7.7 following the menu choices available, noting the e-mail address of any mailing list(s) you would like to join, and following the joining instructions.

a Look in on the ongoing discussions as the e-mails come in to you, along with all your normal, personal e-mails.

b When you want to, send your own message to the mailing list by e-mail, using as the address <name of mailbase@jiscmail. ac.uk>.

References

Barzun, J. and Graff, H. E. (1985) *The Modern Researcher*, London: Harcourt, Brace, Jovanovich.

Brown, L. D. and Kaplan, R. E. (1981) 'Participative research in a factory', in Reason, P. and Rowan, J., (eds.) *Human Inquiry: A Sourcebook of New Paradigm Research*, Chichester: John Wiley & Sons: 303–314.

Clark, I. (1999). 'Corporate human resources and "bottom line" financial performance', *Personnel Review*, 28: 4: 290–306.

Edmondson, A. and Moingeon, B. (1998) 'From organizational learning to the learning organization', *Management Learning*, 29: 1: 5–20.

Fiedler, F. E. (1967) *A Contingency Theory of Leadership Effectiveness*, New York: McGraw-Hill.

Fransella, F., Bell, R. and Bannister, D. (2003) *A Manual of Repertory Grid Technique*, London: Wiley.

Garratt, B. (2001) *The Learning Organisation: Developing Democracy at Work*, London: Profile Business.

Hosking, D. M. and Morley, I. (1988) 'The skills of leadership', in Hunt, J. G., Baliga, B. R., Dachler, H. P. and Schriesheim, C. A., (eds.) *Emerging Leadership Vistas*, Boston: Lexington.

Hunter Brown, C. J. and Faulkner, A. (1998) *Information Search Guide*, Milton Keynes: Open University.

Kotler, P. and Kotler, N. (1998) *Museum Strategy and Marketing: Designing Missions, Building Audiences, Generating Revenue*, London: Wiley.

Likert, R. (1961) *New Patterns of Management*, New York: McGraw-Hill.

London, M. (1988) *Change Agents*, London: Jossey-Bass.

Mann, R. D. (1959) 'A review of the relationships between personality and performance in small groups', *Psychological Bulletin*, 56: 241–270.

Misumi, J. (1985) *The Behavioural Science of Leadership*, Ann Arbor, MI: University of Michigan Press.

Ouchi, W. I. (1981) *Theory Z: How American Business can Meet the Japanese Challenge*, Reading, MA: Addison-Wesley.

Parlett, M. (1981) 'Illuminative evaluation', in Reason, P. and Rowan, J., (eds.) *Human Inquiry: a Sourcebook of New Paradigm Research*, Chichester: John Wiley & Sons.

Parsons, T., Bales, R. F. and Shils, E. A., (eds.) (1953) *Working Papers in the Theory of Action*, Glencoe, Ill.: Free Press.

Pfeffer, J. (1981) 'Management as symbolic action: the creation and maintenance of organisational paradigms', in Cummings, L. L. and Staw, B. M., (eds.) *Research in Organisational Behaviour Vol. 3*, Greenwich, Conn.: J.A.I. Press.

Schön, D. A. (1983) *The Reflective Practitioner*, London: Temple Smith.

Sharp, J. A., Peters, J. and Howard, K. (2002) *The Management of a Student Research Project*, Aldershot: Gower Publishing.

Smith, P. B. and Peterson, M. F. (1988) *Leadership, Organisations and Culture: an Event Management Model*, London: Sage.

Stogdill, R. M. (1948). 'Personal factors associated with leadership: a survey of the literature' *Journal of Psychology* 25, 35–72.

Stogdill, R. M. and Coons, A. E. (1957) 'Leader Behaviour: its Description and Management', Columbus, OH: Bureau of Business Research, Ohio State University.

Weick, K. (1995) *Sensemaking in Organizations*, New York: Sage.

Winship, I. and McNab, A. (2000) *The Student's Guide to the Internet*, London: Library Association Publishing.

A guide to empirical work

In Part 2, we dealt with various aspects of scholarship, seeking to manage the conceptual and practical complexity of a project in a rigorous way. We dealt with the argument and rationale whereby you support your statements with appropriate evidence, working in a complex management environment in which there are varying expectations of your role. We saw that there are two forms of evidence with which you build this argument: secondary data, material collected by other people which you turn into information in the course of your literature review; and primary data, material that you collect yourself. The ways in which you collect these data, and the ways in which you turn the data into information, are the subject-matter of this final section of the book.

8 Planning empirical work

- To define the different kinds of research design available to you and to help you in choosing a design appropriate to your particular research question
- To provide you with several alternative approaches to sampling, in order to encourage you to think through the scope and scale of your data-gathering activities
- To help you to finalize your plan of empirical work

At a glance

Empirical work needs to be carefully planned in advance. As we saw in Section 5.2, the practitioner field can be very messy and complicated. If you are to make sense of it, you will need to adopt a structured approach. The steps required to design the approach are described and three distinct types of design – exploratory, descriptive, and causal – are defined. This tripartite scheme provides a way of classifying the different types of design available to us and some of these designs are briefly outlined.

Empirical work has to be generalized from the particular circumstances in which you collect your data; as a rule, there is no point of coming to conclusions which only apply to the particular people from whom you gathered those data. We introduce two approaches to generalization: sampling and replication, and go into sampling in some detail (leaving the details of replication over to Chapter 9). Finally, the practicalities of empirical work are discussed.

8.1 Planning a design

You leave the house in the morning, get in your car, turn the ignition key, and your car won't work. There is no forward movement whatso ever. Your life comes to a standstill, your blood pressure rises, and you have an important meeting in 90 minutes' time. You switch into your Keystone Cops mode, rush into the garden shed, bring out the spare battery you just happen to have there, and fit it in place; you run round to the coal-shed and bring out the can of petrol you always keep on hand for emergencies, and pour it into the petrol tank. You put water into the radiator and oil into the bit of the engine with the filler cap on top; and you put some brake fluid into the brake reservoir down at the side. All this has taken an hour and you have to rush back indoors to put on a new coat since you got oil all over the one you were wearing, but it's done. Now you can try the key in the ignition again. After all, that's what makes cars work, isn't it – electricity and petrol, water and oil?

In a way, yes. But in point of fact, no, not in this instance, and for a rather subtle reason. Your analytic framework was unsuited to your problem. It isn't necessarily that your conceptual model is oversimplified; nor are you using the wrong conceptual model (the one pertaining to regular weekly servicing rather than one-off emergency startups), though that is part of the difficulty. What is wrong is that your conceptual model is disorganized and inefficient. It's pure Laurel and Hardy; it lacks *design*.

Let's try a different approach. Think a little before acting. But what should you attend to: what kind of data would seem to be relevant to your problem? The answer lies in designing your approach so that you:

- try various possibilities one by one in a controlled manner
- eliminate possible alternative explanations
- avoid tests which will tell you that two possible causes are at work but which make it impossible to decide on their relative importance
- use a conceptual model which is suited to the problem in hand.

Very well then, turn the key in the ignition, listen, and look. Does the engine fire? Well, no, not really: so it must be the starter motor, the solenoid, the battery, or an empty tank. At a stroke, you have eliminated oil, water and brake fluid as the source of the problem. They're irrelevant to the problem you're dealing with at present. Do the headlights come on? Yes: so the problem can't be with the battery. Turn the key in the ignition and listen again. You notice that the engine doesn't even cough, let alone fire. It's unlikely to be an empty tank. In point of fact the problem is much more immediate. Turn the key again: you hear a clicking noise. So the solenoid is doing its job, and, by elimination, it must be the starter motor that's at fault. Other factors could be involved (maybe even your wiring), but they aren't the immediate problem.

That has taken you just one minute, so there is time to call out the AA, ring your garage, or failing all else, order a taxi to take you to work. Yes, your knowledge of solenoids, starters and so on was relevant, but, much more important, it was the approach, the *design* you adopted, which solved the problem you faced.

Design has been defined as the deliberately planned 'arrangement of conditions for analysis and collection of data in a manner that aims to combine relevance to the research purpose with economy of procedure' (Selltiz *et al.* 1981). The idea behind a design is that different kinds of issues logically demand different kinds of data-gathering arrangement if your data are to be:

■ relevant to your thesis or to the argument you wish to present

■ an adequate test of your thesis (i.e., unbiased and reliable)

■ accurate in establishing causality, in situations where you wish to go beyond exploration and description, to provide explanations for whatever is happening around you

■ capable of providing findings that can be generalized to situations other than those of your immediate circumstances.

You have to have some knowledge in order to put together an appropriate design and that is one purpose in doing a literature review; but knowledge, unstructured by an analytic framework and without a careful design, leads to inefficient and inaccurate data collection. Choosing a design is one of a number of steps you take in planning your empirical work. Figure 7.2 showed the earlier steps. It summarizes the development of a research question, as we discussed in Section 2.4 (choice of question) and Section 5.1 (the ontological underpinnings), and it illustrates the development of the conceptual analysis and analytic framework (Section 5.3) through the work which you do on your literature review (Section 7.5).

Now you need to complete the remaining steps shown in Figure 8.1.

■ Choose a research design: the data-gathering approach which will investigate the issues you have identified, and which will serve to help to establish or negate the hypothesis you have in mind, or which will best help you build an argument that justifies the belief statement.

■ Next, you decide on an appropriate research method with which to apply the research design.

■ The method you choose will determine the way in which you plan to generalize your findings once the data have been collected; at this point, you are deciding on your sampling or replication plan.

■ And finally, you make use of a number of techniques to gather the data themselves.

Design and sampling form the subject-matter of this chapter. Once you have a design, you can decide on a method and one or more techniques, and these are outlined in the chapter which follows, together with some material on approaches to replication.

Research designs can be classified into three types: exploratory (in which you identify the key issues the better to understand your research question); descriptive, in which you are clear about the issues and seek to describe them systematically and precisely); and causal, in which you seek to establish the reasons for outcomes (Ghauri and Gronhaug 2002: 48–52). Table 8.1 lists a variety of different designs under each of these headings.

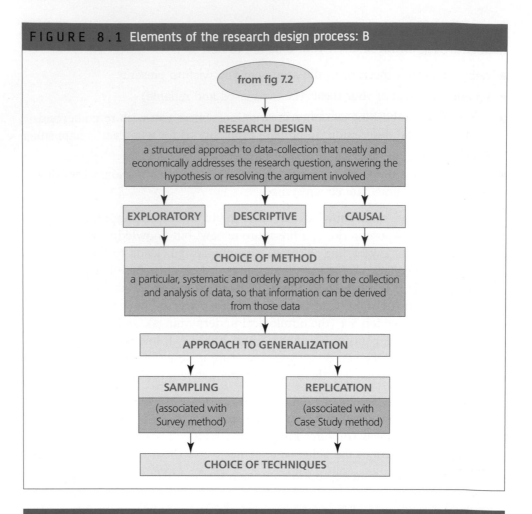

FIGURE 8.1 Elements of the research design process: B

TABLE 8.1 Types of design

Exploratory
- information-gathering (what are the issues at first glance?)
- critical incident assembly
- objectives achievement (direct and inferred)

Descriptive
- marketing research reports
- single case study (describe past, present and future)
- unstratified survey (describe views and opinions)
- systematic examination of contrasting modes of operation

Causal
- stratified survey (identify systematically different views; establish if due to those differences)
- time-sampling (the influence of factors over time)
- comparative case study (the impact of systematic differences)
- before-after (the impact of a one-off intervention)
- independent-dependent variation (controlled experiments)

Exploratory designs

Most straightforwardly, exploratory designs are adopted in order to discover what the issues might be, for more detailed investigation using descriptive and/or causal designs. They can however be used in their own right. Evaluation research, for example, which assembles information about the processes by which organizations achieve their objectives, sometimes uses a variety of exploratory designs on a stand-alone basis. To ask *if formal objectives have been achieved*; or to obtain a statement of espoused objectives, observing operations to identify the actual objectives being worked towards, and to *compare espousals with actuality*, are two common variants (Parlett 1981).

Descriptive designs

Some descriptive designs, like the simple *market research investigation* and the *single case study*, are straightforward. The intention is to identify the crucial features of the organization or situation under study and describe the features, and the issues which arise, as accurately as possible.

Other descriptive designs are more involved. An *unstratified survey* may lack the more complex sampling arrangements of a stratified sample in which you look for the ways in which different types of people differ systematically in their answers (see below); but it is possible to relate the answers people give to different questions, in ways which provide quite rich and detailed descriptions of their views. Do people who indicated that they were in the lower band of incomes in your question about take-home pay say that they prefer a particular product in your subsequent question about the brands which they can recognize?

Causal designs

To use a causal design is to go beyond simple exploration and description and to look for the reasons of the events or situations being studied. Data collection and analysis are carefully arranged so as to identify the forces involved. In the simplest case, for example, if you believed that female employees without children are likely to have different views of the glass ceiling effect than older females with families, it is obvious that you need to keep the answers of these two different types of respondent *separate*. To lump all of their answers together would not illuminate the influence that family commitments might, or might not, have on their views.

Some causal designs are more complex. For example, suppose that you are examining the strategic options available to your company in addressing overseas markets and want to survey different companies to identify the possibilities open to yours. Your ultimate purpose is to identify the factors that make it simple for companies in your market to operate overseas and so you decide to arrange the possibilities along this dimension: are they easy, or more difficult, to implement.

Making comparisons on the basis of ease-or-difficulty seems logically appropriate, given the risks and expenditures involved in overseas investment and given that the issue presents itself as one of choosing one of a set of alternative actions. So, in your industry it may be that joint ventures are viewed as somewhat difficult, and direct exporting is seen as easier. However, it may be that import quotas apply in the overseas country, and so you might also wish to consider manufacture under licence as a way of overcoming this form of trade barrier, placing this option more towards the 'easy' end of the range for your company; and so forth.

Taking this particular approach, the *examination of contrasting modes of operation,* would lead you to look at companies which practise these forms of trade, who represent extreme positions on the range, and who are willing to give you the information you need. Once you had decided on this form of design, then you might decide that the comparative case study seems most appropriate as the method to use.

But this design would be *predestined* to fail if the main issues which you wanted to explore concerned the development and growth of a department and company over time. Here, examining contrasts seems illogical and inappropriate, and it makes much more sense to try and track the change in some way and possibly, to establish the causes of change.

One way of doing this would be to systematically collect the data at various time intervals yourself. Alternatively, if you were working with secondary data as part of a library-based study, you would arrange to have access to archival data which systematically represent that time. In both these cases you would choose what is known as a *time-sampling* design. Your chief design consideration in the basic descriptive account would involve the accuracy and reliability of your sampling of what is happening or has happened. If you took the next step, to explain the causes of development and growth, then you would need to obtain sufficient background information to show which factors have influenced and which factors have not influenced, the changes.

On the other hand, if the issues you had identified related to a major, one-off change occurring in the organization, then in order to describe the change, you could arrange to gather data on some key indicators both before and after the change, in a another kind of causal arrangement, the *before-after* design. If you wish to *explain* change, rather than simply *describe* it, in other words – glance back to Table 7.8 – you need to establish that:

- these changes were associated with the indicators
- the indicators had their impact before the changes not after and that
- they were the most relevant to the events involved and that other factors which might have been responsible were not involved.

If conditions were right and appropriate data were to hand, it is just possible that you could choose a *field experiment* as your method; alternatively, some form of survey would be required.

Making design decisions

What all these examples have in common is that the shape of your data-collection, the factors and events which you decide to notice, and those which you decide to ignore – in a word, the conditions – are arranged and structured deliberately, in order to cast the brightest possible light on the issues you are investigating. Where you intend to explain as well as describe and analyze, you have to arrange things so that you can exclude competing explanations which are not involved, as well as being able to identify the plausible explanations. It would be pointless to make systematic comparisons by looking only for similarities; to observe a process by making an observation only once; to investigate change without some notion of what went before, as well as what is happening now – hence the need to familiarize yourself with these various alternative designs.

With one exception, it is difficult to provide you with more detailed guidelines on the planning of the design of your empirical work at this point; it all depends on your topic, and particularly, on your hypothesis, or on the personal thesis which you are addressing. Indeed, if the purpose of a thesis is to state the conclusions which you believe your data will support, and to help identify the kind of data which would refute such conclusions (see Section 5.3), a good thesis is one which clearly expresses your design, so that the design – what you have to do to establish the thesis – is obvious from the way in which your thesis has been stated. Having said that, I will be providing more detailed guidelines on design when I describe the range of different methods and techniques which are open to you.

ILLUSTRATION 8.1

Michal Stepinski is a Polish manager following an MBA programme offered at the Warsaw Instytut Komercyjny, a private university which gives the degrees of a British university under a carefully monitored licensing arrangement. His topic deals with business reorganization and development during times of economic and social change. There are many possible factors involved and the initial stages of his work are exploratory, to identify the more important factors at play. His hypothesis is that those companies which grew successfully during the 1990s managed to resolve what he calls 'critical issues': issues which are dangerous to the survival of one kind of firm, but less so for another. In arranging to collect information about a range of SMEs over a five-year period, *critical incident assembly* seems the obvious design to use. He will look for happenings which proved turning points for some companies, but which were unproblematic for others; and in a subsequent, causal stage of the study, he plans to interview some of the chief executives using a *comparative case study* design, to identify what exactly happened in their companies that made the incidents critical, or unproblematic. (For example, why *should* the absence of professional marketing expertise have made the difference for a newly reorganized, privatized and regionalized construction company, while being less apparently catastrophic for a large steel works which remained in state ownership and did not reorganize into smaller companies?) And thus, the two designs he has chosen follow naturally, one might almost say inevitably, from his thesis.

The exception mentioned above concerns the matter of sampling and representation. A good design will involve a decision on which data sources to address, and how to address them in order for your conclusions to be both valid with respect to your thesis, and generalizable beyond the situation in which the addressing is done.

 Now take some time to do activity 1 in the Project Guide.

8.2   Representation and sampling

Which companies to study; which departments to include; which people to question, are all design decisions. Your readers are not especially interested in the companies, departments, or people for themselves, but for what they represent (an industry; a type of department; a particular sort of employee); and, in general, empirical work is only worth doing if your local findings are organized in such a way that they can be generalized to other companies, departments, or people like the ones you studied. Alternatively, it is worthwhile if you can specify the circumstances under which, and the situations to which, your specific findings apply. This latter form of generalization arrangement depends on a technique called replication, and will be dealt with in Chapter 9 in the context of comparative case study method. The former kind of generalization arrangement depends on sampling.

Sampling can be defined as the deliberate choice of a number of units (companies, departments, people) – the **sample** – who are to provide you with data from which you will draw conclusions about some larger group – the **population** – whom these units represent.

In order to draw a sample, you have to know how many units are in the population and how this total is made up from units falling into various subgroups in which you might be interested. This may already be available as a published staff list, for example, if the units are employees; or as a directory list of companies for the market you are exploring, if your focus is at the company level. Alternatively, you may have to draw it up yourself. Such a list is called a **sampling frame**. The size of your sample and the way in which you draw it are matters for design and will affect the validity and generalizibility of the conclusions you draw.

There are two ways in which you can draw a sample. **Non-probability sampling** involves identifying and questioning informants because you are interested in their individual positions, roles, or background experience. It is likely that you will want to pose different questions to them accordingly. The population they represent consists of all the varied members of the industry, company, or department that falls within the scope of your topic, and they may represent these somewhat loosely, or, indeed, not at all. In other words, you are interested in variety – in idiosyncratic viewpoints – and seek to exemplify the range of different views in the population. In this situation, the proportion of the population whom you choose to talk to (or the probability of being chosen as a respondent) has no particular significance, other than making things manageable in the time available to you.

In contrast, **probability sampling** involves you in identifying and questioning people because they are members of some population (an industry, type of company, department and so forth) and you want to ensure that your assertions are valid for your respondents and directly generalizable, without further inference, to that population. You pose the same questions to each sample member. So, for example, if 75 per cent of your respondents reply in a particular way (e.g. that they are in favour of some course of action), you would be willing to conclude *directly*, without further inference, that their whole industry, company, or department would have replied identically (e.g. 75 per cent of them would also have been in favour) had you asked everyone. In this situation, the proportion of the population whom you choose to talk to (or the probability of being chosen as a respondent) has an important bearing on the validity of your conclusions and on their generalizability.

Most in-company based projects deal in relatively small samples. You are more likely to be using nonprobability sampling methods and you can generalize your conclusions by means of inference and triangulation (see Section 9.2). However, some in-company, and many undergraduate projects and most of those which involve a questionnaire survey, have the potential for you to use probability sampling methods, and thereby to draw direct conclusions to your population as well.

Non-probability sampling methods

A variety of strategies is possible, each following a different rationale and each of them reflecting the constraints within which you must work.

Accidental sampling

Accidental sampling involves the choice of a sample from the population whose views you want to discover, on the basis of convenience only: for example, because you can get access to them, because you can't obtain the funds or other forms of support to cast your net more systematically, or because your sponsor is uncomfortable in having you talk to some more systematically representative sample of that population.

There are drawbacks. You might very well find yourself in a situation where the organizational pressures prevent you from using any other method, but your sample results may be biased with respect to the population as a whole, and sampling theory provides you with no systematic means of estimating the size of the bias. Given the pressures, you may have no choice but to work with an accidental sample. What you can and should do is to report your judgement of the nature of the bias, as a matter of scholarship rather than sampling theory; that is, make a list of the possible sources of bias given your thesis, the issue you're investigating and the related issues, and discuss them in your project report.

Purposive sampling

Purposive sampling involves choosing people whose views are relevant to an issue because you make a judgement, and/or your collaborators persuade you, that their views are particularly worth obtaining and typify important varieties of viewpoint. Several arrangements are possible:

- Key informant technique (Tremblay 1982) by which people with specialized knowledge about the issue in question are selected for interview. (See Section 10.3 for further particulars.)

- Taking 'slices through the organization' (Reeves and Harper 1981a) selects people because of the positions they occupy in the organization. You might choose a vertical chain of command from chief executive down to first line manager, working within one or more business functions; a horizontal line to include people in a colleague relationship at one particular level within the organization; or a diagonal slice down the chain of command and across functions.

- 'Snowball sampling' (Reeves and Harper 1981a) is a technique by which new respondents are selected following the recommendations of people to whom you have already put your questions; as you proceed, the number of respondents grows like a snowball.

The drawback with purposive sampling is that can never be quite sure whether the basis for seeing people as 'typical' isn't gradually changing as you work through your sample. While it is a useful sampling technique for many situations, it should be avoided when you are exploring issues arising from changes that happen over the duration of your empirical work, and the members of your sample are differentially involved in, or affected by, the changes. In these circumstances, some people will be less typical than others on some aspects you are investigating, equal on others, and more typical on others again!

When using this method, you should report the possible error sources in your discussion of results. You might particularly want to do this collaboratively, by asking your respondents their own views about how typical they are and about the assumptions they are making in talking to you.

Quota sampling

Quota sampling involves a choice of respondents, who represent the diversity in the population, in the same proportions as the diversity itself. You need to know what this diversity looks like before you start; you then continue to select people into subgroups as they become available to you until the quota is achieved.

ILLUSTRATION 8.2   Take Alan Berger as an example. Alan works for a local authority in which 20 per cent of the managers have a prior job history in the private-sector and feels that this is relevant to a study of the decision to privatize cleansing department services being made in the local authority. He decides to represent this diversity by ensuring that the sample he talked to consisted of people from a private sector background and a public sector background in the same proportions, 20 per cent and 80 per cent respectively.

Alternatively, if you cannot achieve quite the quota required and your sample is large enough, then provided your questions gave answers in a quantitative form, you could choose people in equal proportions and apply a weight to the results within each subgroup to reflect the population proportion. This can get complicated, though and you may want to refer to Churchill (1998) for an overview of further particulars.

The main drawback with this method is that, while it splits the sample into subgroups to reflect diversity in the proportion in which it occurs in the population, it does not give each person in the population an equal chance of being selected into the sample. You simply bring each person into one or other subgroup until you have the total number of people required by that subgroup, and the people you didn't get round to have no chance of being included. This might distort your conclusions due to an uncontrolled or unrealized influence.

ILLUSTRATION 8.3

For instance, suppose Alan Berger were to bring in respondents on the basis of availability, by working from the more junior managers upwards until his quotas were achieved. But a person's position in a bureaucracy is likely to be related to age, so the people old enough to have had private sector experience would be more likely to be in more senior positions. So you might find yourself introducing a bias due to seniority and age into the 'private-sector-experienced' group without realizing it.

Non-probability sampling methods have the advantage of flexibility and are particularly useful in the first familiarization cycle through the issues under investigation. They afford a better opportunity for collaboration with your respondents than probability methods and allow great scope for inference and judgement in interpreting results. You can find a useful presentation of additional forms of non-probability sampling and an excellent discussion relating particularly to small samples, in Miles and Huberman (1994) or Robson (2002).

Probability sampling methods

All of these involve a deliberate and explicit selection of respondents into the sample from the population, made in advance of your data-gathering. The essential thing here is to choose sample members at random, so that each population member has an equal chance of being selected and so that the particular combination of people whom you select into the sample is no more or no less likely to have been chosen than any other combination. The mechanics of the process are straightforward, and are shown in Table 8.2; this procedure lies at the heart of each of the following probability sampling methods.

Simple random sampling

This involves a straightforward sampling frame of all the people in your population (whether this is an industry and organization, or department), not classified in any other way. You will be generalizing the results from your sample onto this population and not beyond it; so, for example, if you decide that you are interested in an issue in which the department is the population and if you draw your sample within this departmental frame, you can't subsequently generalize any direct conclusions about how people outside the department would have answered your questions. Of course, this isn't a problem: if you know in advance that you want to generalize beyond the department to the organisation, make the organisation your population and sample within that. If you seek to apply your findings to a whole industry, make that your population; and so on.

The disadvantage with this arrangement is that you lump everyone in the sample together, without making any further distinctions. If that is what you want, that's fine. Suppose, however, that you are interested in generalizing findings to subgroups of the population as well as to the whole – for example, to see whether males answered systematically differently to females; salaried employees as opposed to wage-earners; managers in production as opposed to managers in marketing, in a study of both functions.

Stratified random sampling

If so, then draw a stratified sample. Divide the population into subgroups on the factor in question, and keep the lists separate in your frame. Choose sub-samples at random, following the Table 8.2 procedure, within each separate list. The sum of each of the sub-samples gives you your total sample size. Table 8.3 shows you some different case examples of stratification.

TABLE 8.2 A procedure for drawing a random sample

- Decide on your sample size in advance. Refer to Ghauri and Gronhaug (2002: 117–119) if you want to compute an optimal figure.
- Take the sampling frame (at its simplest, a list of the population), and number each person; note whether the highest number has one digit (a population no larger than nine people!), two digits (maximum 99 people), or three digits (maximum 999).
- Obtain a set of random number tables (these are published separately, e.g. Murdoch and Barnes (1998) and are reproduced as an appendix in many statistics textbooks); ignore the fact that the numbers are printed in blocks across the page.
- Stick a pin at random into the tables, then move systematically up, down, or across the columns of numbers: focus on every single digit, or every pair of digits, or every triplet of digits, depending on your population size.
- When this is the same as a number you allocated to a person in the sampling frame, choose that person for your sample.
- Continue; if you come across the same number again in the random number table, ignore it and go on to the next.
- Stop when you have the sample size that you want.

As you can see as you work through the table, it is procedurally important to keep track of the number of people in each subgroup. This is especially so if your design is more ambitious and you are stratifying in more than one way: for example, if you want to contrast the responses of line managers as opposed to

TABLE 8.3 Alternative levels of stratification: different cases

A In a study of an entire company, you decide that the company is the population.
Total number of employees (let's say) is 1000; this is your **population**. If you choose 40 per cent of the employees at random to be your **sample**, you end up with 400 people, whose responses you are prepared to generalize directly to all 1000.
This is an unstratified random sample.

B If in the same study, you wanted to focus **only** on the salaried staff (of whom there are 300) and ignore the 700 wage-earners.
Total number of salaried employees is 300 people, this is your **population**. If you were to choose 40 per cent of these at random, you'd have a **sample** of 120 people.
Note, you can **only** generalize to the other 180 salaried employees, and not to the 700 wage-earners. It is still an unstratified random sample, but the population is different to Case A above.

C You're back with the population of Case A, and decide to stratify all 1000 employees on the basis of their salary status, choosing 40 per cent of each group, and drawing at random within each group. The 1000 are your **population**.

Sampling frame summary	Population	Sample
Salaried employees	300 × 40%	= 120, the first sub-sample
Wage-earners	700 × 40%	− 280, the second sub-sample
Total	1000	400, the total sample

The 400 people are now a random sample stratified by salary status.

D You decide to stratify on the basis of a second factor, sex of employee, taking 40 per cent of each subgroup to provide your subsamples. The 1000 are still your population.

Sampling frame summary	Population			Sample		
	Male	Female	Total	Male	Female	Total
Salaried Employees	270	30	300	108	12	120
Wage-earners	350	350	700	140	140	280
Total	620	380	1000	248	152	400

You have sampled at random within each subgroup of the sampling frame summary, taking 40 per cent of each subgroup. The 400 people are now a random sample stratified by salary status and by sex. Note how the subgroups add up, as they should, to the appropriate stratum totals shown in Case C. Note also that the 12 female salaried staff subsample is as representative of all the female salaried staff as the 108 male salaried staff subsample is of all the male salaried staff. The fact that there are fewer of them is a property of the population (the regrettable situation in which there are fewer females than males in managerial/ professional positions) than of the sampling technique.

managers in specialist functions (a first stratification), and within this, males as opposed to females (second stratification).

Stratified random sampling is the most powerful means of generalizing findings based on samples to populations; its disadvantages are ones of sheer practicality. It can be very time-consuming to draw up lists of large numbers of employees, while travelling costs to scattered locations, if it's that sort of project, can be prohibitive. (Remember, you are choosing truly at random from the population, so combinations of locations separated by large distances are as likely to occur as combinations next door to each other.)

Cluster sampling

Sometimes called 'multistage sampling', cluster sampling addresses these kinds of issues. Instead of sampling from within each subgroup on a particular stratum, a subset of subgroups is chosen at random and the others are ignored. This subset becomes the sample; additionally, if the numbers of people involved are still too large with respect to the intended sample size, simple random sampling is done within each of the subsets.

This is the most common form of probability sampling. There are technical disadvantages concerned with the efficiency with which your sample data give you information about the population characteristics when cluster sampling is compared with stratified random sampling, but I would imagine that these factors are likely to be less important to the validity of a management project than the various issues and constraints I reviewed in Section 5.2.

A final thought: the census

In conclusion, it is worth remembering that sometimes, topics can be handled well by putting your questions to everyone in the population; in other words, by conducting a **census**. Some topics in the small business sector, or case studies in small sectors such as private healthcare, can fall under this heading: especially if you are carrying out a cross-sectoral, generic industry project. In this situation, you are covering the entire population rather than sampling, and again, while validity is a matter of appropriate technique in asking your questions, generalizability beyond the boundaries of your organization or department is a matter for logical inference and reasoning, where the scope of your project involves comparisons with other kinds of organization or sectors. A census has one powerful advantage if you are taking a quantitative approach. Your statistical reporting does not need to test whether your results are due to sampling error, the results of the analysis (averages and differences between sub-samples in particular) being immediately meaningful.

 This is a good point at which to pause and tackle activities 2 and 3 in the Project Guide.

8.3 The practicalities of design

As you can see, one of the most important design aspects of your empirical work concerns the decision you make on which is your population, which is your sample of that population and which other populations are involved in the thesis you wish to establish. These decisions depend very much on your precise topic, argument, and thesis and you will want to consider involving other people in discussing your design with this in mind: certainly your sponsor, and probably your tutor. Moreover, if you have accepted my comments on project work as a collaborative endeavour (the interpretivist view expressed in Section 5.2) then you will want to involve the people you'll be surveying – the people in the population concerned – in these design decisions.

Whichever approach you take, you are likely to encounter the following practical questions.

Sample size

How many people should you have in your sample? The answer to this question varies depending on the kind of question which you want to ask and the form of sampling you adopt. In the case of accidental sampling, the pressures of the situation result in a total 'by default'; if you intend to work with a purposive sample, the sample size will be determined by your feeling that you have approached all the relevant people, a feeling reinforced by the advice you are given by your tutor and sponsor (and, in the case of snowball sampling, a feeling tempered by the advice of your respondents). If you are using one of the probability sampling methods, then it is possible to determine the sample size statistically, bearing in mind the proportion of the population to sample in order to achieve a given level of accuracy; you can find a good introduction in Ghauri and Gronhaug (2002: 117–119) and a more detailed account in Hemry (1990).

Reading these you will discover that you need to know quite a lot about the population before you can calculate the required sample size (including an estimate of the proportion of the population which has the attribute or attributes about which you want to ask questions). Moreover, in practice the accuracy of your results will depend much more on the variety of different groups and subgroups in your population and how much time and effort you can afford to spend, rather than on sheer size. So, as a start, look at what, say, 10 per cent of your population would look like. If there are only ten people in the population, the resulting single respondent is unlikely to be representative of the ten whatever sampling method you adopt and you would of course conduct a census. At the other extreme, if the population is 1000, then you could proceed. However, this does depend on people's reasons for not responding, and what inferences it is feasible for you to draw will depend on your design. For example, if you are dealing with issues which incline you to stratify your sample in several different ways (by level in the organization and by type of job, say), you may well discover that there are few, or indeed no, people in some of the combinations of level and job type in which you are inter-ested, even in organizations with relatively large numbers of employees!

The simplest way round this problem is to collapse categories in one or more of your strata. (Instead of working with six job levels and ten different types of job, in other words, find a rationale in which it makes sense to classify job levels into three rather than six, and job types into four rather than ten, for example.) Alternatives might be to ignore categories with small numbers of people, combining them into a single, 'Other' category on the stratum in question; to cluster-sample from only those categories which have large numbers of people; or indeed to eschew probability sampling altogether and to use quota sampling or purposive sampling approaches instead. You will find a good discussion of some of these alternatives, with an excellent illustrative case study, in Reeves and Harper (1981a). Notice, though, that the inferences that you can draw from your data – the information you can extract – will be subtly different, depending on the actual alternative you choose.

Response and non-response

'What do I do if I planned to see 25 per cent of the sales staff and only 10 per cent had time to respond: won't this bias my comparison with the 25 per cent of the technical staff I planned for, all of whom provided me with data?' In a word, 'yes'. But, depending on how you are asking your questions, there are three ways round the problem.

- In a stratified random sample in which your data consist of numbers and percentages, it might be possible to weight your results in making comparisons between disproportionately responding groups, as mentioned previously.

- As you will see in Chapter 11, if you are using postal questionnaires or planned interview schedules, these should always involve a chase-up stage, in which you ask people again for their help. This works, though never completely and only if you've planned the time to do so!

- Alternatively, if your population is large enough, it is good practice to have a reserve sample, chosen in the same way as your main sample, from which you can randomly substitute people to approach.

It also depends on the kinds of questions you are asking. Other factors, such as acceptability to management, costs of implementation, the existence of powerful influence groups, or sheer practicality, may have a greater bearing on the chances of your conclusions being accepted as sensible than minor variations in sampling accuracy.

In all cases, you must keep track of the **response rate**: the number of people who returned your questionnaires or agreed to be interviewed, as a proportion of the intended sample size, bearing in mind the size of the population as a whole. This is especially important if your sample is stratified and there are differing numbers of people in each stratum. Table 8.4 provides you with an example; you'll notice that it develops example D of Table 8.3, and the totals agree: as they should!

A table of this kind should be part of any dissertation since it does three important things. It:

a summarizes the sampling frame, i.e. informs your reader of how large the population is and what proportion you intended to sample

b gives an indication of how successful you were

c enables you to interpret the results you receive in terms of any biases arising because different types of respondent were unevenly represented in your final group of respondents.

So, if you glance at the figure, you will see that the reasonably good return rate of 54 per cent was achieved overall, and this was comparable for males and females taken separately. This is heartening; Baruch (1999) reviewed 175 questionnaire-based studies reported in five major journals and found that a return rate of 60 per cent +/− 20 is typical of the well-designed study where respondents are not top managers; a return rate of 36 per cent +/− 13 is characteristic in the latter case. It seems as though very senior managers have less time or interest to spare. Return rates, incidentally, are also lower in commercial surveys; Baruch (1999: 422) reports figures in the range between 10 per cent and 20 per cent for marketing surveys, for example.

There is much that you can do to increase the response rate, and a list of practical suggestions is given towards the end of Section 11.1 in discussing postal questionnaire return rates.

Often, though, what is more important than the overall response rate is the rate for key subgroups of your sample, especially if your design involves several layers of stratification. Where rates vary substantially between subgroups, you need to be careful of the inferences you can draw. Glance again at Table 8.4: all of the very small number of salaried females replied, compared with only half of the salaried males. In this population, there is something about being a salaried employee that makes one more likely to be interested enough to respond; and this may, or may not, be the same factor that is responsible for the 100 per cent response rate for the salaried females. Whether this is a significant factor, or some sort of bias, depends on the question being asked and the issues being investigated; but, unless you have

TABLE 8.4 Sampling frame summary and returns received

	Males			Females			Total		
	Sample	Return	%	Sample	Return	%	Sample	Return	%
Salaried Employees	108	64	59	12	12	100	120	76	63
Wage-earners	140	69	49	140	70	50	280	139	50
Total	248	133	54	152	82	54	400	215	54

Note: the figures represent, respectively, the sample size you aimed for; the number of returns; and the returns as a percentage of the sample aimed for.

a table of this kind, for each major issue you are investigating, you won't be able to pick up all the nuances that have an effect on the accuracy of your conclusions. This kind of analysis of returns received might also trigger ideas for your subsequent data analysis; in this case, that there might possibly be an interaction between sex of respondent and salary status, and it could be worth looking for this interaction in the answers to the particular questions posed.

Interpreting your data must *always* be a matter of presenting and discussing the possible sources of error, as well as the more direct inferences and conclusions which the data suggest. If you look ahead to the discussion of project presentation in Chapter 13, you will notice that so many of the errors of reasoning which merit divine retribution are those in which error sources have been ignored; and this does seem to be a particular problem at undergraduate level and especially when considering sampling errors in particular.

While this sort of mistake is less common at Masters level, you are liable to make others, arising from the sheer complexity of what you're doing. Consider: you are working with more than one issue; it's conceivable that you will have to ask different kinds of questions with different kinds of people for each separate issue, so that, in effect, you may find yourself handling several different populations as you apply several different methods and techniques (a survey; a number of case studies; a set of key informant interviews) to address all the issues. Sorting out which are your populations, which are your samples, and which are the outside groups to which you want to generalize will need a clear head in the first place; and keeping track of different sources of error, arising from variations in return rate, will require discipline in reporting in the second.

Combining sampling methods

'I know what I need to do; but none of the schemes which you describe seems to fit my situation. Ideally, I need to do a mixture of all of them.' Fine, and why not? If you are clear enough about your situation to be able to recognize that, then only a little further thought will suggest the particular combination of methods to adopt.

Some common combinations are as follows:

■ Accidental sampling as you become aware of issues to explore, followed by a systematic slice through the organization to investigate the issues in detail.

■ Purposive sampling (especially key informant technique to help you to identify issues), followed by a quota sample of people who may have systematically different views or perspectives on the issues.

■ A key informant sample to identify issues, with a horizontal slice of relevant managers and perhaps a stratified random sample of their subordinates categorized into departmental subgroups.

■ Some form of purposive sample, followed by a stratified random sample of employees categorized into managerial versus operative subgroups: this is a common pattern for many undergraduate, questionnaire-based survey projects.

■ Selltiz *et al.* (1981) suggest one more. Cluster sampling (e.g. to select particular departments) with the advantages of representativeness that this brings, followed by a quota sample (e.g. within each department, stratified by role or position on issues of interest) with the advantages of economy of effort which quota sampling permits.

You might like to read their discussion on this theme, of combining probability and non-probability samples. There is also a good discussion of some of the factors to bear in mind when designing empirical work with managers, in Reeves and Harper (1981b).

Finally, as mentioned earlier, there is one special situation when, in order to be representative, you do not sample within a population at all; instead, you replicate positions along one or more issues or variables. This is when you use the comparative case study method, and the details are given in Section 9.2.

8.4   In conclusion: timetabling for empirical work

This chapter started with a reminder of the complexities involved in the management world you are exploring, and a reassurance that this complexity can be simplified provided you adopt a straightforward approach to the planning of your empirical work. Once you have decided on a design, and chosen the methods and techniques which you will use (see Chapter 9 and the remainder), all that's left to do is to prepare a data-gathering timetable and to stick to it.

If you have followed the guidelines outlined in Section 4.2, and carried out the activity described in the Project Guide for Chapter 4, you will already have an outline timetable for your project, and a Gantt chart, or at the very least a list of dates and deadlines recorded in your diary. As time goes on you will be able to flesh out this outline, bearing in mind the need to spread your attention evenly over the major issues you identify during the time that will be available to you. As you begin your data collection, you will identify further questions to ask and issues to explore; you will also want to go over familiar territory in more detail, as I suggested in Section 5.3. These will be unpredictable at the outset, so be prepared to amend the timetable from time to time.

How can you plan for the unpredictable? It helps if you can think of the empirical phase of your project work as progressing through four stages: preliminary analysis (often known as the 'pilot stage'), main analysis, synthesis, and implementation, for each main issue which you are addressing. Table 8.5 shows what is involved at each stage, and reveals that the process is periodic: within your work on each major issue, there are stages where your attention expands as you explore all the ramifications in question; and there are times where your attention contracts, as you summarize what you have learnt and pause to take breath before tackling the next stage involved. Martin and Spear (1985), who are the source of this table, point out that you should always plan to 'stop the expansion just before it gets too big to handle', and that you shouldn't expand your attention again until 'you feel you have your information well under control'. The preliminary analysis is the stage at which you think carefully about matters of design; the main analysis, where you put the design into effect.

It is likely that the project work of in-company based students will involve them in empirical work on several major issues, so that the process described in Table 8.5 is cyclic as well as periodic. That is, you will be repeating all the stages of Table 8.5 once for each of the major issues you address. It is very likely, as I mentioned at the start of this chapter, that you will find yourself working on different issues at the same time, being at different stages with each. This usually happens because you are waiting for people relevant to an issue to become available to talk to you, waiting on questionnaire returns, and the like. Keep track of where you've got to in your diary!

Undergraduates are more likely to have taken on a project in which there is only one main issue under investigation, and so they are more likely to go through the cycle just once.

TABLE 8.5	Expansion and contraction phases involved in project work	
Preliminary analysis (pilot stage)	Opening up the issue Looking at associated issues Identifying stakeholders Testing other questions to ask	Expansion
Main analysis	Following up leads Collecting data Searching for alternative viewpoints	Expansion
	Selecting key aspects Summarizing findings Relating them to what's already known	Contraction
Synthesis	Generating alternative courses of action	Expansion
	Selecting the best next step	Contraction
Implementation	Contacting people involved in the next step Examining alternative time schedules	Expansion
	Selecting a particular plan for the next step Taking the next step	Contraction
Choice	Completion of empirical stage, or Addressing next major issue: back to	Contraction
Preliminary analysis	Above	Expansion

After Martin and Spear (1985)

★ Finally, please address activity 4 in the Project Guide.

'Come in, Andreas, pour yourself a tea, that's right. Make yourself comfortable.' Sergeant Andreas MacSean opens the ring binder he's using as a research diary, shifts his biro over to his left hand, and sips at his tea. 'Now.' says the Chief Superintendent. 'You asked to see me about your project.'

'That's right, Sir.' Andreas is taking an undergraduate degree at one of Ireland's technological universities, attending on a part time basis for four nights a week over four years. He is speaking to the Director of the Garda Staff College at Templemore, where he works as a training instructor. The Director is being supportive; he is pleased with Andreas, sees him as a hard-working young man, and views the final year project as an opportunity to conduct some worthwhile research that would be generally useful within the police force, while satisfying Andreas' degree requirements.

'I thought I might look at job satisfaction among the sergeants. You were talking about it just the other day, and I know that AGSI are interested in it as well.'

'Now that *is* a good idea,' says the Chief Superintendent. 'Can you tell me a bit about what it would involve?'

'Well, Sir. It would take me about nine months from start to finish. That's to cover the 1700 sergeants overall – about a thousand uniformed, 300 detective sergeants, and another 400 clerical and admin. What we know about their views on pay and conditions, resourcing, and team spirit in the stations is very unsystematic; it's really just what we hear from the inspectors and superintendents who come here on courses, and they're not really the best source of information about what the sergeants are thinking. Let's ask them all, and find out.'

'Ah, now, I'm not sure we can afford to ask everybody. But if you approached, say, one in every four of them, would that be enough to keep your tutor happy?'

'I'll check, Sir, but that seems about right. I wonder if you could help me with a letter of support to go out with the questionnaire?'

'Yes, I can do that,' replies the Chief. 'I'd better have a word with the training department in Dublin, as well, and clear the way for you to talk to them. I happen to know that they're concerned that things are different for a sergeant in the Dublin Metropolitan Area than it is in the rest of the country. I don't know that people's attitudes are that much different; there again, their jobs certainly are, so it might be. All right then, let's do it. Let me know what else you might need, and who you want to talk to. I can give you a small travel budget. Keep me informed, and we'll meet in a month's time and review progress. Oh, and Andreas – go easy on the pay aspects. There's not a lot the Garda can do about that issue, you know! It's all up to the politicians in the Dail.'

Andreas has the opportunity to conduct a causal study as well as a simple exploratory one. In the exploratory phase, he decides on a simple information-gathering design, to identify what the issues are. He knows from his studies that employee attitudes concern pay and working conditions in particular; and from his own service, that resourcing issues can be problematic. Once a Section Sergeant (a senior sergeant in charge of a shift) in Co. Mayo before his present posting, he knows that how the sergeants and officers on all the shifts in a station get on with each other is very important too. But what else matters to people? He decides to interview a half-dozen sergeants to be sure he is aware of all the issues before committing himself to a questionnaire to over 400 people!

You might like to help Andreas think through the research design and sampling required for the causal phase of his research.

a What kind of design is appropriate to the situation?

b What kind of sampling is appropriate?

c Bearing in mind that he can only afford to approach one in every four of the country's sergeants, draw up a sampling frame summary to match this design (a table like section D of

CASE EXAMPLE 8.1   Design and sampling (cont.)

Table 8.3). Assume that there are twice as many uniformed sergeants in the country districts as there are in the Dublin Metropolitan Area (DMA); that the reverse is the case for detective sergeants; and that the numbers of clerical and admin sergeants are equal in both country and DMA. Round the numbers up or down as necessary, and show the population and sample in two different parts of the table, as in Table 8.3 part D.

d How can Andreas draw the samples?

Answers to Case Example 8.1

a Andreas has mentioned three different kinds of sergeant, while the Chief Superintendent has noted that the views of the DMA and country sergeants may differ. It looks as though the nature of the sergeant's job, and his or her location, may make for a difference in attitudes. The obvious causal design to use is a stratified survey.

b Stratified random sampling is the appropriate form with only three types of sergeant. There are

actually many more kinds of sergeant in An Garda Siochana, the Irish police force, if the various admin and clerical types are spelled out in detail: up to 14 different categories. Working with this longer list, Andreas could consider cluster sampling to simplify the detail.

c Identify the number of cells your table will require. The 'nature of the job' stratum will have three levels (uniformed, detective, clerical and admin) and the 'location' stratum will have two levels (DMA and Country), making a two-way table with 3 × 2 = 6 cells in all. You have sufficient information in the case example to make up a table that looks like the following; (it will differ by one or two people here and there depending on which cells you rounded up). Put in the column and row totals first.

d Often tedious and problematic, devising a sampling frame and drawing the random sample is simple in this case. Andreas approaches the personnel department and asks for a list of all the sergeants in the country. He can then use the procedures described in Table 8.2 to draw the sample.

TABLE 8.6 Sampling frame summary for the Andreas MacSean case

	Population Nature of the job				Sample Nature of the job			
	Uniformed	Detective	Clerical/ Admin	Total	Uniformed	Detective	Clerical/ Admin	Total
Location								
DMA	334	200	200	734	83	50	50	183
Country	666	100	200	966	167	25	50	242
TOTAL	1000	300	400	1700	250	75	100	425

Based on data in Jankowicz and Walsh (1984) as originally reproduced by kind permission of An Garda Siochana.

Project Guide

By now, your project work will be well on its way, and it is difficult for me to indicate activities with very specific examples. You may have to modify the following activities to suit your particular circumstances. However, you should still be in a position to carry them out, amended or otherwise, if you are to complete your project successfully and deliver your dissertation on time. The last activity acts as a self-diagnostic check on just this matter.

1 Begin working on your research design

a If a positivist approach is sensible, write down your research question in your diary. Below it, list five hypotheses which might relate to it. For each hypothesis, try and identify the variables involved.

Or, alternatively:

b If an interpretivist approach is more useful, make a note of the key issues that your research question and your personal thesis suggest may be relevant.

In either case:

c State the research design which would best address the hypotheses or issues. You may find that a single design will address all of them, or that you need more than one.

You will find that you cannot complete this activity in detail until you have considered the research method and techniques which are available to you; but you will be coming back to this matter in the Chapter 9 Project Guide. For the moment, please try make a first approximation.

2 Begin thinking about methods and techniques

a Turn the pages of the remaining chapters of this book. Just that, skim-read it, to get an impression of the range of techniques available to you. Look particularly carefully at Section 9.2.

b Make an initial, very broad choice. Will you be more likely to carry out your research using the explicatory methods, case study method, survey method, or a found experiment?

(Again, you will be returning to this matter after completing Chapter 9.)

3 Begin thinking about your sampling

For the moment, just identify the population(s) with which you will be dealing:

a If your project is in-company based or a generic industry study, and depending on your answers to activities 1b) and 1c) above, ask yourself how many populations you are dealing with. This is quite simple:

- will you be asking all your questions of the same group of people; or

- will each different set of variables, or issues, require different respondents?

Another way of putting this is to ask yourself which people you will wish to generalize your findings to: just one group (e.g. 'all the companies in this sector'); or several (e.g. 'all the companies in this sector'; and 'all the companies which supply them').

b If your project is a library-based one, it is likely that you won't be asking empirical questions of a lot of people, though you might need to interview just one or two people about the information you obtain, collate, and build into an argument by means of library-based desk research.

- what sort of people are likely to be involved?

4 Check that you're on schedule

a Find the research proposal you prepared as activity 5 in Chapter 2, and the Gantt chart you prepared as activity 2 in Chapter 4 (a copy might be in your research diary!).

b How far have you got? Congratulations if you're on schedule or, indeed, if you're ahead of yourself!

c If you've fallen behind, how serious is the situation? Resolving it might call for a word with your sponsor at work, or with your tutor in the university. Are you likely to need to reschedule your job responsibilities, or arrange for a different pattern of involvement in your other academic subjects; or just a more disciplined personal approach? Could you, conceivably, require an extension on submission of your dissertation from your tutor? Don't worry about any of these things, but do take some constructive action.

References

Baruch, Y. (1999) 'Response rates in academic studies: a comparative analysis', *Human Relations*, 54: 4: 421–438.

Churchill, G. A. (1998) *Marketing Research: Methodological Foundations*, London: Thomson Learning.

Ghauri, P. and Gronhaug, K. (2002) *Research Methods in Business Studies*, Harlow: Pearson Education.

Hemry, G. T. (1990) *Practical Sampling*, London: Sage.

Jankowicz, A. D. and Walsh, P. (1984) 'Researching the Sergeant's role', *Garda News* 3: 8: 6–13.

Martin, J. and Spear, R., (eds.) (1985) *Project Manual, Block VI of Technology, a Third Level Course*, Milton Keynes: Open University Press.

Miles, M. B. and Huberman, A. M. (1994) *Qualitative Data Analysis: an Expanded Sourcebook*, London: Sage.

Murdoch, J. and Barnes, J. A. (1998) *Statistical Tables for Science, Engineering, Business, Management and Finance*, London: Palgrave Macmillan, 2nd edn.

Parlett, M. (1981) 'Illuminative evaluation', in Reason, P. and Rowan, J., (eds.) *Human Inquiry: a Sourcebook of New Paradigm Research*, Chichester: John Wiley & Sons.

Reeves, T. K. and Harper, D. (1981a) *Surveys at Work: Student Project Manual*, London: McGraw-Hill.

Reeves, T. K. and Harper, D. (1981b) *Surveys at Work: a Practitioner's Guide*, London: McGraw-Hill.

Robson, C. (2002) *Real World Research: a Resource for Social Scientists and Practitioner-Researchers*, Oxford: Blackwell.

Selltiz, C. S., Wrightsman, L. S. and Cook, S. W. (1981) *Research Methods in Social Relations*, London: Holt, Rinehart & Winston.

Tremblay, M. A. (1982) 'The key informant technique: a non-ethnographic application', in Burgess, R., (ed.) *Field Research: a Sourcebook and Field Manual*, London: Allen and Unwin.

Methods and techniques

- To review the main research methods available in management and business project work, assisting you in choosing one which is appropriate to your topic and research design
- To provide an overview of the techniques available to you, using a standard framework
- To help you finalize your approach to representation and generalization in the light of the research method you have chosen
- To help you to complete your plan for empirical work, summarizing it by amending your project proposal
- To present the rationale for a short pilot study, helping you to execute it

At a glance

People often select their research activities somewhat casually, underestimating the technical requirements and the time required. An interview, for example, is just a conversation with a purpose: and we all conduct conversations every day, don't we? A questionnaire is just a list of questions to which we want answers: what could be simpler than that? My purpose in this chapter is to provide you with a set of guidelines by which to approach the methods and techniques which you will be using, and to help you to match them to your sampling and design requirements, following the plan outlined in Figure 8.1.

First, I clarify some terms, particularly those two words, 'method' and 'technique', and explore the distinction between qualitative and quantitative techniques of analysis. Second, the methods are described in some detail, together with an outline of the circumstances in which you would be likely to choose one of them rather than another. As we saw in Section 8.2, which method you work with will determine your approach to representation and generalization, and this is issue is developed when material on the Case Study method is presented.

Regardless of the method or techniques which you will be using, there is a standard set of issues and activities which pertain. These are presented in the form of a framework of general guidelines to apply whenever you are use a particular research technique – a framework which I shall use to organize the detailed material on individual techniques when these are presented in Chapters 10 and 11.

In conclusion, material is presented which pulls all the foregoing together. You are asked to update the research proposal which you began in Chapter 2 and developed in Chapter 5, and to make an initial test of your plans for empirical work by conducting a small pilot study.

9.1 Methods and techniques: some definitions

You may have noticed in your earlier reading that these two terms are often used interchangeably. This sometimes leads to confusion, particularly in discussions of qualitative versus quantitative approaches. Some basic definitions are in order.

Research methods

In our context, a **method** is a systematic and orderly approach taken towards the collection and analysis of data so that information can be obtained from those data. There is a difference between the two, as you will recall from Section 7.4. Data are raw, specific, undigested and therefore largely meaningless; information, in contrast, is what you get when data have been arranged in such a way that uncertainty is lessened, queries resolved, and questions answered. Everything you do in your empirical work should be directed to the one end of gathering and presenting data from which information can be easily and simply derived.

Several different methods are commonly used in business and management project work and your choice would vary according to the nature and scope of your topic and thesis, the sources of data you are using, the purposes you have in gathering data, the amount of control you are prepared to exert in obtaining these data and the assumptions make when you analyze them. The main methods available to you are:

- *Explicatory method:* in which you direct your questions at people and at written sources, concerning issues and events in the past in order to understand the present and predict the future, making judgements about the data using historical review, drawing conclusions based on the themes you recognize in interview and observational material by means of ethnographic technique or a variety of biographical analysis techniques.

- *Case-study method:* in which you use a variety of techniques in the workplace setting to explore issues in the present and in the past; as they affect a relatively complete organizational unit (single case study) or group of organizational units (comparative case study); which represent different possibilities or stances for the organization concerned; and in which you look to the future by means of the recommendations you make.

■ *Survey method:* in which you direct your questions at relatively large groups of people who represent some larger population, in order to explore issues largely in the present.

■ *Experimental method:* by means of a found or field experiment, in which you identify the relative importance of one or more variables in situations (and these are limited in business project work: see Chapter 5!), where a focus on variables rather than issues makes sense.

At first glance, it might appear that the first pair of these methods lend themselves more to qualitative, and the second pair to quantitative, analysis; one thinks of biographical and ethnographic accounts in the first case, or tables of questionnaire results or of the values taken by variables in the latter. This is misleading and, as we saw in Section 5.3, there are times when one wishes that the qualitative-quantitative distinction weren't so prevalent. An increasing number of people have pointed out (see e.g. Jankowicz 2003a; Stevenson and Cooper 1997) that the kind of analysis of data pertaining to these four kinds of method depends less on meanings versus counting and more on one's ontology and epistemology. It is possible to take a 'quasi-experimental' approach to archived data in order to examine the relative importance of different variables; or a 'quasi-judicial' approach to survey data, in which the researcher makes judgements in categorizing meanings. Robson (2002) states this argument very well.

What matters is the *rigour* with which the method is used (an argument for the occasional borrowing of analysis techniques from methods usually associated with positivist thinking when one is using explicatory method or case study method, provided the borrowing retains relevance), while addressing the meanings which your respondents ascribe to the issues you are researching (an argument for retaining constructivist values when using survey and experimental method). Numbers, the product of quantitative approaches, may or may not be relevant; understanding the respondents' intended meaning, the jewel of the qualitative approach, is always paramount.

Research techniques

Techniques, in contrast to methods, are particular, step-by-step procedures which you can follow in order to gather data, and analyze them for the information they contain. As Bennett (1986) suggests, they tell you *how* to do something rather than *what* you are doing, or *why* you are doing it. There are many techniques relevant in project work. In the remaining chapters I have grouped the most relevant under the following headings:

■ *Semi-structured, open-ended techniques*: the conversation, the individual interview, the key informant interview, and the focus group.

■ *Fully structured techniques:* the structured questionnaire, and the structured face-to-face interview, together with material on Internet, postal and telephone variants.

■ *Additional techniques:* the repertory grid, attitude scaling, and the observational techniques of structured observation and the field experiment.

As with methods, so with techniques: what is important is that you don't regard the more structured techniques as better or in some way more 'scientific' simply because they lend themselves to quantitative analysis, or because many studies go from the qualitative to the quantitative as understanding progresses. As you will recall from Chapter 5, everything depends on the level of understanding which is possible in the management environment, and structure and quantification are, in themselves, no guarantee of freedom from error. In dealing with unstructured, conversational interview technique, for example, Mishler (1991) makes the same point when he says:

'Alternatives to the standard approach, like unstructured interviewing, tend to be viewed as faulted variants . . . I am arguing, instead, that the standard survey interview is itself essentially faulted and that it therefore cannot serve as the ideal ideological model against which to assess other approaches.'

Academic rigour

'All very well', you might say, 'but what am I expected to do when I set out to do my empirical work? The answer is quite simple, and is in three parts:

■ choose a method which suits the research question

■ use one or more appropriate techniques in order to identify the meanings which your respondents convey to you in their utterances and their behaviour

■ analyze your data to identify these meanings in a rigorous way.

The definition given above, and the material in Section 9.2, will enable you to address the first two of these matters (with Chapters 10 to 12 providing an account of techniques of data collection and analysis in depth); it remains to specify what 'rigour' involves. Table 9.1 provides the basic specification.

Neither approach is best in itself. Use the method that is most appropriate to the kinds of questions you wish to ask at the time, in the sort of environment and with the sort of research question which you have adopted. As I argued in Section 5.2, that environment usually requires that you make constructivist assumptions about what counts as data and what counts as evidence This suggests that, regardless of whether your analysis is qualitative or quantitative; whether you work with the top or the bottom half of Table 9.1 as it were, you should remember the following:

a You should set out to identify meanings from your respondents' point of view, regardless of whether you think in terms of issues or variables. Your understanding is ontologically no better or worse than theirs. When you collect your data, do you provide your respondents with a good opportunity to enlighten you? Their views will reflect their stance and the data available to them and so, if you're being rigorous, you need to cover and understand all the possible stances, stake-holdings and constraints acting on them, rather than just a subset. Are all the relevant issues or variables covered?

b You need to monitor the extent to which the explanation which you arrive at makes sense to your respondents. Research is collaborative, as I argued earlier, and it is usually simple to ask them! Does their answer to this question add anything to your understanding? Does it, even if 'misguided' or 'erroneous' in

---

TABLE 9.1 Ensuring rigour

In the qualitative approach

1 Express each issue you wish to investigate as clearly as you can	A pilot study can be useful to identify the issues . . .
2 Familiarize yourself with the situation in depth: build a 'rich picture' of the meanings involved	. . . and in providing the depth required. Eat the data, sleep on the data, have dreams about the data
3 Identify themes, and potential explanations	Record the data as you go, and start analysis at an early stage: categorize, codify, look for trends and themes from the start
4 Use these explanations to search for additional evidence	See if your explanations further confirm or negate the themes you identified . . .
5 Consider alternative explanations	. . . if the original explanation doesn't fit the new data, altering the categories which you use to identify themes
6 Pay attention to the less obvious as well as the more obvious	As a way of enriching your understanding of themes, and of checking the generality of your explanations
7 Check the accuracy and consistency of your data	When you press your respondents, are their responses consistent with the data you previously obtained?
8 Check the reliability of your data	Does a different technique applied to the same respondents give the same results?
9 Cross-check your explanation	Does a new set of respondents who, according to your explanation, ought to think the same way actually respond similarly; what of those respondents whom you'd expect to think differently?

In the quantitative approach

1 Identify the variables involved and ignore those which you feel aren't	Either by means of a pilot study; or by identifying an existing model in the literature and mapping it onto your own situation
2 Measure the values taken by the variables	As accurately and reliably as you can, counting the number and the weight, or importance, of people's responses
3 Generalize from single observations	What is happening on average; over what range do values vary?
4 Examine the relative importance of the variables	What is more frequent and what is less? Are the values of different variables similar or different and is this significant or irrelevant?
5 Identify the relationship between the variables	As the values of one variable increase, what happens to the values on the others?
6 Identify the causal structure of the variables	If values of variable B change when the values of variable A change, and don't when the values of other variables change, it may be that A causes B

After Miles and Huberman (1994) and Robson (2002)

the light of your own more comprehensive account, sensibly and systematically reflect their own stance, stakeholding and constraints as you understand them? What is the degree of 'fit' between their answers and yours, and can you account for any mismatch? Your explanation and understanding are rigorous to the extent that yours can comprehend and account for theirs.

c   You should also monitor the extent to which your explanation matches other researchers' explanations and theories. Is it compatible? It doesn't have to be the same, so long as the similarities and differences are explicable. Can you describe, clearly and accurately, how your account fits in to the general body of knowledge on the topic of your research?

Given my assumption that the qualitative and quantitative distinction is less profound than the constructivist-positivist distinction (see Section 5.2), you won't be surprised to know that it is possible to combine qualitative and quantitative analysis techniques (see Jones 1988 for the argument in detail, and Siehl and Martin 1988 for an interesting case example taken from the study of organizational culture).

While considering definitions and usages, you might find it helpful to note the following in passing: a *datum is* the result of a single observation, while *data* are what you get when you repeat the observation or make several different observations. 'Data' is the plural of 'datum'; so it's incorrect to say, for example, 'my data has been arranged in tabular form'. In a similar vein, you might note that 'methodology' is not just a grand sounding substitute for 'methods'. **Methodology** is the analysis of, and rationale for, the particular method or methods used in a given study, and in that type of study in general. So, if your regulations require you to provide a section in your project labelled 'methodology', you are required to provide a rationale or argument for the approach you adopted to the data, and a simple description of the methods and techniques that constituted that approach would *not* be sufficient.

 Please pause at this point and, in the light of the foregoing, tackle activity 1 of the Project Guide.

9.2   Choosing and combining methods, qualitative and quantitative

Other than the general comments made in Section 8.1 on the matching of designs to methods, and the comments made in defining the different methods above, there is no straightforward decision rule which compels you to choose one method for one set of circumstances and another for another. As you can infer from the discussion, many different factors influence your choice. Moreover, you might find yourself using more than one method or technique, in combination, either because your design calls for it, or because you want to use the results from one method or technique to cross-check the results from another: an approach known as **triangulation**. The rationale for triangulation is expressed well by Kane, who represents archival techniques, questionnaires, interviews, and participant observation as potentially overlapping in scope:

> 'If you had to stake your life on which of these is likely to represent the most accurate, complete research information, you would choose the centre' (of the overlap) 'in which you got the information through interviews and questionnaire, reinforced it by observation, and checked it through documentary analysis . . . Here, you are getting not only what people say they do and what you see them doing, but also what they are recorded as doing.' (Kane 1985: 51)

The purpose of this section is to outline some of the advantages and disadvantages of each method, and to describe some common combinations, with a few words on the some specific techniques that are particularly helpful in, and associated with, each method, together with information on where to find a detailed account of the techniques mentioned here. Chapters 10 to 12 will then present other techniques, semi-structured, fully structured, and additional, which are not especially associated with any one method, in full detail.

Your best approach would be to treat the material on methods as a set of general suggestions and take advice whenever you are in doubt about which approach is most appropriate. The source should be your tutor or sponsor as usual. However, you should also look at written accounts of method and procedures which appear in the literature you have reviewed. I don't say this lightly. One of the reasons for reviewing other people's work in your field is to discover how they resolved problems of methods, techniques and design in investigating issues similar to your own. If in doubt, then, follow the current practice as written up in the journals and books which describe empirical work done in similar circumstances to your own.

However, always remember that you use more than one method or technique in order to triangulate or develop earlier findings; resist the temptation to take on too many different techniques simply because it sounds impressive in your initial proposal document, or on the contents page of your final project document.

Explicatory method

This is a group of methods which have a number of characteristics in common:

- They all focus on the personal and social meanings of phenomena as experienced by the people being studied.
- Their main contribution is made by drawing out the implications of those meanings for the group or organization being studied, and for organizations like them, extrapolating from the initial personal meaning or implication of those experiences.

Some, like the ethnographic method, are commonly, and in my mind wrongly, associated with the qualitative approach. However, it is possible to study meaning in quantitative ways, as in historical review and some forms of biographical analysis.

They have a further characteristic in common however. They share a stance towards the way in which findings are presented, in the form of a 'rich' or 'thick' description which combines three things: detail and accuracy of observation of events; participant comments on the events being observed; and participant comments on the researcher's questions about those events (Holliday 2002: 108). This description is in the form of a connected account, using tables, diagrams, and particularly, verbatim quotations to illustrate the argument the researcher is making. Chapters 5 and 6 of Miles and Huberman (1994) are a very good source of displays well suited to explicatory method, although they don't provide you with any information on one particularly useful technique, the *repertory grid*. The latter is described in Chapter 12 below, with fuller details in Jankowicz (2003b).

The explicatory account is not a simple description, and requires a critical appraisal of alternative and competing meanings taken from the events and issues explored. This can be demanding. On the one hand, you need to keep a certain distance from the material, to avoid imposing your own external perspectives on it; on the other, you should avoid the adoption of a privileged, all-knowing neutrality that would depersonalize the participants you are describing and over-intellectualize the events taking place. The answer to this dilemma, according to Holliday (2002: 176–177), is twofold: first, you need to stay close to the particular events and meanings involved rather than developing 'typical' composites for interpretive purposes. Second, you are encouraged to admit the presence of your own perspective as author of the final interpretations present in your account, as you explain how your review is relevant to the current issues which make up your topic at the start, and present the implications for current practice, throughout and in conclusion.

Ethnography

Probably the most well-known explicatory method, ethnography aims to describe the social experience of the groups being studied from their own point of view, presenting an account of what they notice as meaningful, in their own language and with their own emphasis and significance. The chief technique associated with ethnography is *participant observation*, as described in some detail in Section 12.2. In some situations this observation may need to be covert, although (Gill and Johnson 2002) suggest that the disadvantages of a covert stance (already discussed in Section 6.2 above, as a matter of research ethics) outweigh the advantages.

A rather more important issue methodologically is the extent to which the observations are direct or indirect, and the relative balance between the two. Most ethnographies are a mixture of *direct observation*, in which the researcher is present and participating when the events take place, and *indirect observation* (the literature on action learning technique being very relevant in the former case: see Weinstein 1998 for an overview and Marsick and O'Neil 1999 for a fuller review). Many management projects are dependent on timing. Either they must be completed in a much shorter time-span than an ethnographic account based solely on direct observation would require, or the key data are available at a time which does not suit the researcher, who cannot be there to observe them. In these circumstances, there is an important place for indirect observation techniques such as *unstructured and semi-structured interviews* with participants; and for the *analysis of internal documents* (correspondence, memos, e-mails and reports).

All of these techniques, and the basic approach adopted within ethnographic method, require you to place yourself into the same setting (mental as well as physical) as the people you are researching, entering it with as few preconceptions as possible. Now, like any investigator, you come to your project with a stock of prior ideas and concepts, both the specific ones which have led you to choose your research question as a valuable one to undertake, and the more general ones which characterize you as a particular human being. These prior beliefs are always with you and cannot be discarded!

However, in the ethnographic approach, you are strongly discouraged from undertaking a literature review on the research question and the related issues being studied, until *after* your main data-gathering is complete, and in this, ethnographic method differs radically from the other three methods described in Section 9.2. You are however encouraged to take an explicitly reflexive stance; reflexive in two senses. *Situational reflexivity* involves you in monitoring your own impact on the events being studied, while *epistemological reflexivity* involves you in a careful reflection on the assumptions you make as you interpret your observations. (See Gill and Johnson 2002, for more on this distinction.)

Within this whole interpretive context lie the issues and themes of importance to the organization as it is today and these can be uncovered using additional techniques of *hermeneutic interpretation*. Why has the organization which has made the data available presented them in just this way? **Hermeneutic technique**, which can be defined as the identification and interpretation of meanings expressed and embodied in a text by detailed study of the text-in-context, but is also used by ethnographers as a framework for identification and interpretation of the meanings expressed in behaviour, requires you to:

■ understand the meanings expressed in individual texts, objects or events

■ identify sub-themes

■ identify clusters of themes across texts or events

■ triangulate with other data, especially documentary

■ check validity and reliability through collaboration with other people

■ place the themes into their organizational context

■ sample key documents systematically, preparing a case report in conclusion.

ILLUSTRATION 9.1

Alma Benson was preparing her study of the impact of the General Motors factory closure on their local suppliers. Her undergraduate business studies degree regulations required the completion of her final year dissertation within a nine-month period, and she realized that, by the time she was able to begin the observational study based on access which she was currently negotiating with several of the suppliers, the most interesting and important events (those relating to the immediate impact of the closure announcement on the shop-floor and the management of the supplier companies) would be over. After discussions with her three chief contacts at the supplier companies and with her tutor, she decided on a four-technique approach, one involving documentary sources, limited non-participant observation, interviews, and a repertory grid study of personal perceptions of the changes. The documents were limited to an overview document on the closure (each supplier company had written an account of the impact of the closure in some form or other), the companies being unwilling to give access to more specific documents, memos and e-mails. However, she hoped to gain an understanding of the social impact of the closure within the supplier companies by a hermeneutic analysis of the three overview documents, prior to the next, observational stage. Her observations would involve attendance at three forthcoming senior staff meetings at which strategy changes would be discussed. She also hoped to interview key managers face-to-face in some detail, while the repertory grids were intended to identify the personal values which the managers were drawing on in making personal sense of the events within their firms following on from the announcement of the closure.

Biographical analysis

There is often great significance in what people remember and in the shape of the story which they seek to tell, taken for their own sake, whether these agree or disagree with others' accounts. Davies (1992) provides an interesting rationale and case study of the value of personal biographies in understanding the historical patterns of behaviour which influence current performance and in providing an account of the way in which personal values underlie, form, and conflict with organizational values; or, as Farrell (1992: 219) puts it in her account of how women managers construe issues of quality, '. . . in all of these biographical stories the personal and organizational themes are inextricably intertwined'.

Biographical analysis requires you to take particular care over accuracy of recall. The main problem you will encounter in using biographical (and historical: see below) methods arises because human memory isn't a literal recording medium like an audio or video tape. People are selective in what they notice, have active memorization mechanisms and are motivated in what they will subsequently remember. Furthermore, they make mistakes! You're advised to use at least two sources of data for information which is crucial to your argument, or important in compiling an official record of what has taken place. You can usually cross-check one written source against another, a written source against the results of an interview, and the results of one interview against the results of another. Particularly, be very careful about accepting the status of your data-source as a guarantee of his or her accuracy of judgement and recall!

ILLUSTRATION 9.2

Colonel Burchard (retd) is the village squire and knows the district intimately. However, this proved no guarantee of the accuracy of his analysis of the reasons why a local stately home and its associated theme park had failed to attract foreign visitors. The MSc (Tourism and Leisure) student doing the project, Peter Tomlinson, was told that 'foreigners don't like theme parks so they've never visited ours', but this struck Peter as contrary to common-sense: hadn't the Colonel heard of Disneyland and the Epcot Centre, for example? It was too late to go back and ask him, but, as often happens when common sense is offended, further, more systematic data collection was stimulated. Peter concentrated on interviews with two sets of estate-workers, which provided data towards a fruitful comparison of the factors involved in developing the grounds of an English stately home into a theme park, with the factors involved in developing a theme park on a green field site. Biographical data were there for triangulation purposes from all three sources, the Colonel's personal history being recognized as an important influence on the way he interpreted the strategic choices facing the stately home.

Biographical analysis can be made to serve two distinct functions. The first provides an 'official record': the best account you can devise, despite human frailty, 'what actually happened', with the results of individual conversations and semi-structured interview techniques cross-checked against archival written records where possible. **Content analysis** would be the technique to use: see Section 10.2. The second function is a study of personal meaning; it provides an account of how and why a person or group of people saw events, especially personal experiences, as they did, to provide you with an insight into values, motives and aspirations. In this case, *hermeneutic analysis* is the appropriate technique. Forster (1994) is a helpful introduction to hermeneutic techniques as used in historical review method, which also provides you with guidelines for use in biographical analysis.

Discourse analysis is a more specialized technique associated with biographical narratives, which focuses on the way in which your respondents draw on differing interpretive repertoires depending on their interpretation of the context in which your interview takes place. The technique focuses on the way in which language is used in given settings, and in a discourse analysis, your task is to identify the context; the various interpretive repertoires; and attempt a matching of one to the other, to arrive at an understanding of the function, from the point of view of your respondent, of the different stories being told. Marshall (1994) provides a basic introduction.

With all of these techniques, it is wise to remember that triangulation, a record of the intentions of your data sources, their representativeness and the internal consistency of the story they tell, are all useful safeguards of the rigour of the information you receive. Aspinwall (1992) on validity in biographical analysis is still worth reading, as is the entire special issue of *Management Education and Development* from which the Aspinwall article comes.

Historical review

The purpose of historical review is to describe what happened in the past, sometimes for its own sake, but more commonly as used in business and management projects, in order to illuminate the present. It is particularly useful for familiarization purposes and to trace the development of the issues which you have decided to focus on in presenting your topic; it may, however, provide the only empirical content of a library-based dissertation.

Here, the importance of an issue is due as much to its provenance as to its content and a longitudinal approach can be very revealing. The historical review is particularly important in projects on financial and accounting subjects, in tracing the current health of an organization, product, or market from the financial and sales records available to you. If you do have access to an organization, understanding the meanings ascribed to key historical events by the employees can be a useful source of hunches or more formal hypotheses which you subsequently explore with different methods, case study method in particular.

You proceed by 'interrogating the data', putting questions to the text as I have described in the 'How to Look' checklist in Section 7.4. You may find that some of the very specific techniques and data-sources used in archival work are especially helpful to you: Hunter Brown and Faulkner (1998) is good in general terms, and Orbell (1987) useful for anyone doing a project with a financial topic in which you need to obtain historical data from organizations other than your own.

You would carry out an analysis of historical financial performance by means of *index and ratio analysis techniques*, using the same indices that you use for evaluating contemporary business performance in case study analysis, and Table 9.2 will remind you of some of them.

If you are dealing with official statistics in any form (data published for public consumption), you will find May (2001) quite thought-provoking. All archival data are produced in a context of political, social, tactical, strategic, stakeholder and even ethical assumptions; where you work with pre-existing archival data, you need to be sensitive to, and carefully examine, the assumptions under which the data were compiled. (This is one reason why I have not chosen to associate interpretivist method with purely qualitative approaches, by the way.)

For example, a good way of arriving at the 'thick description' characteristic of any explicatory method, and of extending the scope of a purely quantitive analysis is to carry out an *audit trace*, which involves the detailed checking of published records (for such variables as the cost of labour, training, materials, plant and the like) by comparing actual final costs against book costs. (These checks would require you to interview the managers involved, to establish their varying – and sometimes, contending – interpretations, so this particular technique is not available to a historical review which is purely library based.) You can find an excellent account of the technique in action, and obtain a good idea of the kinds of contribution which this technique can make to the development of theory, in Clark (1999: 305–306).

Case study method

Case study method is used when your thesis focuses on a set of issues in a single organization, and you want to identify the factors involved in an in-depth study of the organization or (to choose a smaller unit of analysis), a single department within it. Alternatively, if you have identified a number of variables whose importance to the present organization you wish to explore, it is possible to carry out a comparative case study, in which you ask the same questions in several related organizations as well as your own.

Yin (2002) compares the case study to the experiment and provides three alternative situations in which one might choose to use the former method in place of the latter:

■ When following a theory which specifics a particular set of outcomes in particular circumstances, a case study of an organization which finds itself in

TABLE 9.2 Financial analysis : some commonly used ratios

Liquidity ratios	
Current ratio:	Current assets/current liabilities
Acid Test:	(Current assets − stocks)/current liabilities
Profitability ratios	
Gross profit %:	((Sales revenue − cost of sales) × 100)/sales revenue
Net profit %:	((Net profit before tax & depreciation) × 100)/sales revenue
Return on total assets:	(Net profit × 100)/total assets
Return on capital employed:	(Net profit before tax and interest × 100)/total capital employed
Return on owners' equity:	(Net profit before tax × 100)/equity capital
Share and dividend performance	
Dividend cover:	Profits available for distribution/dividend paid
Price-Earnings ratio:	Market price per share/earnings per share
Funds management	
Debtors' collection period:	(Debtors × 365 days)/sales revenue
Average payment period:	(Creditors × 365 days)/purchases
Stock turnover:	Cost of sales/closing stock
Ability to borrow	
Debt ratio:	(Current liabilities × 100)/total assets
Capital gearing ratio:	(Fixed interest capital × 100)/shareholders' funds, where fixed interest capital = (long-term debt + debentures + overdraft + short-term loans − current cash assets)

After Lancaster and Massingham (1988: 309)

those circumstances is helpful for a critical test of the theory and its applicability to that organization.

- In order to identify the distinguishing characteristics of an extreme or rare situation in which an organization or organizational unit might find itself. You would be concerned to compare and contrast, and you would have to be careful to do more than simply describe.

- When you are given access to an organization, or a process within an organization, which has rarely if ever been studied. You need to be careful with this rationale for using a case study, since business organizations operate in a rapidly changing environment and one might argue that every situation is new, and poses unique problems that would repay your study. A useful touchstone would be to ask yourself (and/or your tutor and sponsor) whether the circumstances are sufficiently interesting that something important will be learnt from the study.

Representation and generalization in case method

In the comparative case study, Yin points out that the design logic is somewhat similar to the logic involved in experimental methods and different from survey methods in particular. The purpose of data-gathering in a comparative case is not to *sample* different organizations (or companies, departments, people, as the case may be) because you wish to generalize your findings to all other organizations (companies, departments, people) of the same type, as you would do in a survey.

ILLUSTRATION 9.3

Phil Chapman is a manager in a local education authority (LEA). His thesis is that new developments in information technology, such as Bluetooth wireless and internet router networking are so expensive that they will only be bought by LEAs if they can be installed in educational as well as administrative settings. He chooses several LEAs, not for the purpose of *sampling* the range of authorities so that the conclusions can be generalized to all, but in order to examine his thesis systematically, asking questions about the policy decisions involved in new technology implementation.

This he does by selecting authorities in which the new developments in IT are used a) purely for educational use b) purely for administrative applications, and c) for both purposes together. There may be 200 LEAs which use information technology only for educational purposes, 400 only for administrative purposes, and 600 for both, but that is not the point. In choosing *just two LEAs of each kind*, and conducting a comparative case study between them, Phil is *representing the different stances*, and obtaining meaningful findings about them, even though he has not represented the population as he would have done if he had done a survey with a stratified sample of 20, 40, and 60 LEAs respectively. A survey might be suitable in a study of users' attitudes and opinions of the new technology, but Phil is concerned with policy issues where a systematic examination of the three different policy stances is what is required.

You achieve representation through *replication,* that is, by compare the organization (company, department, people) you're studying with others in a systematic way, exploring different possible stances to the issues you are examining, or examining different levels of the variables involved. See Miles and Huberman (1994: 173–176) for more details of this distinction.

Replication is fundamentally different from sampling. In a study using survey method, organizations (companies, departments, people) are selected into a sample to be representative of some population. In contrast, organizations (companies, departments, people) are chosen for a comparative case study to be representative of different possible positions or stances, *regardless of the relative frequency of these stances in the population.*

The data in a case study are obtained largely through the *analysis of written documents,* and by means of *interview technique,* as with the explicatory methods; in addition, **stakeholder analysis** is also available: see e.g. Burgoyne (1994).

Planning a case study

Case study method will involve you in at least four stages of work. Bennett (1986) lists them as follows:

1 Determining the present situation

2 Gathering information about the background to the present situation

3 Gathering more specific data to test alternative hypotheses about the important factors in the present situation

4 Presenting recommendations for action; and, where you have the time and the power to have influenced events, evaluating the outcomes of these recommendations after they have been implemented.

Yin (2002) offers a similar list which emphazises the need to be clear about the unit of analysis (the level at which you are conducting the case study), while Hartley (1994) provides a reminder that the approach taken in a case study should be based on some particular theoretical stance, which you should state explicitly at the outset. Call this the prologue to step 1 in the list given above.

The case study is an attempt to be comprehensive. You will have to engage in description and analysis of the full richness and variety of events and issues in the organization or department in question. Richness and variety, however, will involve you in the full messiness and complications which arise in the real situation which you are describing, as I outlined in Section 5.2, that is why a sampling approach that seeks to generalize conclusions as if conditions were identical in other organizations isn't possible.

A difficulty with this method, then, is that you lay your design open to the influence and interruptions arising from day-to-day events to a somewhat greater extent than with survey and experimental method, and you might care to review Section 5.3 for ways of handling this situation. The need to triangulate by using multiple sources of evidence to check out and confirm initial conclusions; the need to manage and maintain a growing database; and the need to construct an inferential chain from thesis, via data-base, to evidence and final conclusions, are all emphasized by Yin (2002), whose brief but comprehensive guide to case study research, now in its third edition, is highly recommended to anyone choosing this method.

It also helps if you have a clear idea of the way in which you intend to present your information. The outcomes of case studies used as a project or research method are usually presented in narrative and tabular form, according to a structured plan which recapitulates, in greater detail, the stages you went through in doing the work. A good way of developing an appreciation for this structure is to consider the way in which you normally work up and present a case study used in class as part of your taught course, since, in effect, this is the kind of structure which your examiner will be seeking to apply in reading your work. Table 9.3 presents one set of headings which are commonly used by students to present their analysis of a classroom case study; at this stage in your programme, you should be familiar with these headings or something equivalent to them. Chapter 7 of Miles and Huberman (1994) suggests a variety of graphical displays which you might find useful in reporting case study results.

If you are following an undergraduate programme, your exposure to the case method in teaching may be somewhat limited, particularly if you haven't yet done much in the field of Strategic Management or Business Policy. You might look at

TABLE 9.3	One set of standard headings used in the presentation of case study analyses in classroom situations
Where do they come from?	Outline the history and background of the organization or department involved in the case
How did they get here?	What goals, policies, strategies and actions led up to the present situation?
What led them astray?	What constraints and difficulties got in their way, and how did they handle them?
Where are they now?	What is the current situation, and what major issues present themselves?
Where could they go to?	What alternative courses of action are available to them?
Where do they want to go to?	What course of action is currently being contemplated by the organization?
Where ought they to go to?	What course of action is optimal, bearing in mind the tradeoffs involved? How does this compare with the course of action being contemplated?
Where will they go to?	Given the tradeoffs and constraints, what course of action do you recommend?
How will they get there?	What needs to be implemented, with what existing and new resources?
How can they get lost?	Since constraints exist and tradeoffs must be made, what major problem sources or pitfalls exist?
How will they know they've arrived?	What are the criteria for success, how will they be recognized, and how can they be applied?

any of the following collections of case studies to familiarize yourself with the kind of information which cases present to their readers; on reflection though, students at any level might want to glance at them as examples of analytic approach and reporting style. O'Cinneide (1986) covers the range of organizations from small-business startups to existing, mature businesses, and takes enterprise, growth and change as his focus. Tyson and Kakabadse (1987) confine themselves to human resource issues at strategic and operational level in a variety of organizations while Gowler *et al.* (1993) focus on organizational behaviour in general. Boisot (1994) contains four fascinating case studies describing the problem of governance in the post-command economies of eastern Europe and China, written in several different styles. There is a good discussion of case study as a research method in Hartley (1994).

Survey method

In contrast to historical review, the survey method draws most of its data from the present. You conduct a survey in order to establish people's views of what they think, believe, value or feel, in order to discover these views for their own sake, or to support an argument that you are presenting, sampling a population of potential respondents in order to generalize conclusions more widely. It is perfectly feasible to carry out a business and management project, at any level, by using survey method alone, without combining it with other methods; however, in some projects, the historical survey, a biographical analysis, or perhaps a brief case study form a precursor, which generates hypotheses or identifies issues which you investigate with a larger group of respondents by means of the survey method itself.

Surveys are particularly useful when one wants to contact relatively large numbers of people to obtain data on the same issue or issues, often by posing the same questions to all. You would use one of the many techniques associated with the survey method in situations in which either the relative frequency with which certain views are held is informative (as in the *structured interview* or *questionnaire*), or in which particular perspectives arising from different expertise bases contribute to a picture of comparisons and contrasts (as in the less structured, *key informant interview*).

The word 'survey' normally indicates human respondents. Your basic data are obtained by talking to people, either face-to-face, by means of the telephone, over the Internet, or by written questionnaire. This gives rise to the main problem associated with survey method. You are dealing with verbal reports, either oral or written and before you can begin interpreting them, you're limited to the data which people are able and willing to report in the first place. As I mentioned in the previous section, the stories people tell you will depend on their interpretation of your reasons for asking! In survey method as distinct from explicatory method, this tends to be treated as an error factor – something that leads to inaccuracies – and different interview and questionnaire techniques provide you with different ways of controlling or allowing for such 'error'. Your choice of survey method as your main research method means that, to a degree, you are prepared to take people at their word – even when you're holding one interview to cross-check what another interviewee said! Ultimately, you have to ask yourself if what you have heard sounds genuine and 'rings true', and, perhaps, look for techniques associated with non-survey methods (*hermeneutic interpretation, discourse analysis, audit tracing,* or possibly *structured observation*) to verify your conclusions.

You present your information in a narrative report, supported numerically and graphically with the main points of each table or figure being stated in words immediately after it. A connected account is then used to summarize the information from a group of tables or diagrams which you have presented on a particular issue or theme.

The field experiment

You would carry out a *field experiment* if you were sufficiently familiar with the situation you were studying, and the events involved, to be able to identify variables whose impact on each other you would observe. You would do so in order to arrive at an explanation of the events, and possibly in order to contribute to a more general theory of such events.

As you will have gathered from Chapter 5, I am not convinced that there are many situations in which you are likely to use this method. However, I have included this section, here and in Chapter 12, for two reasons. First, there is no doubt that some undergraduate projects (particularly those in the human resource field), which confine attention to a single issue, usually professional, taken independently from the usual flow of organizational events, can base themselves almost entirely on this method. Second, as suggested in the discussion of academic rigour earlier (see also Table 9.1), the experimental method provides a rationale for a number of techniques of data presentation designed to test hypotheses in survey work.

In an experiment, the data are gathered by observation of a tightly predefined range of behaviour under controlled conditions. In the simplest case, you confine your attention to two variables, and look for a pattern of association between the two. For example, you might want to demonstrate that attendance on a training course makes a difference to managers' job performance. 'Attendance on the course' is the first variable, and, let us say, 'supervisor's ratings of the manager's performance' is the second. You would gather ratings for a sample of managers, tabulating the ratings under two headings, 'Did attend' and 'Didn't attend', and look for higher ratings in the former case.

Suppose that is exactly what happened; then what you could conclude is that the two variables are related. However, you couldn't say anything about the direction of the relationship, that is, the cause. (For all you know, supervisors only sent their best people on the course, as a reward for past performance, and the course made no difference. If so, it was the high supervisor ratings that influenced the presence on the course, rather than the presence on the course influencing the supervisor ratings!) Of course, if all you want is to demonstrate that the two variables are related, this isn't a problem. For example, there are many situations (especially in survey work) in which you want to identify patterns in your observations: that males answer questions systematically differently from females, managers in one function from managers from another, and so on, and the idea of stratifying your sample to identify such patterns by looking for associations in your data makes explicit use of this rationale.

However, if you want to say something about the cause of the relationship, you need to do two more things. First, you must arrange events so that you can be reasonably sure about the sequence of the association (which variable makes a difference if it happens first, and which doesn't). The easiest way is by design: in any study of change, it is wise to obtain two sets of observations, using a *before-after* design. So, in our example, you could obtain supervisor ratings of the managers' performance before and after the time of the course, for the managers who attended, and for those who did not attend. You would conclude that the course had a causal impact on performance if the difference between 'before' and 'after' ratings was greater for those who went on the course than for those who didn't. This may not always be possible, however. If it weren't possible in the example given above, you would somehow have to ensure that supervisors sent their staff on this particular course regardless of their opinions of their job performance, so that performance could have no prior influence on course participation.

Second, you must eliminate the possible influence of other, alternative variables. In the example given above, you would need to convince yourself that only attendance on the course influenced performance, by controlling the impact of other factors that could possibly account for the performance. It is plausible, for example, that managers with a heavy and stressful workload didn't have the time to attend the course, while the ones who went were the unstressed managers with a light workload. It could just be, then, that the final ratings of job performance were due to the stresses of a heavy workload, rather than to course attendance. (High workload = stress = can't cope with the job = poorer ratings and no time to go on the course. Low workload = no stress = copes with the job = higher ratings and has time to go on courses.) Just because your results are consistent with your expectations, doesn't make them valid.

Generally speaking, the way to eliminate the effects of external factors is by some form of control. Drawing a sample of managers who are matched in some way – equal in status on the whole range of possible factors that could form an alternative explanation for your observations – is sometimes practicable. But this does require you to know enough about your population to be able to anticipate the factors which need to be controlled; and it also assumes that you have sufficient power to arrange control (in our example, that you have the freedom to influence who attends the course, and who does not attend).

This may not be the case, and you have two alternatives. First, you could draw a purposive sample by deliberately deciding to observe only those people whom you knew to be equal on the factors requiring control. Second, you could simply sample at random from your two different groups (in our example, from among those attending the course, and those not attending the course), and assume that the effects of the various factors involved would cancel each other out. In both cases, you would need to start with a fairly large population, and know quite a lot about the people involved.

On very rare occasions, you may have sufficient control to be able to dictate, in effect, how people arrange themselves into groups for your research purposes. You would be operating in the realm of the controlled, *laboratory experiment* (for all that it occurred in the workplace) rather than the **field experiment** as such, and you would be able to carry out some very powerful work albeit on a restricted number of variables. However, this situation is beyond the scope of my account, and if you were faced with such an opportunity, you need to look elsewhere for guidance. Bennett (1986) will give you a flavour of the issues involved in control, and there are many textbooks of experimental design which you can turn to for further particulars. Orr (1998) is particularly relevant for work in the public sector, while Berger and Maurer (2001) is a more general text. Field experiments are reported in a fairly standardized format, in which you specify the sample size and provide details of procedure and design in terms of three kinds of variable:

- The **independent variable**: the one which you regard as possibly the cause of the effect you're observing, and which you take control over by, for example, assigning people to different groups with respect to that variable.

- The **dependent variable**: the one which you hope will express the effects of your activities (which you hope depends on the independent one) and which forms the focus of your observations.

- The **controlled variables**: the ones which would get in the way of your causal explanation and whose effects you have therefore tried to eliminate.

 Glance at Case Example 9.1 to explore the rationale underlying the choice of a method in practice.

 Then make your own choice of method: please address activity 2 in the Project Guide.

9.3   A framework of general guidelines for empirical work

Before you started this chapter, I would imagine that you saw the preparation of your empirical work as a matter of organizing some questions to put to your respondents. So it is, but remember: your job is to gather and present data in order for your reader to arrive at information. Before you can ask useful questions of your *respondents*, or interrogate your written sources, there are some important questions which you must ask of *yourself*. These are shown in Table 9.4. The questions that you will be devising to pose to your respondents are such a small part of the whole process that I have had to outline the item in bold so that you can find it in the table! Ignore these questions and you will end up with lots of data, and very little information. So, whichever research method you plan to use, before using the particular technique you have in mind, run through the questions and think though the answers in detail before committing yourself to data collection and analysis.

Each of the questions is discussed in more detail below. They are also used as an organizing framework for the presentation of material about each of the techniques in Chapters 10 to 12, so the material which follows here is a general introduction to the more specific material covered in those chapters.

Design

The representation method (sampling or replication) and the design format, are the two main issues which you will need to address. The latter refers to the actual design used, whether examining contrasting modes of operation, time-sampling, a before and after design, and so on. These have been described in Section 8.1.

TABLE 9.4   A checklist to be used in preparing the questions to ask
1 DESIGN For each major issue to be investigated, what kind of sampling method is appropriate? What size of sample should I choose? Should I combine several sampling methods? Should I stratify the samples? What kind of design format is appropriate?
2 ELICITATION What kinds of steering instructions should I provide, and how are these best provided given the questions I wish to ask? Are there any expectations which my informants are likely to have of me and my role, which might influence or bias their response? How should I address this issue and, particularly, how can I involve the respondent in this procedure? What answer format is appropriate to each question? **What is the question which I wish to ask?** How should I record the answers which I receive?
3 ANALYSIS What methods are appropriate in analysing the answers I receive, given the questions themselves, the format in which answers are to be given, and the way in which responses will be recorded? What kind of summarizing method is most likely to be relevant to these kinds of answers?
4 WRITE-UP What sort of approach and style are likely to be appropriate in writing up the kinds of information I am likely to obtain? While I can't provide a firm answer as yet, are there any kinds of information which is more likely to appear as an Appendix; what other kinds will be essential to my argument and should appear in the body of the text?
A pilot study will answer many of these questions

There is only one further point to be made at this stage and, though it may seem banal, it's often neglected. When it comes to the use of particular techniques, design is a matter of small details as well as of the grand plans for arriving at accurate descriptions and causal explanations which we have been considering hitherto. For example, if several questionnaires are sent to a central location in each of a number of companies, is the addressee informed about how he or she is to distribute them to the respondents? How are the completed questionnaires to be returned, centrally or individually? Simply addressing a large envelope containing questionnaires and a generalized covering letter may not be sufficient. The procedures by which the various techniques are administered are an appreciable design consideration.

Elicitation

Elicitation, the actual asking of questions, involves you in four kinds of activity.

Steering

This is the first. You have to tell your respondents how they are meant to tackle your questions: in which order, which ones to answer and which ones to miss out, and so on. I'm sure you can anticipate Section 11.1 in expecting that in a questionnaire, for example, steering instructions of this kind are printed in front of each question, or group of questions. You know the sort of thing: 'If you answered "Yes" to Q2, please skip Q3 and go straight on to Q4'.

It may come as a surprise, however, to hear that *all* techniques involve some sort of steering instructions, not simply postal questionnaires. Nevertheless, it's true. If you are using interviews for your survey, you still have to prepare a set of steering instructions aimed at yourself as the interviewer, and this activity is as important as the preparation of the questions which you will be asking. In an observation study, your very presence as an observer, and the way in which your role has been presented to the people you're observing, will act as a form of steering: legitimizing some kinds of answers, priming respondents to expect you to be interested in some kinds of events and not in others, whether you intend this or not. All of the material on the management of perceptions in Section 7.2 applies.

The form of answers

This calls for another kind of activity, well in advance. Whatever method you use, your respondents will expect to be informed of how they are to make their answers to your questions, either literally in the form of instructions to 'Please choose the alternative that best expresses your views on this question', or metaphorically in the case of experiments, by being told that only one form of behaviour, that which gives data on the dependent variable, will be attended to by the experimenter. You will have to provide explicit instructions which specifies the form of answers, for each question or group of similar questions which you will be asking. Even in an informal, relatively unstructured conversation, the form of answer is implied by the process, as opposed to the content, of the conversation and the questions involved, and you will need to plan and prepare this in advance.

Eliciting answers

At last: this is what it's all about! Well, yes, provided all the other activities have been attended to. There are more detailed guidelines on how to ask questions in order to elicit answers, in the relevant sections on particular techniques; at this point, it's worth noting that very often, the precise wording of your questions will be influenced by the other three elicitation activities, as well as being determined by the nature of the data you were attempting to obtain.

For example, in an interview exploring the development of a strategic plan, you might say 'Please tell me how many meetings with other Division Heads you attended on this issue' if you choose to make an inference about the importance managers ascribed to the plan, and you would record each answer in the form of a number. In contrast, your question would be worded 'Please tell me in your own words how you felt about the plan at that time' if you felt that inferring importance from frequency of attendance was too intrusive, and you were looking for a verbatim response which conveyed your respondent's meaning directly. You would then record the answer as a literal quotation.

Furthermore, the way in which you would analyze answers to these questions would depend on the wording. The first example would call for a tabulation of the answers given to you by all the interviewees to whom you posed this question, while the second would demand some form of content analysis of their varying verbatim answers.

Recording

Recording answers, then – the particular form in which you do so – is also something which you have to decide in advance, for each question or group of similar questions which you plan to ask your respondents. A verbatim record, or some form of quantitative tally (defined as some mark you make on behalf of each respondent to record his or her answer: a tick in the simplest case, or a ranking, rating, or number in more complex instances) cover the possibilities.

Analysis

This is an activity in which you do two things. First, you familiarize yourself with your recorded data until you perceive patterns emerging, either those which you had in mind when you sought to build your argument or explore the thesis by posing the question you did; or fresh patterns, which are new and unexpected. Second, you have to tabulate the data in such a way that these insights or perceptions are informative: obvious rather than hidden, lost in a maze of primary data.

Perceiving

This involves a great many different techniques, from content analysis and hermeneutic analysis to the calculation of frequencies and proportions all expressed in the form of tabular and graphical displays; together with a variety of analytic statistics, the latter being particularly common in the case of experimental method. In all cases, what you are doing is bringing together the responses of all your respondents (keeping subgroups separate in the case of samples which you have clustered or stratified), to see what general findings and trends emerge.

As I suggested in discussing the elicitation of answers above, you will need to have thought through the analysis methods in advance, in order to design the questions you wish to pose. However, once your data have been collected, the information they contain may not be obvious to you and, within the limitations posed by the form which your data take, you might wish to explore. (The kinds of patterns you are able to perceive depend in part on the type of numbering possible to you, and Table 9.5 defines them.) A very good way of exploring is to set your data up in a standard statistical package (see Table 4.4 for an overview of various

TABLE 9.5 Types of data		
Type	**Definition**	**Attributes**
Nominal	Used simply as labels to categorize types of observation. If instead of labelling your data columns '1', '2', '3' and so on, you could have labelled them 'animal', 'vegetable', 'mineral', then you've been using nominal numbering.	The numbers can only be used to indicate similarity or difference. Example: '1', '2' used to stand for sex categories 'male' and 'female'.
Ordinal	Used to stand for items in an ordered series. If the numbers '1', '2', '3' are equivalent to 'first', second', 'third', you are using ordinal numbering.	The numbers are used to indicate similarity or difference, and relative importance. Example: '1', '2', '3' used to give the position of horses in a race, coming in first, second, and third.
Interval	Used to indicate the degree of difference between items. If the difference between '1' and '2' is the same as the difference between '2' and '3', you are using interval numbering.	Indicate similarity or difference, and relative importance, and size of the difference on a constant scale. Example: 'John received 70% for his assignment, Mary 65%, and Alan 40%. Mary's work was closer in standard to John's than it was to Alan's.
Ratio	Used to indicate the relationships between items on scales which have a true, physical zero. Salary scales, the time scale used for duration, scales of length such as the metric and imperial scales all have a zero point.	Indicate similarity, difference, relative importance, and absolute difference. Example: 'Peter is paid twice as much as Mary' is possible because the scales used for earnings (e.g. the '£' scale) have a true zero, so 40,000 is twice as much as 20,000.

Statistics computed with nominal and ordinal numbers are known as **non-parametric**. They lack certain attributes which stem from those listed in the right-hand column above. Statistics computed with interval and ratio numbers are known as **parametric**, and have those attributes. So, for example, it is possible to compute the arithmetic mean of a set of *finishing times* of a horse over a series of races but only the median *position* of that horse over the series.

software packages, and the appendix to Miles and Huberman (1994) for a useful review of qualitative analysis software), trying out the various statistical measures that apply.

Analysis is often a matter of exploration: casting data in one form, then another; analyzing it one way, then another, to see what emerges. That is not to say that you don't have a number of personal hunches, or more formal hypotheses, which you wish to test or issues you want to verify, in which some particular way of inspecting your data hasn't been decided in advance. Rather, I wish to emphasize the richness of your data, given the kinds of management issues being investigated, and the value of familiarizing yourself with these data thoroughly in order that the unexpected can be recognized and novel information identified. Information doesn't reach out from the data and grab you by the throat!

Summarizing

Having identified findings, trends, and meaningful patterns in the data; having obtained information, in other words, you need to cast the data into a final form which expresses the information involved, as clearly and obviously as possible; some form of numeric table, graphical display, or list of verbal points or quotations, is usually the final step in an analysis. As you will see if you glance at Miles and Huberman (1994), Perceiving and Summarizing are closely interdependent. Saunders *et al.* (2003: 340) provides a classification of different forms of descriptive statistics (pie charts, line graphs, histograms and the like), while Siegel and Castellan (1988) do the same for analytic statistics, with an emphasis on the nonparametric statistics in particular.

Write-up

You may feel that thinking ahead to the time when you write up your information is an unnecessary activity at this stage. However, a little time spent in considering the kinds of write-up which your design, your questions, and their analysis make possible, is very advisable even now, with further particulars left until you begin writing, having cast your eye over the material in Chapter 13.

Presenting

Presenting findings is frequently a matter of style. You may as well know in advance that some types of design and questioning lend themselves to one presentation style, and others to another, especially if you have personal preferences for one of them. For example, a project in which the empirical stage is largely dependent on a series of interviews with key informants may call for a content analysis, followed by a narrative account of the main findings of the analysis. In contrast, a highly structured questionnaire may require you to tabulate rankings and ratings, presenting much of your information in numeric form. Are you more comfortable with one form rather than another?

MBA and other post-experience students may have a topic in which they need to combine several different forms of questioning, analysis, and reporting. It would be wise to think these through, to the presentation stage, well in advance, so that you know which issues you will deal with, and present, in which way. In general, presenting findings involves two distinct activities:

- presenting content: the substantive information which you have prepared from your data, in the context of the argument you are developing
- presenting evidence about the accuracy and credibility of this information.

You would do the latter by showing that the substantive information is consistent with other information which you have obtained, either primary (empirical data you gathered yourself) or secondary (consistency with the findings and ideas of other authors as obtained in your literature review), as part of the argument your project document presents. You may add to the weight and credibility of your presentation by citing any measures of reliability of the particular techniques which you used in your data analysis, at this point in your text. There is more on this in Section 11.2, in the discussion of content analysis.

Locating

Locating your results in the right place is probably the most important influence on the way in which your reader obtains information from the data which you will be presenting. As you carry out your analysis (and especially during the summarizing stage of analysis), you will need to decide where in your project document the different kinds of results will be presented. What sort of material should you present in your text and in what order; how should findings be related to objectives; which should be confined to an appendix, and which displayed in the main body of your account?

To put it into a nutshell, you should aim to present information in just the right quantity at just those places where they will support your argument best, *at just the point at which you imagine your reader will require them if he or she is following the argument as you intend it*. As well as writing your project document, you should be tracking how your reader is following it, at every point in the text you are creating!

ILLUSTRATION 9.4

Jean Weston has submitted a very interesting and workmanlike CIPD professional project on the topic of Infectious Diseases at Work. A major key to success lies in her decision (prompted, it must be said, by her tutor) to reorganize her material as initially presented, so that technical descriptions of various bacterially-propagated infectious diseases were confined to an appendix. As originally placed, in the main body of her text, they were long enough, and detailed enough, to have obscured her findings on health and safety practices among employees potentially exposed to infection hazards in a local authority cleansing department, to the point at which the reader had great difficulty in discerning the information from the wealth of data which she had supplied.

In principle, this issue is straightforward enough: present just the material which is required to establish your findings in the body of your text, and additional, illustrative, or highly technical material in an appendix. In practice, it depends very much on the kind of finding which you are trying to establish, and the particular way in which your data support the argument you're presenting in arriving at your information. As a rough guide, that means that direct findings (classification headings and frequency counts thereunder, totals, averages, trends, other descriptive and analytic statistics) should go in the body of the text, together with sufficient of the data which gave rise to them for the reader to understand that your argument and conclusions aren't arbitrary. The remainder would then go to an appendix. More specific guidance is given, where necessary, in the account of the various techniques in Chapters 10 and 11; you might like to skim-read these now if you have not already done so.

Next, please address activities 3 and 4 in the Project Guide.

9.4 In conclusion: your proposal and your pilot study

At this point you might argue that the answers to some of the procedural questions posed in Table 9.4 are arbitrary, since you might see several ways of answering them, and have no way of recognizing which is more likely to lead to success. The purpose of the proposal document is to make a first stab at this issue; and the purpose of the initial pilot stage of your project, to resolve any doubts. If you look back to Section 4.2, and Table 4.2, you will recall the importance of timetabling for the piloting of your questions with an appropriate subsample; you may, at this point, find Table 4.3 with its standard times for project activities useful too. Section 8.1 discusses the idea of preliminary analysis in the context of design, and you might find that a glance back at Table 8.1 is also helpful.

Updating your project proposal document

This is a good time to finalize your choice of research design, choice of method, and sampling plan, putting all of this information together coherently with the material you have already prepared in the Project Guide for Chapter 2, exercise 5, as amended in exercise 3 of the Project Guide for Chapter 5.

Section 2.5, you will recall, provided you with some standard headings to use in starting a project proposal document:

- the topic
- the rationale
- the objective

- the research question
- the provenance table.

The following additional headings are standard ways of completing a document of this kind.

- *The methodology*, itself composed of the choice of, and rationale for, each of the following:

  a A *research design,* chosen to suit the particular research question and dependent on whether exploratory, descriptive, or causal work, or a combination of these, is planned.

  b A *method* by which the research design will be addressed.

  c The approach towards, and arrangements for, *representation*. The main choices here involve a description of which stances you intend to *replicate* and variables to examine, if you have decided on the comparative case study as your method; or, a description of the nature of the population and how it is to be *sampled*, with details of the samples size(s) provided, if you have decided to use survey method.

  d A brief description, with rationale, for the main research *techniques* to be used. The chief mistake when you're planning the techniques is to include everything: 'interviews with senior managers and customers, two questionnaires, one to customers and one to staff, participant observation of employees, focus groups to establish the main issues, and comparative case studies of selected competitors' may be an indication that you haven't really thought things through. (When I act as a tutor myself, it's usually that plural in the word 'questionnaires' that starts the warning bells ringing.) Be selective.

  and

- *A research timetable*, which may be in the form of a detailed Gantt chart, or a simple statement of the time to be spent on each main project activity.

Table 9.6 provides an example, building on the Project proposal document presented in Table 2.3 and Case Example 2.3.

Most institutions that require a project proposal include a request for personal contact details. The proposal, once approved by your tutor, will be used as a convenient aide-memoire for your early tutorials (he or she is likely to have several tutees doing a project at any one time!) and as a quick reference of how best to communicate with you when he or she wishes to contact you.

 Now, please draw on the above to address activity 5.

Planning a pilot study

As soon as you have received feedback on this proposal, and gained some confidence that your plans are appropriate, you may find yourself carrying out a more complete pilot study of your final data-collection technique(s).

TABLE 9.6 Marco Testa's completed project proposal document. Post-experience Masters level. Compare with Table 2.6

Topic	A comparison of production efficiencies and quality standards in the US, UK and Danish companies
Rationale	The US headquarters sets competitive strategy with respect to a global marketplace, and determines product differentiation in the local companies (with several manufacturing units within the USA and units in the UK, Denmark, Canada and elsewhere). In-company indicators of labour efficiency, machine utilization, output and rework suggest that the unit which does things its own way with relatively little collaboration with Head Office is apparently the most efficient. This suggests a need for synergy: a better integration of manufacturing systems across all units, bearing cultural factors in mind.
Research Objective and Research Question	To compare the production and quality standards of the US, UK and Danish factories using a range of standard internal indicators, bearing in mind the national differences. What accounts for the differences in their claimed efficiency? Initial discussions suggest a thesis that cultural differences do not entirely account for production differences but do account for the approach to communication; implications for changes felt to be necessary will most probably be for the soft systems than the hard systems in each location.

Provenance	Area	Field	Aspect + concepts/reading
	Strategic Management	marketing and distribution	demands made on manufacturing (new products, batch sizes, customer base, quality standards) Denison 'Corporate Culture and Organizational Effectiveness' Edwards 'Managing the Factory' Pande 'What is Six Sigma?'
	Operations Management and Production Technology	support functions (planning, quality, engineering); reliability of equipment and processes	Kettinger and Grover on Business Process Re-eng.
	HRM	policy and procedures	selection, training and motivation
	Globalization	cultural differences: national culture; NB Hofstede and Trompenaars	Tayeb 'Management of a Multicultural Workforce'
	International business	conditions of trade	Elashwami and Harris 'Multicultural Management' Jaques 'Changing Culture of a Factory'
	OB and HRD	group dynamics and sociotechnical systems considerations leadership theory, esp. communication, participation, performance management	Bion 'Experiences in Groups' Neale 'Performance Management' Vroom and Yetton 'Leadership and Decision Making' NB: systematic scan of *Human Resource Development International* journal!
	Finance	cost/management accounting	Identical transfer pricing policies? Innes and Mitchell on Activity-based costing Investment decision/return on capital

TABLE 9.6 Marco Testa's completed project proposal document. Post-experience Masters level. Compare with Table 2.6 (cont.)

Research Design	Initially descriptive, and then causal. The three factories (US head office; the UK company; and the Danish company) will be systematically compared with each other, examining those processes and facilities on which comparison is possible and ignoring the facilities and products which are specific to a given site for which there is no equivalent in one of the other two sites.
Method	A comparative case study. Objective indicators and benchmarks exist for some of the information, but the key issues reflect stakeholder preferences among senior staff, national differences, and different regulatory frameworks, and so several different types of respondent must be approached in each location, using different techniques for each component, and so a rich picture by case study is preferred to a single survey-method-based review.
Representation	Comparative case study implies replication. Here, the main variable is the national one. Cultural differences are expected to play a part, but these do not entirely account for production differences. Legal requirements, reporting standards and practices, and varying quality standards are also likely to be involved. a It is not possible to replicate different levels of these three factors systematically within each location, so it is proposed to interview a group of at least three people in each location who are known to have worked in all three locations as a substitute. b Differences in stakeholder positions are expected between the Head Office and other two locations; so it is planned to speak to three senior (head of function/department) people with similar responsibilities at each site and seek similarities and differences between Head Office versus 'regions' (the other two). c A review of internal documents and procedural guides, with discussion and observation on how these are followed in the three different locations, will address the hypothesized national differences, which are expected to affect communication between the sites on issues such as quality setting and benchmarking in particular. d Each Production Manager, and 30% of each of the remaining categories should provide a return of 100 questionnaires from each company. Covering values, culture, leadership, communications, performance management; some Trompenaars scales may be incorporated.
Techniques	a semi-structured interviews, 3 – 4 people × 3 locations = 9 – 12. Views on the relative importance of policy views and disagreements among stakeholders, communication issues, and different national frameworks to be addressed. b key informant interviews, 3 × 3 = 9; telephone or internet interview following initial face-to-face sessions as required. Policy differences to be covered. c Archival search: systematic collation and comparison of company histories, organization charts, approaches to operations management (e.g. 6–Sigma in UK versus a local scheme in Denmark), operating process figures, performance data, quality standards, financial parameters esp. costing practices, governmental and state legislation/regulations. I will have assistance with this in each of the locations. d Questionnaire: mixed structured and semi-structured questions covering the soft systems aspects using random sample of Production Managers, Supervisors, Engineers (N.P.D. and process engineering), machine setters and production operatives in each of the three locations.

TABLE 9.6 Marco Testa's completed project proposal document. Post-experience Masters level. Compare with Table 2.6 (cont.)

Timetable	
NB I have been seconded on a 60 per cent basis to this project	
Month 1:	finalize topic with tutor and sponsor; methodology, method and techniques; start literature review. Tutorial.
Month 2:	Start pilot study in UK company, focusing on semi-structured and key informant interviews. Tutorial.
Month 3:	Complete pilot, start development of questionnaire, continue reading.
Month 4:	Complete archival search; complete bulk of literature review. Tutorial.
Month 5:	Semi-structured and key informant interviews in UK, USA and Denmark (company funding available for one week in each location)
Month 6:	Write-up interviews, do telephone and internet followups as required, complete questionnaire.
Month 7:	Despatch questionnaire, write introduction, Literature Review, Methodology sections of Dissertation. Tutorial.
Month 8:	Begin questionnaire analysis, begin write-up of pilot study and archival study results; despatch chase-up questionnaires to non-respondents.
Month 9:	Bulk of questionnaire analysis work; write-up of main results. Further round of telephone follow-ups. Discuss with sponsor. Tutorial.
Month 10:	Write-up of discussion, conclusions, recommendations. Tutorial?

Generally speaking, you **pilot** your empirical work by asking the questions that you intend to ask, in the form you intend to ask them, of a small number of people taken from the same population as your sample. You then analyze the answers in the way you have planned, to see if the results are indeed likely to give you the kind of information which you are seeking. This is your last opportunity, before committing yourself to the time and effort involved in your main data collection, of making sure that the issues mentioned in this chapter have been adequately resolved. Use the standard framework presented in Section 9.3 and Table 9.4 to establish:

- That the design will address your research question, that the method suits the design on which you've decided, and that your approach to representation is appropriate.

- That the techniques are suitable. Specifically, how you will handle the practicalities of each technique: the partiality of your respondents' memory; their ability and willingness to respond; the sheer volume of data with which you'll be faced, some more and some less informative; and the problem of accurate inference-making from the data before you.

- That the wording of your questions, the steering information, and the instructions on answer format are appropriate; that your arrangements for recording answers will work.

- That your plans for analysis of the data from each question are likely to give you the kind of information you need. Is it going to be easy to express the information in the table, or bar-chart, or pie-chart that you have had in mind?

- Finally, will the findings be informative to your readers, given the way in which you anticipate you'll be reporting them?

 If possible, carry out activity 6 at this point.

Naturally, some of these issues can only be addressed in the light of the specific techniques available to you. The following chapters cover them in detail.

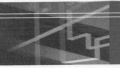

CASE EXAMPLE 9.1   Choosing a method

Xie YanShao, the Chinese student whose early thinking about his topic you helped to shape in Case Example 2.4, has been progressing his plans. You will recall that he was particularly interested in the development of e-retailing in China, and decided to focus attention on the ways in which existing retailers might make better use of the business potential of the internet. His provenance table emphasized the importance of buyer behaviour, marketing strategy, and branding; issues within the promotional field were also important. The main thrust should be to try and understand how consumers are moved from using websites for informational purposes, to using them for online purchasing, by looking at companies which have, and have not, had success in the latter. He decided on the following research question: 'What is it that the two successful companies have done with their websites, in getting people moving from information to sales, that is different to what the less successful companies have been doing?'

Xie recognizes that the question calls for a descriptive design, that of examining contrasting modes of operation. This fits his initial thinking about the importance of comparison as the ontological approach which applies. Now, what research method could he use?

Explicatory method, with its emphasis on personal meaning, might be suitable. His question does concern how websites are seen by the consumer. In a country where there is no equivalent to Section 75 of the Consumer Credit Act 1974 (Tang 2003) which provides protection against fraud, user perceptions are rather important! An ethnography is going to take too long; a biographical approach seems misplaced; perhaps a discourse analysis would be useful in identifying consumers' stances towards the company websites. But on reflection, Xie notes that he already knows something of people's views – he has already identified two contrasting orientations, one which sees the site as an informational showcase and the other as a point of sale – and that he really needs a different

method to address the issue of how consumer behaviour has been changed from the former to the latter in the companies concerned.

He considers running an experiment which examines the impact of different website formats and designs in changing people's behaviour, but rejects the idea since he isn't sure of what the variables are. That was why he chose a descriptive design in the first place: to discover what has worked for the two companies which have viable web-based sales, and what they did that differed from the companies which have not made this transition. That leaves the case method and the survey.

Tease out the issues involved, and advise Xie. Which method to adopt? A case study or a survey? Comments on the techniques to use would also be helpful.

Answers to Case Example 9.1

The choice of method here depends very much on whether the companies in question already knew, and how well they knew, what consumers were looking for when they designed their sites. Some of the issues are as follows.

Case study method

A comparative case study would certainly provide the contrast which Xie's design requires. How did the 'selling' companies' induce people to use the shopping basket and payment facilities on their site? Granted that all the sites Xie wishes to study provide a payment facility, what was it about the former sites that engaged consumers' propensity to purchase as well their interest in information? What was it about the other sites that kept consumers coming back for information, but prevented them from purchasing? This sort of study would concentrate on the layout and content of the sites, and ask questions about what buyer concerns were appealed to and what needs they addressed.

CASE EXAMPLE 9.1   Choosing a method (cont.)

But to be useful, it does assume that the site designers already knew what the consumers were looking for. A necessary first step for Xie would be to talk to appropriate staff in the companies' marketing and sales departments to identify the kind of evidence underpinning their beliefs about their customers. Had the 'sellers' systematically surveyed their customers? Perhaps their success stemmed from their designers' creative knowledge applying professional IT standards? Or were they relying on *general* experience of their industry that was better-informed than the 'information-givers'? Or were they just lucky?

This also raises the issue of whether the 'selling' companies were successful because they were correct about consumers' needs and concerns, or successful despite themselves! An internet-based questionnaire to consumers of both companies would be a way of checking this, helping to build up a rich picture of both types of company. Within this comparative case study, a sampling approach representative of the general population would probably be less appropriate than an approach which replicated different levels of purchasing propensity; that is, asked equal subgroups of people who had and had not bought, from each kind of site, what there was about the sites that made them buy from one kind of site but use the other kind only for product information.

Survey method

As an alternative to the case study method, an approach based on survey method would certainly be indicated if there was no evidence from initial discussions that the 'selling' companies had a clear picture of why they were successful. The focus would shift from an emphasis on 'branding' (what accounts for purchasers' trust and choice in the case of the 'selling' firms in particular) to one in which general attitudes to innovation and the adoption of on-line purchasing practices were addressed. Rogers (1995) could be used to provide an organizing framework of issues to cover (relative advantage; compatibility; complexity; trialability; observability), with examples of the four sites' web pages used as the focus for discussion. An internet-based questionnaire would focus attention on experienced IT users; conclusions of greater generality would be obtainable by using postal questionnaires; while interviews would make for greater generality still. (Note how the population being sampled is different in each case. And note how the particular techniques, interview and questionnaire, can be used within both case study method and survey method.)

In the reality on which this case study is based, the approach chosen used a small team of interviewers who followed a brief-interview, checklist-based approach to interview a sample of 400 people stratified by age. The design emphasis on contrast was preserved, but shifted towards comparisons between conventional versus electronic purchasing systems. The conclusions were applied to the companies described earlier – those that succeeded in selling and those whose sites were used just for informational purposes. The interviews were held solely in urban locations since a Chinese rural sample would not have extensive, if any, computing experience (Tang 2003).

Project Guide

1 Revisit your research design

a Look again at the initial notes you made when you carried out activity 2 in the Action Checklist for Chapter 8.

b How and in what order do you plan to measure the variables you identified, assuming you have adopted a positivist approach? In the case of a field experiment, what are the names of the variables and what data-collection technique will you use: observation or some form of questioning? Look ahead to Section 12.3 and make some provisional notes. In the case of a survey, which questions will allow you to allocate each respondent to the strata required by your design, and which questions will provide you with the basic information? (For example, look again at Table 8.3: two questions would be required, one to ascertain the sex of the respondent and one to identify their payroll status, before any question about how much they earn could be analyzed.) Do this for each variable you have in mind; and return to it after reading Chapters 11 and 12 in detail. Or, alternatively:

c How many questions will you need to obtain information on each of the issues your interpretivist approach has identified as relevant? And, in both cases:

d Does your research design address the hypotheses or issues with which you're working? You may find that a single design will address all of them, or that you need two designs (e.g. a *before-after* arrangement to identify the consequences of some strategic decision taken by the company you're studying, coupled with a *time-sampling* of the documents, minutes of meetings and the like, through which the decisions were implemented at an operational level).

2 Choose the main research method you will be using

By now you are clear about your ontological and epistemological assumptions, and know whether your topic and your personal preferences incline you to a more constructivist or positivist stance. Review Section 9.2 and choose the main method! Be wary of an approach which commits you to more than one method and many different techniques.

3 Revisit early plans for the techniques which you plan to use

a Do so on a tentative and provisional basis, after a thorough review of Section 9.2 above, and an initial reading of Chapters 10 to 12.

b Make up a shortlist of any of the textbooks, referred to above, which you will need to look at to learn the details of the main technique(s) you will be using.

c Read them! You will find a lot of useful and detailed information in Chapters 10 to 12 which follow, but it is nevertheless useful to have ready access to any texts offering a more detailed treatment of any technique on which you are particularly dependent.

It is of course rather difficult to finalize this step before you have looked at Chapters 10 to 12. However, even if you sketch out your initial thoughts (activity 3 of the Chapter 8 Project Guide) just enough to help you address activity 4 below, that would be very useful.

4 Consider your plans for representation

a Decide on your overall approach in the light of your choice of method: sampling of a population if you plan to use survey method, or the replication of different stances if you plan to conduct a comparative case study:

b With survey method, for each technique you plan to use, work out in outline what your population and what your sample consist of – how many people, how chosen, and how stratified (if applicable). Draw up a sampling frame summary, locating the sources of information which will allow you to construct it.

With case study method, determine and state the rationale for your choice of company or companies. If you plan a comparative case study, ask yourself what the main variables are, on which an examination of systematic differences would be valuable. Can you find companies for each stance: each level of the variable(s) in question?

If you find any of the above activities problematic, then you might revise your intentions about the type of sampling (perhaps a non-probabilistic sample rather than a probabilistic one?); reconsider the technique (or, more likely, the mix of techniques) you plan to use. It may not be too late to consider a different method.

5 Complete your project proposal document

To the details you have already provided in doing activity 5 of Chapter 2, as amended when you tackled activity 3 of Chapter 5 (under the headings of Topic, Rationale, Objective, Research question, and Provenance Table), add the following:

a An account of the methodology, including a statement of your design, a statement of the main method by which you will address the design, your plans for representation (sampling or replication), and an initial statement of the main techniques to be used.

b A research timetable: you might wish to insert the Gantt chart you prepared in activity 2 of Chapter 4, amending it as required.

6 Plan and conduct your pilot study

As soon as you are ready, carry out your pilot study. In the meantime, please think through the following:

a Satisfy yourself that all is well on each of the questions listed in the section on the pilot study above, as far as you can at this stage.

b Attend to the minutiae as well as the grand plan. Locate two to five respondents. Go through the details of finding them, arranging time with them, informing them of what you are doing, putting your questions to them, and analyzing the kinds of responses you obtain as you have planned: will all this work with your main sample?

c Make whatever alterations might be required in both a and b.

References

Aspinwall, K. (1992) 'Biographical research: searching for meaning', *Management Education and Development* 23: 3: 248–257.

Bennett, R. (1986) 'Meaning and method in management research', *Graduate Management Research* 3: 3: whole part.

Berger, P. and Maurer, R. (2001) *Experimental Design with Applications in Management, Engineering and the Sciences*, Duxbury.

Boisot, M., (ed.) (1994) *East-West Business Collaboration: the Challenge of Governance in Post-Socialist Enterprises*, London: Routledge.

Burgoyne, J. G. (1994) 'Stakeholder analysis', in Cassell, C. and Symon, G., (eds.) *Qualitative Methods in Organizational Research*, London: Sage.

Clark, I. (1999) 'Corporate human resources and "bottom line" financial performance', *Personnel Review* 28: 4: 290–306.

Davies, J. (1992) 'Careers of trainers: biography in action, the narrative dimension', *Management Education and Development*, 23: 3: 207–214.

Farrell, P. (1992) 'Biography work and women's development: the promotion of equality issues', *Management Education and Development*, 23: 3: 215–224.

Forster, N. (1994) 'The analysis of company documentation', in Cassell, C. and Symon, G., (eds.), *Qualitative Methods in Organizational Research*, London: Sage.

Gill, J. and Johnson, P. (2002) *Research Methods for Managers*, London: Sage, 3rd edn.

Gowler, D., Legge, K. *et al.* (1993) *Case Studies in Organizational Behaviour*, London: Paul Chapman.

Hartley, J. F. (1994) 'Case studies in organizational research', in Cassell, C. and Symon, G., (eds.) *Qualitative Methods in Organizational Research*, London: Sage.

Holliday, A. (2002) *Doing and Writing Qualitative Research*. London: Sage.

Hunter Brown, C. J. and Faulkner, A. (1998) *Information Search Guide*, Milton Keynes: Open University, 2nd edn.

Jankowicz, A. D (2003a) *The Gift of the Grid*, A paper given at the XV International Conference on Personal Construct Psychology, Huddersfield, July.

Jankowicz, A. D. (2003b) *The Easy Guide to the Repertory Grid*, Chichester: Wiley.

Jones, M. O. (1988) 'In search of meaning: using qualitative methods in research and application', in Jones, M. O., Moore, M. D. and Snyder, R. C., (eds.) *Inside Organisations: Understanding the Human Dimension*, London: Sage.

Kane, E. (1985) *Doing Your Own Research: Basic Descriptive Research in the Social Sciences and Humanities*, London: Marion Boyars.

Lancaster, G. and Massingham, L. (1988) *Essentials of Marketing: Text and Cases*, London: McGraw-Hill.

Marshall, H. (1994), 'Discourse analysis in an occupational context', in Cassell, C. and Symon, G., (eds.) *Qualitative Methods in Organizational Research: a Practical Guide*, London: Sage.

Marsick, V. J. and O'Neil, J. (1999) 'The many faces of action learning', *Management Learning*, 30: 2: 159–176.

May, T. (2001) *Social Research: Issues, Methods and Process*, Milton Keynes: Open University Press, 3rd edn.

Miles, M. B. and Huberman, A. M. (1994) *Qualitative Data Analysis: an Expanded Sourcebook*, London: Sage, 2nd edn.

Mishler, E. G. (1991) *Research Interviewing: Context and Narrative*, London: Harvard University Press.

O'Cinneide, B. (1986) *The Case for Irish Enterprise*, Dublin: Enterprise Publications.

Orbell, J. (1987) *A Guide to Tracing the History of a Business*, Aldershot: Gower Press.

Orr, L. L. (1998) *Social Experiments Evaluating Public Programs with Experimental Methods*, New York: Sage.

Robson, C. (2002) *Real World Research: a Resource for Social Scientists and Practitioner-Researchers*, Oxford: Blackwell, 2nd edn.

Rogers, E. M. (1995) *Diffusion of Innovations*, Glencoe Ill. The Free Press.

Saunders, M., Lewis, P. *et al.* (2003) *Research Methods for Business Students*, London: Prentice Hall, 3rd edn.

Siegel, S. and Castellan, N. J. (1988) *Nonparametric Statistics for the Behavioural Sciences*, Maidenhead: McGraw-Hill.

Siehl, C. and Martin, J. (1988) 'Measuring organisational culture: mixing qualitative and quantitative methods', in Jones, M. O., Moore, M. D. and Snyder, R. C., (eds.) *Inside Organisations: Understanding the Human Dimension*, London: Sage Publications.

Stevenson, C. and Cooper, N. (1997) 'Qualitative and quantitative research', *The Psychologist* 10: 4: 159–160.

Tang, LinQi. (2003) E-mail personal communication to A. D. Jankowicz 2 August 2003.

Tyson, S. and Kakabadse, A. P., (eds.) (1987) *Cases in Human Resource Management*, London: Heinemann.

Weinstein, K. (1998) *Action Learning: a Practical Guide*, Hampshire: Gower Press.

Yin, R. K. (2002) *Case Study Research: Design and Methods*, London: Sage.

Semi-structured, open-ended techniques

- To present the procedural details of four semi-structured, relatively open-ended data-gathering techniques: conversational technique; the individual interview; the key informant interview; and the focus group, following the standard framework presented earlier
- To outline the procedure for content analysis of material obtained by interview techniques
- To help you to progress your project; and particularly, the empirical stages of your own project work, by considering and working through the practical implications in the event that you decide to use any of the techniques presented in this chapter

At a glance

All four techniques presented in this chapter are semi-structured. In other words, they involve you in asking questions whose content and sequence aren't fully specified in advance. The first three address individual respondents, while the last, the focus group, is a technique for helping people to discover and express their views by means of a group discussion. You would use all of them in situations in which you have a clear idea of your purpose, a general idea of the kinds of content which you wish to explore, and a rough notion of the sequence in which you will do so. You allow both the content and the sequence to vary with different respondents, in order to be sensitive to the way in which your interaction with particular individuals is progressing. The techniques are also open-ended. That is, they use a form of questioning in which your respondents are encouraged to answer in their own words. While you might have some hunches about the kind of answers to expect, you wouldn't be prepared to specify them in advance.

Because they are relatively unstructured and open-ended, they provide you with large amounts of rich, fertile, but disorganized data.

In turning these data into information, your main task during analysis is to classify and categorize what has been said, using *content analysis* technique.

All of these techniques can be used with the explicatory methods, and with case study method. However, they have an additional purpose when they are used with the survey method. In survey work, they are the means by which you conduct an initial, relatively unstructured pilot study in order to identify the questions to ask, the answer categories to provide, and the sequence to be followed in the more structured main study.

10.1 Conversations and storytelling

During your project period, you naturally spend a lot of your time talking informally to other people. Some of it is gossip, some is storytelling, and some involves conversations. All of it is valuable, often in a rather vague and unspecified way, in providing you with background about the personalities, procedures, culture and values of your organization. Here is how to make this information more accessible and organized. The headings follow the standard framework shown in Table 9.4.

Design

A straightforward way of providing an explicit focus is to turn a spontaneously occurring chat towards some purpose related to your project, controlling and maintaining the dialogue to this end. Sometimes, however, as Burgess (1982) indicates, you can initiate a conversation with a clear, project-related intention in mind, and this raises the possibility of holding a series of preplanned conversations in which you follow a rationale by which you group your respondents according to their job title, role, or status within the organisation. Are the data you're likely to get from Marketing different from those obtainable from Production, for example? Is the culture, and hence the 'flavour' of your conversations, likely to differ systematically according to the division or region in which you do your informal, conversational wandering around?

Elicitation

Elicitation requires you to listen properly. This means knowing how to:

- keep quiet without interjecting your own stories into the narrative, using your own comments to clarify the other person's meaning or elicit fresh meanings from him or her, rather than to initiate fresh topics of your own
- be sensitive to the non-verbal signals as well as the verbal, so that you can
- hear the emotions and feelings expressed by your informant, as well as the words.

However, this is anything but a passive process! You have to track what the respondent is saying; provide the usual feedback that pertains in any sort of conversation, unsupported by the greater formalities of structured interview technique; and you have to remember as much of what is said as possible since this is a conversation and note-taking is not possible.

Steering

In a structured interview, steering is always done directively. You tell your respondents how you want them to address your questions, often as a result of their answers to previous questions. For example, 'I'm asking this question because you said you had shop-floor experience before becoming a manager; now, bearing that experience in mind, could you tell me . . .' In a conversation, steering is a matter of conveying your purpose to your respondent, possibly in so many words, but more frequently by implication through the direction your comments and follow-up questions may take. If your respondent has already given you his or her thoughts, then exposing your own can stimulate additional material; sharing your own feelings (assuming they are relevant and it's done in response rather than in initiation) can deepen the affective content of the answers you hear.

Directiveness is a matter of degree, and you might find Table 10.1 useful in illustrating the range of possibilities.

You could consider extending the range of your conversations to include *storytelling*. The accounts which your respondents provide are obviously important with explicatory method, but can form a useful part of case study and survey methods too, if you consider that, as well as offering content, they are good indicators of your respondent's quality of experience, assumptions about self, and the organizational values as perceived by your respondent. Located at the relatively non-directive end of the range of possibilities, storytelling also requires you to tolerate considerable deviation on the part of the respondent, who is allowed to 'ramble on' since the length of the narrative, and the language used, provide information about the importance of the topic to the speaker, and his or her circumstances respectively, quite apart from the content of the account being provided. This can be a simple account of whatever is to the forefront of the speaker's mind as he/she replies to your invitation; this technique is often known as the *focused* or *informal* interview (May 2001).

It can, in contrast, literally be a story; in other words, an account with characters and a plot. Mair (1989; 1990) provides a rationale for the value of this form of storytelling as a form of psychological and sociological investigation, and Boje (1994) a thought-provoking account of why it matters to examine the assumptions underlying the stories we tell in and about organizations. Tommerup (1988) provides an interesting example, which focuses on the stories employees of Hughes Aircraft told about a succession of their chief executives, as a way of understanding the culture of the organization involved. (If you need a review of the basic material on organizational culture to provide a conceptual underpinning to the narratives you gather, you'll find Pheysey 1993 a convenient handbook of basic ideas.)

To return to technique: *self-characterization* is a very effective non-directive procedure for eliciting personal stories (Kelly 1991). You ask your respondent to describe him or herself, in the job being done, from a separate but sympathetic viewpoint.

Format

When you hold a conversation, you tell your respondent about the format in which you would like your questions answered by the way in which you use spoken English, by the way in which you respond to non-verbal signals, and by your mutual use of a variety of social skills. In other words, there aren't any particular techniques other than the ones you dispose of as a language user, and you would not make a deliberate statement of the form 'Please indicate your preferences by ranking the alternatives'.

TABLE 10.1 The range of non-directive elicitation and steering	
Parallel monologues	Pinteresque dialogue: 'questioner' concerned with his/her own issues, 'respondent' with his/her own; no steering occurs
Gossiping	Steering occurs mutually: respondent's direction steered, somewhat loosely, by the questioner's issue, and vice-versa; several topics or themes involved
Storytelling	Other than an indication by 'questioner' that he or she's willing to listen, steering left to the discretion of the respondent: respondent tells his/her story and determines the issues
Informal conversation	Steering occurs mutually, though often on one issue as determined by one of the participants
Research conversation	Steering by questioner within the bounds of the respondent's story and questioner's purpose; respondent takes the dialogue where he or she wishes
Semi-structured interview	Steering by questioner to cover certain previously identified issues within a topic predetermined by questioner; broad direction preset by questioner
As above	With firmer steering given by means of: a 'devil's advocate' questions: respondent presented with an opposing point of view to clarify his/her position b hypothetical questions to discover respondent's reactions in certain circumstances c questioner asserts an 'ideal' position, to discover how respondent sees the ideal d questioner offers interpretations to seek agreement and/or stimulate counter-arguments
Structured interview	Steering by questioner following predefined topic, issues and sequence; other material offered by respondent treated as marginal or ignored

ILLUSTRATION 10.1

John Davis is interviewing Jayanti Patel about himself and his company, as part of a study of ownership succession in Asian-owned small businesses. How does he see himself after 30 years of hard work in setting up and growing the firm? John establishes good rapport as he collects some basic background and biographical information about Jayanti and his intended successor (his son who, alas, is reluctant to take over the small corner shop in question, and who will also be interviewed), John addresses Jayanti as follows. 'I'd like you to tell me a little about yourself, and how you feel nowadays about the business. But could you tell it as a story? A story about Jayanti Patel and the firm, as if you were a friend who knew him very well, and liked him a lot.'

'Okay. Well! Perhaps the first thing to know about Jayanti is that he is a hard worker. He knows that you cannot make a success of a venture without caring about it, and you can tell that a person cares about what he is doing is by the extent of his effort, isn't it? He works hard, sometimes he has worked too hard, but always knowing that he was building a stable future for himself and his family. And until recently he has been pleased with the results he has achieved. The business has a steady turnover, he has been clever in building up links with good suppliers, and he is known as an honest and successful person in the Asian community and among his customers. But now the time has come to step down and his son, who is also conscientious and hard-working, and has always been his successor in his eyes, has told him that he wishes to begin studies to be a lawyer and eventually read for the Bar. Well. Of course he understands the boy's wishes – this is a fine ambition – but he is an only child and I really don't know – sorry, Jayanti! – really doesn't know what to do.'

At this point John is ready to ask Jayanti about the options available to him. Keeping the business ticking over in case his son's plans about study are not fulfilled? Employing a nephew as a manager? Selling the business outside the family? John is ready to switch to conventional reporting if he talks about the options themselves, but to retain the third person if he wishes to explore the feelings involved. Notice the two *essential* aspects of self-characterization technique. You make sure that the interviewee talks about themselves in the third person, using 'he or she' rather than 'I'. And you encourage a sympathetic and understanding viewpoint by asking the interviewee to 'speak as if they are describing someone they like very much'. The rationale here is that a sympathetic account will legitimize a warts-and-all account. By being affectionate about themselves, the interviewee will feel comfortable in telling all sides of the story.

Now, it isn't my place to teach you English (with one exception, and that is in Section 13.2). However, some points are worth noting.

- The tone of a conversation is something which is set mutually.
- To some degree, you can shape and model the form of your respondent's answers deliberately by the form of language you're using yourself, if you choose to do so. So, interest shown in the other person creates interest in yourself; the extent to which you use metaphors in your utterances will influence their use by your respondent; agreeing, nodding the head, and

appropriate eye-contact induce your respondent to expand on his or her material; and so forth.

- Your role as an interviewer, whether in a highly structured survey interview or in a non-directive conversation, is never neutral, and the meaning of your respondent's answers is something created by both of you. If this issue intrigues you, glance at Mishler (1991) or, in somewhat more detail, in Phillips and Jorgensen (2002: 81–83). A project that uses explicatory or case study method will demonstrate an awareness of this issue in its discussion of methodology, and will avoid oversimplifications of the 'only objective methods were used' variety.

Eliciting answers

The content of the questions you wish to interject into the conversation is entirely up to you, relating as it does to the purpose of your conversation. You may find it helpful to examine the material on structured interviewing in Section 11.2, however, since some of the material, especially on the sequencing of topics to be discussed, is relevant.

Recording answers

With one exception, you would be unlikely to be doing much recording in an unstructured conversation. The place for the tape-recorder or the notepad and pencil is in one of the other forms of semi-structured technique, and you will find yourself largely dependent on your memory as a recording medium. It's good practice to make a few notes in private as soon as possible after the conversation, however. Obviously, you will record the gist of what you remember, but you should also highlight any points which you might want to explore in more detail in subsequent conversations with your respondent, or by means of a more structured technique. Your project diary is probably the best place for this, even if you intend to use a separate record book for your data.

The exception pertains to the highly structured analysis technique, pioneered for conversational data by Sacks, in which tape-recordings are made: see Ten Have (1999).

Analysis

Perceiving

With that exception, the analysis of data that you have obtained conversationally is fairly unstructured. There are few structured techniques to apply, since you have relatively few data recorded systematically, and there is a danger that your analysis would be invalid if you used a technique which demands more robust data than those at your disposal. Analysis is still possible, however, and an informal content analysis of the various conversations you have had is very useful. See the description in Section 10.2. However, analysis of conversational data is as much to do with yourself as with the material your respondent has provided. Useful questions to ask yourself are as follows:

- How do the data I have obtained today compare with the other data I have already obtained? Are there any apparent trends? How frequent are various kinds of answers in comparisons to others? What picture seems to be emerging?
- What concepts and research from my background reading seem relevant to the data I have obtained?
- How did I personally feel about the conversations at the time I had them?
- Did the answers ring true?
- How can I confirm any initial impressions I formed?
- How much of myself went into it, does this matter, and to what extent do I need to discount it?

A useful way of perceiving patterns in your answers to these questions as you mull over the narrative is to record the answers in the form of a memo to yourself. Miles and Huberman (1994: 72–76) have some useful ideas on how you can be systematic about this technique, and prompt the thought that a simple classification and content analysis of a set of such memos is a useful way of developing a set of propositions for more formal investigation later on in your data-gathering activities.

More formally recorded conversational materials can be analyzed using the full rigours of the detailed approach described in Ten Have (1999), but you may not have time for it. Phillips and Jorgensen (2002: 148–153) suggest that substantial meaning can be derived from just four useful questions applied whenever you work with written text, however formally or informally you have recorded it. They are shown in Table 10.2 and are at the heart of *discourse analysis* technique,

TABLE 10.2 Analytical strategies in discourse analysis
Comparison   of the text with other texts of the same subject-matter. What assumptions about the subject-matter are being taken for granted in each. Are these explicit and recognized by the story-teller?
Substitution   of a word or phrase in the text with a different one, to see what difference it might make. Does it make a difference if we substitute the word 'sacked' for the word 'let go' in an account of a redundancy scheme, or is there sufficient information in the rest of the account to establish the speaker's emotions and feelings of control versus helplessness?
Exaggeration of detail   Take a phrase whose significance is not obvious and exaggerate it; under what assumptions and conditions might it make sense?
Multivocality   Is there more than one voice in a given piece of text? Is the speaker speaking at several levels; is it possible to discern the influence of other people in what is now being said by one person?

after Phillips and Jorgensen (2002:148–153)

particularly useful with the biographical and historical variants of explicatory method.

Summarizing

This is a matter of presenting the main themes mentioned and issues raised, in the form of a set of summary points. It is unlikely that these will be quantified in any way, unless as simple frequency counts of how often different views were expressed, under a simple set of nominal-category headings (see Table 9.2). The categories might be based on an analytic framework found in, or developed as a result of, your literature review; or they may be constructed there and then, as you look at the data, by means of the content analysis. Some statement of the limits of their usefulness, bearing in mind the extent to which you put yourself into the data, is wise.

Write-up

Presenting

If your recording was fairly informal, you won't be able to include large amounts of data in your project document. You will be limited to impressions, judgements, summary statements and so forth. There are, nevertheless, two situations in which you have to present such impressions. First, if your regulations require you to describe the organization in which you carried out the project (particularly common in professional and diploma programmes), then your impressions of the organizational culture, climate, and values will form a useful supplement to the more factual material concerning your organization's ownership, structure, market and customers.

Second, whether recorded using the memo technique or not, initial impressions are often a very good source of ideas for subsequent data-gathering using more structured techniques. In outlining your choice of topic, issues explored, and choice of design and techniques, it is useful to include a statement of these impressions in your project document as part of your rationale for doing so.

Locating

So, if you do report them formally, the results of conversational technique are presented in the body of the text of your project, rather than as an appendix. They are often an integral part of your argument.

In conclusion

All of this may seem that I'm making a mountain out of a molehill. If you would do all of this anyway, that's fine. However, if some of this is new to you, or helps to legitimize your feelings that informal methods are 'allowed' in project work, that's even better. But remember the message I expressed in Chapter 5: while the techniques being used may be relatively unstructured and open-ended, the responsibility for ensuring their accuracy is still there. That means that there's a need to check your impressions; a need to have repeated conversations with the same respondent and with others; and, almost always, a need to check your conclusions by using other semi-structured techniques, or to progress to a more formal stage of your data-gathering by using a structured technique, in a pilot-main study format.

If you intend to use any of the conversational techniques described here, please work through activities 1 to 4, to the extent that they apply, in the Project Guide.

10.2 The individual interview

As indicated in Table 10.1, a semi-structured interview differs from a conversation because the topic and issues to be covered have been determined in advance, because you have previously determined the sample of people whom you intend to contact, and usually because your attempt to prevent biases from affecting your data occurs *before* data collection rather than after.

Design

The design of a series of semi-structured individual interviews starts with an explicit statement (use your diary!) of the purpose in holding the interviews. It helps if you think of the purpose as some central issue which you need to resolve: a major question which arises from a particular facet of your thesis, or a critical part of your argument which you need to substantiate empirically. Thinking about this major question suggests a number of aspects, each of which merits one or more questions to be put to your respondents. Usually, the aspects are listed in no particular order (with the exception that the more straightforward, easy-to-answer, descriptive and less personal aspects should be dealt with at the start of your interview). Under each aspect, then, you list a number of questions which you intend to cover with your respondents. You're prepared to be flexible about the order in which you will pose them, depending on how each interview progresses; but it is important that you obtain answers to all of them by the time any one interview is complete. As a secondary issue, you intend to remain open and sensitive to new aspects, issues, and answers offered to you by the interviewee.

By this stage, you will have identified the population you're dealing with, drawn a sample using an appropriate technique (see Section 8.2), and specified the strata or groupings, if any, of respondents within the sample. The plan is to cover the ground with all of your respondents and analyze the results according to the sub-groupings (whether managers in one department answer systematically differently to managers in another, for example).

As you can see, an important difference between the conversation and the semi-structured interview lies in the way in which you plan to minimize bias. In the conversation, bias is handled indirectly, by repeating conversations on a particular issue with the same or different respondents, or by triangulation (using some different technique and looking for compatibility). In the semi-structured interview, while these other techniques are open to you, you reduce bias by means of a careful design of the interview itself – biases arising from the sequence in which you address subject-matter, from any inadvertent omission of questions, from unrepresentative sampling, and from an uncontrolled over- or under-representation of subgroups among your respondents (the purpose of Table 8.4, you will recall).

Among the design decisions you make, probably the most far-reaching pertains to the communication medium which you intend to use. You have a choice of three: the traditional face-to-face encounter, the telephone interview, and the e-mail interview. Table 10.3 provides a comparison of the main semi-structured techniques.

Elicitation

In the conversation, effective elicitation is a matter of linguistic and personal intuition and flair; in semi-structured interviewing, elicitation is often regarded as a matter of skill, and I would imagine that you will be familiar with the idea of 'interviewing skills' from some part of your taught course, or from your earlier reading. In a sense, the semi-structured interview demands greater skill than the fully structured interview. For a start, there's more face-to-face, 'on the hoof' flexibility and adaptability involved, precisely because the social encounter hasn't been fully structured in advance. Moreover, the purpose of a semi-structured interview is often to obtain information about personal, attitudinal, and value-laden material, and you are likely to be dealing with matters which call for social sensitivity in their own right.

This subject is a large one, and the best I can do is to refer you to one or more of the following: Edenborough (2002), Gillham (2000), King (1994), and Torrington (1991). Most deal with matters of interviewing skill while the last offers an in-depth treatment of interviewing in an HR and personnel context.

You will discover that the particular skills required vary, depending on the medium of communication. Internet-based interviewing using e-mailer facilities is a viable alternative to the traditional face-to-face and telephone-based formats, but it has its limitations. The near-impossibility of maintaining anonymity and, despite the use of various kinds of smiley, the absence of all non-verbal cues in particular, are among the issues mentioned in Table 10.3. However, it also has advantages compared with other techniques, combining informality with the creation of a permanent, analysis-ready record of what was said by interviewer and interviewee.

Steering

This is a matter of two contending forces: a directive force on the part of your respondent, in the sense that he or she has a role in determining the sequence of questions and the way in which these are to be interpreted; and a deliberate, explicit but not rigid effort on your part, in bringing the respondent back to the main flow of the interview when the occasion is right. (Rather like sailing, in fact: the wind provides both energy and direction, while your hand is at the tiller to harness this energy and channel the direction onto the bearing you want.) Whyte (1982) is particularly good on this topic, and offers you a scale of 'restrictiveness' which you can use to increase or decrease the directiveness of the dialogue at any one point. This is shown in Table 10.4.

TABLE 10.3 A comparison of the main interview techniques

H stands for high, M for medium, and L for low levels of the characteristic shown at the left.

Characteristic	Face-to-face interview	Telephone interview	e-mail interview
Design and sampling issues			
Control over inclusion of all population in sample	H	M	H
Control over selection of respondents into sample	H	H	H
Chances of answers being given by someone else	L	L	L
Sensitivity to distortion by respondent substitution	M	H	L
Chance of controlling bias due to selective non-response	H	H	H
Refusal rate	M	H	L
Response rate with varied populations (public-at-large)	H	L	L
Response rate with homogenous, highly-selected populations, if incentivized as below	H	H	M
Elicitation issues			
Likely acceptability of longer list of questions	H	M	L
Likely success of complex questions	H	L	M
Likely success of open-ended questions	H	H	H
Likely success of steering questions	H	H	M
Likely success of boring-but-necessary questions	H	H	L
Likely success with personal and sensitive questions	H	L	M
Likely success in avoiding missed questions	H	H	H
Issues of bias			
Likely success in establishing anonymity/ confidentiality	M	M	L
Chances of avoiding bias due to social desirability of answers	L	M	H
Chances of avoiding 'interviewer' bias	L	M	H
Chances of avoiding contamination by others	M	H	H
Administrative issues			
Amount of time required	M	L	L
Potential costs	H	L	L
Control over costs	H	L	H
Sensitivity of costs to geographical distance from respondents	L	M	L
Feasibility of assistance being available to investigator	H	M	L

After Curasi (2001), Dillman (2000; 1978), Frey (1983), Selwyn and Robson (1998)

Format

In the semi-structured interview, you avoid the use of pre-set answer categories. However, you can of course influence the options available to the interviewee, and this is a matter of degree. The least directive approach is the **projective** form of questioning, in which you ask a fairly vague or apparently unrelated question, and take the answer, not at face value, but as indicative of a perception, belief, personal value or motive which, you infer, predisposes your respondent to answer in that way.

For example, instead of asking the respondent to state what he or she thinks of their own effectiveness as a manager, you might ask a general question about managers as leaders, in the form 'how would you define leadership?', or, more directively, 'what are the constraints that managers in the company must handle?' You would interpret the answer as an indication of your respondent's own effectiveness. As you can see, projective questioning is very context-dependent; nevertheless, the following general guidelines apply:

- Projective questions in which you are looking for answers about perceptions are easiest and safest to handle. Questions designed to elicit personal values and, particularly, motives, require the greatest amount of sensitivity on your part.

TABLE 10.4 Varying the directiveness in steering a semistructured interview	
Non-committal utterance ('uh-huh'); Nod of the head	Encourages respondent to continue on same topic with minimal influence on direction of answer or introduction of new question; though a pattern in the utterances, e.g. only nodding when the same point is made, can reinforce development or repetition of the same point
Repeating interviewee's last utterance verbatim but with a questioning inflection	Increases the encouragement to expand on the same point
Probing the last utterance	Raising a question on the same point or remarking on it: interviewee encouraged to develop the point
Probing the idea just before the last utterance	More directive because it doesn't follow the interviewee's lead to the same extent that probing the last utterance would
Probing an idea expressed earlier in the interview	A deliberate choice by the interviewer to go back to something the interviewee said earlier
Introduction of a new question on the same general theme	More directive exercise of interviewer control
Introduction of a new theme	More directive still
After Whyte (1982)	

- Projective questions calling for answers about the respondent's immediate boss, and about his or her colleagues, are likely to be more tricky than ones which refer to the respondent him- or herself.

- Using projective questions requires a high level of pre-existing rapport. Your respondents would be unhappy if they construed your questions as 'loaded', (which they are) and intrusive or possibly malevolent (which they're not).

- Before using one, always consider the alternative of being straightforward about your difficulty. A form of words 'Look, I feel shy about asking this question, but I'd appreciate your help as I think this issue's very important', followed by a direct, *non-projective* question, is often safer and just as effective.

- The more projective questions you use, the more you have to interpret the result, and the more your own judgement will influence the validity of the answers received.

If you haven't encountered this form of questioning before, glance at (Schlackman 1989); written by a very experienced market researcher, this short article is a very convenient compilation of eight different verbal and graphical projective techniques.

The most directive format for answers in a semi-structured interview is one in which you follow an open-ended question with an indication of the context or scope of the answer you expect. For example, a sentence beginning 'What did you do when the marketing proposal was rejected . . .?' (an open-ended question) might be completed with the words '. . . how did you handle the staff who'd prepared it?' if you want to limit the answers to issues of delegation rather than issues of personal reactions, alternative proposal development, or anything else. Clearly, completing the sentence with the words '. . . did you recognize a training need in the staff who prepared it . . .', (pause), '. . . or did you put it down to the opposition from other departments?' would turn an open-ended question into a closed question, more appropriate to a fully structured interview technique.

The e-mail interview format is particularly informal. As Selwyn and Robson (1998) argue, the influences of status, gender, age, and race are less dominant in e-mail communication, and the asynchronous nature of the medium permits interviewees to respond when they feel comfortable.

Eliciting answers

Again, the content of the questions is up to you. You might note, though, that the semi-structured interview is a good technique for questions dealing with feelings and attitudes, and any situation in which you are uncertain about the range of possible answers you are likely to obtain. It's commonly used with the case study method, and fairly frequently in the first stages of survey work.

Recording answers

You should do this as systematically, thoroughly, and completely as you can. If your design requires you to carry out a large number of relatively brief interviews (20 minutes or so), you will probably cover the ground adequately by making hand-written notes during the interview (having asked your respondent's permission at the outset). Read over and revise them immediately afterwards, and make an appointment for a very brief subsequent meeting (five minutes or so on the same day as your interview) to resolve any issue which looks important and wasn't properly recorded in your notes. An elegant alternative is to telephone your interviewee to express your thanks for the interview, using the phone call to clarify anything you missed in your notes.

Ideally, your notes should be in the form of a précis rather than a paraphrase or synopsis (see Figure 4.2 for examples of each); it is very useful to record key points, or particularly interesting or apt expressions, as direct, word-for-word quotations, for subsequent use in your write-up.

You may wish to consider the use of a tape-recorder if your interviews are any longer than half an hour. If you plan to use one or other of the hermeneutic narrative analysis techniques, then you simply have to make a tape-recording, and turn it into a transcript, regardless of the length of your interview. The most important factor, and one which first-timers often forget, is the time it takes to make the transcript: at least seven hours of work for every hour of interviewing if you are to do it properly (see Table 4.3) A written, literal, word-for-word text which records all the 'ums' and 'ers' is an essential prerequisite to any form of analysis, since it is impractical to make an analysis directly during playback.

The great advantage of an e-mail interview is that it provides a permanent record of what was said. 'The text from e-mail interviews can easily be tailored for any word processing package or computer-based qualitative analysis package with a minimum of alteration . . . this also eliminates any errors introduced through incorrect transcription' (Selwyn and Robson 1998).

Analysis

The main technique associated with semi-structured interviews is called *content analysis*. With the growth in popularity of interpretivist approaches, this is, nowadays, a generic term for the core of the activity in such techniques as narrative analysis, discourse analysis, or, more generally, qualitative analysis as presented in Robson (2002) or Holliday (2002: Ch 5). A comprehensive set of readings is provided in Neuendorf (2002). Where these techniques differ is usually in the use made of the result of this basic procedure.

As the name suggests, the purpose is to describe the content of your respondents' utterances systematically, and classify the various meanings expressed in the material you have recorded. There are alternative ways of analyzing this kind of data. You might find yourself presenting information in the form of a connected narrative (in a study following the case study method, for example), or by means of a series of verbatim quotations taken from the interviews. Indeed, researchers who come from an ethnographic background and those who use discourse analysis, would be very uncomfortable with the bottom half of Table 10.5 below, preferring to stop short at an identification of the main themes being expressed.

However, all reporting of semi-structured interviews assumes that you present findings which are representative of what was said, and all forms of content analysis provide their own ways of checking the reliability of the categorizations obtained. Content analysis is also important in the analysis of more structured interview and questionnaire materials: see Chapters 11 and 12.

Perceiving

Content analysis is, very literally, a perceptual activity. You engage in a process of active perception and judgement which classifies the answers you obtained. It involves five stages:

- preparation, in which you identify your unit of analysis (what counts as an utterance to be classified: a word? sentence? whole conversation?)
- categorizing, in which you either use a set of categories taken from the literature, or devise a set of categories of your own by reading over your written transcript. These will be used to classify each utterance by means of
- coding, in which you assign each utterance to one and only one category
- tabulating, in which you count the number of utterances under each category
- illustrating, in which you present the categories and list the assertions under them: all, or a representative set.

Table 10.5 provides you with a procedural guide and a worked example showing the result of a simple content analysis of the answers to one open-ended interview question.

As mentioned earlier, it is essential that the categories which you construct are reliable. If you are using categories drawn from a pre-existing theory or rationale, then it is important that, before you use them to classify your data, you make a brief, explicit list of the defining characteristics of each category: that is, of the signs that you will be looking for in order to put each assertion into one category rather than another. Reliability is a bigger problem in those situations in which you have no pre-existing categories in mind and have to draw them up in the first place as a result of reading, and perceiving, the dominant themes in your interview transcripts. This is because there is no pre-existing list of defining characteristics and because you have to invent these, as well as the categories themselves.

In either case, the issue of reliability boils down to a simple question. Would someone else perceive the same categories as you did? The way to answer this question is to be literal about it. Hand a photocopy of the uncoded transcripts to a colleague whom you ask to recognize categories for him- or herself. You would then compare the two category sets, your own and theirs, and argue over them until something more useful emerged and agreement on the defining characteristics was obtained. This would then be tested by seeing if you were both agreed on the coding, i.e., on the assigning of utterances to categories. You should consider involving one or more of your respondents in this role, assuming that the anonymity of the other respondents' material can be preserved. (See the rationale presented in Section 5.2: if you're working collaboratively, they are often very well qualified for this particular task.)

TABLE 10.5 A procedural guide to the tabulation and presentation of content-analyzed data

The steps to follow	Example
Specify the sample:	All 33 members of New Product Development department
Indicate if stratified and how:	17 in the Industrial Products division, 16 in the Consumer Products division
Indicate how many responded in each stratum (to provide columns for the table):	32 (17 and 15 + 1 unavailable on day of interview)
Prepare the unit of analysis:	The whole of the respondent's reply is treated as a single entry under analysis: one category, regardless of number of sentences
Prepare the data:	A transcript of the 32 conversations with the relevant part of the interview highlighted; each coded with a number, 1 to 6, according to the categories below

The steps to follow	Example
Specify the categories, how derived, and what defines each category (to provide the rows of the table)	Derived from consideration of all the data; defining characteristics given in italics 1 *Plan inappropriate* in view of what *competitors* are doing 2 *Plan unviable* since the proposed *divestments inappropriate* 3 *Plan unviable* since planned *acquisitions don't match company policy* 4 *Plan viable* but needs *further development* 5 *No view either way* 6 Miscellaneous

(Code the data)		Industrial products		Consumer products	
		n	%	n	%
Tabulate the data, calculating percentages, using the total of each column as the base for each column	Plan inappropriate in view of what competitors are doing	8	47	7	44
	Plan unviable since the proposed divestments inappropriate	4	24	3	19
	Plan unviable since planned acquisitions don't match company policy	3	18	3	19
	Plan viable but needs further development	1	6	1	6
	Miscellaneous	0	0	1	6
	No view either way	1	6	0	0
	No Answer	0	0	1	6
	TOTAL	17	101	16	100
Check that total percentages sum to 100 allowing for rounding errors	Presenting in whole numbers here, so after dividing by the column total, round back to the nearest whole number				

TABLE 10.5 A procedural guide to the tabulation and presentation of content-analyzed data (cont.)	
Prepare a verbal description of the table, to be used when presenting the table in the project document	**Illustration:** 'The majority of respondents (82%) expressed unfavourable views about the plan, the most common being that competitors' activities were insufficently taken into account. This is true in each of the divisions in which the respondents are located. Only a small minority (one person in each division) felt the plan was viable, and that with reservations; one further person refused to commit him/herself. The miscellaneous comment concerned some of the personalities involved and does not add to the information expressed.'

Summarizing

Your data consist of frequency counts under nominal categories (see Table 9.5) and so tabulation is the obvious way of presenting the information available. Simply count the number items in each category, perhaps stratified according to your sampling design. This will reveal relationships and permit a variety of descriptive and analytic statistics to be carried out on the numbers. If you are less concerned with the numbers, then a list of the various utterances, or representative examples, can be reported in a table in which the columns are the category headings. Miles and Huberman (1994 Ch 5) provide other alternatives to the table of numbers, as do Morris *et al.* (1988) and Robson (2002).

As presented, tabulated information of this kind is formally identical to what could have been obtained by a structured interview or questionnaire question (often due to the unit of analysis being set to be equal to the respondent's entire utterance in response to the question, regardless of how many sentences were involved), and many of the reporting conventions of the more structured techniques apply: see Chapter 11.

This isn't surprising. The answer categories for fully structured interviews and questionnaires were obtained through content analysis in the first place, whether the categories derive from some theory, or are developed from a pilot study, or are developed informally 'in one's head' on material obtained by conversational techniques. Structured techniques may look more 'objective' because the answer categories are specified before the questions have been asked, but where do you think these categories came from? Someone, somewhere, has carried out some form of content analysis in order to arrive at them in the first place and has had to grapple with the resulting problems of reliability in categorization.

An alternative approach to tabulation, in those situations where the relative frequency of different types of response is less important than the identification of different meanings expressed by the respondent and their careful and reliable interpretation by the researcher, consists of the *quasi-judicial* or *explanation-building* (Yin 2002) technique: a technique associated particularly with case study method. The basic procedure is to:

- examine some of the data (whether these have been categorized or not)
- check whether they can be understood in terms of a particular explanation taken from the literature or from previous pilot study work
- check whether this explanation still holds water when further data have been examined
- revise the explanation as required, until it can account for *all* of the data.

Used as a way of summarizing the information in the empirical data, the explanation-building approach can also be used as a design factor in your work. In other words, if you are using case study method, the decision on which cases to use can, (after the choice of an initial set of cases), be deliberately deferred until initial data analysis has led to the development of an informative explanation for what is going on. Further cases are then chosen in a search for instances which would prove exceptions to the explanation, forcing the development of an alternative, more comprehensive explanation which can explain more of the cases – more of what is going on, in other words. There is more on this earlier, in the context of replication logic: see Section 9.2.

Robson (1993: 380–381) provides a fascinating example of explanation building technique used to account for the conditions under which people embezzle company funds. Another instance is presented in Table 10.6, based on a study I once conducted for the Benefits Agency, investigating, *inter alia*, the situations in which sanctions must be applied in the case of security breaches committed by Agency employees working as counter clerks dealing with benefit claims. Possible explanations were considered for their fit with the observations, each one being rejected in succession until an explanation which matched all of the observations was found. The particular technique exemplified here (and in Robson 1993) is known as **negative case analysis** (Kidder 1981). What is important is that the final explanation fits all known cases in the data set (which achieves the generality argued for as a characteristic of all research (see Section 8.2) while providing a precise definition of the issue being investigated. Here, the number of respondents giving one kind of reason rather than another is irrelevant to understanding. What is important is that the understanding is achieved when *all* of the respondents, and all of the observations, have been accounted for in a single explanation.

Write-up

The results of semi-structured interviews can be presented in a variety of ways, from the continuous narrative which blends empirically obtained information together with your own interpretative comments, to a formal, tabular summary accompanied by the results of statistical tests.

Presenting

There's no more to be said about the **narrative account**, other than to remind you to be careful in the inferences you draw from your information. Tables 7.8 and

13.2 will remind you of the pitfalls involved. Tabular presentation is exemplified in Table 10.5, and described in more detail in Section 11.1. However, there is a third way of presenting semi-structured interview material, and that involves the use of **illustrative quotations**.

You can give a highly informative presentation of your findings by stating the main issues you were exploring in the interviews, and, for each issue, presenting the relevant categories from a content analysis, with one or more verbatim quotations taken from the interview transcripts in order to illustrate the points being made. The impact of a list of verbatim statements can have a dramatic impact on your readers – statements which all say the same thing (grouped under their category headings, you will recall), but in slightly different ways, with all the weight of experience, the awareness of practical detail, and the practitioner wisdom of the people whom you interviewed in gathering the data.

You will recall from my account of the general framework in Section 9.3 that your write-up should always include some information on the reliability of your

TABLE 10.6 An example of explanation building using negative case analysis	
Explanation	**Case evidence**
1 Sanctions pertain only when a counter clerk commits a fraudulent activity to his or her own benefit (e.g. paying a benefit cheque to his/her own bank account).	
	but interviews with counter clerks show that some activities don't involve personal benefit (e.g. making an overpayment to a claimant who is personally known to the counter clerk)
2 Sanctions pertain when a counter clerk commits an act which defrauds the Agency, regardless of who gains from that act.	
	but interviews with counter clerks show that some acts are security breaches, which don't involve fraud (e.g. leaving their computer terminal switched on and unattended, in plain view and reach of the claimant)
3 Sanctions pertain when a counter clerk deliberately breaks the rules laid down by the Agency, regardless of whether these involve fraud or breaches of security.	
	but the interviews also show that some of the rules are underspecified so it's difficult to assess the deliberateness (e.g. spending insufficient time in investigating a claim, just in order to meet the monthly targets of completed claims)
4 Sanctions pertain when a counter clerk malevolently and clearly breaks the rules laid down by the Agency, regardless of whether these involve fraud or breaches of security.	

Based on cases in Jankowicz (1996)

findings, and the argument was first stated in Section 9.2 in the discussion of triangulation. This is the place to include any evidence you have obtained on the reliability of your content analysis category system. This evidence can be of two kinds. You can provide evidence by rational argument, in which you describe what you did to make sure that the categories were robust:

- perhaps they came from other people's published work, and are commonly used in this kind of research
- perhaps you devoted substantial time and effort into pre-researching the definitions of each category, and referred carefully to these definitions each time you categorized your evidence (in which case, show the definitions in your account to demonstrate that they are unambiguous).

Alternatively, you can ask a friend to repeat the content analysis independently and *measure* the extent to which you are both agreed on the way in which utterances have been allocated to categories. Two statistical indices are provided in the procedural guide given as Table 10.7.

Locating

By definition, a narrative account blends empirically derived information with reasoned argument, and would therefore appear in the body of the text. Either spread out in crucial locations over most of your project document (as in the case of many generic and library-based projects: see Figures 3.2 and 3.3), or confined neatly within the boundaries of an 'empirical section' (a little like Figure 3.1). A tabular presentation which focuses on numbers and proportions would more likely be presented in an empirical section, each table followed by a verbal statement of the information presented as in Table 10.5. As you will see in Chapter 13, the place for long lists is normally the appendix. However, if you're careful in your selection, and can present your argument in an interesting and, possibly, entertaining way, here is one situation in which a longish list of verbatim quotations from your respondents can be placed in the main body of the text, as a supplement to the tabular account. It isn't primarily there to add interest, however, but to move your argument onwards at key stages in your presentation.

 If you intend to use the general interview technique described here, please work through activities 1 to 4, to the extent that they apply, in the Project Guide.

10.3   The key informant interview

Key informant interviews differ from other forms of interview largely because respondents are chosen on the basis of their idiosyncratic, specialized knowledge rather than being randomly chosen to sample the range of issues you are investigating and this has important consequences for design. According to Tremblay (1982), the technique is especially useful in:

TABLE 10.7 Procedural guide to reliability calculation in content analysis

Purpose: To demonstrate the absence of idiosyncrasy in the allocation of responses to categories when coding those responses. Would someone else arrive at the same allocations? Also, to demonstrate the extent to which a careful discussion of category definitions has increased the reliability of coding.

Procedure:

1. Record the category into which you have coded each item.
2. Record the category into which a colleague has independently coded each item.
3. List the categories down one side of a sheet of paper or spreadsheet.
4. Repeat them along the bottom of the paper or sheet.
5. Into the cells of the matrix thus formed, enter the number of items you and your colleague have placed in each cell.

Your content analysis is reliable to the extent that you both agree: so all of the items should lie on the diagonal of this matrix, with no outliers.

Example: steps 1 to 5 result in:

Colleague's list Your list	Comms. Probs.	Prod. Diffs.	Define Mkt.	Will. Coop	Client Knowl.	Total
Communication problems	15	1	2	4	2	24
Production difficulties	–	10	–	2	–	12
Defining the market	3	–	12	1	–	16
Willingness to cooperate	5	2	–	14	1	22
Client's product knowledge	2	4	–	–	16	22
Total	25	17	14	21	19	96

A simple percentage agreement score

1. Sum the items which lie along the diagonal, and express this sum as a percentage of the total number of items:

2. $100 \times \left(\dfrac{15 + 10 + 12 + 14 + 16}{96} \right) = 69.8\%$

Intuitive enough, but biased by the sheer number of categories: the fewer the categories, the easier it is to get a large percentage by chance; impossible to compare percentage agreement scores across separate content analyses which have different numbers of categories. You need to find a way which removes the effect due to chance.

TABLE 10.7 Procedural guide to reliability calculation in content analysis (cont.)

Cohen's Kappa (Cohen 1960)

The number of codings on which you both agree, minus the number of codings for which agreement would be expected by chance given the marginal totals; as a proportion of the total number of codings minus the number of codings for which agreement would be expected by chance.

To find the level of agreement due to chance

1 Find the proportion of the total codings which each person has allocated to each category.	You	24/96=0.25	12/96=0.125	16/96=0.17	22/96=0.23	22/96=0.23
	Colleague	25/96=0.26	17/96=0.17	14/96=0.15	21/96=0.22	19/96=0.20
2 Multiply together the corresponding proportions (yours and your colleague's); sum the result.		(0.25 × 0.26) +	(0.125 × 0.17) +	(0.17 × 0.15) +	(0.23 × 0.22) +	(0.23 × 0.20)

= 0.2079

= 20.79

3 Multiply this sum by 100

Now subtract this from the number of codings on which you agree; and also, subtract this from the total number of codings; divide the first result by the second.

$$\text{Kappa} = \frac{67 - 20.79}{96 - 20.79} = 0.614$$

Cohen's Kappa is a very common measure of agreement, and it is worth using it as a supplement to the simple percentage agreement score. In both cases, your objective is to discuss the result with your colleague, exchange views of what exactly you mean by each category, and repeat the whole content analysis and coding, with the objective of improving on the level of agreement. (Repeat both analyses after you have done the coding afresh and trust that the value you compute the second time round is higher!)

Actually, there is a more accurate agreement measure than Kappa. Kappa ignores the fact that, in most instances, you and your colleague will have more agreements than disagreements, and assumes that you have a fair idea of the kinds of errors you are likely to make – an assumption that may not be warranted in the first of your two codings. If you are in a situation in which the absolute degree of agreement is important to your argument, rather than the fact that you can improve on your first coding, use the measure described in Perrault and Leigh (1989).

- Defining the essential characteristics of some issue by drawing on the personal experience and understanding of the people involved. The way in which such concepts as 'organizational learning', or 'customer orientation', are understood and interpreted in practice in your particular organization, for example.

- Identifying the boundaries, constraints and extremes within which these definitions are seen to apply.

- Increasing your knowledge of the issue itself.

Design

This technique uses purposive, 'snowball' sampling (see Section 9.2): you take the guidance of your early respondents into account in choosing subsequent interviewees. Moreover, you also involve early respondents in determining the kinds of questions you will ask of your subsequent interviewees. As a result, your advance planning must include arrangements to prevent your respondents from running away with the design, and you do this in two ways. First, by determining the criteria for respondent choice in advance, bearing in mind:

- their role, job title, and position in the organization

- their likely knowledge of the issue involved

- their willingness to help, and potential articulateness in doing so

- their likely perspective on the issue, so that idiosyncratic views can be controlled.

Second, by recording subsequent deviations from the list of people you initially chose as interviewees, presenting both the initial and final list as a table in your write-up, and commenting on the likely differences this might have caused to the information which you obtain.

ILLUSTRATION 10.2

So, for example, in a study of senior staff views on some policy decision which will affect the company's brand image it might be appropriate to interview the managing director and the heads of the finance and marketing functions. Talking to all three may suggest that the HR function has a key role in the development of the company image (Martin and Beaumont 2003), which merits an interview; and that the production head has strong views which disagree with those expressed by the head of finance, and should also be interviewed.

Elicitation

Since this is a form of semi-structured interview, all the general comments made in Sections 10.1 and 10.2 apply, with the following specific pointers.

Steering

For any one respondent, you would proceed from the general to the particular, asking questions which define terms and determine broad boundaries before proceeding to particular details. As the sequence of interviews progresses, you incorporate questions which check the information you have obtained from your early respondents, and look for particular viewpoints and comments on these early impressions from the current respondent's perspective, always remembering to cover the general ground with the current respondent first.

Format

The comments made under this heading in Sections 10.1 and 10.2 apply.

Eliciting answers

Again, the actual content of the answers depends on your purpose, which I cannot anticipate here. Remember, though, that the individual expertise of your respondents is what matters with this technique, and so you might wish to include some questions which help to establish this expertise. For example, how long the person has been in his or her job, or any particular professional background which might have helped to formulate their views.

Recording answers

The comments made under this heading in Section 10.2 apply: you will need some form of recording medium and in the case of longer interviews, this might well involve a tape-recorder. Bear in mind that different expert interviewees might offer you data expressed in the language of their particular expertise. Thus, an accountant might give you a table of financial ratios, or a senior manager, a page showing the results of a SWOT analysis. Take these when you leave, in addition to any personal record you make, even if you have no current plan to present them during your write-up.

Analysis

Data obtained from key informant interviews are well suited to a content analysis in which the categories reflect the major perspectives arising in the interviews.

Perceiving

As before, you are identifying what people have said and the emphasis which they have given it. Do people with different roles or expertise bases converge on an agreement about the issues involved, or do their individual perspectives vary in significant ways, perhaps as stakeholders of important but divergent positions? How frequently do different people express these similar or dissimilar views? How does their position and role affect the nature of the data which they provide? Moreover, which data are as you would expect, and which are informative because they are surprising?

Summarizing

As before, you would do this by means of a narrative account and/or by counting the number of people who have given different kinds of answers. Bearing in mind that it is the individual respondent's specialist views which are particularly important, and that there may only be one of each kind of interviewee (one Chief Executive, one Group Chief Accountant, and so on), you may want to present information initially under job title headings, before going on to summarize the views on which there is agreement and the views on which there is disagreement, concluding with a statement of the significance of the main viewpoints.

Write-up

There is little more to say under this heading that I haven't already implied under the headings immediately above, and in Section 10.2.

Presenting

What makes your data informative to the reader is its provenance: who said it and why, as much as what was said! And so:

Locating

Locating your findings in the main body of the text, preceding and illuminating the findings of a larger probability sample drawn from employees in general, is a common, and very informative, way of proceeding. If you have lots of findings from individual job holders, one respondent for each job, you might consider making these an appendix, and just presenting a summary in the main body of the text. If so, you would need to make sure that the list of job titles was shown as a table in the main body, when you describe the sample of respondents.

> This would be a good point at which to read Case Example 10.1.

> If you intend to use the key informant interview described here, please work through activities 1 to 4, to the extent that they apply, in the Project Guide.

10.4 The focus group

This is a form of group interview in which the data arise from dialogue and general discussion among participants, rather than from a dialogue between yourself as investigator exploring his or her story with a single person as respondent. Though it has gained a degree of notoriety in recent times, when used to identify general social reactions to various party-political initiatives (and, some would argue, to substitute for such initiatives), it is in fact particularly useful for discovering the range of views and attitudes present within an organization or part of it. It offers a good opportunity to observe the processes by which people interact, and hence to infer something of the culture and climate of the organization, as well as providing you with data about the content of people's views on the issues which you are exploring. Carey (1994), whose useful procedural guide makes a good supplement to the account which follows below, suggests that the focus group is particularly useful for:

- needs assessment
- the subsequent development of questionnaires, where you may wish to identify the concerns people have and the language in which they talk about these concerns, to provide a vocabulary for the questions you will be writing
- the interpretation of previously obtained research results, especially where these may appear to be puzzling or contradictory.

Because the technique involves a number of people in interaction, your control over the sequence of questions dealt with is less than in the one-to-one interviews described above, and the data are somewhat more difficult to analyze; moreover, your questions need to be restricted to publicly expressible material. So if you use focus groups in your project work, you might consider triangulating by using one of the individual forms of interviewing as well.

Design

If your purpose is simply to familiarize yourself with the variety of views on a topic, a pair of focus groups will do; however, if you are examining different perspectives, or exploring a variety of issues on which people's views are likely to vary depending on their role or company position, you will need to organize a larger number. (One group alone is never sufficient, since the data may simply reflect individual personalities, raising problems for the generalization of your findings to your organization as a whole.)

Each group should consist of similar kinds of people with enough in common that they can enter into a discussion about the topic in question, but preferably unfamiliar with each other on a regular, day-to-day basis. The latter may seem surprising, but consider: if they know each other and communicate regularly, your participants take a lot of things for granted. Yet these are just the things (values, norms, assumptions and beliefs based on a common organizational rather than personal history), that you want to uncover, by the skilful and careful way in which you conduct the discussion. Ideally, you create a situation in which the focus group is led to *discover* them for you. While it's appropriate to mix people doing different kinds of job at the same organizational level, Krueger and Casey (2000) are probably correct in suggesting that you shouldn't mix people across organizational levels, for the above reason and the additional one that people in supervisor–subordinate relationships to each other may be inhibited in what they are willing to say to each other.

Table 10.8 lists the main factors involved in designing focus group activities, most of them self-evident. Notice the distinction made between the focus group

TABLE 10.8 Procedural guide to designing and conducting a focus group

Determining purpose
- what kind of information is being sought?
- why is it being sought: what project issues will it illuminate?
- consider involving members of the organization (but not future focus group participants) in identifying issues, questions and type of focus group participant to recruit
- who else will have access (including feedback to the focus group participants themselves)?
- a written statement of the above, for discussion with people who will use the results: stakeholders and other interested parties in the organization, tutor, sponsor

Determining number and size of groups
- one to four groups for fairly structured, exploratory work
- 6 to 8 groups for relatively unstructured work requiring full content analysis of data
- 4 to 12 people in each group: small groups may be biased by existing relationships between participants, individual expertise, uncooperative respondents; larger groups raise difficulties in controlling and recording subgroup conversations
- not too large so that everyone has the opportunity to talk
- add 20 per cent extra to each group to allow for 'no-shows'

Determining focus group participants
- which different categories of people will be involved?
  - Members of different departments?
  - Holders of different types of post?
  - Members of different professional groups?
  - Advisory/service groups?
  - Customers/clients, potential or actual?
  - Big customers/small customers?
- different focus groups for different categories

Determining timetable
- a day or so to determine questions, especially if these are developed cooperatively
- a half-day for preparation, briefing of other people involved in observation/recording
- a half-day per focus group activity
- a further day for preparation and administration of recordings, per focus group
- a week or so for typing transcripts
- another week for analysis
- a week for write-up and report

Also
- provide refreshments
- ask permission to tape-record
- check any views which may have been the result of inaccurate first impressions of one another's status or value as a contributor
- encourage open expression, discourage self-censoring, legitimize free expression as much as possible

After Carey (1994); Krueger and Casey (2000); Morgan (1997).

members and other people in the organization, whom it may be possible to involve in the design of the group. You'll recall the rationale for, and value of, doing so from Section 5.2. In the case of focus groups, there are two good ways of involving people in a cooperative venture:

- By discussing your purpose, and the sort of information sought, with the kinds of people in your organization who would be most interested in, or affected by, the conclusions and recommendations of this part of your project. Involve them in planning, and consider the possibility of using one or two of them in acting alongside you as group facilitators (always assuming that this doesn't bias your results); take feedback from them after they have seen the results.

- By feeding back the results to your focus group members.

Elicitation

You elicit data in a focus group by **facilitating** ('leading', 'moderating' are synonyms) a group discussion focused on a particular topic. You do so by posing a sequence of questions which stimulate, maintain and direct the flow of discussion; this discussion needs to:

- be broad-ranging but relevant
- provide data that are as specific, concrete and detailed as possible
- explore feelings with sensitivity, while bearing in mind the personal context.

To do this well requires some experience of group discussion and a fair degree of interpersonal skill. If you are a beginner, and intend to base the bulk of your empirical work round the focus group technique, then a careful reading of Krueger and Casey (2000) will give you an excellent start.

Steering

A relatively small number of questions (five to eight, no more) are posed, ordered from the more general to the more particular and preceded by a statement of the purpose in holding the group and a number of statements in which you set the context for the discussion.

It is useful to think of the set of questions as a route within which discussion will be channelled, and, in contrast to the semi-structured interview, it is best not to diverge from the predetermined order in which you ask the questions.

Indeed, the skill in focus group facilitation lies less in the posing of the questions, and much more in:

- making appropriate interjections and probes to maintain discussion on a particular question
- tolerating silences at points where these might encourage fruitful *sotto voce* comment

- anticipating the flow of discussion and steering it away from 'dead-ends'
- legitimizing varying viewpoints
- preventing some individuals from dominating the discussion at the expense of others.

Format

As with all the other types of semi-structured interview, your questions are open-ended; as with the individual interview, you can delimit the form of answer by adding a qualifying statement to the question. In contrast to these however, you are advised to avoid direct 'why' questions, since these can inhibit the flow of discussion. Use a 'what prompted/influenced you?' or a 'what sort of features attract you to/lead you away from?' form of question instead. Other than these format guidelines, focus group technique explicitly avoids any attempt to indicate the form in which answers are to be provided, because the 'answers' to questions are often an emergent property of the discussion, to be identified during the analysis, rather than a specific response to a direct question.

Eliciting answers

What you will ask depends on your purpose. Since the intention during the group is to stimulate a natural and free discussion, and all of your attention will be devoted to matters of interaction and process, it is good practice to memorize in advance the questions you intend to ask, and the possible follow-up probes for each.

Recording answers

For similar reasons, you won't be able to make extensive notes during the focus group. If you want to capture complete verbatim utterances, use a colleague in an assistant facilitator role, whose entire job it is to act as a scribe. You will depend on the tape-recorder for the bulk of your recording needs, however.

Analysis

An adequate analysis of material obtained from a set of focus groups takes plenty of time. This is partly because written transcripts have to be prepared from the original tape-recordings – (remember Table 4.3? Seven hours of transcription for every hour of interaction recorded!) – partly because the analysis procedure itself is fairly unstructured and partly because of the additional safeguards you have to provide in order to preserve the validity and reliability of the information you obtain.

As soon as possible after each focus group is completed, you should sit down, with your co-facilitator if you used one, listen to the tape recording and discuss the main themes which you see as emerging. These should be summarized in a brief written report which reflects your discussion of themes, sub themes, relevant participant characteristics, key utterances or phrases used by the participants, notes on significant non-verbal incidents and an impression of the mood and feelings expressed in the group. The value of a co-facilitator (someone who was also there!) is immense: can you agree on the contents of this report? Here's the important matter of reliability again. If you are working without a co-facilitator, then each point in the notes should be written with the following questions in mind:

■ How can I prove it?

■ What evidence can I cite?

Perceiving

The next step is to use this initial impression as a guide and organizing framework to the written transcript of all of the focus groups you have conducted, bearing your topic and project issues in mind. You will have a mass of raw data in front of you, and your aim will be to simplify it by perceiving, summarizing, and providing evidence, so as to identify the themes and sub-themes which emerged in the discussion. Inevitably, as with all semi-structured work, something of yourself will go into this analysis. You will have had a number of hunches, expectations, and propositions related to the thesis of your project before you come to the data, and these will form a background against which you look for the themes themselves. How best to prevent them from prejudicing your findings while using them to guide and inform all your efforts?

You have two main possibilities. The first is to stick closely to the *raw data* themselves, carrying out and presenting a content analysis along the lines discussed in Section 10.2. Alternatively, you can stand back from the data a little, and write an *interpretation*, based on your prior hunches and on the material in front of you, with supporting evidence in the form of verbatim quotes that reflect consensus and key disagreements. Memos written to yourself (see Section 10.1 above) could be content-analyzed as evidence. Somewhere between these two extremes lies the possibility of providing a descriptive account: a summary, with relatively little interpretation, of the data before you, again, supported by evidence in the form of direct quotations. Krueger and Casey (2000) provide you with some useful examples of each approach.

Whichever approach you adopt, you're setting out to discover themes in the data. You do so by:

■ reading through all your summaries to *identify* potential themes and trends

■ reading through all the transcripts, identifying the material which followed in response to each of your questions, to *refine* your perceptions of themes and trends

■ listening again to all the tape-recordings, looking for evidence to *confirm* the results of the previous step

■ bearing in mind the membership of the different focus groups that you conducted, and the way in which this may influence the themes which people expressed.

You need to listen to the meanings expressed in the words people use, the context in which things were said, and the consistency with which these were said; in all of this, as Krueger and Casey (2000) put it, you're trying to 'find the big ideas'.

Summarizing

The results of all this activity are summarized in the form of a series of statements. Each statement expresses a main theme and is followed by evidence in the form of a narrative account of the gist of what was said, with some information about the degree of consensus with which it was said, and some illustrative quotations.

Opinions are divided about the way in which consensus is expressed. Some authors feel that there is no place for numeric data (along the lines of a content analysis which states how many utterances were coded under each category or theme), while others suggest that, so long as the numbers are only used to give an impression of the impact or main thrust of the feeling (percentages and the like), numeric data can be useful, particularly in contrasting the strength of feeling on an issue between focus groups consisting of different kinds of people.

I would advise you take the latter approach, but avoid the temptation of carrying out any statistical tests of significance on these numbers. In other words, you can use them in a descriptive way, to identify the 'main thrust' of consensus; to do any more would be to make unwarranted statistical assumptions. Many of your focus group members will make repeated statements on one theme, which on feedback to the group turn out to be relatively lightweight; while others make just one, quiet, but deadly-effective utterance, which sums up the mood of all. Here, a frequency count would be misleading.

Write-up

You would write up your findings as a single account and not group by group.

Presenting

Krueger and Casey (2000) provide a number of examples suited to one-off reports. As your own presentation will be just a part of a more complete document, I would suggest that you present the context, followed by a set of headings each of which represents one of the themes you identified, with a descriptive summary and a list of relevant quotations. One or two tables which summarize the main thrust of the trends on a particularly important issue (especially if these express some difference of emphasis between different categories of participant) would also make sense; but, generally, the presentation of the information in focus group technique, in contrast to questionnaire technique, is not structured round tables.

Locating

This account would be placed in the main body of the text, preceded by an account of the issues and themes which you selected for investigation by the focus group technique. A summary and conclusions might follow immediately, or form part of a broader statement which summarizes the results of accompanying individual interviews or any other technique which you have used. The place for a full report, or summaries of the findings of each separate group if they are particularly pertinent, would be in an appendix.

 If you intend to run a focus study as described here, please work through activities 1 to 4, to the extent that they apply, in the Project Guide.

10.5 A note on the validity of what you're doing

Chapter 5 presented an argument to the effect that project work done in the style of a study, rather than according to the rules of hypothetico-deductive method, is more likely to cope with the realities of in-company existence. If this is true, then some of the techniques described in this chapter are quite sufficient to provide you with realistic and valid information, on a stand-alone basis. They are quite good enough to help you build an argument round a conceptual model, or support some thesis you wish to establish (or to reveal lack of support if the evidence as you're forced to perceive it is such!). Others, like the conversational technique, may require triangulation, or supporting evidence obtained by using one of the other techniques. You should always remain aware of the sources of error that face you, and the first step in doing so is to re-read the description of the technique you wish to use, paying particular attention to the methods for coping with error.

Having said that, it's also true that any of the techniques described in this chapter can be used as a means of piloting and developing categories and hypotheses for the more structured techniques which are described in the following chapter, the validity of which will be all the stronger because of the rigorous work you have already put in. When used for pilot work in this way, any of these techniques could be used on its own.

 Before finishing with this chapter, please address the last activity in the Project Guide, whether you have done any of the other activities, or not.

Arranging a set of key informant interviews

Maria Delmer works for a company which owns and manages three care homes for the elderly, and, as an assistant in the head office administration department, is involved with the decision to introduce a quality system into the organization, ISO9000 and Investors in People being the two under active consideration The company is a responsible concern, run energetically according to the entrepreneurial style of its private owner. Each of its homes provides a ward with full nursing care as well as the usual mix of sheltered and supervised care accommodation.

She decides to focus her dissertation on the company, the arguments for each quality system, and on the process by which the decision is made and conveyed to the employees. She will probably use a questionnaire with the latter to identify attitudes, but also to identify their perceived training needs arising from whichever system is adopted. As for the process of adoption, she suspects that staff in different departments at head office and in the various homes will have different interests and

concerns about the system to be introduced, and so she decides to use a series of key Informant Interviews at the beginning of her study.

Clearly, the managers of each of the three care homes should be interviewed. Certainly, she will need to talk to the Chief Executive, given that the company is privately owned and very much the creation of this dynamic entrepreneur. She suspects that there will be a variety of different views among senior staff in the company, and she needs to ensure that she elicits them in an even-handed way.

Following the approach outlined in Section 10.3 above, and after completing exercise 1 in the Project Guide below, she draws up the following table, intending to build on it as she conducts a series of key informant interviews.

1 What sort of sampling arrangement would you advocate?

2 If some of her respondents are unavailable, how can Maria ensure that their viewpoint is represented in her interviews?

Interviewee	Role/reason	Note	Date seen
Arthur Kozubal	Chief Executive, Leeds Head Office		
Alma Wilson	Manager, York	keen on IiP	
Michael Norris	Manager, Darlington	quality champion	
Johnny Kozubal	Manager, Leeds	Arthur Kozubal is his uncle	

Answers to Case Example 10.1

1 As with many situations for which a key informant interview is suited, the respondents' views are likely to be based on their position in the organization and their stakeholding in the issue under consideration. Maria already feels that Johnny Kozubal, the manager of the care home at the head office site, is likely to take whatever view his uncle, the Chief Executive,

adopts. She knows that Alma Wilson favours the IiP scheme. While the whole idea of introducing a quality system was Michael Norris', she suspects that he is currently quite open to which scheme it should be: he has already made his mark with the MD and Board in convincing them of the bottom-line impact of attending to quality.

In order to represent both sides of the argument, for IiP or for ISO9000, she decides to adopt a snowball sampling technique. She

CASE EXAMPLE 10.1   Arranging a set of key informant interviews (cont.)

knows that Johnny will agree with Arthur, and so she decides to ask each of them who in the company, they feel, has a reasonable argument for whichever option they *don't* favour, whichever option that might be. She decides to ask Alma Wilson at the end of her interview, for the name of someone who, Alma feels, may have something to say in favour of her contending scheme, ISO9000. Following the same rationale, she will ask Michael Norris for the name of someone who agrees with his own view, and someone who disagrees with his own view. Thus, she hopes that the people who have a stakeholding, and new people known by the latter to have a interest, have the opportunity to outline their views, without snowballing in a way that results in a bias towards just one point of view. This will result in four additional interviewees, for a total sample of eight people.

2 If anyone isn't available on the day, Maria will need to arrange substitutes, or wait until the intended interviewee is available. Someone who works closely with the individual in question, and is likely to face the same issues of quality as the 'missing' interviewee, should be aimed at if substitutes are required. The same 'which people might I talk to, who might have a different view to your own?' question would be asked.

Project Guide

If you plan to use any of the techniques mentioned in this chapter, then you will need to carry out the following activities for each one. If you don't intend to use these techniques (are you sure? Not even for pilot work?) then please address the last activity and then press on to the next chapter.

1 Arrange the design and sampling for the technique you will be using

a In a single column of a page of your research diary, make a list of the issues which you intend to investigate with this particular technique; note any issues which you will not be able to cover, and consider which other technique you will use, and in what order.

b Go through activity 4 in the Project Guide for Chapter 9 and work though it in detail. You're not planning now, you're committing yourself to action!

c How does the sample you are drawing for this technique compare with any other samples you will be drawing? Are you working with the same people throughout; are they different? If they are different, then give each an identifier ('Sample A'; 'Sample B' etc.) and, in a second column of the page you used for question a above, note which issues will be addressed by which sample.

d Commit yourself to some diary dates and plan how long it will take you to complete your data gathering with this technique. You may find it useful to refer to Table 4.3 at this point.

2 Prepare for data-gathering

a Organize any recording equipment you will need

b Organize help for any of the techniques which need a colleague for the data-gathering or analysis stages, well in advance

c Discuss what you are about to do with your sponsor and (if you need help with the technical details) your tutor

d If you don't have a computer of your own, now is the time to book a machine in your university department, find out the time of day when machines are most likely to be available if your university doesn't run a booking system, checking that the required software is there.

3 Construct your instrument

a Where the technique requires it, construct the list of questions you intend to ask, following the guidelines given above.

b In doing so, you need to bear in mind the way in which you plan to analyze the data you will obtain. The best way of doing this is to write an outline of the methodology chapter of your dissertation – the first draft of the account of your analysis – since this forces you to think the analysis through in detail. So, in a few sentences, what exactly will you have done, what steps will you have followed, when you have analyzed all of the data? Write this down now!

c Having thought it through at this level of detail, if you find that the analysis you're planning isn't possible, review and amend exercises 1 and 2 above.

4 Go to it!

a Complete your piloting according to the plan you prepared in activity 6 in the previous chapter.

Bear in mind that you may be using a mixture of techniques drawn from Chapters 11 and 12 as well as the present one (which may make a difference to how and when you utilize the present technique . . .).

b Do it!

c Analyze the data as you have planned, following the guidelines in this chapter and any related authors recommended above.

5 Continue your write-up

a By the time you are ready to collect data, you should have completed the write-up of your introductory chapter, and the literature review. If not, it would be wise to do so at this stage!

b Prepare a first draft of the methodological section of your dissertation. Now that you are about to collect data, you should be able to provide a coherent rationale for the method you are using, and to state the techniques you plan to adopt. Revisit the research proposal which you prepared in activity 5 in Chapter 9 and expand the information you gave there, into a connected account which describes what you are about to do and gives reasons for it, in the light of your research question.

References

Boje, D. M. (1994) 'Organisational story-telling: the struggles of pre-modern, modern and postmodern organisational learning discourses', *Management Learning*, 25: 3: 433–461.

Burgess, R. G. (1982) 'The unstructured interview as a conversation', in Burgess, R. G., (eds.) *Field Research: a Sourcebook and Field Manual*, London: George Allen & Unwin.

Carey, M. A. (1994) 'The group effect in focus groups: planning, implementing, and interpreting focus group research', in Morse, J. M., (eds.) *Critical Issues in Qualitative Research Methods*, London: Sage.

Cohen, J. (1960) 'A coefficient of agreement for nominal scales', *Educational and Psychological Measurement*, 20; 37–46.

Curasi, C. F. (2001) 'A critical exploration of face-to-face interviewing vs computer-mediated interviewing', *International Journal of Market Research*, 43: 4: 361–375.

Dillman, D. A. (1978) *Mail and Telephone Surveys: The Total Design Method*, Chichester: Wiley.

Dillman, D. A. (2000) *Mail and Internet Surveys: the Tailored Design Method*, London: Wiley, 2nd edn.

Edenborough, R. (2002) *Effective Interviewing: a Handbook of Skills and Techniques*, London: Kogan Page.

Frey, J. H. (1983) *Survey Research by Telephone*, London: Sage Publications.

Gillham, R. (2000) *The Research Interview*, London: Continuum Books.

Holliday, A. (2002) *Doing and Writing Qualitative Research*, London: Sage.

Jankowicz, A. D. (1996) *Personal values among public sector employees: a methodological study*, Paper given at the 3rd Conference of the European Personal Construct Association, Reading, UK, April.

Kelly, G. A. (1991) *The Psychology of Personal Constructs*, London: Routledge.

Kidder, L. H. (1981) 'Qualitative research and quasi-experimental frameworks', in Brewer, M. B. and Collins, B. E., (eds.) *Scientific Enquiry and the Social Sciences*, San Francisco: Jossey-Bass.

King, N. (1994) 'The qualitative research interview', in Cassell, C. and Symon, G., (eds.) *Qualitative Methods in Organizational Research*, London: Sage.

Krueger, R. A. and Casey, M. A. (2000) *Focus Groups: a Practical Guide for Applied Research*, London: Sage, 3rd edn.

Mair, M. (1989) 'Kelly, Bannister, and a story-telling psychology', *International Journal of Personal Construct Psychology*, 2: 1: 1–14.

Mair, M. (1990) 'Telling psychological tales', *International Journal of Personal Construct Psychology*, 3: 1: 121–135.

Martin, G. and Beaumont, P. B. (2003) *Branding and People Management: What's in a Name?* CIPD Research Report, Wimbledon, CIPD.

May, T. (2001) *Social Research: Issues, Methods and Process*, Milton Keynes: Open University Press, 3rd edn.

Miles, M. B. and Huberman, A. M. (1994) *Qualitative Data Analysis: an Expanded Sourcebook*, London: Sage.

Mishler, E. G. (1991) *Research Interviewing: Context and Narrative*, London: Harvard University Press.

Morgan, D. L. (1997) *Focus Groups as Qualitative Research*, New York: Sage, 2nd edn.

Morris, L. L., Fitz-Gibbon, C. T. *et al.* (1988) *How to Communicate Evaluation Findings*, London: Sage.

Neuendorf, K. A. (2002) *The Content Analysis Guidebook*, London: Sage.

Perrault, W. D. and Leigh, L. E. (1989) 'Reliability of nominal data based on qualitative judgements', *Journal of Marketing Research*, xxvi, May: 135–148.

Pheysey, D. C. (1993) *Organisational Cultures: Types and Transformations*, London: Routledge.

Phillips, L. and Jorgensen, M. W. (2002) *Discourse Analysis as Theory and Method*, London: Sage.

Robson, C. (1993) *Real World Research: a Resource for Social Scientists and Practitioner-Researchers*, Oxford: Blackwell.

Robson, C. (2002) *Real World Research: a Resource for Social Scientists and Practitioner-Researchers*, Oxford: Blackwell, 2nd edn.

Schlackman, B. (1989) 'Projective tests and enabling techniques for use in market research', in Robson, S. and Foster, A., (eds.) *Qualitative Research in Action*, London: Edward Arnold.

Selwyn, N. and Robson, K. (1998) *Using e-mail as a research tool*, Social Research Update series, Guildford, Surrey, University of Surrey. WWW http://www.soc.surrey.ac.uk/sru/SRU21.html accessed 12 April 2004.

Ten Have, P. (1999) *Doing Conversation Analysis: a Practical Guide*, London: Sage.

Tommerup, P. (1988) 'From trickster to father figure; learning from the mythologisation of top management', in Jones, M. O., Moore, M. D. and Snyder, R. C., (eds.) *Inside Organisations: Understanding the Human Dimension*, London: Sage Publications.

Torrington, D. (1991) *Management Face to Face*, London: Philip Allan.

Tremblay, M. A. (1982) 'The key informant technique: a non-ethnographic application', in Burgess, R., (eds.) *Field Research: a Sourcebook and Field Manual*, London: Allen and Unwin.

Whyte, W. F. (1982) 'Interviewing in field research', in Burgess, R. G., (ed.) *Field Research: a Sourcebook and Field Manual*, London: George Allen & Unwin.

Yin, R. K. (2002) *Case Study Research: Design and Methods*, London: Sage, 3rd edn.

11 Fully structured techniques

- To present the procedural details of two fully structured, data-gathering techniques: the questionnaire and the structured interview, following the standard framework presented earlier
- To describe a variety of delivery variants: postal and internet-based questionnaires, computer-assisted personal interviews and telephone interviews
- To revisit the topic of research ethics, as it applies to matters of anonymity and confidentiality
- To help you to progress your project; and particularly, the empirical stages of your own project work, by considering and working through the practical implications in the event that you decide to use any of the techniques presented in this chapter

At a glance

All of the techniques presented in this chapter are **fully structured**. In other words, the content, layout, question sequence and answer format have been determined in advance, in such a way that there is little that your respondent can say or do which would make you deviate from this set pattern. This approach is not as inflexible as it might seem, and several ways of providing an open-ended element (the use of verbatim responses and 'other, please specify' answer alternatives) are described.

The different techniques by which you interact with respondents (face-to-face, postal, electronic and telephone) are outlined within each of the two main sections.

The value of the structured approach is that it allows you to standardize your questioning to such an extent that a more numerate, statistically-based analysis is possible, and permits you to test out hypotheses quantitatively should you wish to do so. Much of the material in this chapter deals with the alternative answer formats which a structured approach makes possible, and the data analysis techniques which pertain. There is also a concern about how to maximize response rates, and a variety of procedures are considered, all of which constitute simple good practice, and some of which arise from the ethical requirement that respondents' anonymity and confidentiality need to be assured.

11.1 The structured questionnaire

You begin the development of a structured questionnaire in more or less the same way as you do the semi-structured interview. In other words, as I described in Section 10.2, an explicit statement of your purpose will suggest a major topic or issue which you wish to explore, and you spend some time in mapping out a number of questions, each of which will provide you with data about various aspects of the major topic. Beyond that, the procedure is substantially different, since you must also provide the steering information, the format of answers, and a system for recording answers to each of the questions, in such a way that your respondent can express his or her intentions straightforwardly without further prompting by yourself. (After all, in the case of a questionnaire, you won't be physically present: you will be interacting at a distance, by post, or by e-mail, web reader, or newsgroup posting.) Furthermore, you will have decided on the format in the light of your plans for the analysis of your data.

At this point, when you see the scale of the task you have devised for yourself, you might consider using a software package such as SNAP (see http.www.Snapsurveys.com/software/softwareprof.shtml) or SPHINXSURVEY (http.www.sphinxdevelopment.co.uk/Products_v4.htm) in which to design your questionnaire. Both products are expensive, but your university should have a site licence, or you may wish to buy an inexpensive cut-down student version of either, suitable if your questionnaire is a simple one. The advantage of this kind of software is that the same package can be used for design and for analysis; if all you are concerned with is a single, relatively brief questionnaire, however, you may feel that the time spent in learning the package is better spent in constructing the questionnaire by conventional means.

Before proceeding, let me establish a convention of terminology. It is possible to elicit data in a variety of ways, and only one of these takes the form of a question (a sentence which ends with a question mark!), to which a number of answers are provided. Occasionally, for example, you will be asking your respondent to look at a set of phrases and tick just one of them as most representative of his or her views; there is no question as such, no answer sentence either. To avoid confusion, let's call the string of words by which you elicit data an **item**, any string of words which expresses a potential answer an **alternative**, and the action a respondent makes to indicate his or her views, a **response**.

Design

A properly devised, standardized technique is likely to be cheaper to administer, may permit you to cover more respondents, may require less skill and sensitivity to administer, and allows your respondent more time to think about his or her responses than any of the semi-structured techniques. Table 11.1 summarizes these and other characteristics of postal questionnaires internet (web-based) questionnaires, and e-mail questionnaires. As you can see, there isn't a single 'best buy' for all situations.

TABLE 11.1 A comparison of the main structured techniques

H stands for High, M for medium, and L for Low levels of the characteristic shown at left.

	Postal questionnaire	Internet questionnaire	e-mail questionnaire
Design and sampling issues			
Control over inclusion of all population in sample	M	L	M
Control over selection of respondents into sample	M	L	M
Chances of answers being given by someone else	M	H	L
Sensitivity to distortion by respondent substitution	H	H	H
Chance of controlling bias due to selective non-response	L	H	H
Refusal rate	H	M	L
Response rate with varied populations (public-at-large)	H	M	M
Response rate with homogenous, highly-selected populations	H	H	H
Questionnaire construction issues			
Likely acceptability of longer list of questions	M	L	H
Likely success of complex questions	M	L	H
Likely success of open ended questions	M	L	H
Likely success of steering questions	M	H	H
Likely success of boring-but-necessary questions	L	L	M
Likely success with personal and sensitive questions	L	M	H
Likely success in avoiding missed questions	M	L	H
Issues of bias			
Likely success in establishing anonymity/confidentiality	H	M	L
Chances of avoiding bias due to social desirability of answers	M	H	H
Chances of avoiding 'researcher' bias	H	H	H
Chances of avoiding contamination by others	M	L	H
Feasibility of assistance being available to investigator	M	L	L
Administrative issues			
Amount of time required to set up and implement	H	M	L
Potential costs	H	L	L
Control over costs	M	H	H
Sensitivity of costs to geographical distance from respondents	M	L	L

After Dillman (1978; 2000), Frey (1983), Coomber (1997)

Maximizing response rate

Response rates can be surprisingly high for the e-mail medium (Anderson and Gansneder, 1995 report a 76 per cent e-mail return rate for an e-mail questionnaire) compared with the very best rate for the postal questionnaire (74 per cent on average using the Total Design Method: Dillman, 2000; though 20–30 per cent is a more usual rate for postal questionnaires), so this electronic medium is certainly worth careful consideration. With a rate of 10 per cent, the Internet (web-based) medium is rather less successful: Saunders *et al.* (2003: 284).

It can be extremely difficult to ensure anonymity in the case of the electronic media and this accounts for some of the comparisons in the first section of Table 11.1. Many e-mail users are not sufficiently technically competent to anonymize the e-mail address which, as Selwyn and Robson (1998) remind us, appears automatically in their e-mail response. While the web-based medium is less vulnerable in this respect, both media place a considerable onus on the respondent to preserve anonymity. For example, Coomber (1997) made a point of reminding his drug-dealer respondents to use the anonymous terminals available in libraries and internet cafes.

Whatever the medium, a careful statement of your purpose is essential. This is a covering note or letter which contains:

■ A statement of who you are and who is supporting you.

■ A statement of the purpose of the questionnaire.

■ A request for help, in which you should primarily try and show how completion of the questionnaire may be of ultimate benefit to the respondent. (Most requests for help state how the questionnaire will be helping the student. While this is a legitimate thing to do, it's best seen as a secondary issue. The reality is that many recipients are more interested in satisfying their own needs rather than yours!)

■ A statement that the respondents' material will be treated responsibly, with a brief description of the confidentiality and security arrangements that pertain. As Gregory (2003), who has a useful chapter on issues of confidentiality, reminds us, respondents expect confidentiality as a matter of research ethics, and expect to be told how you will preserve it.

■ An expression of thanks in anticipation.

In general, you obtain cooperation by adopting a cooperative stance: by creating a sense of ownership among your respondents and by adopting a negotiating approach in bringing together their interests with your own legitimate needs to satisfy your formal project requirements.

Much of the work in what is a very well-researched field has been summarized by Dillman (2000). His 'Tailored Design Method' draws on exchange theory in social psychology, Blau (1964) and Thibaut and Kelley (1959) to suggest that collaboration is maximized when:

- respondents are in some sense rewarded for cooperation
- these rewards outweigh the costs in terms of money, time and effort
- the respondents are convinced that they can trust you.

Table 11.2 summarizes the major factors and examples are given at the right of the table. While you are unlikely to achieve the same outcomes, not having the various resources of a survey centre to hand, it should be possible to raise rates to a level of 50 per cent for postal questionnaires, 30 per cent for Internet, and 60 per cent for e-mail based compared with the 5–10 per cent you might expect from an unsolicited, cold-contact approach. Mehta and Sivadas (1995), for example, achieved a 45 per cent return rate for an unsolicited postal questionnaire, a 40 per cent rate for its e-mail equivalent, but a 63 per cent rate when an initial e-mail requesting participation preceded the e-mail questionnaire.

ILLUSTRATION 11.1

Andreas MacSean, you may recall, carried out a study of job satisfaction among police sergeants in An Garda Siochana, the Irish Police Force. (Glance again at Case Example 8.1.) He sent out his 425 questionnaires and received 285 returns, a 67 per cent response rate, pleasingly high for a postal questionnaire. While he used all the applicable factors listed in Table 11.2, in retrospect he feels that there were three techniques in particular which account for the high level of return.

First, he despatched the questionnaires from Garda Headquarters in Phoenix Park, with a covering letter from the Assistant Commissioner, Personnel and Training. Police sergeants have a very keen sense of priorities and are quite effective at not doing things they feel they don't have time for. It seems that the letter was successful in supporting a view that this particular survey was important. Second, Andreas arranged for the AC to mention that he had received some sponsorship and funding from the Association of Garda Sergeants and Inspectors, the respondents' own professional body. Finally, he sent out a chase-up letter, together with a fresh copy of the questionnaire, three weeks after despatch of the originals.

By now, you will be clear on the form of design to use, will have decided on the size and nature of the sample which you wish to draw and will know enough about the issues you wish to explore to have decided on a particular sampling method. If this is still unclear, you would be advised to do one or both of the following:

- Re-read Section 8.2 on representation and sampling, and Section 8.3 on design and on sample size.
- Discuss the results of any semi-structured technique which you have already used with your tutor or sponsor in order to work out the design and sampling implications of the present phase.

If you have divided your sample into subgroups of respondents (by quota, stratified, or cluster sample methods), or if you are interested in the responses of

TABLE 11.2 The factors which maximize response rates in survey work	
Factors maximizing response	**Examples**
1 Rewarding the respondents by	
■ Showing that you value them and their help	Sharing information on why and how they were chosen; personalizing communications
■ Expressing this verbally	Saying 'thank you' in writing or orally, in advance as well as after data return
■ Viewing them as experts you wish to consult	Telling them why their knowledge is relevant Appealing to their personal expertise
■ Showing how the study supports (or at least is not in conflict with) their values	Showing how the research is relevant to issues which currently concern them
■ Offering tangible rewards	Where available, a token payment to establish 'ability to deliver'
■ Making the questions and method used to pose them interesting to the respondent	Good technique in using the particular data-gathering method involved
2 Reducing costs to the respondent by	
■ Making the task appear brief	Evidence of clear structure (layout and clarity of questionnaires; brief summary of points to be covered in interview)
■ Reducing the mental and physical effort involved	Clarity of expression of questions asked; simplifying data return; making appointments to suit respondent; chasing up non-replying respondents two weeks after initial issue
■ Eliminating the possibility of embarrassment	Making more personal questions easy to answer by a) avoiding them! b) appropriate wording c) appropriate sequencing; informing about anonymity and security arrangements
■ Avoiding any impression of subordination	'Asking a favour'; but also, involvement in design/ evaluation of the questions being asked
■ Eliminating any direct monetary cost	Supply of prestamped, preaddressed return envelope; paying your way in interview situations where a meal is involved; meeting direct expenses
3 Establishing trust by	
■ Providing some token in advance	A confirmatory thank you card or phone-call before the questionnaire is returned/interview conducted
■ Establishing status and legitimacy	Reference to your university; use of letterhead/logo; reference to in-company sponsor/support
■ Building on pre-existing reward-cost outcomes	Reference to previous relationships between you/supporters and the respondent; appeal to mutual friends where snowball sampling is appropriate

After Dillman (1978; 2000)

different kinds of people irrespective of sample subgrouping, then the major design issue which remains is for you to prepare items to be used to identify, record, or confirm your respondents' membership of the various subgroups.

For example, if you have a sample stratified by number of years of service in the organization, you will need to develop a item which gets your respondents to tell you how many years they have served. With some forms of sampling, you would have found this out in advance, needing to know it in order to draw up the sample subgroups in your sampling frame; but though you may know this for each subgroup in total, you may not know it for each named individual. In any case, it is essential standard practice to confirm information of this kind. Similarly, if you intend to break down people's responses on any other basis, quite apart from their membership of a sample subgroup (for example, because you are exploring a topic and have subgrouped respondents according to their views on that topic), you must make sure you provide an item which will allow you to group in this way.

There is more on this in the analysis section below; for the moment, let me stress that good design involves you in identifying, in advance, two entirely distinct kinds of item: those which provide you with straightforward descriptive data, and those which will help you to turn these data into information by analyzing responses according to the categories of people in whose differing patterns of response you're especially interested. Do the males respond differently from the females? The head office staff differently from those in the branches? The group who responded 'yes' to question 12 – do their responses to question 15 look any different to those of people who responded 'no' to question 12? And so on.

Elicitation

Designing the items themselves is an iterative process. You will find yourself cycling through the activities outlined below several times, for each item you are preparing, as you refine it for eventual use. Table 11.3 is intended as an aid in this activity. You should use it as a checklist to be applied to each item as you develop it.

You may find it helpful to write each item on a filecard, to allow for subsequent amendment and reordering as necessary. Other important details will also be written on this filecard, so make sure you buy a pack of the larger, 6″ × 4″ cards.

Steering

Your first concern will be for the sequence in which you will present your items to respondents. Next, you will need to decide if a given item is to be answered by all respondents, or is to be skipped by some respondents because of the way they answered items earlier in the sequence. You might like to number each card in the order in which that item is going to be presented to respondents, writing the substantive item itself on the card in capital letters. Generally speaking, items which elicit personally sensitive data, those dealing with feelings or which require

TABLE 11.3 Procedural guide to item construction

Design and sampling

1 How is the respondent's membership of sample subgroups ascertained or confirmed? In internet-based surveys, use e-mail to provide a pin number to enable you to identify the respondents as belonging to the intended sample. (Other people may see your survey and decide to respond!)

2 Does this particular item do the above, as distinct from providing substantive data?

3 In an e-mail survey, is the material appropriately personalized so it stands out from other e-mails?

Elicitation: steering

1 What form of words is most appropriate for the steering instructions?

2 Is the item in the right place in the sequence? (Straightforward and factual towards the start, more difficult, intrusive, attitudinal items towards the end.)

3 Is it led up to in a natural way? Does it come too late or too early in terms of arousing interest?

4 Is the response likely to be biased by responses to previous items?

Elicitation: format

1 What response format is most appropriate for this item? In internet survey work, placing an 'X' inside brackets or using radio buttons works well with free-choice and multiple-choice formats.

2 Where free-choice and multiple-choice formats are used, does each set:
   - Cover all the possible alternatives?
   - Provide categories that are mutually exclusive?
   - Provide an appropriately worded 'don't know' category?

3 Where rating-scale format is used, is the scale:
   - Anchored at each end and at various points by a suitable operational description?
   - Centred with a middle point so that genuine indifference can be indicated? (Unless you suspect that people will 'sit on the fence': in which case, use an even number of alternatives.)
   - Of no more than nine points (people can't apply a consistent framework over more than nine)?

4 Where a set of rating scales is used:
   - Are position preferences and 'yes-saying' controlled for?
   - Is social desirability controlled for?
     (In the first case, by wording the item such that agreement with the meaning expressed in the item means ticking the right-hand end of the scale for some items, left-hand end for others; the second case requires appropriate wording, or the use of paired comparison techniques.)

5 Where ranking format is used:
   - Is the respondent told whether tied ranks are acceptable?
   - Asked to rank fewer than 12 or so alternatives? (Again, there are problems in being consistent when ranking large numbers of alternatives: use paired comparison format if necessary.)

6 In internet-based work, are drop-down boxes used only for choosing among many alternatives?

TABLE 11.3 Procedural guide to item construction (cont.)

Eliciting answers

1 With respect to item *content*:
- Is this item really necessary to the issue being explored?
- Are several items required to cover the issue? (E.g asking what the person thinks in one item, and then asking how strongly a person feels in the following item – rather than trying to pack it all into a single item.)
- Will the respondent have the information required for a valid response? (Consider using information cards, 'flashcards', and boxed graphic displays to remind about possibilities.)
- Is the item sufficiently concrete and specific? But also
- Is the item general enough and free of spurious concreteness?
- Will the response really indicate an informed judgement, or just elicit a stereotype?
- Is it too specific, personal, too early or too late in the sequence to be answered honestly?

2 With regard to item *wording*:
- Does the item elicit the response without being too long or complex?
- Is the vocabulary simple and clear? (This is a questionnaire, not an intelligence test!)
- Does it avoid obscurity? (E.g. does 'PC' stand for a non-Macintosh computer, any personal computer, political correctness, or a police constable?)
- Does it avoid undefined qualitative words? (E.g. words like 'quite', 'usually', 'frequently'.)
- Is the basis for answering specified? (E.g. are you looking for a neutral, informed, personal, behavioural, ethical, or moral basis underlying the response?)
- Does it mislead through hidden implications or words evoking stereotypes? (E.g. 'International Manager'; 'Good European'.)
- Is it too personal? (E.g. 'How much do you earn?' – better provide broad bands and ask the respondent to tick one.) But also, can it be expressed more directly if required?

Recording answers

1 Is the respondent told explicitly how he or she is to indicate the response? (Ticking one alternative, ticking more than one alternative, ranking, rating, filling out a table, answering in his or her own words.)
2 Is the respondent asked to check the consistency of responses? (E.g. ensuring that percentages sum to 100; knowing what to do to indicate an equal preference.)
3 Will the item require illustrative graphics, or a flashcard to summarize the alternatives?
4 Is the respondent asked to check that essential details have been provided? (E.g. name, job.)

Analysis

1 Is the planned method of analysis consistent with the wording of the item and its content? See Figure 11.1 on methods of analysis to be used after the questionnaire has been returned – but make sure that this issue is considered when the item is first being written!

After Kornhauser and Sheatsley (1976); Dillman (1978; 2000)

some thought, and those concerning issues on which the respondent may not have made up his or her mind, should come later in the sequence. Factual and more straightforward information should come first; an interesting, personalized, but not over-intrusive first question is particularly recommended in e-mail and internet-based work.

Clearly, some personal data are factual and straightforward. Given assurances about confidentiality, no one will mind giving you their name, department name, or, assuming it's relevant, their sex. It is important to have these, particularly if your sample is divided into subgroups and these data are to be used in cross-tabulating other, less personal data. Your inclination will be to put them at the start of your questionnaire, but consider: some people are very sensitive about certain factual details about themselves (e.g. age, salary, union membership). A common practice in cases where personal details include sensitive, as well as factual data, is to put all the personal details questions together at the end of the questionnaire, the rationale being that by then, rapport will have been established with the respondent.

As your set of items develops and you realize that the sequence will depend on the individual's responses to previous questions, you will need to add a form of words which tells the respondent which question to address next. 'If you chose alternative a to this question, please skip question 16 and go on to question 17'; or, 'If your answer to the previous question was "Yes", please give a reason in your own words in the space provided below', are some possible examples of explicit steering instructions. You might like to write these onto the filecard in lower case lettering, below or above the words which express the substantive content of the item itself. In internet-based survey work, page layout within the available window is important. Keep an eye on the physical length of the item so that, when transferred from the index card to the software version, excessive scrolling or paging is avoided; particularly, avoid the need to scroll or page down halfway through a set of steering instructions. Alternatively, consider the possibility of automating the steering where possible: see Dillman (2000: 376–401). Occasionally, whole sections of the questionnaire must be skipped depending on the responses to previous items and you will need to keep track of whole wodges of filecards. If you are constructing your questionnaire manually rather than with the help of a software package and you find yourself constructing several such contingent sequences of questions, you will find that a simple flowchart is helpful for recording the order of the cards, and for keeping track of the alternative sequences through them. This may seem a little pedantic but is useful when you, or the member of a pilot group of respondents on whom you're testing out your questionnaire, wonder if a better questionnaire sequence is required.

Whether you need to keep track of the items in this way depends partly on how long your questionnaire is going to be. Common sense suggests a dilemma: people like attractive, well-laid out questionnaires with plenty of space on the page (especially if you include some open-ended items); on the other hand, they lose interest if the questionnaire has too many pages. There is more on this issue in the eliciting answers section below; for the meantime, as a rule of thumb you might consider using filecards and a flowchart if your questionnaire is longer than ten items or three pages of final typescript.

Format

A variety of response formats is available to you, the most common being the fixed-alternative forms (multiple choice, free choice, ranking, and rating), and open-ended forms.

Multiple-choice format is the most common and straightforward: you ask your respondent to choose a single alternative from a list of several which you provide. You always include an 'Other, please specify' alternative, which gives the respondent the opportunity to respond in his or her own words because none of the alternatives you have provided expresses what he or she wishes to say. With some kinds of question an appropriately worded 'Don't know' alternative will also be informative without causing offence. *Free choice format* allows the respondent to choose one *or more* alternatives and, again, you should offer an 'Other, please specify' alternative. *Ranked format* asks the respondent to put all the alternatives into rank order on some quality specified in the item. In this case, using an 'Other, please specify' alternative is not advisable since analyzing the item will be very difficult, and so you need to have thoroughly pre-researched ranked format items, to be sure that your set of alternatives is completely exhaustive without the 'Other' alternative. *Rating format* involves the respondent in assigning 'points' to each alternative, and usually provides a scale by which he or she can do so. Finally, *Open-ended format* simply states the item and requests the respondent to answer in his or her own words.

These formats are exemplified in Tables 11.4 and 11.5, (with the exception of rating scales, which are described in Section 12.2). As you ponder over the content of each of your items, you should decide which answer format is most likely to provide you with the most useful data about your respondent's views, being easily analyzed for the information contained in the data it will provide.

In other words, the format isn't something you can decide without thinking ahead to the time your questionnaires have been returned and your data are available for analysis. On the one hand, if the format doesn't match the wording of the item to the appropriate analysis method, the item will confuse the respondents and the results will lack validity; on the other hand, a format that is inadequate in this regard will also confuse yourself, when you have to get down to the mechanics of the analysis and realize that you haven't thought things through. Indeed, one of the most common reasons for missing a project submission deadline arises when a student leaves the detailed planning of his or her analysis until all the data are in!

Different kinds of question content may call for different answer formats. Try not to change format too often; in other words, consider dividing your questionnaire into separate sections so that all the multiple-choice questions are together in one section, and the rating scales in another. Within any format, make sure that the exact way in which respondents are asked to make their response remains consistent throughout the questionnaire. For example, if you are using multiple-choice format, ask your respondents to indicate their choice by a tick, or by underlining the alternative, or by circling it, but not by a mixture of all three! (See Gillham, 2000 for more on answer format and questionnaire layout.) Using 'X's within square brackets is increasingly popular with multiple-choice and free-choice formats used in e-mail questionnaires (Dillman 2000: 376–401), as is the use of drop-down boxes in internet-based questionnaires, where the same set of alternatives is offered in a series of rating-scale items; see Dillman (2000: 392–394).

TABLE 11.4 The structure of a questionnaire item

The questionnaire is aimed at the Chairs of Boards of financial institutions (banks, discount houses, insurance companies, merchant banks, venture capitalists, and government funding organizations).

Components	Text as it appears in the questionnaire (italics excepted: these refer to the notes below)
Item	Q.8 *IN YOUR VIEW*, WHAT IS THE MOST IMPORTANT PRIORITY FOR THE *CHAIRMAN* OF A FINANCIAL INSTITUTION?
Recording instructions	Please put a X in the brackets beside the *ONE alternative* which best describes your view
Alternatives	a To understand the basic concepts which underlie the various forms of financing which the institution offers to its clients. [ ] b To foster an entrepreneurial spirit in which appropriate levels of risk can be contemplated and evaluated. [ ] c To encourage the development of a clear, and commonly shared, vision of the institution and its future. [ ] d To ensure that the corporate strategy and mission permeate decisions taken by staff at all levels. [ ] e To develop an appropriate organizational structure, and avoid alterations to it. [ ] f To remember the paramount importance of the shareholders when setting objectives and evaluating priorities. [ ] g OTHER: Please specify in your own words, in the space below. [ ]
Steering instructions	Q.9 which follows is aimed at *privately* owned financial institutions. If you are a *public* (government) funded organization, please skip Q.9 and go on to Q.10.

Notes on the text in italics

IN YOUR VIEW	A personal viewpoint is being elicited (as distinct from, say, a corporate or Board view).
CHAIRMAN	It is tempting to use 'Chair' or 'chairperson' but following evidence that the practice among this population is to use 'Chairman', the latter is used to match expectations of respondents. A difficult choice: do you stick to your principles or maximize return rate?
ONE alternative	The item is written in multiple-choice format, i.e. choose just one item from several.
Public/private	Analysis will require you to tally crosses in each box across the whole sample. The sample has been stratified on this basis, so the tallies will be totalled separately for each of these two subgroups.

Eliciting answers

Now you come to the specification of the item content. This consists of two parts: the item itself, and the set of alternatives. As Table 11.3 suggests, there are issues of both content and wording which you should bear in mind as you write. A good

TABLE 11.5(a) Procedural guide to the analysis of multiple choice responses				
IN YOUR VIEW, WHAT IS THE MOST IMPORTANT PRIORITY FOR THE CHAIRMAN OF A FINANCIAL INSTITUTION? Please put a cross inside the brackets beside the ONE alternative which best describes your view.	Public f	Public %	Private f	Private %
To understand the basic concepts which underlie the various forms of financing which the institution offers to its clients.	4	10.0	8	13.3
To foster an entrepreneurial spirit in which appropriate levels of risk can be contemplated and evaluated.	2	5.0	12	20.0
To encourage the development of a clear, and commonly shared, vision of the institution and its future.	9	22.5	15	25.0
To ensure that the corporate strategy and mission permeate decisions taken by staff at all levels.	6	15.0	11	18.3
To develop an appropriate organizational structure, and avoid alterations to it.	8	20.0	7	11.7
To remember the paramount importance of the shareholders when setting objectives and evaluating priorities.	5	12.5	4	6.7
Fulfilling responsibilities to government.	5	12.5	0	0
No answer	1	2.5	3	5.0
Total Sample	40	100.0	60	100.0
(Total respondents)	39		57	

A straightforward analysis.
- In the two f (frequency) columns, tally all the responses in each category across the sample, keeping the two subgroups separate. Report the tallies, together with the information about the number of people not answering the question.
- The total of tallies downwards plus the 'no answers' plus 'don't knows', if any, must equal the sample size and must always be reported.
- Where subgroups exist and are of unequal size, calculate percentage values and report these next to the basic frequency data.

item is strictly necessary, covers appropriate material, is suited to the comprehension and knowledge level of the sample, is appropriately specific, avoids stereotyped answers and comes in the right place in the questionnaire sequence. Moreover, it's worded precisely, doesn't take a knowledge of in-house or professional acronyms for granted, is non-threatening, avoids vague words and indicates the basis on which the response is to be made.

TABLE 11.5(b) Procedural guide to the analysis of free-choice responses				
HERE IS A LIST OF PRIORITIES TO WHICH A CHAIRMAN MIGHT SUBSCRIBE. Please place a X against any one *or more* which you feel are important.	Public f	Public %	Private f	Private %
To understand the basic concepts which underlie the various forms of financing which the institution offers to its clients.	16	11.3	25	12.0
To foster an entrepreneurial spirit in which appropriate levels of risk can be contemplated and evaluated.	3	2.1	49	23.6
To encourage the development of a clear, and commonly shared, vision of the institution and its future.	38	27.0	57	27.4
To ensure that the corporate strategy and mission permeate decisions taken by staff at all levels.	25	17.7	38	18.3
To develop an appropriate organizational structure, and avoid alterations to it.	30	21.3	21	10.1
To remember the paramount importance of the shareholders when setting objectives and evaluating priorities.	18	12.8	18	8.7
Fulfilling responsibilities to government.	11	7.8	0	0.0
No answer	1		3	
(Total Sample)	40		60	
(Total Frequency for those who responded)	141	100.0	208	100.0

Not quite so straightforward since, in free choice format, each respondent chooses as many boxes as he or she wishes.
- In the two frequency columns, tally all the responses in each category across the sample, keeping the two subgroups separate. Report the tallies, together with information about the number of people not answering the question.
- Notice that the total at the bottom of the columns represents the sum of tallies or Xs, and *not* the total of respondents. Use the sum of tallies as your 'total' when working out percentages, and not the total of respondents.

It is possible that you will construct the alternatives from the knowledge of the issues which you gained by your earlier use of less structured techniques: conversational, key informant interview, focus group, or whatever. Your piloting of the questionnaire may also suggest new alternatives. The alternatives may be ones which you informally judged to be appropriate as a result of that earlier experience, or they may be categories which you explicitly derived from a full content analysis of the earlier data. Their content will depend on this prior thinking, while their wording will depend on the answer format which you have chosen, as well as on

TABLE 11.5(c) Procedural guide to the analysis of ranked responses

HERE IS A LIST OF PRIORITIES TO WHICH A CHAIRMAN MIGHT SUBSCRIBE. Please rank them from 1 to 7 to express your own view of their relative importance. '1' means 'highest' and '7' means 'lowest' priority. They *are* priorities, so no two can have the same rank.	RESPONDENTS (Public-sector only) There would be as many columns here as there are respondents, plus a column for the sum of ranks. (Only the first and second respondents' columns and the total of all 39, are shown in this example.)			PUBLIC SECTOR
	1st,	2nd ...	... Sum of 39 respondents	Sums, ranked
To understand the basic concepts which underlie the various forms of financing which the institution offers to its clients.	5	7	178	5
To foster an entrepreneurial spirit in which appropriate levels of risk can be contemplated and evaluated.	7	6	242	7
To encourage the development of a clear, and commonly shared, vision of the institution and its future.	2	1	56	1
To ensure that the corporate strategy and mission permeate decisions taken by staff at all levels.	3	2	125	3
To develop an appropriate organizational structure, and avoid alterations to it.	1	4	109	2
To remember the paramount importance of the shareholders when setting objectives and evaluating priorities.	6	5	168	4
Fulfilling responsibilities to government.	4	3	214	6
No answer			1	
Total Sample			40	

- The analysis of ranked data involves two steps:
  a Sum the rank given to each alternative, *across* the sample or sub-sample, left to right across the respondent columns, (as in the first two columns above, which show only the first and second respondents' ranks), into a column of rank sums for the whole subgroup (the third column above).
  b Rank these sums, the lowest getting rank 1, and put the resulting values into another column (the fourth column above).
- You would repeat both steps for each subgroup (public sector, private sector) in the overall sample, *and then report just the ranked sums for each subgroup*: not the intermediate calculations.
  You would however report the number of people not answering, as usual.

the guidelines outlined in Table 11.3. Add the item and the alternatives onto your filecard.

The wording of your item and alternatives has a great bearing on the final length of the questionnaire and, clearly, if the questionnaire is perceived as too long the responses are likely to be careless, or indeed non-existent, and return rates may well drop by some 5–10 per cent through this factor alone (Dillman 2000: 305–306). Some items may require a brief sentence of background and rationale; some demand a longish list of alternatives, while others, the open-ended ones, require you to provide about three inches of space into which your respondent will write their response verbatim. If you begin to get the impression as you prepare your filecards that the questionnaire is simply going to be too long, you might decide to use an entirely different technique, the face-to-face structured interview being the obvious alternative to choose.

How long is 'too long'? Well, that depends on many factors, especially those which help to retain your respondent's interest in your topic, layout on the page and the like (see Table 11.7 in the later section on response rates). Howard and Sharp (1983) offer a useful rule of thumb for postal questionnaires when they suggest that anything longer than ten pages, or taking longer than 15 minutes to complete, is likely to be too long. Dillman (2000: 372) considers a variety of factors which influence respondents' attention in e-mail questionnaires and predicts a future in which e-mail questionnaires will be used particularly with short (3–5 question) surveys of small samples of respondents whose names are already in a database and a fast turnaround of a few days is required.

Recording answers

When you have specified the alternatives, you must then decide on the wording you will use to instruct the respondent on how he or she is to make a response. You might imagine that most sensible people would be able to work it out for themselves just by looking at the item. However, as you'll realize from your ruminations on answer format, different formats call for different recording methods: see Tables 11.5. If you don't tell the respondent which of these answer formats to use, you will end up assessing the respondent's intelligence rather than his or her responses to the item in question, thus increasing the unreliability of the data you collect. Add the wording of the recording instructions onto your filecard.

The words in which you tell your respondents how they are to tackle the item (the format instructions and recording instructions) have a great influence on the perceived style of your questionnaire and these in turn play an important part in the respondent's decision to cooperate with you. The word 'please' is at your disposal and the only issue is whether including it with the recording instructions of every item isn't a bit repetitive. Make a judgement when you've seen how the whole set of filecards reads.

By this time, each card is beginning to look crowded. It contains:

■ a number indicating its place in the questionnaire sequence

■ the wording of the steering instructions

- the wording of the item
- the wording of the alternatives
- the wording of the recording instructions.

Shuffle the cards into sequence and give them to a friend for an initial overall piloting of the item wording and sequence. Compile them into a typed A4 format, to provide a master of your questionnaire ready for photocopying for piloting as described in Section 9.4, and for eventual use, after amendment, with your main sample of respondents.

Analysis

There are a great variety of techniques available, from the simple description of sample responses by means of frequency counts over item alternatives, to a more complex use of analytic statistical tests, single or multivariate, for a single sample or for various sub-groupings of your sample, the latter made possible by the fact that your questionnaire is highly structured. I cannot provide an account of all of them, but you will find a brief account of the main descriptive methods helpful, followed by an indication of the existence of analytic statistical measures and a reference to further information. I have however included one analytic statistic, the Chi-square test, since it is so useful when you cross-tabulate your data (breaking down the answers to one question by the answers to another); or for looking at how two sub-samples compare. My concern at this stage is to provide you with an overview just sufficient for you to be able to complete the writing of your questionnaire items, bearing in mind the type of analysis which you intend to carry out. If you are looking for a good overview of statistical methods, Blaikie (2003) provides a general text; if you are nervous of statistics but want to see what might be possible for you, Diamontopoulos and Schlegelmilch (1997) is quite comforting and has examples keyed to SPSS, a very popular analysis package; while if you are familiar with statistics but need a quick reference text which will remind you of many of the formulae and procedures, then Collis and Hussey (2003) is ideal.

Set a cut-off date for the return of the questionnaires, incorporating a period for any chase-up or re-posting you have planned in the case of tardy respondents (see Section 4.2). Begin your analysis on this date. Compile all your returns and look through them all, rejecting any respondents who have omitted or botched responses to so many items that their questionnaire is unusable. (If a respondent has omitted a response to just one or two items, you can treat him or her as a 'no answer' when analyzing those items; too many non-responses, or too many improperly answered items, mean that the questionnaire must be rejected.)

From this moment on, treat the analysis of the resulting set of questionnaires as an accounting exercise. In other words, you have to account for the total number of respondents in this resulting set in your analysis of each question. Responses to tables have to add up to this total and the subtotals of subgroups must sum to this same total. The sums of response alternatives plus 'don't know' plus 'no answer' responses must sum to this total – in short, your reader must get a clear picture of the answers of the sample as a whole, across all of the items, and this is only possible if you account for all of the returns in your presentation of the results of *each* question.

Perceiving

As Tables 11.4 and 11.5 indicate, your first step is to do a brief content analysis (see Section 10.2) of the 'Other, please specify' responses to find a few (one to three, usually) additional categories to add to your list of alternatives for each of the items. Your analysis will then be carried out on the full set of alternatives. (Look at the alternatives in Tables 11.5 in contrast to Table 11.4: the alternative 'Fulfilling responsibilities to government' has been added to the former, reflecting the views of five public-sector respondents who said as much in their own words.)

Next, you have to aggregate the data across all respondents. Finally, you look for patterns in the data, in order to discover the information contained. You might do this for the data as a whole, or you might aggregate within subgroups of respondents and there are two ways of doing the latter.

First, if your sample is clustered or stratified, you will need to examine the responses of people within the different clusters or strata, in order to draw comparisons or make contrasts. So, for example, if the sample is clustered on the basis of salary status (salaried versus wage-earning), you would keep the data separate for each of these groups (see Table 8.4). Second, as we have seen earlier, it is possible to obtain unexpected and interesting information by cross-tabulating: breaking down the answers to one question, by the answers to another. So, for example, if you asked respondents to specify their length of service with the organization, you could see if long-serving respondents answered systematically differently from short-serving respondents, even though you didn't originally stratify the sample by length of service.

Indeed, when you're exploring an issue, it is possible to break down the answers to each item by the answers to every other single item, provided your sample is large enough and that you haven't got too many alternative answers to the items involved. The availability of user-friendly microcomputer packages such as STATVIEW, SPSS or GBSTAT makes this sort of exploration very straightforward and tempting, but you should consider the costs:

- You end up with masses of data and you need time to identify the usable information you increase the risks of making a Type 1 error if your package allows the automatic calculation of analytic statistics, due to the repeated use of a statistic when a smaller number of usages could have been possible. (If you are familiar with statistical analysis, note the danger. If you're not, ignore the point – you shouldn't be using the statistics the package offers, so seductively, in the first place!)

- You may become confused about the generalizability of your findings.

The last point needs some explanation. If you are working with a sample split into subgroups (by cluster or stratified sampling), you have kept control over the sample and can validly generalize your findings to the population. So, if you had stratified by length of service, a statistically significant difference in answers to a particular item between long-serving and short-serving members of the sample would indicate a real difference among long- and short-serving employees in your population. In contrast, if you hadn't stratified by length of service, but did a break-down of answers to a particular question by length of service anyway, any difference between the long- and short-serving respondents would be true of the sample but not necessarily of the population.

Explore the data by all means, but focus your primary attention on the issues, hunches and hypotheses which you developed originally as relevant to your topic and research question. Keep it simple: you are looking for patterns in the data, which usually boils down to three things:

- Is there a trend?
- In the case of comparisons (e.g. between subgroups) are the answers the same?
- If not, is there a trend to the contrasting answers: have the respondents answered systematically differently?

At the simplest, descriptive level, you report plain frequencies under nominal categories, tallying and reporting the number of people who chose each alternative answer. See the procedural guide in Table 11.6. As you can see, the way in which you lay out and present these tables may make a difference to how obvious and perceivable the actual relationship is. If you're comparing the responses of different subgroups of different size, you should turn the frequencies into percentages within each subgroup and report both. Multiple-choice, free-choice and ranked formats involve different variations on this theme, as illustrated in Table 11.5.

At a more complex, analytic level, you compute an appropriate analytic statistic which informs you if the difference or trend in the data is statistically significant, that is, large enough to represent an actual difference or trend in the population, rather than only occurring 'by chance' in your sample, i.e., as a result of factors which you haven't anticipated, didn't control, or aren't even aware of. Chi-square is particularly useful for indicating whether the relationships in a cross-tabulated table are significant, and the procedural guide given in Table 11.7 explains the rationale and shows you the computation involved, working with the data from Table 11.6. (There is a different computational procedure which you could use when working with a 2×2 table, which gives a slightly more statistically accurate answer, but the difference isn't worth worrying about: the formula I have used is a general one, suitable for a table with as many columns and rows as you please and it was convenient to use a 2×2 table as an example.)

Remember, too, that whenever you establish the statistical significance of your data, while you have provided the best possible proof that your information expresses what is happening in the population, you have not necessarily said anything about the meaning – the psychological significance – of your informa-tion. The two are distinct and the latter depends on the rationale that lies behind the relationship you're examining, which in turn depends on your design, as I've presented in Section 8.1.

TABLE 11.6 Procedural guide: summarizing and presenting patterns in data

Sometimes trends in the data are difficult to perceive by the reader unless you present them appropriately.

In Example 1, tallies have been converted to percentages by summing downwards in the conventional way to find the total of responses in each subgroup. Percentages refer to the proportion of all males and all females in each salary band.

In Example 2, tallies have been summed across, to find the total of responses in each salary band, and these band totals have been used in calculating percentages. These now refer to the proportion of each salary band that is either male or female.

	Example 1				Example 2				
Salary band £,000	M f	M %	F f	F %	Salary band £,000	M f	M %	F f	F %	Total
>=38	1	1.4	0	0	>=38	1	0	100.0	0	100.0
36–37.9	10	14.2	3	2.9	36–37.9	10	3	76.9	23.1	100.0
34–35.9	5	7.1	2	1.9	34–35.9	5	2	71.4	28.6	100.0
32–33.9	5	7.1	4	3.8	32–33.9	5	4	55.6	44.4	100.0
30–31.9	1	1.4	1	1.0	30–31.9	1	1	50.0	50.0	100.0
28–29.9	8	11.4	9	8.6	28–29.9	8	9	47.1	52.9	100.0
26–27.9	7	10.0	9	8.6	26–27.9	7	9	43.8	56.3	100.1
24–25.9	8	11.4	11	10.5	24–25.9	8	11	42.1	57.9	100.0
22–23.9	9	12.9	16	15.2	22–23.9	9	16	36.0	64.0	100.0
20–21.9	12	17.1	32	30.5	20–21.9	12	32	27.3	72.7	100.0
18–19.9	4	5.7	12	11.4	18–19.9	4	12	25.0	75.0	100.0
<18	0	0	6	5.7	<18	0	6	0	100.0	100.0
Total	70	99.8	105	100.1						

Running the eye down the two percentage columns of Example 1, it's apparent that males tend to be distributed in the upper salary bands, but the relationship isn't especially obvious; (the arrangement of the columns doesn't help either). Running the eye down the columns in Example 2 makes the relationship very clear indeed: the values systematically decrease downwards for males and increase for females.

Once you suspect a relationship or trend, then presenting the data as a 2 × 2 table can make it more easily perceived (though you're presenting fewer data, so the 'split' needs to be made in the right place!). Examples 3 and 4 use the same raw frequency data on male and female salaries as Examples 1 and 2.

In Example 3, the lower values are in the top row and the larger values are in the lower row: no sign of a relationship.

In Example 4, the relationship is revealed as an effect along the diagonals: larger values in the top left and bottom right, and smaller ones in the bottom left and upper right.

	Example 3			Example 4	
	M	F		M	F
>−30	22	10	>=24	45	39
<30	48	95	<24	25	66
Total	70	105	Total	70	105

TABLE 11.7 Procedural guide to the computation of Chi-square

Comments

You would work out the value of Chi-square if you have a table of nominal categories arranged vertically and horizontally, and you felt the data in this sample suggest that there might be a trend or relationship in the population. It is particularly useful when you are comparing two columns of figures which are tallies, for two separate subgroups of a sample, of responses which have been categorized using the same set of answer categories for both subgroups: as in Examples 1 and 2 in Table 11.6. The computation does *not* work with percentages, but with the original frequencies.

Rationale

Take the simplest case: a 2 × 2 table, such as Example 4 in Table 11.6.

Salary	Males	Females
>= 24,000	45	39
<24,000	25	66
Total	70	105

Is there a trend? In the population from which this sample is drawn, do the males earn more than the females? Or is this just sampling error: an accidental characteristic of this particular sample? Well, how big would the top left and bottom right figures have to be; how small would the bottom left and top right figures have to be, before you decided that the relationship in this sample was so large that you couldn't put it down to chance and concluded that it was true, in the population? (Remember, we're assuming that you've done all you can to draw a representative sample!) Look at these two cases:

Salary	Males	Females		Salary	Males	Females
>= 24,000	33	51		>= 24,000	69	15
<24,000	37	54		<24,000	1	90
Total	70	105		Total	70	105

You'd conclude there was no trend

You'd feel pretty sure there was!

And in these four examples, your certainty that there is a real trend in the population increases, from left to right, below.

38	46	43	41	53	31	63	21
32	59	27	64	17	74	7	84
70	105	70	105	70	105	70	105

Computing Chi-square

You follow the same rationale. You work out the chances that the figures you actually obtained are so different from the 'no-trend' pattern that you can no longer continue to believe there's no trend; and so you conclude that there *must* be a trend, beyond the level of chance.

1 If you haven't already done so, work out all four marginal totals and the grand total.

2 ... for each observed figure, work out its expected value if there was no trend, by multiplying its two marginal totals together and dividing by the grand total

Observed: the figures you actually obtained

Expected: the figures you'd get with these marginal totals if there were no relationship

TABLE 11.7 Procedural guide to the computation of Chi-square (cont.)

Salary	Male	Female	Total	Salary	Male	Female	Total
>= 24,000	45	39	84	>= 24,000	33.6	50.4	84
<24,000	25	66	91	<24,000	36.4	54.6	91
Total	70	105	175	Total	70	105	175

Now, what would the figures look like if indeed there wasn't any trend? Well, that's determined by the marginal totals. So to find out what the 'no-trend' figures would be ...

That's $(84 \times 70) / 175 = 33.6$; $(84 \times 105) / 175 = 50.4$; $(91 \times 70) / 175 = 36.4$; and $(91 \times 105) / 175 = 54.6$. Next, notice that your certainty that there is a trend depends on the difference between the observed figures and the no-trend, 'expected'.

3 So, summarize your degree of certainty by summing the differences between observed and expected, as a proportion of what you'd expect if there wasn't any relationship (first squaring the differences to get rid of awkward minus signs). This gives you the value of Chi-square.

$$(45 - 33.6)^2 / 33.6 = 3.87$$
$$(39 - 50.4)^2 / 50.4 = 2.58$$
$$(25 - 36.4)^2 / 36.4 = 3.57$$
$$(66 - 54.6)^2 / 54.6 = 2.38$$

Total = 12.40 = Chi-square

Statisticians have worked out all possible combinations of differences for you and published the results in a table called the 'Table of critical values for Chi-square'. Using this, you can find out how certain you can be that there is a real trend in your data – that the sample reflects a real trend in the population, rather than just an accidental sampling error. You can find this table printed in any statistics textbook, or any collection of statistical tables, e.g Murdoch and Barnes (1998). An extract, relevant to a 2 × 2 table, is shown here.

Critical values of Chi-square where the prediction is of a directional relationship between two variables in a 2 × 2 table (one-tailed)

p	0.10	0.05	0.025	0.01	0.005	0.0005
1 df	1.64	2.71	3.84	5.41	6.64	10.83

4 Look in the body of the Chi-square table (for the example above, in the row marked '1 df'). Going from left to right, find the value nearest to and smaller than the value you calculated for Chi-square. At the top of that column you'll find the probability that the value you calculated was accidental rather than reflecting a real trend. With our own data, the nearest-and-smaller-value to 12.40 is 10.83 at the very right of the table. Now look immediately above to the top row, where the corresponding probabilities of values as large as the computed value are shown. For our own data, 10.83 corresponds to a probability of 0.0005, or five chances in ten thousand; and so 12.40 must have an even lower probability of occurring as a chance outcome. So we can accept this difference in the sample as representing a real difference in the population out there, with very little chance of being wrong.

5 By convention, 0.05, five chances in a hundred, is the conventional value for deciding to trust the data, or continue in the conservative belief that sampling errors are at work. So, if

TABLE 11.7 Procedural guide to the computation of Chi-square (cont.)
the probability corresponding to the value of Chi-square which you calculated was greater than 0.05, you would have to conclude that there is no real trend in the population, and that your actual data reflect sampling error.
6 If you're working with a table larger than 2 × 2, then (C − 1) × (R − 1), where C is the number of columns and R is the number of rows in your table, gives df: in other words, tells you which row of the table of critical values for Chi-square to refer to in step 4 above. Use row 30 in this table if the value of (C − 1) × (R − 1) is 30 or greater.
7 A final caveat. If in a table larger than 2 × 2, you have an expected value of less than 1.0, or if more than 20 per cent of the cells have expected values of less than 5.0, you should collapse rows and/or columns – combine categories, in other words – until this criterion has been met, before calculating the total for Chi-square. If you're working with a 2 × 2 table already, collapsing categories will make the test rather pointless, since it's a diagonal relationship you're looking for. Use Fisher's Exact Probability Test instead: see Siegel and Castellan (1988: 123).

Before leaving the subject of analysis, perhaps a final few words about using a computer are indicated. With a sample of fewer than 100 people and a questionnaire of 15 items or so, you will probably finish the job faster if you do most of the analysis by hand, with a calculator for any percentages calculations or analytic statistics that an individual question may require. That assumes you don't have an appreciable number of cross-tabulations. The reason is simple: it takes time to learn how to use one of the packages I have mentioned, to cross-check your understanding with some sample data which you have hand-computed and then key in all of your main data. In any case, you really ought not to use a microcomputer-based statistics package to compute analytic statistics unless you know enough about the statistic to be able to do it by hand. Worst of all is the student who runs every computer-based statistical test in sight and then goes to look for a tutor to interpret the results!

With samples of 200 and over, the time lost in learning the system and inputting the data is amply repaid by the speed and convenience of a computerized analysis, while between 100 and 200 sample size, it can be difficult to say, and depends very much on the number of cross-tabulations and analytic statistics you need to compute.

If you're using a computer for analytic statistics, the manual that comes with the package will provide a good guide to the versions of the formulae used and a statement of the assumptions entailed in each. Users of SPSS are well served with many good manuals; Green and Salkind (2002) is particularly useful, though aimed more at a behavioural sciences than a management audience.

Summarizing

In the case of questionnaire data, this involves you in casting the data into a form which best displays the trend or relationship to your reader, a knack which develops with practice. It boils down to two things: highlighting the relationships you have identified, as we saw in Table 11.6; and choosing a graphical form in which to display them. The most common alternatives to a simple tabular form are the frequency distribution, the bar-chart, and the pie-chart, labelled with the item alternatives as appropriate, and with the results of any analytic statistics superimposed. See the Figure 11.1 procedural guide for some examples.

Write-up

Presenting

Questionnaire results are presented according to a common pattern as follows:

- The purpose of the particular section of the questionnaire is stated; then, for each item in the section the wording of the item itself is presented, without steering instructions or recording instructions.
- The format is stated, if it isn't obvious from the data.
- The data are presented, in **tabular** or graphic form, with the alternatives shown in the appropriate position in the table or graph, and making sure that every member of the sample is accounted for. Each table or figure must have a number and a title; the axes of a graph must be labelled.
- A verbal statement is made of the information contained; the foot of Table 10.5 provides an example.
- General comments or statements are made to link the item just presented to the item to be presented next. What I have in mind here is that there should be a logical, step-by-step progression of ideas and discovery across the set of items as your argument is built.
- A summary of the findings of the section is provided, in the form of bulleted statements. (The point I am making now is part of a bulleted statement: a clause, sentence, or short paragraph beginning with a small black circle and being part of a list, the whole set being inset from the left margin!) By the time your reader has got to the end of the section, he or she is likely to be forgetting the earlier findings you presented and needs a summary of all that have been presented so far.

Locating

All of the above is placed in the main body of the text, either in one single major section (Figure 3.1), or in several different sections in which different issues and aspects of your thesis are explored and relevant ideas taken from reading are presented (Figure 3.2). It should be followed by a general summary of the findings, in the form of a connected narrative and should precede a discussion of the implications of these findings.

Supporting data, data to amplify your findings, and less relevant information are presented in an appendix. People often wonder how much to provide in their appendices. That depends on the nature of the work they're doing, but you

FIGURE 11.1 Procedural guide to simple data descriptions

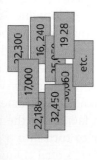

...a confused mass of data (being the salary figures of the 70 male managers shown in Table 11.6); points on an underlying continuous distribution

Continuously Distributed Data

Information can be extracted from this confusing mass of data by drawing up a frequency table and expressing the figures as a *frequency graph*, *histogram*, or *pie-chart*.

1 If you don't already have one in the form of a set of questionnaire item alternatives, create a set of 5–15 mutually exclusive intervals of equal size, standing for categories into which you can code each item.

2 Count the number of items in each interval across the sample and list the resulting totals in a column of frequencies.

3 Check that the total of the frequency column equals the sample or subgroup size; if not, repeat step 2.

Frequency Graph: a graph of intervals along the horizontal axis and points indicating frequency of occurrence along the vertical axis. The points can be joined together to show a distribution.

Histogram: exactly the same, but with the points along the vertical axis indicated by horizontal lines, joined to their neighbours.

Salary Freq. Intervals (£,000)		
>=38	1	
36–37.9	10	
34–35.9	5	
32–33.9	5	
30–31.9	1	
28–29.9	8	
26–27.9	7	
24–25.9	8	
22–23.9	9	
20–21.9	12	
18–19.9	4	
<18	0	

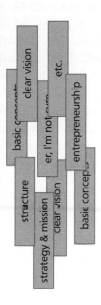

...a confused mass of data (being the 40 Xs placed into one or other of the 8 multiple-choice alternatives of Table 11.5a): distinct data with no continuous dimension underlying them

Data in Discrete Categories

Information can be extracted from this confusing mass of data by tallying in groups and expressing the figures as a *bar-chart* or *pie-chart*. While the bar-chart looks, at first glance, like a histogram, and while pie-charts are used for both continuous and discrete data, you can't use a histogram or, worse, a frequency graph, for discrete data. The figures express the number of tallies allocated to distinct, non-continuous categories.

1 If you haven't already done a content analysis of new verbatim data, create a set of mutually exclusive questionnaire item alternatives. Usually, though, if you're working with a structured questionnaire, you already have the item alternatives: the boxes people mark with an X.

2 Count the number of responses in each box (tallying) across the sample and then list the resulting values in a column, each next to its item alternative

3 Check that the totals of these values equal the sample or subgroup size; if not, repeat step 2.

Bar-chart: a diagram of item alternatives along the horizontal axis, and frequencies up the vertical axis. Vertical bars are drawn whose height is proportional to the tallies. If the bars are touching each other, that is only for visual purposes: remember they represent non-continuous categories. (Think about it: you can have a salary of £27,999 and 50 pence but you can't have an alternative between 'basic concepts' and 'entrepreneurial spirit'!)

Item Alternatives	Tallies
To understand the basic concepts...	4
To foster entrepreneurial spirit...	2
To encourage the development...	9
To ensure that the corporate...	6
To develop an appropriate...	8
To remember the paramount...	5
Fulfilling responsibilities to...	1
No answer	5
Total	40

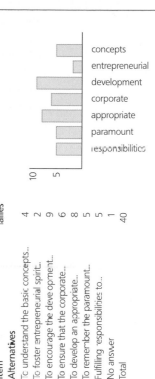

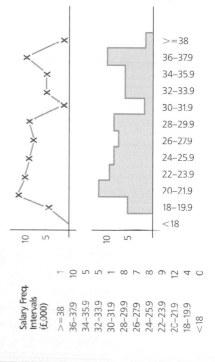

might find the following guidelines useful. First, the questionnaire itself must be appended; second, supporting data which can be sensibly organized in some way should be appended (for example, the table which you analyzed to recognize a particular finding, before you recast it into the form presented in the main body of the text; or a list of 'Other, please specify' responses grouped into the categories which you added to your list of alternatives). Unorganized raw data that are simple lists of responses must not be appended. So, for example, you would not include a table like 11.5(c) anywhere in your dissertation; but you would provide the rightmost column (the Public Sector ranked sums), together with the ranked sums for the Private Sector respondents (not shown in that table) and you would do so in the main body of the text rather than in an appendix, since a two-column table of this kind reports a main finding without computational details.

 This would be a good point at which to read Case Example 11.1.

 If you intend to use the structured questionnaire techniques as described here, please work through activities 1 to 5, to the extent that they apply, in the Project Guide.

11.2 The structured interview

A glance at Tables 10.3 and 11.1 will remind you of the advantages of the interview in comparison with the questionnaire. As far as business and management project work is concerned, probably the most important of these relate to the ease with which you can express complex ideas and cover the ground thoroughly. As Chapter 6 suggested, matters of business strategy, policy, and practitioner concern are often difficult to break down into a small number of unambiguous, single questions. The advantage of the face-to-face interview over the questionnaire is that you are present yourself, and can, within the structure you have previously designed, amplify the meaning of the items, and explain the intentions behind your questions, in a way which isn't possible with the structured, postal questionnaire.

Every structured interview follows a written interview guide: a document which looks very much like a questionnaire, and provides item sequence details, steering instructions, items, alternatives and recording instructions. In fact, all of the information which you would have recorded on filecards in order to turn into a questionnaire (as described in the previous section) is also, with occasional changes to wording, required in preparing a structured interview guide. Use filecards in the same way.

Computer Assisted Personal Interviewing (CAPI) software fulfils the same function, the items, their sequence, the response format and alternatives, and prompts which provide a steering function being presented by a laptop computer. The ability to present alternative sequences through the set of items depending on respondents' prior answers is a frequently mentioned advantage of CAPI technique, but it would appear (Bryman and Bell 2003: 121) that some respondents may feel uncomfortable with this form of technology.

The purpose of the conventional guide or the CAPI technique is to ensure that you handle the interview in essentially the same way with each of your interviewees. Memory can fail you, you might be tired, the need to explain your intentions to a particular respondent may cause you to forget the thrust and direction of your question sequence, something which your respondent says may be so interesting that you go off on a complete tangent – if you're not careful, a structured interview can turn into a semi-structured interview, an e-mail interview or even a conversation, which is fine if that's what you want; but if you're reading this chapter rather than Chapter 10, I assume that your intention is otherwise!

Because of the close similarity between interview guide and questionnaire, I will assume that you are familiar with Section 11.1 and confine my material to issues that are unique to the structured interview. I also assume that you are familiar with the material on semi-structured interviews in Section 10.2 – some of the material is related and the rest forms a useful contrast of which it's useful to be aware.

Design

Apart from the need to be explicit about the items which will be used for breaking down answers to other items (see the relevant material in Section 11.1) and the general issues of design, there are no particular points to be made here.

Elicitation

When you elicit data in a structured interview, you follow your previously designed guide, but react appropriately to the verbal and non-verbal signals by which your respondent indicates his or her understanding of the items and their alternatives, to the level of interest which your respondent expresses, and to the digressions and comments he or she initiates.

Steering

So, just as with the questionnaire, you prepare steering instructions in advance. However, in this case, they consist of notes to yourself. In reacting appropriately to your interviewee, you will need to use techniques from the more directive end of the range shown in Table 10.1. In other words, you take the initiative in introducing new themes as you move from one section of your guide to the next, you determine the items and their sequence within each section, and you're active in redirecting the respondent's attention when the conversation momentarily diverges from the course you have set.

You can set the direction from the start of each main section, by providing a fuller rationale for the direction you are taking than you would be able to in a questionnaire. Decide on the wording in advance and write it into your guide at appropriate places. As the interview progresses, you will find yourself responding in one of five ways, depending on what the respondent says and does:

- Recording responses and proceeding to the next item in the sequence as you receive a direct response.

- Amplifying the wording or meaning of an item if the respondent misunderstands the item as first expressed. If you feel in advance that some items will require an amplifying phrase, you should write an appropriate form of words, in brackets after the main item, in your interview guide.

- Maintaining the flow of the interview after a digression by the respondent, bringing him or her back to your sequence as skilfully as you can without further action.

- Remembering and perhaps noting a comment which, while it's a digression, has a bearing on a subsequent item. When you get to that item, you can refer back to the comment the respondent made.

- Noting and responding appropriately to any other comment which you hadn't expected, and therefore hadn't planned for in preparing the guide, but which is nevertheless relevant to the theme of your work, before proceeding with the main sequence as before. When designing the interview guide, you might like to leave a wide margin at the side of each page in which you can record such comments. You might also use this 'personal margin' to record any significant non-verbal activities which you feel might be useful during analysis.

Format

As with questionnaires, most interview guides tend to present similarly formatted items together: it would be unusual to jump from a multiple-choice item to a rating item to a ranking item and back throughout the whole sequence of items. So you need to give the format instructions just once before the set of items in question, with an occasional reminder of the format, in advance of the item itself. 'Now, for the next four questions I'm going to give you a number of alternatives, and ask you to rank them . . . ' (several items later) '. . . and again, how would you rank the following?' Decide on the wording of the format instructions in advance and write them onto a filecard at an appropriate point in the sequence.

Eliciting answers

Your cards, and the resulting interview guide (or the CAPI software if you are using it) will show the item itself and the set of alternatives you regard as responses to the item. When you prepare the interview guide leave sufficient space in which you can write down *verbatim* responses to any open-ended items being used. Record these literally rather than attempting a précis or synopsis. You elicit answers in one of three ways:

- By reading out the item and the alternatives. Because you will keep the interview guide in front of you as you conduct the interview, the respondent won't have any record of the item and the alternatives, and is likely to forget the alternatives soon after you have stated them. To prevent this, it is useful to prepare a set of **flash-cards**: stiff cards bearing all of the alternatives, typed in block capitals and preferably in a large typeface, which you hand to the respondent as you read out the item. It would certainly be feasible, but is not good practice, to show the respondent the screen where CAPI approach is used, since the layout and personal steering instructions would be a distraction. Use flash-cards just as you would with a conventional, non-CAPI approach.

■ By reading out the item, listening to the response and doing an instant content analysis before classifying the response under one of the alternatives written in the interview guide. When preparing the guide, you may need to include a brief statement of the defining characteristics beside each alternative, to help you in classifying the responses appropriately: see Section 10.2 under the 'analysis' heading for further particulars of content analysis.

■ By reading out an open-ended item and recording the verbatim response, for subsequent content analysis.

I say 'reading out', and, if you're to ensure reliability, you will need to stick to the same form of words, and as far as possible, similar procedures, with all of your interviewees. However, a series of readings from a script makes for no eye contact and a very dull social encounter, and the ideal to aim for is a thoroughly practised procedure: not necessarily a completely memorized script, but sufficient familiarity so that an occasional glance at your interview guide, or the screen of the laptop, is sufficient to remind you of where you are, what you need to say, and where you'll be heading next.

Recording answers

You'll be doing that yourself, as I've implied already. In contrast to the semi-structured interview, this is a straightforward procedure, since you know what format of answer to expect, and you have all the relevant alternatives in front of you. You record the responses in the interview guide itself (or, with CAPI, by keying in to the laptop). The guide has been prepared and laid out appropriately and at this point you're acting as scribe for the respondent. As you will have gathered from the foregoing, you have little use for a tape-recorder if the structured interview is your main data-gathering method.

Analysis

Perceiving and summarizing

These are almost exactly the same as in the questionnaire: see the appropriate headings in Section 11.1. The only difference (and this isn't universal practice, but is nevertheless a good one), is that you should scan all the interview guides before you start the analysis, to see if you have written any comments in the 'personal margin' which might be relevant to your handling of individual items.

Write-up

Presenting and locating

Again, the procedures used in the questionnaire will apply.

 If you intend to use the structured interview techniques as described here, please work through activities 1 to 5, to the extent that they apply, in the Project Guide.

11.3	Telephone interviews: convincing respondents of your bona fides

The telephone interview can be a very convenient way of contacting your respondents, especially if they work for your own organization but at distant locations. You might argue that it's just a face-to-face structured interview with the non-verbal behaviour removed, as it were, and that the general guidelines for the interview apply. However, there is a little more to it than that, precisely because the face-to-face element is missing, and good telephone interview technique provides lessons in interviewer–respondent relationships which are relevant to any form of structured survey in which people unknown to you are surveyed. Response rates, in the USA at any rate, seem to have decreased over the years (Dillman 2000: 28), so it is all the more important to think through your approach and carefully adapt your technique to this particular medium.

Imagine that you are sitting at your desk, or at home, and the telephone rings. A strange voice asks you if you wouldn't mind answering a few questions for a survey they are conducting. How would you react, especially if you'd been in the middle of an important task and the questions appeared to be a little personal? Much the same, you might imagine, as if you had received an unsolicited questionnaire. How can one best establish one's personal *bona fides* and minimize intrusiveness when dealing with strangers?

The approach is taken from Dillman (1978; 2000) and Frey (1983), both well worth reading if the telephone survey is to be your main data gathering technique. They provide you with excellent guidelines on design and procedure, though their comments on sampling (directory based or random dialling) are more appropriate to marketing surveys of the general public than to in-company business project work.

First, just as in the postal variant, where a letter accompanies the written questionnaire, you should send your respondents a brief letter or memo which says enough to provide assurance, but not sufficient to dispel curiosity, which gives an approximate time and date in the near future and which additionally provides a return telephone number for the respondent to use if the proposed time is inconvenient. Provide the name of an appropriate senior person (your sponsor or tutor) and their phone number in case your respondent wishes to check you out. Use headed paper, your university's or your organization's as appropriate. Do all you can to assure the respondent that you are not selling anything, or requesting an act of charity.

It's wise to give some thought to the best time to call your particular respondents; this will involve a decision on whether the best place to contact them is at home or at work. Once you start the phone calls, keep a careful record to prevent you calling people twice over, just as you keep a record of despatches in the case of the postal questionnaire. Keep a note particularly of other people answering your intended respondent's phone, and information on when your respondent will be available for interview. It is very easy to forget such details when you're engaged in making a series of phone calls to a variety of people.

The remaining guidelines apply particularly to the telephone interview itself. Make the call as planned, and check that the time is convenient, calling back if it isn't; give your respondent a fair opportunity to refuse, by stressing that participation is voluntary.

You need to have prepared your opening comments very carefully (it's here that most refusals occur), to include your name, where you're calling from and why, information on how the respondent's number was obtained, a reminder of the letter you sent, and a statement of how long the interview will take. Offer an alternative time (even though you've already stated the current time in your earlier letter)!

If the respondent has any questions, answer them fully, and then start on your interview guide. The items should flow sensibly and obviously, from one to the next: unlike the face-to-face interview, you don't have quite the same freedom to explain apparent inconsistencies. The first items should capture attention and relate directly to the purpose of the interview, with the personal background items kept until the end. Because you're not able to show your respondents a flash-card which summarizes a large set of alternatives, you will need to split longer items up into two or more stages: the first which asks for a general expression of their views and the second which examines the issue in more detail depending on the initial response, asking for a statement of how strongly they feel, for example. Both Dillman (2000) and Frey (1983) provide detailed examples.

When you have finished, say thank you and describe what will happen next, in the form of feedback on some of the results if you have planned to provide this.

> If you intend to use the telephone interview technique as described here, please work through activities 1 to 5, to the extent that they apply, in the Project Guide.

11.4　Anonymity: procedures and ethics

One of the underlying themes of this chapter concerns response rates and much of the material deals with the various techniques by which high rates may be achieved. But there is an ethical, as well as pragmatic, aspect to all of this. One of the best ways in which you can encourage cooperation is by making and communicating adequate arrangements to encourage a feeling of safety among your respondents. This, as a matter of research ethics rather than thoughtfulness or mere politeness; you might wish to review Table 3.1 at this point. There is a good general rule to apply. Unless you have explicitly obtained your respondents' agreement to mention them as providers of particular items of data, you should use the information they give you anonymously. There are various levels of security involved.

Once given, a promise on your part not to reveal names must be kept. Your data could then be labelled, in your own records only, with the name of the respondent only so that you don't confuse the respondent's data with someone else's.

The use of a simple letter or number code by which to identify the set of data given you by a particular respondent is a very common procedure for ensuring anonymity. You keep a list of names and corresponding code numbers in a safe place. The use of codes is essential if this degree of anonymity has been requested and you are following a before-after or similar design which involves you in going back to your respondents. Don't just remove their names from their data set, or you won't be able to put the two sets of data together again for analysis! If you have used number codes in drawing up a random sample (see Section 8.2), the number you used then can be used as your anonymity code.

Anonymity is also provided by the use of data which have been partially or completely processed (tables, percentages, distributions, or general narrative summaries), so that individual responses, whether previously identity-coded or not, aren't reported in your project report. This is also a very common form of arrangement and is used in combination with the previous one. You store raw data identified by an identity code, and you report processed data in which the individual provenance or ownership isn't identified.

Of course, with some kinds of information, your in-company readers, being lively and curious people, will try to work out who said what; this is particularly likely with small samples or stratified sub-groups.

Finally, there may be situations in postal questionnaire work in which your respondents don't even wish *you* to know who said what. You state on the questionnaire that the respondents don't have to identify themselves, you provide no identification marks on the questionnaires, you put the questionnaires into envelopes and despatch them. It gets a little more complicated if you have to approach the respondent again, e.g. in the case of a before-after design. You could adopt double-blind procedures based on the list of respondents and the code numbers which you have allocated, with the help of an assistant. This can get complicated; something much simpler, which works very well, is to ask respondents to provide their own code number, based on, say, the year, month, and day of birth of a close relative, and to remember to use the same code on the two separate occasions (Selltiz *et al.* 1981).

Of course, no security system is perfect. Even with double-blind procedures, if your intentions were evil you could get together with the other person and decipher the coding arrangements. It is your job to assure your respondents that your intentions are benign.

You have another ethical responsibility and that is to keep your data in a secure place. At the simplest level, they should be kept under lock and key. More sensitive

ILLUSTRATION 11.2

Jonathan Tully is presenting his dissertation to the Board, in the form of an executive summary of his dissertation. He is showing one of three key tables as an overhead projector transparency. It shows answers to a multiple-choice question about a recent marketing strategy decision on which he has polled a wide range of head office staff, broken down into four main departmental groupings: Trade Sales, Retail Sales, Export (Europe), and Export (Gulf). The table shows that the home staff disagree with the export staff on one of the issues. He hands out a single-sheet handout of 30 verbatim quotations from managers in each of these departments to give dramatic impact to the dry table of figures. The table shows that there are just five responses from the Export (Gulf) department, and reading his handout the marketing director guffaws: 'Ah, yes, this must be old Fred, and I don't agree with him but I know just what prompted the comment. He's always had a bee in his bonnet on the subject; wait'll I see him and pull his leg about it!' He does just that, and Fred gets straight on the phone to Jonathan with a very angry complaint.

Jonathan feels aggrieved. How was he to know that the marketing director would make the connection between the figure '5' against Export (Gulf) in the table, and a separate list of verbatim quotations? On reflection, though, he realizes he has made a big mistake. He should have combined the Trade plus Retail figures in the table into a Home Sales category, and the Europe plus Gulf figures into an Export category, the larger number of staff in each of these larger categories being enough to make it impossible to attribute the quotation to Fred, since other people in the combined category are associated with the view in question. He could have trimmed the quotation to make it less obviously in Fred's vernacular. Or, of course, he could have found someone else whose quotation was less readily identifiable. All he can do is to apologize to Fred and hope the issue blows over, for the damage has been done.

data can be kept in a safe: you might ask your tutor if he or she has access to one in the department. If you keep data in computer file, ask your computer technician if he or she has one of the many commercially available security programs, and install it in your micro with your own unique password. If your computer is on the networked university system you should make sure that you keep your data on your own drive rather than a generally accessible drive; if this isn't possible to arrange, save the data to a floppy disk (two so you have a backup!) rather than keeping them on a hard drive.

Under the terms of the Data Protection Act (1998), any respondent has the right to a printout of his or her data entries: see Table 3.3. You should check the implications with the member of staff in your department or teaching institution who has responsibility, and be prepared to supply a printout of the respondent's own data to the respondent if he or she requests it.

Before finishing with this chapter, please address the last activity in the Project Guide, whether you have done any of the other activities, or not.

CASE EXAMPLE 11.1   Identifying patterns in cross-tabulated data

Maria Gowling, whose plans for an undergraduate dissertation you last encountered in Case Example 2.2, has completed her data collection. Her research question investigated the extent to which women in traditionally masculine organizations experienced greater stress than women in traditionally female occupations, as compared with men in those two kinds of occupations. She was fortunate to gain the cooperation of the Fire Service through her uncle, who introduced her to the Fire Service College at Moreton-in-Marsh at a very good time, just as the College was extending its research activities in several ways, through an annual research conference, and via increased support for networking among national organizations interested in fire safety. They agreed to sponsor the despatch of questionnaires to 200 staff in line-operational grades. Her neighbour, a nursing tutor, arranged some initial interviews but was particularly helpful in introducing her to a colleague, Joanna Rawson, who was conducting research into stress among nurses herself, sponsored by a small research grant from the King's Fund. Joanna agreed to include some of Maria's questions which overlapped with her own interests, in a questionnaire she was about to distribute to 350 NHS nursing employees. As a result of this help, Maria's final returns from both organizations were as follows:

female staff in the Fire Service to make her research design viable. She addressed her research question through a design which provided for a series of comparisons between male and female non-managerial grades of staff. The actual material being compared was based on the outcomes of some initial semi-structured interviews with five staff from each organization. Initially, Maria had intended to choose a standard questionnaire as suggested by her reading in such compilations as Stewart *et al.* (1984) and Price (1997). However, her tutor suggested that she might find it very time-consuming to review and choose an effective measure, quoting Cohen *et al.* (1998) as a general source, and particularly Rick *et al.* (2001: 91) to the effect that she would do better to use her interviews to identify reactions to job hazards, or simply symptoms of stress experienced by both types of employee in the two actual organizations concerned, incorporating just these indicators in a short, checklist questionnaire she devised herself, rather than using a standard measure.

One of the questions concerned how well the respondents slept, 'unproblematic sleep' being defined in terms of how easily the respondent could get to sleep both initially and after waking in the night, and absence of unpleasant dreams, during the previous two weeks. Her results for this question were as follows:

	FS	NHS
Despatched	120	350
Returned (male)	70	30
Returned (female)	14	90
Returned Total	84	120

	FS			NHS		
Question 7	problems	no problems	Total	problems	no problems	Total
Male	13	57	70	10	20	30
Female	11	3	14	28	62	90

Maria's early discussions with both these sponsors led her to abandon her attempt to look for differences between managerial and operative grades of staff: there simply weren't enough senior

In the Fire Service, the proportion of females reporting problems is certainly greater than the proportion of males, while in the NHS, the proportion of females reporting problems seems slightly

less than the proportion of males. This looks promising for Maria's research question. She recast her question 7 data in line with the research question as follows: 'women in traditionally masculine occupations have greater difficulty sleeping than women in traditionally female occupations'; and 'men in traditionally female occupations have greater difficulty sleeping than men in traditionally male occupations'. This gave her two tables as follows.

There seems to be some relationship between sex and type of organization, strongly so for females and less so for males. But is this sampling error or is it the same for the population? If you feel comfortable with a statistical analysis, calculate Chi-square for each of these two tables, and check its statistical significance against the benchmark figures shown in the extract from the Chi-square statistical table shown below.

Q7 Staff reporting sleep problems

	Female respondents			Male respondents		
	FS	NHS	Total	FS	NHS	Total
Yes	11	28	39	13	10	23
No	3	62	65	57	20	77
Total	14	90	104	70	30	100

Critical values of Chi-square where the prediction is of a directional relationship between two variables in a 2 × 2 table (one-tailed)

p	0.10	0.05	0.025	0.01	0.005	0.0005
1 df	1.64	2.71	3.84	5.41	6.64	10.83

Answers to Case Example 11.1

Your computations should look as follows.

First taking the Female respondents,

Q7 Female respondents

	Observed			Expected		
	FS	NHS	Total	FS	NHS	Total
Yes	11	28	39	5.25	33.75	39.00
No	3	62	65	8.75	56.25	65.00
Total	14	90	104	14.00	90.00	104.00

$$(11 - 5.25)^2 / 5.25 = 6.30$$
$$(3 - 8.75)^2 / 8.75 = 3.78$$
$$(28 - 33.75)^2 / 33.75 = 0.98$$
$$(62 - 56.25)^2 / 56.25 = 0.59$$

Total	- 11.65

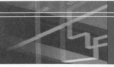

CASE EXAMPLE 11.1   Identifying patterns in cross-tabulated data (cont.)

Looking in the Chi-square table extract shown above, the nearest-and-smaller value to 11.65, our value for Chi-square, is 10.83, which corresponds to a probability of 0.0005 that these results could have been obtained merely by chance. We conclude that

Maria's belief about the females is supported: they do indeed experience this form of stress more in the masculine environment of the Fire Service than in the NHS.

And next, the male respondents.

Q 7 Male respondents						
	Observed			**Expected**		
	FS	**NHS**	**Total**	**FS**	**NHS**	**Total**
Yes	13	10	23	16.1	6.9	23.00
No	57	20	77	53.9	23.1	77.00
Total	70	30	100	70.00	30.00	100.00

$$(13 - 16.1)^2 / 16.1 \quad = \quad 0.60$$
$$(57 - 53.9)^2 / 53.9 \quad = \quad 0.18$$
$$(10 - 6.9)^2 / 6.9 \quad = \quad 1.39$$
$$(20 - 23.1)^2 / 23.1 \quad = \quad 0.42$$
$$\text{Total} \quad = \quad 2.59$$

Looking in the Chi-square table extract shown earlier, the nearest-and-smaller value to 2.59, our value for Chi-square, is 1.64 which corresponds to a probability of 0.10 that these results could have been obtained merely by chance. So the probability of this value of Chi-square being obtained by chance lies between 0.10 and 0.05; this is not sufficient to achieve significance, since the conventional level used by statisticians is 0.05 or five chances in a hundred. We conclude that Maria's belief about the males is not supported: it would be unsafe to conclude that in the population, males experience this form of stress more in the female environment

of the NHS than the male environment of the Fire Service.

It may well be, of course, that the NHS, with its three professional cultures (the managerial, the nursing, and the medical) presents less of a strong female culture than the Fire Service presents a male culture. But, if the analysis of the other results were to show a similar pattern, that view would be argued in the discussion section of the dissertation, where initial beliefs about what is going on are examined and revised in the light of the empirical findings – rather than in the empirical section, where the data are presented.

Project Guide

Project Guide for Chapter 11

The suggested activities here are somewhat similar to those at the end of Chapter 10 (though there are some additions). If you plan to use any of the techniques mentioned in Chapter 11, then you'll need to carry out the following activities again. If you don't intend to use these techniques, then look at activity 1 and then press on to the next chapter. As in Chapter 11, though, the first of the following activities pertains!

1 Check your design and sampling

a In a single column of a page of your research diary, make a list of the issues which you intend to investigate with this particular technique; note any issues which you will not be able to cover and consider which other technique you will use, and in what order.

b Go through activity 4 in the action checklist for Chapter 9, and work though it in detail. You're not planning now, you're committing yourself to action!

c How does the sample you are drawing for this technique compare with any other samples you will be drawing? Are you working with the same people throughout; are they different? If they are different, then give each an identifier ('Sample A'; 'Sample B' etc.) and, in a second column of the page you used for question a above, note which issues will be addressed by which sample.

d Use a third column for any stratifications you intend to make in the sample.

e Commit yourself to some diary dates and plan how long it will take you to complete your data-gathering with this technique. You may find it useful to refer to Table 4.3 at this point.

2 Prepare for data-gathering

a Arrange to have a suitable number of survey documents copied; this should be the sample size plus, say, ten in the case of a questionnaire (double this amount in the case of the before-after study which asks the same questions!).

b Five copies of the interview guide in the case of the structured interview or telephone interview – you're bound to lose or spill coffee on at least one of the copies!

c Make appropriate postal arrangements as required. Who will be paying for the stamps in a postal questionnaire? Ask your tutor or sponsor. Academic institutions which do a lot of survey work might, conceivably, make some pre-franked standard return address labels available to you.

d Set out a record book for the outcomes of each call, and follow-up action required, in the case of a set of telephone interviews.

e Maintain a record of correspondence (times, dates, summary of content) if you plan a long series of e-mail interviews with each respondent. A shorter series needs no separate record provided that both you and each respondent use the auto-reply function when corresponding with each other, which automatically retains the text of previous exchanges. Don't throw any of the previous e-mails away, though!

f Organize help for any of the techniques which need a colleague for the data-gathering or analysis stages, well in advance.

g Discuss what you are about to do with your sponsor and (if you need help with the technical details) your tutor.

h Again, if you don't have a computer of your own, now is the time to book a machine in your university, check that the required software is there, and that the machine will be available to you when you want it.

3 Construct your instrument

Where the technique requires it, construct the list of questions you intend to ask, following the guidelines given above. Familiarize yourself with SNAP or SPHINXSURVEY if you are using software. Alternatively, use a humble set of filecards; decide on the sort of data you expect to elicit for each issue you're covering; decide on the number of questions you will need for each issue; their format (follow Table 11.4) and their sequence and content (follow Table 11.3).

In doing so, you need to bear in mind the way in which you plan to analyze the data you will obtain. The best way of doing this is to write the first draft of the account of your analysis that you will provide in your dissertation document, since this forces you to think the analysis through in detail. (See activity 6(b) below.) So, in a few sentences, what exactly will you have done, what steps will you have followed, when you have analyzed all of the data? Write this down now! Now look at Tables 11.5a, b and c and choose an appropriate format for each question.

Having thought it through at this level of detail, if you find that the analysis you're planning isn't possible, review and amend exercises 1 and 2 above.

4 Double-check the ethical implications

a Glance at each of the steps in activities 2 and 3 above, using Table 3.1 as a template.

b Check particularly that you have not compromised the principles of informed consent and the issues which follow: voluntary participation, protection against any consequences of non-participation; anonymity; confidentiality; and feedback.

c Revise your arrangements if any of these are compromised.

d Sign any formal declarations or proposals which your department may require.

5 Go to it!

a Pilot your technique as outlined in exercise 6 in Chapter 9. Bearing in mind that you may be using a mixture of techniques drawn from Chapters 10 and 12 as well as the present one (which may make a difference to how and when you utilize the present technique).

b Do it!

c Analyze the data as you have planned, following the guidelines in this chapter and any related authors recommended above.

6 Continue your write-up

a By the time you are ready to collect data, you should have completed the write-up of your introductory chapter, and the literature review.

b Prepare a first draft of the methodological section of your dissertation. Now that you're about to collect data, you should be able to provide a coherent rationale for the method you are using and to state the techniques you plan to adopt. Flesh out the few sentences you wrote for activity 4(b) above. Revisit the research proposal which you prepared in activity 5 in Chapter 9 and expand the information you gave there into a connected account, which describes what you are about to do and gives reasons for it, in the light of your research question.

References

Anderson, S. E. and Gansneder, B. M. (1995) 'Using electronic mail surveys and computer monitored data for studying computer mediated communication systems', *Social Science Computer Review*, 13: 1: 33–46.

Blaikie, N. (2003) *Analyzing Quantitative Data*, London: Sage.

Blau, P. M. (1964) *Exchange and Power in Social Life*, New York: John Wiley & Sons.

Bryman, A. and Bell, E. (2003) *Business Research Methods*, Oxford: Oxford University Press.

Cohen, S., Kessler, R. C., and Gordon, L. U. (eds.), (1998) *Measuring Stress: a Guide for Health and Social Scientists*, New York: Oxford University Press.

Collis, J. and Hussey, R. (2003) *Business Research: a Practical Guide for Undergraduate and Postgraduate Students*, London: Palgrave Macmillan.

Coomber, R. (1997) *Using the Internet for survey research*, Sociological Research Online. WWW http://www.socresonline.org.uk/socresonline/2/2/2.html, accessed 15 April 2004.

Diamontopoulos, A. and Schlegelmilch, B. B. (1997) *Taking the Fear out of Data Analysis*, London: The Dryden Press.

Dillman, D. A. (1978) *Mail and Telephone Surveys: The Total Design Method*, Chichester: Wiley.

Dillman, D. A. (2000) *Mail and Internet Surveys: the Tailored Design Method*, London: Wiley.

Frey, J. H. (1983) *Survey Research by Telephone*, London: Sage Publications.

Gillham, R. (2000) *Developing a Questionnaire*, London: Continuum.

Green, S. B. and Salkind, N. J. (2002) *Using SPSS for the Macintosh and Windows: Analyzing and Understanding Data*, London: Prentice-Hall.

Gregory, I. (2003) *Ethics in Research*, London: Continuum.

Howard, K. and Sharp, J. A. (1983) *The Management of a Student Research Project*, Aldershot: Gower.

Kornhauser, A. and Sheatsley, P. B. (1976) 'Questionnaire construction and interview procedure', in Selltiz, Co., Wrightsman, L. S. and Cook, S. W., (eds.) *Research Methods in Social Relations*, New York: Rinehart and Winston, 3rd edn.

Mehta, R. and Sivadas, E. (1995) 'Comparing response rates and response content in mail versus electronic mail surveys', *Journal of the Market Research Society*, 37: 4: 429–439.

Murdoch, J. and Barnes, J. A. (1998) *Statistical Tables: for Science, Engineering, Business, Management and Finance*, London: Palgrave Macmillan.

Price, J. L. (1997) 'Handbook of organizational measurement', *International Journal of Manpower*, 18, 4:5:6 whole part.

Rick, J., Bryner, R., Daniels, K., Perryman, S. and Guppy, A. (2001) *A Critical Review of Psychosocial Hazard Measures*, Brighton, Institute for Employment Studies, University of Brighton; also WWW, http://www.hse.gov.uk/research/crr_pdf/2001/crr01356.pdf, accessed 15 April 2004.

Saunders, M., Lewis, P. *et al.* (2003) *Research Methods for Business Students*, London: Prentice Hall.

Selltiz, C. S., Wrightsman, L. S. and Cook, S. W. (1981) *Research Methods in Social Relations*, London: Holt, Rinehart & Winston.

Selwyn, N. and Robson, K. (1998) *Using e-mail as a research tool*, Guildford, Surrey, University of Surrey; also http://www.soc.surrey.ac.uk/sru/SRU21.html accessed 12 January 2004.

Siegel, S. and Castellan, N. J. (1988) *Nonparametric Statistics for the Behavioural Sciences*, Maidenhead: McGraw-Hill.

Stewart, B., Hetherington, G. *et al.* (eds) (1984) *British Telecom Survey Item Bank*, Bradford: MCB University Press.

Thibaut, J. W. and Kelley, H. H. (1959) *The Social Psychology of Groups*, New York: John Wiley & Sons.

12 Further techniques

- To present the procedural details of two additional data-gathering techniques: the repertory grid, and the structured rating scale
- To outline two approaches to the observation of people as employees, focusing on structured observation and presenting the found experiment as a form of highly structured observation
- To help you to progress your project; and particularly, the empirical stages of your own project work, by considering and working through the practical implications in the event that you decide to use any of the techniques presented in this chapter

At a glance

The first technique presented, the repertory grid, is valuable for open-ended, exploratory work prior to the use of more structured techniques, but can also form the basis of an entire study conducted along interpretivist principles. It is a curious hybrid, being highly structured but with contents completely determined by the respondent. The second technique, attitude scaling, may be used in its rough and ready form as part of a structured questionnaire or interview guide, and can, if properly developed, form the entire empirical core of a project, especially at undergraduate level. The remaining material represents an approach to the observation of people at work, and is given in two contrasted variants, structured observation and the field experiment. I include the former because I believe the skills to be highly relevant to project work, and the latter because, if one is to use experimental method at all (see Chapters 5 and 9), the relevant techniques should be well understood.

All of these techniques are sufficiently different from those presented in Chapters 10 and 11, and from each other, that my standard scheme of headings (Design, Elicitation, Analysis, Write-up) isn't very helpful in outlining them. What follows is a more connected account, but the relevant matters arising under each of these headings are dealt with.

12.1   The repertory grid

Most of the techniques I have outlined in Chapters 10 and 11 require you to make assumptions about the way in which your respondents are likely to view the issues under investigation. For example, all of the fully structured techniques require you to specify the alternative answers from which respondents must choose. What happens if the respondents don't find these alternatives helpful, though? What if they view the issue in a completely different way? With a semi-structured technique, you can back off to a degree and change the basis of your dialogue to one which matches the respondent's assumptions while you're talking together, but, with a structured technique, the best you can do is to provide 'Other, please specify' alternatives at appropriate points.

The repertory grid allows you to address the respondent's assumptions and personal understanding of the issues *directly*, without the slightest need to anticipate the alternatives which he or she has in mind. It is particularly useful whenever you want to identify the individual's perspective and view things from his or her own point of view, whether as part of a pilot study in order to determine what your subsequent questions and alternatives should be, or as a detailed form of key informant interview. It's less a case of 'Other, please specify', and more a case of 'No other: *you* specify'.

The technique involves three phases of activity: conducting a form of structured interview with the respondent; analyzing the individual results; and aggregating the results of several interviews into an overall set of findings.

The grid interview

The purpose of a grid interview is to elicit your respondent's constructs. A **construct** is a way in which the respondent thinks about the issue you are investigating; a particular way he or she has got of giving meaning to, i.e. construing, the issue in question. In sum, it's an active perception of how things are from the respondent's point of view. Now, the ways in which meaning is expressed vary enormously depending on the subject-matter, from single adjectives and noun phrases like these,

Pleasant	–	Unpleasant
Solvent	–	Insolvent
Strategic	–	Operational
Niche product	–	Commodity product

to more complex sentence structures like these:

Likely to slow the growth of the company	–	Likely to foster expansion
Insufficient managerial experience	–	Substantial managerial experience

But what all constructs have in common is that they're always expressed as a *contrast*, like the examples listed above. You can't understand what a person means by 'Good' without knowing what he or she has in mind as a contrast: to say 'Good' as opposed to 'Poor' is to express a very different meaning to 'Good' as opposed to 'Evil'. Go on: try it out explicitly, by saying to yourself (as in 'this is a good piece of work'), 'Good–Poor'; and then, 'Good–Evil'. Don't you feel the weight of the connotations and implications of the latter 'Good' as they unfold into your awareness?

The grid interview consists of four components:

- The *topic*, in which you agree the subject-matter under discussion.
- The elicitation of *elements*, in which you arrive at examples or components of the topic for further discussion.
- The elicitation of the *constructs* themselves.
- The *rating* of elements on constructs, to identify the particular meanings being expressed.

The interview itself is conducted in ten steps, which are listed in Table 12.1. Each step must be followed faithfully, and it's in that sense that the interview is highly structured; however, the content of what you discover is completely in the hands of your respondent, and in that sense, the grid interview is entirely open-ended. Figure 12.1 shows an example of the results of this procedure: it's a completed grid sheet which records the results of an interview with a lecturer, in which his constructs about the teaching methods he uses are recorded. The constructs are laid out on either side of the ratings and the meaning being expressed can be identified by a simple convention as follows. The left-hand end of each construct specifies the '1' end of a 5-point scale, and the right-hand end of each construct specifies the '5' end of a 5-point scale.

If you follow this convention, you can read back what this respondent thinks of the various teaching techniques. Look at the first column of ratings, for example, in which the meaning of element 1, the Lecture, is expressed; '5' on the first construct, so it's seen as a technique that the lecturer can prepare by himself; '3' on the second construct, so it needs some preparation on the part of the students but is not dependent on such preparation to succeed; '1' on the third construct, so he sees a danger of being remote from the students when lecturing; and so on. He sees it as potentially boring for the students, doesn't particularly enjoy lecturing, feels that the lecture tends to teach specifics, views it as a relatively inexpensive technique in terms of staffing costs and preparation time, requiring little equipment; emotions, he feels, play little part in the learning experience; and its effects are less enduring than some of the other techniques. You can pack a lot of information into a repertory grid!

The best way to learn the technique is to conduct a grid interview with yourself, following the steps outlined in Table 12.1. Choose some topic which sounds interesting, which you would like to think through construct by construct. May I suggest 'My friends and colleagues' as a topic, and a list of five different friends/colleagues

TABLE 12.1   Eliciting a repertory grid

The basic procedure is in 10 steps

1 Agree a topic with your respondent and write it onto the sheet.
2 Agree a set of elements, and write these along the diagonals at the top of the grid sheet.
3 Explain that you wish to find out how he or she thinks about the elements, and that you'll do this by asking him or her to compare them systematically.
4 Taking three elements (nos. 1, 3 and 5), ask your respondent 'Which two of these are *the same* in some way, and *different* from the third?' Provide assurance that you're not looking for a 'correct' answer, just how he or she sees the elements.
5 Ask your respondent why: 'What do the two have in common, as opposed to the third?' Write down the thing the two have in common, in the first row on the left side of the grid sheet; and the opposite of this (the reason the third element is different) in the same row on the right of the grid sheet, making sure that you've obtained a truly bipolar expression – a pair of words or phrases which express a contrast. This is the person's construct.
6 Check that you understand what contrast is being expressed; use the interviewee's words as much as possible, but do feel free to discuss what he or she means, and to negotiate a form of words that makes sense to you both.
7 Present the construct as a rating scale, with the phrase on the left standing for the '1' end of the scale, and the phrase on the right standing for the '5' end of the scale. A form of words like this: 'Now, the words I've written down on the left: imagine they define the "1" end of a 5-point scale. And that the words I've written down on the right define the "5" end of a 5-point scale.'
8 Ask your respondent to rate each of the three elements on this scale, writing the ratings into the grid as he or she states them. 'I'd like you to rate each of the three elements on this scale; give each of them one of the numbers, 1, 2, 3, 4 or 5, to say which end of the scale they're nearest to' or words to that effect. Occasionally, check that the directionality of the scaling is preserved, i.e. that your respondent shouldn't be using a '1' when he or she is offering a '5' and vice versa.
9 Now ask the respondent to rate each of the remaining elements on this construct. Having only rated three elements so far; now you complete rating the rest.
10 Your task is to elicit as many different constructs as the person might hold about the topic. So, repeat steps 4 to 8, asking for a fresh construct each time, until your respondent can't offer any new ones; use a different triad of three elements each time: nos. 2, 4 and 6; then 1, 2 and 10, and so on. Aim to obtain 8 to 12 constructs in all.

A few additional pointers: once you're familiar with the above procedure

■ You don't always have to actively offer three elements; you might ask your respondent to look at all the elements together, and for him or her to choose any three which express a particularly strong contrast that hasn't yet been offered as a construct.

■ If you get the feeling that a construct is too vague (e.g. 'good leader–bad leader' where the elements are people) you can always ask 'In what way?' and press for a more behaviourally specific definition of each end of the construct, writing these into the grid sheet.

■ Alternatively, if you're trying to discover constructs which are more basic/fundamental to your respondent, don't record the construct offered, but ask him/her, 'which end of the construct do you prefer – and why?' Express the reason given as one end of a new construct, which you then record in the grid sheet together with its opposite.

FIGURE 12.1 An example of a complete repertory grid

Topic: Teaching Methods
Elements: 9 different teaching methods/ learning situations
Constructs: 10 constructs elicited from the lecturer
Ratings: or a 5-point scale

Construct		1	2	3	4	5	6	7	8	9		Construct
Other people in preparation	1	5	4	4	2	5	3	2	1	1	1	I can prepare this by myself
Succeeds even if students haven't prepared	2	3	5	4	2	3	1	3	4	2	2	Requires some preparation on the part of the students
Instructor can be remote from students	3	1	5	3	3	4	2	3	2	5	3	Greater involvement with students
May bore the students	4	1	3	2	4	4	4	3	5	4	4	Usually interests the students
Less enjoyable for me	5	2	1	5	4	3	3	3	5	4	5	More enjoyable for me
Learning comes from specifics	6	2	3	3	3	4	1	4	5	5	6	Many possible sources of learning
Expensive in terms of staffing and preparation	7	4	4	3	4	2	4	3	1	5	7	Economical in terms of staffing and preparation
Requires equipment	8	4	5	3	2	1	3	5	4	5	8	No equipment: talking and doing
Emotions play a small part in learning	9	1	3	2	5	3	3	3	4	5	9	Emotions must be engaged for learning to occur
Effects more enduring	10	4	5	3	3	3	2	1	1	1	10	Effects less enduring

Elements

9	Experience in general
8	Overseas Exchange
7	Company Visit
6	Structured Exercise
5	Residential
4	Role-play
3	Seminar
2	Tutorial
1	Lecture

Constructs

at work as the elements? Just to make things interesting, add two further elements: 'Myself as I am now', and 'Myself as I'd like to be' as elements number 6 and 7. Use a photocopy of Figure 12.2 on which to work. Write the elements into the diagonal lines at the top of the figure, and use the spaces at the left and the right to write in the ends of each construct. As soon as you've elicited each construct, rate all the elements on the construct using a 5-point scale, following the convention that the left end of the construct defines the '1' end of the scale, and the right end of the construct defines the '5' end of the scale. Put the rating of each element into the appropriate box in the row of boxes devoted to the construct with which you're working.

As you go through this grid, you may learn a few new things about your views of your friends: things which hadn't occurred to you before, since you had never thought quite as explicitly, or as hard, about this group of people before. A grid is a very good way of getting to the root of an issue, by expressing perceptions explicitly. And, of course, of identifying an individual's personal constructs; for if someone else were to repeat this exercise, both the constructs, and the elements, would be different. Each respondent proposes his or her own rating scales, automatically ensuring their personal relevance and meaningfulness, as well as providing their own ratings. Perhaps you can see the potential value of the technique as part of a key informant interview?

In practising with your own grid as I suggest, you may, likewise, learn something new about *yourself*. This could arise from the content of the constructs you have about your friends and colleagues, or from the way, now that you come to think of it systematically, that you rate particular individuals on particular constructs; and particularly, the element 'Myself as I am now' as compared with 'Myself as I would like to be'! Or it might come from a consideration of the kinds of constructs you discover you're using. Are they all evaluative, or are some purely descriptive? (Incidentally, while the left- and right-hand ends of a construct have to be opposite in meaning, they don't have to express a positive–versus–negative evaluation. The construct 'technically skilled–socially skilled' is quite neutral and descriptive, unless of course the topic is one which demands technical skills and not social skills, or vice versa.) Do feelings predominate? Do the constructs concern activities and action?

Working through the grid, you may also wonder about some of the finer points of the procedure, and these are summarized in Table 12.2. If these don't cover all of your queries, then look in Chapters 3 and 4 of Jankowicz (2003), a procedural guide aimed at beginners.

Finally, you might become curious about the possible applications of repertory grid technique. Grids have been used predominantly in the personnel and training field (job analysis, performance appraisal, training needs analysis, training course development, employee mentoring and counselling, team building), but there are also some applications in the study of financial decision making; in assisting in the development of business policies and strategies by management teams; in the field of market research (during the 'qualitative stage'); and in quality control (to identify the factors involved in subjective judgements about product quality).

FIGURE 12.2 Grid sheet for recording elements, constructs and ratings

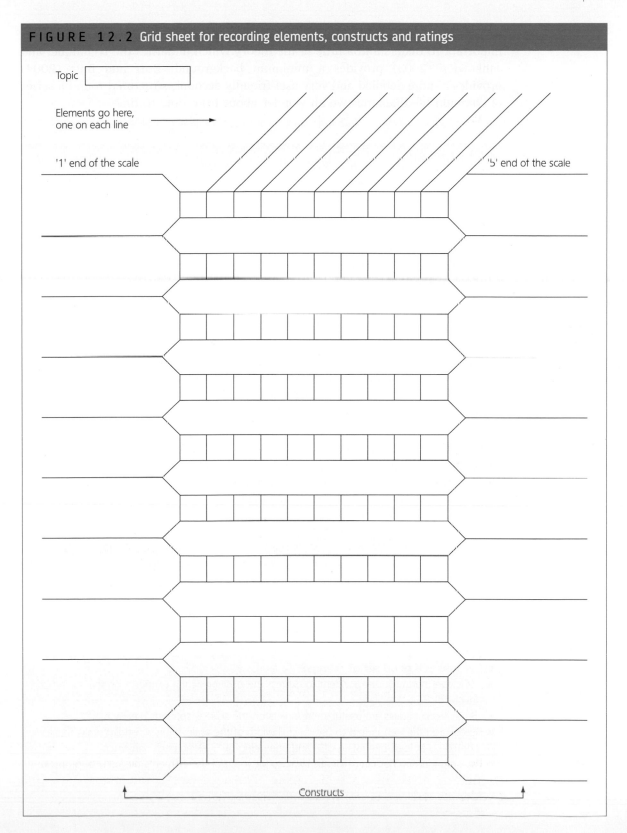

Topic [   ]

Elements go here,
one on each line →

'1' end of the scale

'5' end of the scale

Constructs

A review of most of these applications is provided in Jankowicz (1990). It's important to understand a little of the theory which underlies the technique, and Jankowicz (2003) provides a minimum background; Burr and Butt (2004) provides a more detailed and very user-friendly account, structured round a series of common life dilemmas we all wonder about from time to time.

TABLE 12.2   Issues and procedures in repertory grid interviewing

What makes a good element?

- A feeling of ownership on the part of the respondent; so, usually you ask the respondent to nominate the elements. But not exclusively; you might want to supply an element that's relevant to the topic, as I did when suggesting you add the 'myself' elements to your own list of friends and colleagues (see text).
- Anything can be an element: people, places, institutions, job responsibilities, different business strategies – the list is endless, *provided* it's not a construct. Avoid words with easy opposites, and words that are qualities rather than actions or things.
- Nouns make good elements; the less abstract, the easier they'll be to handle.
- Verbs and clauses are useful, but more tricky. Use the '-ing' form, i.e. Not 'To make a decision' but 'Deciding'; not 'The delegation of responsibility' but 'Delegating'.
- A usable set of elements (i.e. one that your respondent will find easy to work with during the grid interview) covers the topic evenly and is 'all of a kind'. Try not to mix abstract nouns with concrete nouns and complicated verbal forms. (How would you construe 'the Olympic Ideal', 'bicycles', and 'Saturday afternoons spent in acting as a sports coach'? It's possible, but messy.)

What makes a good construct?

- Whatever expresses your respondent's meaning fully and precisely.
- A pair of words or phrases which are opposites, and as specific as possible. Don't accept as an opposite, the same words with the word 'not' stuck in front of them. 'Good–Not good' doesn't convey much meaning, whereas 'Good standard–Poor standard' tells you it's not a case of 'Good' as opposed to 'Evil'.
- Encourage your respondent to be as specific as the topic demands. Avoid 'motherhoods' by asking 'in what way exactly?' Thus 'Performance adequate–Performance inadequate' conveys much less meaning than '>10% return on capital employed – <10% return on capital employed' if the topic deals with financial performance, and less meaning than 'Experienced enough to carry out the more difficult tasks – Requires constant monitoring and checking' if the topic involves an employee performance appraisal.

What makes a good set of ratings?

- Whatever helps your respondent to express the position of the elements on the construct involved.
- 5- or 7-point scales are useful; more points on the scale is spurious precision.
- Encourage the respondent to use the full width of the scale: if it is a 5-point scale, there should be at least one rating of '1'and one rating of '5' along each construct.
- Use ratings, and not ranks; identical values for some of the elements are quite appropriate.

Analysis of a single repertory grid

Having completed a grid yourself, you will appreciate how straightforwardly you can read the data back from another person's grid.

■ Read the elements.

■ Read the constructs.

■ Look at the extreme ratings: where are the '1's and where are the '5's; what does this tell you about the position of elements on constructs, and the meanings being expressed?

Whether this is informative depends on what you would have expected the respondent to say before you looked at their grid! However, more detailed analyses are possible, all of which involve answering questions about the relationships expressed in the grid.

■ What are the relationships between the elements? To find out which elements are construed similarly, and which ones differently, take the elements in pairs, find the absolute difference between the ratings on each construct, and sum these differences down the grid across all the constructs. When you have done this for all the element pairs, the lowest sum will indicate the most similarly construed elements, and the highest, the most differently construed. Whether this is informative depends on the topic of the grid and the particular elements involved. For example, in your own grid, if the most different elements were 'Myself as I am' and 'Myself as I'd like to be' that would surely be thought-provoking!

■ What are the relationships between the constructs? To find out which constructs are rated most similarly, use the same procedure of summing differences between pairs of ratings, but this time, work across the grid taking two constructs at a time. Bearing in mind that a construct is bipolar scale (one with two ends!) you need to do this twice over, once for each pair of constructs, and once for one member of each pair reversed (i.e., with the ratings changed from 1 to 5, 2 to 4, 5 to 1 and 4 to 2, and with the two ends of one of the constructs changed over from right to left). There is more on this in Jankowicz (2003: 108–110).

This sort of difference analysis is most informative when you have prior grounds for supposing that some differences will be high and some low, or when you are investigating a particular hunch about the way in which your respondent thinks. You might care to go back to your own grid and look at the difference between each of your elements and the 'Self as I am' element. Which of your friends and colleagues do you construe as most similar to yourself? Who is matched most closely to 'Myself as I'd like to be', that is, who comes closest to your ideal?

It is possible to carry out more powerful and complete analyses of single grids using cluster analysis and principal component analysis, both of which focus on differences between ratings as we have done above, but these techniques are beyond the scope of this book. You will find more about this in Jankowicz (2003: 118–139), and the associated website, http://www.wiley.co.uk/easyguide. Another useful site is at http://tiger.cpsc.ucalgary.ca:1500/, where you will find a suite of platform-independent software which you can use to elicit and analyze repertory grids.

Aggregating the results of several grid interviews

Calculating difference scores for selected comparisons on more than a few grids can be very time-consuming. Very often, what you are looking for in a group of grids is an organized listing of all the different constructs which the sample of respondents holds about some common topic. Assuming that you have used the same set of elements with all your respondents, it's a straightforward task to carry out a content analysis of all the constructs. Glance again at Section 10.2 on content analysis, and Table 10.5 for the general procedures involved; your unit of analysis would be each individual construct, and you would pool all the constructs of the whole group of respondents before proceeding with the content analysis.

The power of a repertory grid content analysis comes from a differential analysis; that is, from asking whether different kinds of respondent provided systematically different types of construct once you have categorized the whole set.

ILLUSTRATION 12.1

Dominique Soustel has just completed 20 repertory grid interviews with the fellow-students on her undergraduate degree in human resource management. Ever since reading Karen Legge's classic book on the professionalization of the HR function (Legge 1978) she has been interested in the process by which people adopt a 'person-orientated' way of thinking about management issues, and has adopted a design in which she hopes to find contrasts between the constructs of ten first-year undergraduate, and ten final year undergraduate, students on a range of common HR activities taken as elements.

She obtains a total of 232 constructs from all 20 interviewees, and carries out a content analysis which categorizes the whole pool of constructs into 12 different categories. She counts the number of constructs allocated to each category, and then looks to see what proportion in each category were contributed by the first year HR students and by the final year students. There are few differences with such categories as 'Concerned with resourcing' and 'Concerned with change management', but she is interested to notice that 42 of the constructs she categorized as 'Concerned with strategy and mission' come from the final year students and only eight from the first year students. She also notices a smaller difference in the very interesting category of 'Interfacing with line managers'. Taken together, she feels that this finding can be used to support her argument about the way in which a concern with corporate and strategic issues is viewed as a capstone to a professional HRM degree programme, coming to fruition at the end, as opposed to being a fundamental underpinning to the whole of the programme, present throughout.

A more grid-specific form of content analysis has been described by Honey (1979). It makes use of the ratings in each of the grids to identify to what extent each construct matches a set of ratings that express, for each respondent, their overall judgement of the topic of the grid. So, for example, a grid can be used in the design of a performance appraisal questionnaire by supplying each respondent with the construct 'Overall, more effective in the job – Overall, less effective in the job' and looking at the relationships between the specific, elicited constructs and this overall construct, by comparing the ratings of each. This kind of approach (described in detail in Jankowicz 2003: 169–176) is particularly suited to the development of appraisal and evaluation systems, where existing rating scales are frequently insufficiently specific to be useful.

Bearing in mind the discussion in Chapter 6, in which the importance of issues rather than variables in project work was emphasized, you will find that the grid interview is a very powerful way of exploring the ways in which managers and professionals think about the issues themselves. Bearing in mind my warnings about the need to avoid contaminating your findings with your own pre-judgements, it is apparent that the grid interview is powerful precisely because it speaks in the language (the constructs), of the respondents themselves. Finally, given the importance of negotiating a place for your own research interests and questions in investigating your respondents' concerns, the use which grid technique makes of negotiation as a form of interaction (in agreeing elements, and in its use of occasional supplied constructs added to the pool of the respondent's own, elicited constructs), seems particularly well suited to business and management project work.

This would be a good point at which to read Case Example 12.1.

If you intend to use the grid techniques as described here, please work through activities 1 to 5, to the extent that they apply, in the Project Guide.

12.2 Attitude scaling

Empirical work for business and management projects often involves the measurement of your respondents' attitudes. (Strictly speaking, 'attitude scaling' involves techniques which can be used to assess strength of feeling, well-being, and personal value preferences, in addition to those states of mind that underlie people's expressed opinions and which we call 'attitudes'.) The measurement always involves the assessment of the strength and direction of response – whether people are strongly in favour, weakly against, slightly unhappy, very upset, and so on.

There are three ways of doing this: by structuring your items into rough-and-ready five- or seven-point rating scales; by using a scale which has been thoroughly pre-researched and published for your convenience; or by developing your own precise scale.

Rough-and-ready rating scale items in structured questionnaires and interviews

You will no doubt be very familiar with this kind of item. In the case of a 5-point scale, the respondent is requested to express the strength of his or her agreement or disagreement with an item, by placing a mark on some point on a scale which runs from 'Strongly agree' to 'Strongly disagree', the scale being represented by a line with four divisions, or by a set of five boxes. Analysis would be by tallying the responses to each item across the whole group or subgroup of respondents, to see how many people answered 'Strongly agree', how many answered 'Agree', and so on. The average score for each item could be calculated for the group as a whole, and for subgroups. This approach is useful and straightforward if you want a rough-and-ready indication of the strength of feelings among the group.

Very often, it's particularly helpful to ascertain people's *reasons* for providing the ratings they did, particularly if they chose the negative end of the scale and you can combine the item with an immediate follow-up item to the effect 'If your response was "Disagree" or "Strongly disagree", please indicate your main reason in the space below', carrying out a content analysis of the reasons given when you present the results. Figure 12.3a provides an example of an item of this kind, taken from a larger set used to measure job satisfaction among police sergeants (Jankowicz and Walsh 1984).

If you require greater precision, however, you may feel a little uncomfortable about this form of scaling. Your respondents' internal scales of judgements may vary substantially, so that someone who is fairly cautious would answer 'Agree' to an item which a less cautious person would answer 'Strongly agree' to, when, for all you know, both hold the same strength of attitude. This sort of thing can be troublesome (especially in situations which evoke caution, e.g. those in which managers appraise their subordinates). What was a 5-point scale turns into a 3- or even 2-point scale because most of your respondents avoid extreme ratings even when one might suspect they are merited.

One very good way round the problem is to express the wording of the item in such a way that you can label each of the scale positions with an **operational description**: a description of an observable event, or a statement of what would have to happen for the respondent to be able to tick one point on the scale rather than another in making a response. Figure 12.3(c) shows an example.

Crude scales of this kind have their limitations, though. The relative strength and direction of the attitudes or feelings need to be established, even after operational descriptions for the various scale positions have been established. By and large, what sort of attitude is held on average; and to what extent do attitudes as extreme as those exemplified exist in the population? How well does the scale perform in practice; how reliable and valid might it be? If you construct simple scales 'on-the-spot' for inclusion in your questionnaire you may not know the answers to these questions. Often, it doesn't matter since you are looking for a general impression of people's views and don't seek very great precision. But there are times when you need a precise scale which has been previously developed to known standards, in which the relevance of the content has been established by prior research, and the measurement characteristics of the scale established.

FIGURE 12.3 Samples of rating scale items (a) The item as in the questionnaire; (b) The item as analyzed; (c) An example of an item with operationalized scale-point descriptions

[A]

Q. 16. How satisfied are you with the sense of teamwork which exists between yourself and other sergeants?

Please indicate your answer by ticking ONE of these boxes

very satisfied   satisfied   neither   dissatisfied   very dissatisfied

☐ ☐ ☐ ☐ ☐

If your answer was 'Dissatisfied' or 'Very dissatisfied', please use the space below to tell us why, in your own words

[B]

Q. 16. How satisfied are you with the sense of teamwork which exists between yourself and other sergeants?

	very satisfied	satisfied	neither	dissatisfied	very dissatisfied	Total	
	70	140	8	22	2	242	n
	28.9	57.9	3.3	9.1	0.4	99.6	%

Mean=4.04

Content analysis of the cause of dissatisfaction

	No of replies
1. There is no opportunity for teamwork; colleagues meet only rarely at work due to shift arrangements etc.	11
2. There is no teamwork, but an attitude of 'I'm alright'. There is no concern for other areas and no cooperation or interest	8
3. Colleagues are interested in teamwork when it will benefit themselves	4
4. No answer	1
TOTAL	24

[C]

How satisfied are you with the services of our technical help-line?
Please rate the quality of our service by putting an 'X' in the box which best espresses your views.

☐ ☐ ☐ ☐ ☐

enquiries always answered fully and promptly	enquiries answered fully though with occasional delay	most information provided within a reasonable time	either the timing or the completeness is usually inadequate	rarely if ever get sufficient information in time

The use of pre-researched attitude scales

Such scales exist and have been published. One source is a two-volume collection put together by a team of researchers and practitioners associated with British Telecom, which you will find referenced either under MCB (1984) or Stewart *et al.* (1984), and it's under the latter entry that it appears in my bibliography. The blue Volume 1 provides a variety of personal satisfaction measures, and is more likely to contain scales assessing personal attitudes; but you should check the yellow Volume 2, to see if there is anything suitable among its collection of organizational measures. A second source which contains accounts of pre-researched attitude scales is an excellent review compilation in the *International Journal of Manpower*, by Price (1997).

It is worth including one or more of these scales in a longer questionnaire or interview schedule, at any level of project, from undergraduate to Masters. You could also use a suitable scale from either of these collections as an adjunct to any semi-structured technique which you are using. In looking at possible scales in either of these two publications, make a note of how the scale which interests you has been designed, how the content has been shown to be relevant to the attitudes being measured, on what size and nature of sample it has been constructed, and any information on its validity and reliability which may be mentioned in the review. Finally, take note of any particular copyright restrictions that might pertain. You will find that the vast majority of authors will give you permission to use their scale for your research without any payment, but you do need to write to ask them first. Author details are provided either in the review, or in the original articles to which the review will refer you.

There may be occasions, however, when there is no suitable pre-published scale, but you still need something more precise than the simple 5-point scale described above.

ILLUSTRATION 12.2

Maria Gowling's undergraduate dissertation is a case in point. Her tutor put her on to an article (Rick *et al.* 2001), which suggests that the use of standard scales for carrying out a stress audit based on listings of psychosocial hazards may not be as robust as a set of locally-researched and designed scales focusing on situations encountered in specific organizational settings. Maria found herself identifying the kinds of stress symptoms experienced by employees in two rather specific environments, the Fire Service and the NHS. As part of her interest in the impact of traditionally male and female settings on employee well-being, she identified several kinds of symptom which reliably characterized male and female employees in one or other setting – you will recall that Case Example 11.1 provides one instance, giving details of sleep problems as an indicator of stress.

This is the kind of research from which situation-specific scales can be developed. It does, however, require a substantial amount of prior work about the content of the attitude in question before a usable scale can be devised.

The development of a precise attitude scale

It is possible to compromise between the rough-and-ready 5-point scale and the fully researched attitude measure, by adopting one of two standard approaches to attitude scale development: *Likert's Summated Ratings Scale*, and the *Thurstone Scale of Equal-Appearing Intervals*. Both techniques specify the content of the subject-matter informally, without the prior research of the kind Maria Gowling conducted in our example above; but devote considerable attention to the development of the psychometric, or measurement, characteristics of the scale.

Both techniques start with the premise that attitudes are complex states of mind. The assumption is that people who hold an overall attitude on an issue may respond one way to one aspect, but very differently to some other aspect of the issue. If one were to assess them on just one scaled item the result would not be very reliable; and so, they proceed by identifying several different items covering a variety of aspects of the issue in question and derive some kind of combined score.

Admittedly, for most business and management projects, this level of precision would be too time-consuming and would be too narrow in scope to be worth troubling over. However, there are some topics, especially at undergraduate and professional level, in which you could do very useful work by making the development of such a precise scale the main thrust of your project. Attitudes to a new policy, working practice, or outside organization spring to mind, especially if the issue is likely to be a recurring one and your organization would like to have a scale for use on repeated occasions.

Figure 12.4 shows the steps involved in each technique. Both of them consist of two stages: a design stage, in which you use a group of people in order to develop the scale; and a usage stage, in which you measure the attitude of a *different* group of people, your actual research sample.

Likert's summated rating scale

Likert's approach is based on the rationale that you can't assess an attitude from a response to just one item. You need several, and you need to put the responses together somehow; if the responses are numeric, then this is usually by addition. Now, if you intend to assess the strength and direction of the attitude by summing the ratings of a number of items, you must first ensure that the items which you're adding together do indeed measure the *same* attitude. The problem is that you have no independent measure of the attitude concerned which would allow you to check this, and so you adopt a 'bootstrapping' approach. That is, you take the total score over all the items as an indicator of 'whatever the scale as a whole measures', and each item is evaluated against this. (Obviously, after you have eliminated the unsuitable items, the total score will be different, and so will 'whatever the scale as a whole measures'; it is likely to be more unified and precise, since the items that you are left with will relate more closely to it.) Basically, the procedure outlined in Figure 12.4(a) develops the coherence of the whole scale, and leaves it up to you, in devising the content of the items in the first place, to ensure that the appropriate attitude is being tapped. To use this particular variant of Likert scaling, you need

FIGURE 12.4 Procedural guide: (a) the Likert summated rating scale (b) the Thurstone equal-appearing interval scale

(a) The Likert Scale

1. Write 50–60 items you believe measure the attitude in question. Cover different aspects.
2. Ask a test panel of 100 respondents to respond to all the items.

'The policy of this government seems to be to give in to as many pressure groups as possible'

strongly agree	agree	neither	disagree	strongly disagree
☐	☐	☐	☐	☐
1	2	3	4	5

3. Cast responses into a table showing each respondent's response to each item.
4. Sum across the table to derive a total score for each respondent.
5. For each item, correlate the scores it received (its column) with the total score column.

respondent no.	item no. 1	2	3	4	... 50	total score
1	3	5	4	1	4	150
2	1	2	2	2	3	50
3	4	3	4	3	3	200
4	5	3	3	4	4	250
.	.	.	.	.	.	.
.	.	.	.	.	.	.
100	2	3	3	1	5	100

6. Items with low correlations don't measure 'what the scale as a whole measures' so they're not tapping the attitude very well: reject them.
7. The remaining items (aim for 20 or so) form the final scale, on which a person's attitude would be measured by summing the scores of the items s/he ticked.

Column 1 correlates highly ($r = 1.0$) with the total score column, so retain the item for the final scale. Column 2 correlates poorly ($r = 0.3$) with the total score column, so reject the item from consideration. And so on, for all items

(b) The Thurstone Scale

1. Write 100 or so items that you believe measure the attitude in question. Cover the whole range.
2. Ask 50 people NOT to agree/disagree, but to judge how favourable/unfavourable each item is, by putting it into one of 11 groups from 1 = very favourable to 11 = very unfavourable.

Example 1 : Item 1 is distributed as below:

very favourable → very unfavourable

group 1	group 2	group 3	group 4	...	group 11
5 judges	15 judges	5 judges	25 judges		
put it here	put it here	put it here	put it here		

No consensus: reject the item

3. An item distributed by the judges as in the first example is unsuitable (since people can't agree on where it lies) and would be rejected. An item distributed as in the second example is, by the same token, usable.

4. You would aim for a final set of 22 items on which judges agree, all spread across the width of the scale.
5. Place these in random order and give to the respondents (the people whose attitudes you wish to measure). Ask them to choose just those with which they agree.
6. The mean of the scale position of those items indicates the attitude, its direction and strength.

Example 2 : Item 2 is distributed as below:

very favourable ← → very unfavourable

group 1	group 2	group 3	...	group 11
1 judge	48 judges	1 judge		
put it here	put it here	put it here		

Good consensus: use the item to measure the '2' position on the scale to understand how correlation works and know how to work it out; or, at least, understand how your software works it out for you! (Note: there is a little fine-tuning required in the procedure outlined in Figure 12.4. When you correlate the column of individual item X against the overall total column – step 5 in the procedural guide – you actually correlate the individual item X values against the column of 'total score minus that person's item X value'. This is to prevent the correlation from being spuriously inflated by the X value contained within each total.)

An alternative approach, if you don't know how to calculate a correlation coefficient, is to proceed according to Figure 12.4(a) up to step 4, and then to focus your attention on two extreme groups of respondents: those whose total scores are highest (say, the top 25 per cent), and those whose total scores are lowest (the bottom 25 per cent). For each item, calculate the difference between the average score on that item of the top group, and the average score on that item of the bottom group. *If this difference is low*, reject the item. Clearly, if the item cannot distinguish between those with high total scores and those with low total scores, it doesn't coherently measure 'whatever the scale as a whole measures'. How low a difference would you use? Well, you're seeking to reject between two-thirds and a half of all the items, to end up with a final set of 20, so a pragmatic rule of thumb would be to set a benchmark value for the difference which would allow you to retain 20 items.

Whichever method you use, you should ensure that the wording of the final set of items is arranged so that agreement with the attitude means scoring '5' for half the items (call them set A), and '1' for the other half (set B). You do this to control any tendency for respondents to answer unthinkingly. When you use the scale with your final sample of respondents, you ask each respondent to choose one of the five alternatives for each item; you then reverse the ratings for the items in set B (by subtracting from 6 in the case of a 5-point scale) to restore the direction in which they are scaled, and sum the ratings of both groups of items to get a total score for the respondent concerned. The lowest possible score is (1 times the number of items) and highest possible score is (5 times the number of items) for a 5-point scale, and so you can place your respondent somewhere between these two extremes.

Likert's method provides powerful and precise attitude measures and, because the end result is a set of 5-point items that look familiar to respondents, people feel comfortable in using them.

There is one problem, however, arising from the fact that individual item scores have to be *added* to get the attitude score. You could get the same score either by ticking the '1' box for half the time and the '5' box for the other half, or by ticking the '3' box every time. Yet surely these are rather different attitudes? The first represents some kind of ambivalence, while the other would appear to indicate neutrality. But the problem is, we don't know what 'neutrality' on such a scale is, and it's a rather large assumption to say it is the middle score on the total scale. Thurstone's technique is designed with this problem of the mid-point in mind, for use when greater precision is needed.

Thurstone's scale of equal-appearing intervals

In Thurstone scaling, the design stage requires people to judge the scale position of each item directly, using a procedure which arrives at a set of final items which are spread evenly across the whole scale, including the mid-point. (At steps 3 and 4 in Figure 13.4(b), the position of a given item on the scale is derived by calculating the median value of all the groups it is put into by the judges; its spread across the groups is derived by calculating the inter-quartile range of the groups it is put into by the judges. Only items with low inter-quartile ranges are selected.)

As you might have anticipated, the validity of the scale obtained by Thurstone's technique depends on the attitudes of the people you first use as judges, and depends on the assumption that people can adopt a neutral stance when asked to act as judges. This issue has been extensively researched and a straightforward guideline has emerged: when choosing a sample of judges for the design stage, avoid people who belong to social groups which are likely to have strong or extreme views on the attitude in question. It would be silly to construct a scale measuring attitudes towards your company's products by sampling only from customers who gave you constant repeat business, on the one hand, or only from customers who had complained about your products in the past, on the other.

If you plan to develop one of these forms of attitude scale, you might want to refer to a more detailed account than the above. Oppenheim (2000) presents a variety of techniques very clearly and provides worked examples. You would also need to have a nodding acquaintance with simple statistical calculations such as those for computing the mean, median, and interquartile range, and with the correlation coefficient as an option in the case of the Likert scale. You might care to check your calculations with your tutor before using the scales with your sample of respondents.

 If you intend to use any of the scaling techniques as described here, please work through activities 1 to 5, to the extent that they apply, in the Project Guide.

12.3 Observation techniques

When all's said and done, and all the semi-structured and fully structured techniques have been taken into account, your eyes are still a very good research instrument. You don't have to depend on extensive dialogue with other people to begin to understand what is going on! However, standing and staring in a disorganized manner will not get you very far, and both of the techniques which I shall outline depend on a more structured approach.

Structured observation

Some of the most interesting and important findings about the nature of managerial work and its problems have been obtained by observational means. Stewart's original research on how managers spend their time (Stewart 1967) asked managers to act as their own observers and record their activities in diary form; it is still quoted as a source of ideas, hypotheses, and guidance in understanding the problems involved in different kinds of management role.

Mintzberg's work on the same issue (Mintzberg 1973) helped to change our views about management as a planned, purposeful activity; its observation categories are still used in studies which seek to relate what managers do, to their effectiveness (e.g. Martinko and Gardner 1990, an article which reproduces Mintzberg's category headings themselves, with some additions). Isenberg's study of middle and top management (Isenberg 1984) has refocused our attention on the importance of the personal interpretations that influence management decision-making and action, helping to legitimize the individual as the unit of analysis in management research; it provides a good account of a semi-structured approach. Finally, if you plan to carry out observations of problem-solving groups, you should take note of Bales' Interaction Process Analysis category system (Bales 1950), reproduced in many basic social psychology and behavioural studies texts (see e.g. Mullins 2001) which led to some very influential findings on group dynamics and influenced early work on leadership style.

If you want to include an observational phase in your project work, two basic procedures are open to you. You can use a pre-existing analytic scheme, such as Mintzberg's; or you can develop and apply your own. In either event, you proceed by preparing a table of basic headings, and, when making the observations, tallying instances of behaviour under those headings as they occur. Mintzberg's scheme can be used as a complete unit, or you might take just the one of his three main category schemes that is most relevant to your needs. He offers schemes for classifying Managerial Events, Purposes of Contact (together with a separate scheme for classifying the Initiator of Contact), and Managerial Roles.

How to develop your own scheme is outlined below. However, some form of scheme is strictly essential, if you are to avoid being overwhelmed by the flood of observations that is potentially available to you in even the simplest business or management situation.

Developing and using your own scheme involves you in a process of analytic induction, a brief account of which is provided in Section 5.3 under the rubric of Grounded Theory. There are several variants of the procedure, perhaps the most influential, because following a fairly standard content-analytic approach, being Strauss and Corbin (1998). Becker and Geer (1982) provide a useful overview when they describe the three stages involved in the case of observation technique:

1 *Selection and definition of problems, concepts and indices*, in which you try and place initially observed single events into a conceptual perspective and begin the search for further indicators of the ideas, concepts, or themes that you think are involved. So for example, if a manager mentions the pace and burdens of his or her particular job, your thoughts might turn to the concept of stress, and you begin to identify ways of categorizing stressors in the management environment; or the notion of time management may occur to you, and a variety of efficiency measures become possible. In this stage, the

credibility and status of your informants, the extent to which the comments were elicited by you or volunteered by the informant, and the extent to which social influences prevail, are particularly important.

2 *Checking frequency and distribution of phenomena,* in which you decide whether the events are widespread enough and typical enough to repay systematic recording, and in which you do the main data-collection itself. How frequent is the comment or behaviour concerned, what forms does it take (the beginnings of a categorization scheme), and do other events confirm the significance and importance of the behaviour in question? This is the place for the collection of observations using whatever category scheme (or schemes: it is likely that the events you're studying will require several) you construct. Other techniques, such as the repertory grid, or a semi-structured technique like the key informant interview, may provide you with the material for a content analysis which results in a category scheme.

3 *Construction of models* which provide a general framework within which the observations can be described, and into which general concepts may be introduced to allow an explanation of the events in question. (On the distinction between a description and an explanation, refer again to Table 7.8.) This model will relate the events to particular factors and influences in the organization being studied, and allow statements about the necessary and sufficient conditions required for the events to occur, statements about what is important and what isn't, and statements which relate the present situation being studied to some wider class of situations as described by the concepts you drew on initially. Here, you are commenting on the significance and generalizibility of your conclusions to other organizations.

This form of observation forms a very useful technique if you are using case study method. During all of this time, you will need to carry pencil and paper and pre-printed category tables (tape-recorders are, as I have mentioned before, a mixed blessing). You will need to tolerate a measure of uncertainty and ambiguity; and you will certainly want to discuss your emerging ideas with other people. For all of these reasons, your role as observer must be publicly known, and you should have taken an early decision on whether you are there as a participant observer or as a non-participant.

The latter is too big a question to be resolved here, since it depends on the specifics of your situation. But in any event, you will always influence the events you observe to some degree, regardless of whether you participate or not; you will always have problems of over-identification with what's going on which need to be guarded against; and you will always encounter situations and events in which things happen so quickly, or which have such personal implications, that the role of the dispassionate observer is difficult to maintain. Jorgensen (1989) is a useful guidebook on these and related issues, and Waddington (1994) reinforces these points in an account which summarizes his classic case study of the Ansells Brewery strike. Depending on whether you are involved in the more systematic stage of data-collection, this may or may not be a problem.

ILLUSTRATION 12.3

Fred Meynell was doing an observation study of activities in a hospital ward, as part of his undergraduate work placement with a national study of hospital work patterns being conducted in the National Health Service, one of his objectives being to draw conclusions about the adequacy of staffing levels on the wards. Being a kind-hearted sort of fellow, he would occasionally help the harassed nurse to turn some of the heavier post-operative patients in their beds during the night shift when assistance couldn't be obtained. Other nurses weren't available to come and help her at certain periods (especially during meal breaks) and his chivalrous nature (for he was the sort of chap who would stand up when a lady entered the room) prevented him from doing nothing to help. Which was, of course, what he should have done, given the objectives of his study: precisely nothing. This sort of over-identification needs to be avoided.

Being a lively and curious person, on a couple of occasions he scrubbed up and dressed in surgical robes to observe an operation immediately after his nightly observation period was completed, taking advantage of the surgeon's mistaken belief that the only 'student' on the wards could be a medical student. In this case, the observations he had taken weren't compromised, and he enjoyed himself immensely. This seems quite an appropriate level of identification with the issues being studied!

There is a very interesting discussion of the personal implications of participant observation in Gans (1982).

The field experiment as observation

As you may recall from Section 9.2, experiments are feasible in those situations in which you can structure events so tightly that control becomes possible. Here, you are concerned with the control of extraneous variables that compete with the independent variable in influencing changes in the dependent variable, and also with the kind of control that permits you to manipulate the independent variable itself. The experiment then becomes a form of highly structured observation, in which you formally ignore everything but these variables, while informally keeping an eye on anything else that might have a bearing on the validity of your findings and their interpretation.

Occasionally, you may be lucky, and discover that events have arranged themselves in such a way that at least two levels of some independent variable fall naturally to hand (one group of managers go on a course and another group don't; one division adopts a new policy and another doesn't). You're faced with a *found* or *natural experiment*, in other words, and you are faced with three problems.

■ To define a suitable dependent variable sufficiently operationally so that informative conclusions about the impact of the independent variable become possible.

■ To ensure that your measurement of the dependent variable doesn't intrude excessively on the behaviour of the people you are observing.

- To find a rationale for deciding which of the variables which you couldn't control matter, and which don't.

I leave it to you to recognize a suitable occasion if it should ever occur. You might find Webb *et al.* (1999) a useful source of ideas, particularly in handling the second kind of problem.

In the normal course of events, however, experiments must be made to happen, and one way to do so is by structuring a form of questionnaire in such a way that the various subgroups of respondents fall into different levels of the independent variable in which you are interested. This has already been suggested as a rationale for the analysis of conventional structured questionnaires (see Section 11.1), and, provided it's possible for you to arrange subgroups according to a precise experimental design, you can obtain an impressively high level of experimental control.

ILLUSTRATION 12.4

A study by Clouse (1990) provides a good example. He presented a group of students with a questionnaire at the beginning and end of a course in entrepreneurship, in order to measure changes in their perceptions of the factors to be taken into account in making business start-up decisions. In this case, presence on the course is the independent variable, and the extent and nature of the changes form the dependent variables. Following a carefully pre-validated procedure, in which the validity of the questionnaire was established and the reliability of the participants' responses demonstrated, he was able to show that there were statistically significant changes in students' perceptions on many of the factors which the entrepreneurship course was designed to influence.

Strictly speaking, as he didn't measure changes among a group of students who did *not* attend the course, there was only one level of the independent variable, and it is technically incorrect to conclude that it was the course which brought about the changes. Indeed, he could, one imagines, have administered his questionnaire twice over to a group of students who did not attend the course for comparative purposes, but he chose not to. However, to provide a control group of this kind would be difficult in many of the situations in which you might plausibly conduct a field experiment of this type, and he used the evidence of questionnaire reliability, and the informal reasoning that the changes were as one would expect given the contents of the course, to attribute the changes to the course itself.

If you find yourself with an issue or topic which lends itself to this approach, the following guidelines should be followed:

- Identify some grouping of respondents which represents *at least two levels of an independent variable* in which you are interested: for example, position in the organization, or known and clearly distinct views on some important issue.

- Construct a questionnaire-based *measure of this variable*. This may be a simple, single question which asks them to state their position in the organization or their views on the issue, as in the above example. Alternatively, it may be a more sophisticated index which is the result of combining responses to several questions. For example, if you wanted to find out whether 'high-flyers' in your organization made systematically better decisions than run-of-the-mill employees, you might have to ask several questions covering such issues as number of years employed, and number and level of positions held in the organization, in order to construct a measure of career progression.

- *Decide on the dependent variable* or variables: some indicator of the issues in which you are interested, that you think may be influenced by the independent variable.

- Construct one or more questions which *assess this variable*. In the case of the 'high-flyers' example, for instance, your questions about the quality of their decisions might be incorporated in the same questionnaire, in the form of technical problems to which there was a recognizable right or wrong answer. (This is essentially what Clouse did: he asked his students to say what emphasis they placed on a number of factors which are necessary for successful business startups, and he checked with existing entrepreneurs and with colleagues that these factors were realistic, and that the judgements being elicited were appropriate.) Alternatively, you might get this information from other sources: in the case of our running example, from their supervisors' views of the adequacy of the decisions they make, or even from some quasi-objective indicator. Salesmen can be judged on the sales they make, bank lending officers by the number of loan defaults occurring among businesses to which they lend, and so on.

- Analyze the data to see if there is any *systematic relationship between the independent variable and the dependent*. In practice, this would involve casting the answers to the questions measuring the dependent variable into a table with at least two columns, one for the first level of the independent variable, and one for the second: high-flyers' responses in one column, and run-of-the-mill employees in the other, in terms of the above example.

- The analysis would involve you in making the assumption of no difference in the responses, and examining them to see if the observed differences were sufficiently large for you to reject this assumption. A variety of statistical tests are available to aid this decision, and you might find the discussion under the Analysis heading of Section 11.1 useful here.

- If the difference were indeed statistically significant, you would be able to *attribute it to the independent variable only if your design permits you to*. As usual, this would have to have been considered at the outset, when you constructed the questionnaire itself. It would include such issues as the robustness, reliability, and validity of the measures you chose; a decision to take repeated measures with the same group of people, as opposed to making separate measures for independent groups of people and the extent to which this might influence the inferences you can draw; and the presence of uncontrolled variables which might plausibly account for the result which you obtained.

Using this version of experimental technique depends on a familiarity with the principles of experimental design in general, and on the use of appropriate analytic statistics, the two being interrelated. Much of this involves standard procedures outlined in a variety of textbooks; Shadish *et al.* (2002) is a definitive text with a distinguished pedigree, and is particularly good on issues of design for field observation.

 If you intend to use any of the observation techniques as described here, please work through activities 1 to 5, to the extent that they apply, in the Project Guide. Activity 2 pertains particularly to the field experiment.

CASE EXAMPLE 12.1   Analyzing a single repertory grid

Phillip Sturton has had a lot of difficulty in identifying a company which would collaborate with his empirical research on the training and development of trainers. None of the consultancies or large organizations whom he approached were willing to allow him to interview a group of trainers who varied in experience, to find out how one becomes an effective trainer. Time was passing, and after a discussion with his tutor he decided to do a library-based project, supported by some interviews within the university. Forced to rely on local resources, he decided to do an internal study of the ways in which less experienced and more experienced staff were perceived as lecturers by their students.

Philip decides to use a questionnaire based on rating scales as his main data-gathering technique, looking to see if more experienced lecturers get systematically different ratings from less experienced lecturers, and on which characteristics in particular. But how is he to identify the characteristics to offer as rating scales? What are the attributes or dimensions of lecturer performance? He decides to do a short pilot study to find out, and does a repertory grid with five fellow-students to see what characteristics they spontaneously apply to their lecturers. Phillip will use the most frequently occurring ones in his final questionnaire.

He sets up the grid as follows. He asks the departmental secretary discreetly for information about how long each of the lecturers responsible for the semester's modules have been teaching, and uses the names of the modules they teach as the elements in the grid. (He could have used the actual lecturers' names, but he doesn't especially want to signal to his interviewees that it is the person's experience that he is interested in. He also feels that his interviewees will be more comfortable if they respond about 'the lecturers who taught these modules', rather than named individuals, even though they do, of course, know who taught them!) As well as requiring his interviewees to rate these elements as the constructs are elicited, he asks them to provide a set of ratings on one additional element: 'An ideally presented module', which he will use in his final questionnaire as a yardstick for evaluating each lecturer.

One of Phillip's completed grids is shown below. The last two lines have been added after the interview, so that you can see how many years' experience each lecturer has.

1 Just for practice, read back the information in the grid for the 'Ideal' element: how does this student construe 'an ideally presented module'?

2 Is there any evidence in this particular grid for Phillip's hypothesis that lecturers with more years' experience are construed more favourably than lecturers with fewer years' experience?

	1	Int Mgt	Strat Mgt	Mkt of Serv	B-to B Mkt	Mkt Res2	Ideal	5
1	Clear and easy to follow	2	4	1	4	4	1	Difficult to follow
2	Makes it interesting	1	3	3	5	3	1	Dull and boring
3	Clear diction	1	4	3	5	4	1	Mumbles a bit too much
4	Easy-going	2	4	2	4	5	2	Tense and nervy
5	An all-rounder	2	3	3	5	2	3	Very specialized
6	Good tutorial skills	2	5	1	2	5	1	Poor at leading discussion
7	Makes me laugh	1	5	2	5	5	2	Very solemn
8	Open to my reactions	1	4	2	5	5	2	Preoccupied with subject
Lecturer		Dr P	Mr A	Ms O'B	Prof K	Ms L		
Years experience		20	2	15	30	1		

CASE EXAMPLE 12.1   Analyzing a single repertory grid (cont.)

Answers to Case Example 12.1

1 In any grid application in which respondents' preferences are to be established, it is very useful to provide for an 'ideal' element. It is tempting to suppose that, because a grid consists of a set of constructs which are used as rating scales, a respondent's preferences are going to be associated with one end, or the other, of each construct. The ratings on the 'Ideal' element show that this is not the case.

For this respondent, the 'Ideal' lecturer is someone whose presentation is clear and easy to follow (rating of '1' on construct 1); who makes the material interesting (rating of '1' on construct 2), and speaks with clear diction when outlining it (rating of '1' on construct 3). However, (see construct 4, a rating of '2', not '1') the ideal is not completely easy-going; and this student prefers (construct 5, a rating of '3') that the lecturer should occupy a position mid-way between generality and specialization. Good tutorial skills are preferred; the ideal lecturer should be amusing but not completely so, and the lecturer should be open to the student's needs (a rating of '2' on construct 8) but, at the same time, just a little concerned with the responsibilities to the subject-matter as well.

2 Since the preferred ends of each rating scale seem to lie on the left, where a rating of '1' pertains, it is tempting to suggest that by summing the ratings down each column and looking for the lowest total, the most favourably construed lecturer can be identified: and on this rationale it would be Dr P. But, as we have noted above, it is the 'Ideal' column of ratings which specifies the favoured characterization of an effective lecturer. *So the way to answer this question is to compare each column, one by one, with the 'Ideal' column.* Sum the absolute differences downwards. So, for column 1, Dr P's International Management course: 2–1 = 1; 1–1 = 0; 1–1 = 0; 2–2 = 0; 2–3 = 1 (absolute differences, remember); 2–1 = 1; 1–2 = 1; 1–2

= 1. The total of these differences is 5. Working out the differences between each column and the 'Ideal' gives the following results.

Lecturer	Dr P	Mr A	Ms O'B	Prof K	Ms L
Years experience	20	2	15	30	1
Sum of differences from 'Ideal'	5	19	4	22	22

Dr P's course is indeed closely matched with the 'Ideal' specification; but Ms O'B's, with a sum of differences from the 'Ideal' column of only 4, is closer still. Two staff with fairly long service histories (20 years and 15 years respectively) whose ratings are closely aligned with the 'Ideal'. Now look at Mr A and Ms L: their sums of differences from the 'Ideal' are 19 and 22 respectively: in other words, their ratings are very different from those specified by the 'Ideal'. It seems as though, for this respondent at any rate, Phillip's hypothesis is supported: the lecturers with more years of experience are more highly regarded.

There is a slight problem, though. Notice that Prof K's sum of differences with respect to the 'Ideal' is rather large; yet he has the largest amount of teaching experience.

So the simple generalization expressed in Phillip's hypothesis is not entirely substantiated. Is this a matter of sampling? In other words, what will the results of the other four grid interviews show: will the relationship between the lecturers' ratings and the 'Ideal' be entirely different? Or is the situation rather more complex than Phillip had imagined? Is perceived effectiveness related to years of experience up to a certain number of years, but then decrepitude sets in, as the very long-serving lecturers become rigid, set in their ways, solemn and unresponsive to student needs?

Again, an analysis using the same sums-of-differences approach of the other four grids will cast light on the hypothesis!

Project Guide

As in Chapters 10 and 11, so here: work through these activities paying particular attention to any details which pertain to the techniques outlined in this chapter, even though you may have already worked through similar activities in using techniques drawn from Chapters 10 or 11.

1 Check your design and sampling

a   In a single column of a page of your research diary, make a list of the issues which you intend to investigate with this particular technique; note any issues which you will not be able to cover, and consider which other technique you will use, and in what order.

b   Go through activity 4 in the action checklist for Chapter 9, and work though it in detail. You're not planning now, you're committing yourself to action!

c   How does the sample you are drawing for this technique compare with any other samples you will be drawing? Are you working with the same people throughout; are they different? If they are different, then give each an identifier ('Sample A'; 'Sample B' etc.) and, in a second column of the page you used for question a above, note which issues will be addressed by which sample. In the case of repertory grid technique, your sampling will usually follow a purposive rationale (as in the key informant interview), but simple stratifications may be possible; an observational study whether structured observation or field experiment will be structured according to the variables involved; while any rating scales you use will take their sampling from the design of the survey technique (interview or questionnaire) in which the scales are embedded.

d   Use a third column for any stratifications you intend to make in the sample.

e   Commit yourself to some diary dates and plan how long it will take you to complete your data gathering with this technique. You may find it useful to refer to Table 5.3 at this point.

2 In the case of a field experiment

In the event that you haven't already done so in activity 2 of Chapter 8, and activity 1 of Chapter 9.

a   Read over the instructions for those activities and do the exercise.

b   Now fine-tune the description of the variables. Take a sheet of paper and write the name of your independent variable(s) at the left, together with a precise description of how, exactly, you plan to measure it/them. If more than one, don't have too many.

c   At the right of this sheet, write in the name of your dependent variable, and how exactly you plan to measure it (i.e. which question(s) will supply the data on this variable?).

d   In the middle of the page, list all the variables which you think could influence the dependent variable, quite apart from the influence of the independent variable. For each one, write down a few words on how you might minimize or control its effect on the dependent variable.

e   Talk to your tutor about a fine-tuning of your design which would provide this control; if your data are quantitative, talk to him/her about the possibilities of a statistical analysis which might partial out the effects of unwanted variables.

3 Prepare for data-gathering

a   Organize any recording equipment you will need. Take a sufficient number of copies of the repertory grid sheet shown as Figure 12.2 (plus some spares); in the case of an observational study, prepare a set of observation sheets pre-printed with the categories into which you will be classifying whatever behaviour or utterances which you observe.

b   Discuss what you are about to do with your sponsor and (if you need help with the technical details) your tutor.

c If you are constructing a rating scale of your own, plan sufficient time with the sample on which you construct the scale, and time for analysis, before you incorporate the resulting scale in the questionnaire or interview schedule to be used with your main sample.

d If you don't have a computer of your own, now is the time to book a machine in your university department, check that the required software is there, and that the machine will be available to you when you want it.

4 Construct your instrument

a Where the technique requires it, construct the list of questions you intend to ask, following the guidelines given above. In the case of a repertory grid, decide on the Elements you will use; decide on the exact wording of any supplied Elements you intend to provide; if you intend to do a content analysis following Honey's technique, decide on the wording of the supplied 'Overall' construct, to best reflect the topic of the grid.

b In doing so, you need to bear in mind the way in which you plan to analyze the data you will obtain. The best way of doing this is to write the first draft of the account of your analysis that you will provide in your dissertation document, since this forces you to think the analysis through in detail. So, in a few sentences, what exactly will you have done, what steps will you have followed, when you have analyzed all of the data? Write this down now!

c Having thought it through at this level of detail, if you find that the analysis you are planning isn't possible, review and amend exercises 1 and 2 above.

5 Go to it!

a Pilot your technique as outlined in activity 6 in Chapter 9. Bearing in mind that you may be using a mixture of techniques drawn from Chapters 10 and 11 as well as the present one (which may make a difference to how and when you utilize the present technique.

b Do it!

c Analyze the data as you have planned, following the guidelines in this chapter and any related authors recommended above.

6 Continue your write-up

a By the time you are ready to collect data, you should have completed the write-up of your introductory chapter, and the literature review. If not, do so at this stage. Prepare a first draft of the methodological section of your dissertation. Now that you're about to collect data, you should be able to provide a coherent rationale for the method you are using, and to state the techniques you plan to adopt. Revisit the research proposal which you prepared in activity 5 in Chapter 9 and expand the information you gave there, into a connected account which describes what you are about to do and gives reasons for it, in the light of your research question.

References

Bales, K. F. (1950) *Interaction Process Analysis: a Method for the Study of Small Groups*, Cambridge, Mass: Addison-Wesley.

Becker, H. S. and Geer, B. (1982) 'Participant observation: the analysis of qualitative field data', in Burgess, R. G., (ed.) *Field Research: a Sourcebook and Field Manual*, London: George Allen and Unwin.

Burr, V. and Butt, T. (2004) *An Invitation to Personal Construct Psychology*, London; Whurr, 2nd edn.

Clouse, van, G. H. (1990) 'A controlled experiment relating entrepreneurial education to students' start-up decisions', *Journal of Small Business Management*, 28: 2: 45–53.

Gans, H. J. (1982) 'The participant observer as a human being: observations on the personal aspects of fieldwork', in Burgess, R. G., (ed.) *Field Research: a Sourcebook and Field Manual*, London: George Allen & Unwin.

Honey, P. (1979) 'The repertory grid in action', *Industrial and Commercial Training*, 11: 11: 452–459.

Isenberg, D. J. (1984) 'How senior managers think', *Harvard Business Review*, 62: 6: 81–90.

Jankowicz, A. D. (1990) 'Applications of personal construct psychology in business practice', in Neimeyer, G. J. and Neimeyer, R. A., (eds) *Advances in Personal Construct Psychology*, Greenwich, CT: JAI Press; 257–287.

Jankowicz, A. D. (2003) *The Easy Guide to the Repertory Grid*, Chichester: Wiley.

Jankowicz, A. D. and Walsh, P. (1984) 'Researching the Sergeant's role', *Garda News*, 3: 8: 6–13.

Jorgensen, D. L. (1989) *Participant Observation: a Methodology for Human Studies*, London: Sage.

Legge, K. (1978) *Power, Innovation and Problem-solving in Personnel Management*, London: McGraw Hill.

Martinko, M. J. and Gardner, W. L. (1990) 'Structured observation of managerial work: a replication and synthesis', *Journal of Management Studies*, 27: 3: 329–357.

Mintzberg, H. (1973) *The Nature of Managerial Work*, New York: Harper & Row.

Mullins, L. J. (2001) *Management and Organisational Behaviour*, London: Financial Times Pitman Publishing, 7th edn.

Oppenheim, A. N. (2000) *Questionnaire Design, Interveiwing and Attitude Measurment*, London: Continuum, 2nd edn.

Price, J. L. (1997) 'Handbook of organizational measurement', *International Journal of Manpower*, 18: 4:5:6 whole part.

Rick, J., Bryner, R., Daniels, K., Perryman, S. and Guppy, A. (2001) *A Critical Review of Psychosocial Hazard Measures*, Brighton, Institute for Employment Studies, University of Brighton. Also at WWW, http://www.hse.gov.uk/research/crr_pdf/ 2001/crr01356.pdf accessed 4 February 2004.

Shadish, W. R., Cook, T. D. and Campbell, D. T. (2002) *Experimental and Quasi-Experimental Designs for Generalized Causal Influence*, New York: Houghton Mifflin, 3rd edn.

Stewart, B., Hetherington, G. and Smith, M., (eds) (1984) *British Telecom Survey Item Bank*, Bradford: MCB University Press.

Stewart, R. (1967) *Managers and their Jobs: a Study of the Similarities and Differences in the Ways Managers Spend their Time*, London: Macmillan.

Strauss, A. and Corbin, J. (1998) *Basics of Qualitative Research: Techniques and Procedures for Developing Grounded Theory*, Newbury Park: Sage, 2nd edn.

Waddington, D. (1994). 'Participant observation', in Cassell, C. and Symon, G., (eds.) *Qualitative Methods in Organizational Research*, London: Sage.

Webb, E. J., Campbell, D. T., Schwartz, R. D. and Sechrest, L. (eds), (1999). *Unobtrusive Measures*, London: Sage (revised edn).

13

Writing it up

- To assist you in planning the preparation and production of your project document within the deadline indicated by your university
- To provide some guidelines on how your material should be formatted and structured
- Bearing the needs of your audience in mind, to leave you with some suggestions about the style in which your ideas should be expressed

At a glance

If you haven't done any previous project work before, you may not have realized to what extent the act of writing, the very activity of composition, influences the development of your ideas and your arguments. This process needs time: time for the materials to be organized; time for you to put your initial thoughts into appropriate words presented in an appropriate order; and time for the reflection which stimulates further ideas. My first task is to help you plan your production so that plenty of time will be available.

The next is to help you in expressing your ideas clearly. You may have a good literature review, entirely convincing results, and some astonishing conclusions to offer, but if you can't express what you want to say in a way that communicates effectively, the outcome will be disappointing. The structure of your document makes a difference; the order in which you present your material likewise. Quite how you organize your material depends partly on the length of the document which your have been asked to prepare, and we examine several variants.

Expressing what you have to say, as clearly as possible and in the most convincing way, depends on your subject-matter and how it is presented, but it also depends on your audience. Different readers look for different things. The holiday-maker boarding a plane expects to be entertained by his block-buster novel; his wife carries a couple of reports in her hand-luggage and hopes to appraise the content and make some business decisions before they arrive at their holiday destination; and her mother, who is travelling with them, enjoys problem-solving and carries a paperback book of crosswords and logic puzzles to keep her mind busy while they're in flight. Your audience – your tutor and your examiners – have equally firm aims in reading your material, and equally firm assumptions about the way in which your material should be presented. You need to follow a number of stylistic conventions when you write, and these are described in what follows below.

13.1   Basic requirements: timing and deadlines

If you think about it, you will recognize that you need to go through three stages in order to construct a completed project document. The first stage involves adding data taken from primary and secondary sources specifically related to your topic, to data taken from your own stock of general knowledge; while the second stage requires you to turn those data into information by building an argument which achieves your project objectives. In the third stage, you draw all this together by writing in a way that communicates the material and the argument effectively.

How much time have you got, overall? Glance back at Section 4.1, and, working backwards from your ultimate deadline, revise the final stages of the work-plan you prepared (in the form of a Gantt chart, perhaps, like the one shown in Figure 4.1), all those weeks ago. Now that you're closer to the deadline, do you need to fine-tune the time available for your write-up? Indeed, the sooner you start writing, the better.

Now engage in some planning on a micro-level. How much time can you make available for your writing during your normal working week, in advance of the final continuous period you have set aside for the write-up? You can produce around six to eight pages of final text (at 300 words to the page) in a day's work during that final phase. Before then, how much time can you spare and how often? It takes a little time to get started on each occasion you sit down to write, so if you don't have a full day, set aside a period of at least two hours long, as often as possible. Try and arrange this for a time when you feel rested and fresh, and for a place where you have all your materials to hand.

Set yourself a target for each session: not a simple word-count, but a content-related objective. For example, to complete a particular stage of your argument, to explain a given idea or set of ideas, or to prepare a given number of tables on a related theme. Take the occasional five-minute break during the session, but don't start doing or reading something else: keep your mind ticking over on the same subject-matter, so that you can return to an intact flow of ideas after your rest. If you find that you haven't achieved your target at the end of the session, then write a brief note to yourself under the heading 'What Comes Next', to remind you of what you had in mind as the next thing to say when you start writing again.

As you come to the end of the time you have allocated for the write-up, check how much there is still to do to achieve the complete, balanced structure described

ILLUSTRATION 13.1

Harold Ramotswe, you will remember from Case Example 4.1, ran into difficulties in managing his time over the project as a whole. He didn't finish collecting his questionnaire data until the middle of October, and he hadn't done any preparatory writing before-hand, so that he had the whole dissertation to write between 1 and 18 November. Allowing time for binding he had barely 13 days. However, Harold remembered his undergraduate days, in which he would sit up from 10 pm until 3 am, fuelled with coffee, revising for his finals. He'd received a First. The same tactic had worked when he was preparing some of his MBA assignments. So: no problem! That's what he decided to do for his dissertation. He would hide away in his room for a fortnight, working long into the night if necessary, and do it all in one marathon session.

Unfortunately, it just didn't work. After a few days, his tutor gave him feedback on a draft of his introduction and literature review. His e-mail contained a variety of comments, most of them having to do with how very disorganized and poorly argued his material was. He had obviously tried to do too much, at the wrong time of day, with ill-digested ideas and insufficient time available for re-reading, reorganizing, and editing the material he wrote. He realized that he simply could not do himself justice in the time available, and had to approach his tutor to ask for an extension.

in Section 3.4. Talk to your tutor if it seems as though you might miss your deadline. At this point, he or she will have three options:

- To ask you to submit the material by the original deadline, complete or not, and give you a mark accordingly – which may be a 'refer', a 'fail' or some other form of unsatisfactory mark.

- To allow you a few extra days taken out of the period allotted to him or her to read the document before submitting the grade to the appropriate examination board, bearing in mind the requirements of external examiners. This may save your life, but it only happens exceptional circumstances.

- To submit no grade to the examination board, making an arrangement with you for submission to the next board. This may be a term, a semester, or a year later, may well hold up your graduation, and might use up one of the two chances which most regulations permit for submissions (including the chance to resubmit work that was initially 'Failed'). There may also be a penalty in the form of deducted marks in one form or other.

Try to plan ahead so that you don't get into this situation!

And the best way of doing so is to pause now, and complete activity 1 in the Project Guide.

13.2   Format and structure

Section 3.4 provided you with some introductory material on the length, layout, timing and structure of your document in order to make you aware of what you were facing. This material is worth a brief second glance now that you are well advanced with your work.

Length

Writing to length is important. You might argue that quality, rather than length, is a primary consideration, and you would be right in general terms. However, some institutions (especially the professional bodies), see the project as an exercise in the communication skills essential to a manager, and feel quite strongly that you should be able to get your message across within a set number of words.

The best way to do this is to divide your maximum length, as specified in the programme regulations, into sections or chapters, allocating an appropriate number of words or pages to each. Writing is not an exact process, and you will find it useful to pretend that you're aiming to produce one more section than you actually need, allocating pages to it when you make this initial estimate, and keeping these in reserve to account for the sections which, once you have written them, turn out to be longer than you estimated. This may seem pedantic, but the discipline is useful. An over-extended project may raise a suspicion that you've 'padded out' your project with unnecessary information, may indicate a lack of originality in what is an undigested compilation of material, and may suggest that you haven't given sufficient thought to the message you are trying to convey.

Layout and makeup

Once you have finished placing words on the page following the suggestions made in Section 4.4, you will need to bind the pages together. Different universities have their own regulations but, as a general rule, Masters and many Diploma project documents need to be bound by a professional bookbinder. The actual colour of the covers is often specified for you. Your institution should be able to give you a list of local bookbinders; allow for a turnaround period of two to four weeks and remember that other students may be needing the same service at exactly the same time as yourself! Undergraduate project reports should at the very least be spiral-bound with a punching-and-binding machine; peg-and-strip arrangements in which the plastic strip is melted to the pegs in a process of heat-treatment, with plasticized card for front and back covers, make for a satisfactory binding. You may be asked to provide a temporary binding first, and more permanent covers after the work has been marked and no major revisions shown to be required.

The wording on the title page, and sometimes on the front cover, is normally as follows: Title; Author Surname and initials; the words 'A thesis' (or 'dissertation') 'submitted to' (name of your institution) 'in partial fulfilment of the requirements for the degree of' (name of your qualification); the month and year of submission. Professional bodies may have their own variant.

Structure

Take a glance at Figures 3.1, 3.2 and 3.3, and now that you're *in medias res*, refresh yourself on the associated discussion in Section 3.5. Now that you have a good feeling for the scope of your project, it helps if you think of yourself as being involved in one of three situations:

The short document

Your work is best structured as a management report, in which the title gives an exact description of what you are doing rather than an allusive or literary gloss on the subject-matter. ('An evaluation of three strategies for overseas trade' is an exact description; 'Coping with cultural differences: implementing trading strategy' contains an allusion to the main conceptual material contained in the document.) It should open with an Executive Summary in which objectives are followed by recommendations; supporting information comes next; a description of methods and techniques is given where recommendations depend on them, usually next but sometimes in an appendix. The arguments for various actions given relevant background information comes at the end. The remaining material should be organized in order to amplify and support this summary, and you might consider labelling the major sections with a hierarchic numeric system (1.0 containing 1.1, 1.2 etc.; 1.1 containing 1.1.1, 1.1.2 etc.), or numbering each paragraph sequentially.

The longer document without implementation

This is probably the most common alternative, and the structure will take one of three forms.

- If your study is a *focused, in-company based* one and your material is straightforward and you are dealing with one main issue or hypothesis, the dissertation will look like Figure 3.1. You will provide just a single literature review following the introduction, and you will discuss, conclude, and make recommendations after presenting your empirical findings.

- If your study is a *focused, in-company based* one but your material is complex, involving several different issues, then, after an introduction and overall description of methodology and literature review, you might prefer to devote subsequent chapters to presenting each issue in turn, each one containing its own literature review, methodology, data presentation and discussion, the whole being followed by concluding chapters of discussion, conclusions and recommendations. This is the pattern illustrated in Figure 3.2.

- If your study is a *generic, industry-based* one, or a *library-based* one (see the discussion in the latter parts of Section 3.1 and Section 3.5) your report may take the form shown in Figure 3.3.

The longer document with implementation

If you have the opportunity to implement recommendations arising from the earlier parts of your project, in which you constructed an argument for some course of action and mustered primary and secondary data in support of a choice from a set of alternatives, your reader will be particularly interested in the outcomes of that action. Your document should be structured accordingly. Make sure that you give sufficient emphasis to the outcomes, presenting fresh data as evidence, discussing the outcomes, evaluating the wisdom of the particular action you recommended, and drawing conclusions for the future. This is really an argument for allowing plenty of pages (perhaps half of your complete document) to everything that followed the action which you initially recommended.

 Take a break now; and address activity 2 in the Project Guide before continuing.

13.3   The use of language

There are many useful accounts which will help you with the humble business of writing. George Orwell's classic essay is one to read now if you haven't encountered it before (Orwell 1957). Strunk and White (1972) provide plenty of useful detail in only 85 pages while Bryson (2004) is immensely entertaining while presenting the essentials of word-meanings and grammar. Turk and Kirkman (1989) provide a comprehensive account which includes many useful pointers to the use of computers in dissertation writing.

The last of these asserts that the notion of 'proper' grammatical English is somewhat outmoded, and argues that you should discover and implement the rules of acceptable usage, and current convention, instead (Turk and Kirkman 1989: 15). Though I might disagree on matters of detail ('datum' or 'data', for instance; 'medium' or 'media'), there's no doubt that you need to be familiar with the style and conventions which apply when you write for an academic audience in the business and management field.

How might we define that elusive notion, 'style'? It's said of *people* that they either have it or they don't; but *literary* style in particular consists of the method or methods by which you obtain the effect you wish to achieve in your reader. Like fashion style, it is something which you deliberately adopt in order to obtain the effect you intend (though it is wise to stick to the rules of grammar and certainly, avoid grammatical solecisms; Strunk and White (1972) and Bryson (2004) provide plenty of useful examples). Table 13.1 lists some recommendations given in Turk and Kirkman (1989), to which I have added some relevant stylistic suggestions which are worth addressing individually.

TABLE 13.1 Devising a style suited to an examiner in business and management

The question to pose	A suitable answer	Stylistic implication
What is your aim?	To build a convincing argument leading to a conclusion which is sensible given the issues investigated and the data obtained.	Ensure your assertions are logical, supported or supportable by evidence, and take exceptions into account. Avoid personal or company opinions and feelings to which the above doesn't apply.
Who are your audience and what is their aim?	To pass you or fail you depending on whether they are convinced by the argument, with the minimum expenditure of time and effort on their part.	Write in an authoritative but not opinionated manner (quote sources!) using simple and readable sentence constructions. Provide summaries where needed.
What attitude do they hold?	Supportive, taking account of any special difficulties you encountered. They're cheering you on, hoping they can pass you so that they don't have to read the document afresh when you resubmit it after an initial failure.	Include conceptual, situational and organizational constraints within your argument and indicate if and how you dealt with them. Personal difficulties are best left to a separate statement.
What is their background?	Already knowledgeable in the field and willing to learn more, of above average intelligence, and used to absorbing large amounts of written information in a hurry.	Reference your assertions, elaborate concepts and ideas only when necessary, include relevant asides selectively to maintain interest. Polysyllabic words and sentences are welcomed; though only if briefer formats do not suffice.
What do they really need to know?	Enough to convince them that you have learnt the relevant parts that they know, together with sufficient new reasoning and data to be convinced by your argument.	Ensure the basics of the subject are covered, summarize periodically, and include self-referential statements indicating that you are tracking the argument you are building.

After Turk and Kirkman (1989)

Your own aims

Don't confuse your aim of building a convincing argument with the aim, and associated objectives, of the project itself. Indeed, weaker students have been known to cite their substantive objectives; the aim of being convincing; and one or more of the objectives given in Section 1.2 and Table 1.1, in sentences such as 'The objective of this dissertation is to examine and evaluate the outcomes of divisionalization on the marketing strategy of the company, to convince you, the examiner, that all the relevant arguments have been marshalled, and to be of assistance to the company'. The objective *of the student's project work* concerns divisionalization and its impact on strategy, and the examiner will refer to this substantive objective periodically to see how well the argument is achieving it. An objective *of the project process* relates to the wish to be convincing, and, while Tables 3.3 and 3.4 suggest that presentation is important in assessment, it's just a part of what is assessed. Finally, the objective *of the project as an educational method* is in a different category altogether. While the examiner may discern ways in which the work might help the company and form an opinion on the extent to which project method has succeeded educationally for the student, he or she is not the best judge of company benefit and will restrain enthusiasm or despair arising from these grounds in giving a mark. Don't confuse categories when stating your objectives!

Try not to be breathless. You can be convincing by sharing your convictions, and expressions of personal opinion are permissible – but only if the evidence warrants it. Statements of company views or policies can be quoted as observations you have made, but you need to be careful about their status as evidence: 'We are a People Company' is a valid report of something you have seen in the company brochure and may state something about the company's espoused image for publicity purposes. Lifted straight from the brochure and used as evidence, however, it doesn't engender confidence that the company does indeed care for the people it supplies or employs.

Your reader's aims

Your examiner will do his or her best to do your work justice when the mark is allotted, but you must make this as easy as possible.

Long sentences are dangerous, since the reader's concentration may be distracted by qualifying clauses. Faced with six other project documents each of between 10,000 and 50,000 words, and the scripts of two or three taught courses to mark (some of which may involve answers to up to four questions from each of a class of 100 people), all within a period which varies between one week and six weeks, your examiner will appreciate everything you do to make the experience of reading your document an interesting and pleasant one, since you are competing for his or her attention with many other people.

That sentence was rather too long, and might have been better expressed as follows. 'The lecturer may be faced with six other project documents to read, each of them 50,000 words long, and yours will be particularly appreciated if it's readable and interesting. There could also be three or four examination scripts to be marked, each one consisting of answers to four questions from each of 100 students. You're competing for attention at a very busy time.'

So, several longish sentences seem a better alternative, especially as they lend themselves to a rhythm which pulls the reader's attention along.

Short sentences command attention.

Your reader's attitude

While being supportive, the examiner would prefer you to keep your personal cries for help separate from an account of conceptual difficulties encountered and methodological problems addressed. A conversation backed by documentation, or a letter submitted with your document, are a better way of drawing the examiner's attention to problems caused by illness, files lost through criminal breaking and entry, and all of the other accidents which have been known to happen to project documents. Justified or not, including them in the document suggests special pleading and is best avoided.

Your reader's background

It is safe to assume that your examiner knows the subject-matter well and doesn't require you to explain simple terms or to plod through basic definitions and concepts. Your problem lies in judging what he or he is likely to view as 'simple' and 'basic', but by the time you are writing the main part of the document you should have formed an impression from the secondary sources you've read. Stop the flow to define and explain:

- when you feel it is critical to your argument
- when you are taking an unusual stance
- when you're trying to do something new with the material to hand.

Although your reader will be used to coping with large volumes of information, you can help by providing bulleted summaries periodically (especially when presenting empirical findings). He or he will find it difficult to handle situations in which poorly-digested data lie congealed within an unclear presentation, especially when both are compounded by errors of thinking and logic. A list of the most criminal errors of reasoning is given as Table 13.2: commit them at your peril.

What your reader really needs to know

In amplifying Table 13.1 and the original suggestions given in Turk and Kirkman (1989), I am addressing the irreducible core of your project document – the essence which remains when the outer layers have been pared away. What is it all ultimately about? Here's a checklist which would seem to apply to all project documents.

TABLE 13.2 Seven errors of reasoning calling to Heaven for vengeance

The kamikaze argument

Your assertions may state a case, or contradict and hence argue with someone else's statements. What they shouldn't do is argue with themselves. Two statements which contradict one another are easily spotted if they're in the same paragraph, and may be recognized even when separated by lots of intervening text – especially if they're strong statements, or central to your thesis. Of course you can change your mind in your project document: but this is best done intentionally, and usually, when the primary data warrant it.

The plain stereotype

Certain phrases are like 'motherhood' and 'apple pie' on the one hand, or 'anarchy' and 'democratic rights' on the other: they may express banalities, seduce the listener into a brainless response, and prevent originality of thought. Take care when you use words like 'leadership', 'participation', 'vital' and 'objective'. Of course there are occasions on which they are exactly appropriate, but these aren't as frequent as you might think. Conversely, there is:

The misinterpreted stereotype

An idea may express a conventional wisdom, and may be couched in stereotyped terms. But you need independent evidence to decide if it's weighty or trivial: to recognize that a stereotype exists is not sufficient to decide if the ideas it involves are in error or, indeed, plausible.

The cardboard cutout

Your project can only sample a person's actions and ideas. The complete individual is more complex than your methods allow. People can appear inconsistent (particularly in behaving in ways that appear to contradict their utterances). That doesn't necessarily prove thoughtlessness or insincerity on their part and you always need independent evidence to establish the position which people hold.

The sloppy consistency

You can usually turn up evidence which leaves your beliefs intact without testing them properly. 'The company survived; the profits were high; therefore the profits led to the survival'. If you believe that, then you're ignoring a multitude of alternative explanations: for example, cashflow. Just because your evidence appears consistent with your beliefs, doesn't make them true.

The articulate nonsense

A manager may be effective but unable to define it or explain it in words. Conversely, the ability to make propositional statements about one's beliefs and actions is consistent with wisdom but isn't a necessary or sufficient condition. An explicit argument isn't necessarily true.

The galloping hypothesis

A plausible possibility can be expressed in one paragraph, taken for granted in the next, and assumed to be true in the remainder of your text. Reiteration will irritate rather than convince, unless you provide some evidence to support your assertion.

After Watson (1987)

- That you have identified your objectives, stated them clearly, and referred back to them in writing your conclusions.

- That you are familiar with basic secondary sources, drawing on them to formulate your efforts within an appropriate academic context.

- That you understand the organizational background sufficiently well to demonstrate that your objectives are appropriate, your topic relevant, and the issues you select for investigation realistic.

- That you can demonstrate that your methods and techniques of primary data-gathering are capable of answering the research questions you ask, being aware of their limitations.

- That you can build a critical argument which pulls all of the above together.

- That you can turn primary data into information which is relevant to your argument, congruent with the secondary data, relevant to the issues you are exploring, and essential to the conclusions you draw and the recommendations you make.

You will provide your reader with all of this only if you provide clear guidelines and signposts through your material, directing and controlling his or her attention. By doing this, you tell the reader that you are capable of thinking through your material to the point at which you have become a very competent *teacher* of what you know about the topic of your research. To be a teacher is to possess knowledge, and to know how it is best shared with the reader; it is a reflexive, self-aware process, and so another suggestion is that you demonstrate your competence by the occasional self-reference. Comment on your intentions, draw attention to weaknesses in your argument (while demonstrating that you can imagine how they can be improved); let your reader know when you are arguing from a position of strength. This needs to be done subtly.

- 'The main weakness in this argument is x, y and z' comments on what you are doing and shows you *know* what you're doing without the explicit intrusion of 'I'. 'The main weakness of my argument . . .' might be appropriate on rare occasions but is likely to lead to excessive self-consciousness as you grope for a consistent style.

- 'Another advantage to this position is that . . .' is entirely appropriate, while 'Yet another advantage . . .' is light and readable, but carries the danger of turning into facetiousness if a long list is to be presented.

- 'It remains to present the views of the senior managers' sample, in order to . . .' shows that you're building an explicit argument; 'I now intend to present the senior managers' views and will next . . .' is a little too plodding, especially if you use it often in building a series of bridges across different sections of your account.

If you take the conclusion that my own style in writing this book is best avoided, that would be entirely correct, since my intentions about my reader were necessarily different from yours. Some project topics lend themselves to a section or chapter written in a very personal, experiential style, where the qualitative and the personal are an integral and intended part of your research design. However, this takes skill to carry off successfully, and you would probably want to take your tutor's opinions on an early draft. In general, then, I would suggest that you follow the excellent advice given in Strunk and White (1972: 60): 'Place yourself in the background' (with a suitable emphasis on the second word as well as the last). The rest of that chapter is worth reading in detail (though to my mind a lot of it is about personal voice, as much as it is about style).

ILLUSTRATION 13.2

Malvina Llull comes from a Catalonian family which settled in the UK seven years ago. She is completing her undergraduate degree, and writing a dissertation on ageism in the UK workforce. As someone who speaks four languages (Spanish, Catalan, French and English), she is aware that words matter and that shades of meaning are important. Having completed a detailed literature review, she knows that much of her central argument is going to turn on the definition and connotations of that term 'Ageism' as it is applied in situations in which the pressures on employee and employer are more than a simple matter of the employee's age. The way in which we think of early and normal retirement; career and succession planning; women returners; and flexible working all interact in determining the behaviour which becomes described in terms such as ageism, and so she starts her dissertation with a section on definitions. 'Ageism is a complex term and takes its meaning in relationship to . . .' is how the introduction to her dissertation begins. 'The following four definitions of the term must be clarified at the outset' soon follows, at the start of the second paragraph. 'What do we mean by . . .?' is a phrase that often recurs, and terms such as 'critical theory' and 'meanings as constructed and construed' are encountered in the first five pages.

Her tutor contacts her with some urgency when asked to provide some e-mailed feedback on her first draft. 'The problem isn't that it doesn't make sense, Malvina', she says. 'Actually, this is a beautifully argued, detailed analysis – but it's in the wrong place! Do you realize that you don't get round to telling me what the objectives of this dissertation are until page 17?'

In an introduction, objectives come first. Then the rationale for those objectives, i.e., an account of why it makes sense to study this topic in this particular way. In an in-company project this will frequently involve an account of the organization in which the research is taking place, and how the research question relates to issues within the organization. A brief account of how the research is to be done, which anticipates but merely introduces the later chapter on methodology, often ends the introductory chapter. It may be necessary to give initial definitions of terms, but their detailed discussion is best left to the literature review, and should never take place before the purpose of the dissertation has been explained!

13.4 On non-discriminatory language and political correctness

There is a stylistic rule which suggests that you use active constructions rather than passive; (*I am writing this clause* in the active voice, while *this clause has been written* in the passive). Unlike the rules which suggest that you should be grammatical and care about the accuracy of your spelling (both of which can be handled automatically if you use a word-processor, the former less successfully than the latter), there will be many occasions on which you will need to break it.

For example, one is occasionally driven to use the passive voice rather than the active when framing phrases that avoid sexist language constructions; indeed, one of the older arguments against the use of non-sexist language is that it leads to awkward sentence constructions. However, there are many good reasons for avoiding sexist terms and constructions in your writing, and in drawing your attention to Table 13.3, I can only suggest that you take it seriously, and accept that a clear style and elegant sentence constructions are compatible with non-sexist language, given a little practice and forethought.

Another argument against non-sexist language is that it reflects political correctness, and that there can't be any place for political correctness in a document which is meant to be the outcome of free and untrammelled intellectual thought. ('*Political Correctness*'. . . It is always worth wondering *whose* 'politics', policies, or belief systems, are being insisted on. When one's being told to be 'correct', who's doing the asking? What special interests are being peddled?) It is important to distinguish between being discriminatory, and giving gratuitous offence (which is, of course, why one avoids sexist or racist terms) and the thoughtless adherence to a 'politically correct' viewpoint.

Take the example of 'spinster' shown in Table 13.3. It is certainly rather unpleasant to use the word as an insult, as the table suggests . . . unless one's purpose was to be insulting, when the term 'bitter old spinster' would be much more effective than 'bitter old unmarried undivorced woman'. (Likewise, 'seedy old bachelor' makes for a more pungent insult, if an insult is intended, than 'seedy old unmarried, undivorced man'.) Clearly, while rudeness and insults have no place in a dissertation, there are places in other forms of writing where insults may be merited, and to propose a blanket ban on insult is to be politically correct: to go beyond the purpose, which is to prevent *gratuitous* offence.

It is, likewise, political correctness rather than an simple avoidance of gratuitous offence to 'update' language according to present conventions. Anachronisms are especially unacceptable if you are *quoting* from an author who wrote before the time when our current conventions emerged. A student once asked me if Bannister's book *Inquiring Man*, first published in the 1970s, shouldn't somehow be excluded from his bibliography since it reveals an unconscious prejudice, and was sent off with a flea in his ear. If the book were written today it would probably be called *Human Inquiry*, but the point is that it was written before the times when this particular convention was adopted. (If for some reason one wishes to convey

TABLE 13.3 Avoiding sexist language: the NUJ Equality Style Guide

Instead of . . .	. . . try
businessman	business manager, executive, boss, business chief, head of firm, etc., businesswoman/people
cameraman	photographer, camera operator
newsman	journalist or reporter
fireman/men	firefighter, fire service staff, fire crews
ice cream man	ice cream seller
policeman/men	police officer, or (plural) just police
salesman/girl	assistant, shop worker, shop staff, representative, sales staff
steward/ess, air hostess	airline staff, flight attendant
chairman	chairperson/woman, in the chair was . . ., who chairs the committee
best man for the job	best person/woman
man or mankind	humanity, human race, humans, people
manhood	adulthood
man-in-the-street	average citizen, average worker
manpower	workers, workforce, staffing
manning	staffing, jobs, job levels
manmade	synthetic, artificial, manufactured
Ford men voted . . .	Ford workers voted . . .
male nurse	nurse
woman doctor	doctor
housewife	often means shopper, consumer, the cook
mothers	often means parents
girls (of over 18)	women (especially in sport)
spinster/divorcee	these words should not be used as an insult
he, his	often means he or she, or his or hers – or sentence constructions can be changed to use they or theirs
Mrs, Miss	if your publication insists on courtesy titles, at least offer women the choice of being called Ms
Mr John Smith and his wife Elsie	Elsie and John Smith
authoress	author – avoid /ess where possible
dolls, birds, ladies, Mrs Mopp	these, and the puns arising from them are not funny
pin ups	are they really news?
spokesman	official, representative

a feeling of the gas-lit early years of the last century, then I dare say that 'man in the Clapham omnibus' is a more effective use of style than 'average citizen'.)

Political correctness is an evil since it constrains freedom of action: see e.g. Phillips (1994). However, it isn't necessarily political correctness to constrain language (for what are grammar, orthography, and style but forms of constraint?) if the consequent impact on thinking makes for the lessening of prejudice and the avoidance of offence, and it is important for you to avoid sexist – and racist – constructions as best you can. Choosing alternatives is often a matter of taste and is best done with forethought and deliberation. If in doubt, follow the excellent advice given in Saunders *et al.* (2003: 470, 471), and ask a member of the social group in question whether a term you are planning to use in naming the group is offensive or not.

> Time to tackle the last activity in the Project Guide.
> And glance at the Case Example: the last one in this book.

13.5 Conclusion

As with the previous section, all of this chapter is about conviction in one form or another. Indeed, this whole book explores ways of convincing someone else that you have something valuable to say and that you have evidence to support it. Your goal, ultimately, is to present accurate and convincing information to your tutor and the examiners; although the relevance and realism of your work is most important, it's the academics, rather than the colleagues in your organization, that your argument has to convince. Prove what you claim.

After losing Calais to the French, Mary Tudor is said to have declared 'When I die, you will find the word "Calais" engraved on my heart'.

Just in case you're ever autopsied, ensure that the words 'I proved it' are written on yours.

I wish you every success in this endeavour.

CASE EXAMPLE 13.1   Language and style

Jan Kowalski completed his five-year Masters in Economics at a Polish university, and has been studying an MSc in International Management in the UK. His second language is German, and while he had sufficient private lessons in English before he came to the UK to meet entry requirements, acquiring fluency during the one-year full-time Masters has, at times, been hard work.

He e-mails you his literature review for feedback. An extract is given below. It is taken from a section of his review in which he is describing knowledge transfer and the ways in which management ideas travel across national boundaries in the global economy. As his tutor, you need to decide:

a Is there a problem?

b If there is, how might it be resolved?

2.3 Communication across different cultures

The process of knowledge transfer in global economy involves the negotiation between organizational actors on the levels of national and also corporate culture. In order to understand the complexity of the global knowledge transfer we need to explore the ways in which ideas travel between cultures in more detail.

2.3.1 Diffusion

Idea-spreading is traditionally discussed in terms of 'diffusion' (Mohr 1969; Levitt and March 1988; Rogers 1995), a process which has 'direction'. This concept is mainly used when describing a transfer of innovation. Diffusion of ideas became a crucial subject for multinational companies. Their ability to transfer knowledge and practices globally often decides their survival or failure on the market. Hence many authors emphasized the importance for understanding the factors determining its success. It resulted in many different approaches to the subject of idea-spreading. How this diffusion works? See the Figure 2.2 which shows Czarniawska's model (Czarniawska and Joerges 1996).

An idea exists within a cultural matrix in which it is embedded. The idea is expressed through corresponding objects and artefacts; these are utilized in particular actions in a societal milieu; and the more important ones become standardized and regulated through a process of institutionalization. In order for an idea to travel by one means or other (a radio broadcast, a book, a training manual, a piece of artwork) it has to be *dis-embedded* from the various cultural assumptions which those processes have brought about. It then becomes understood within a new culture only by being *re-embedded* into the processes which apply to objects, actions, and institutions of its kind *in the new culture*. Each arrow in the figure stands for an act of translation – linguistic, behavioural, social and institutional.

For new idea to succeed it must be considered in terms of its usefulness to replace existing ideas *in accordance to recipient's criteria*. Successful knowledge transfer is not conclusive with copying all the elements of an idea chain from location A to B. Instead, it should copy the role and function that the idea plays in culture A into culture B. For this reason ideas and practices may undergo transmutation following their transfer (Edwards and Ferne 2004). Boyer, Charron *et al.* (1998) refer to this process as to *hybrydisation*. The original function of an idea and the practice in the donor unit may be irrelevant to the purposes assigned to it in the recipient unit. This may apply even to highly 'codified' practices and ideas. The new function may emerge out of the process of translation not as the one originally intended. The impact of translation is thus in part a function of the way in which the recipient culture institutionalizes the new practice. A given idea might not operate in

CASE EXAMPLE 13.1   Language and style (cont.)

the same fashion in the recipient as it does in the donor. Hence actors in the recipient culture might need to adapt it to pre-existing patterns of behaviour and power relations (e.g. Szulanski 1996; Ortiz 1998).

Answers to Case Example 13.1

I'm sure you will have noticed one difficulty immediately. The material is of a high standard, but it is very obviously from someone who does not have English as his first language. Some of the ideas are rather complex, and Jan is to be congratulated: except in one place, it is generally comprehensible. At times, though, discerning the meaning is hard work for the reader.

■ The vocabulary is sometimes weak. ('Successful knowledge transfer *is not conclusive with copying* all the elements of an idea chain from location A to B'.)

■ The idiom and expression are not English ('The new function may emerge out of the process of translation not as the one originally intended'; a more comfortable idiom would be something like 'after translation, an idea may come to be used for purposes different to those originally intended'.)

■ There is considerable uncertainty over the use of the definite and indefinite article. (Although in English, 'the' is meant to be used when talking of a particular identified object and 'a' when talking about a member of the general class of such objects, English usage is in fact rather capricious. Consider 'The first act of governance in a newly instituted university is to convene *an* Academic Board'; 'I am attending Academic Board'; 'the Academic Board minutes are ready'; 'Academic Board minutes are ready'. The second item has no article whatsoever, and the last item has two distinct shades of meaning, one of them being exactly the same as the previous item!)

All of this poses considerable difficulties for people whose first language lacks definite and indefinite articles.

What to do? If the whole dissertation is like this it may lose marks for presentation, and if key meanings are obscured, it will lose marks for substance.

■ At the very least, you will need to advise Jan to allow additional time for re-reading the whole text, paying greater attention to language, and correcting it where he can.

■ But there are limits to this process, and he may wish to find a native-English speaking friend who might read over the whole document and suggest appropriate re-wordings. (This is rather time-consuming, a saintly role for girlfriends, boyfriends, partners or spouses . . .). This would seem appropriate, since you as the tutor have seen the original work, will see the final result, and be able to judge that the latter is indeed Jan's own work and has not been improved in substance, only in English expression.

But this does raise another kind of problem. Look again at the third of the four paragraphs. It stands out from the rest. Compared with the rest, it is suspiciously good English. Has Jan succumbed to temptation and, knowing that his English is not quite perfect, 'borrowed' the description of the main item of this account from another author, without attribution? If so, this would be plagiarism, and would have two consequences:

a you would have to talk face-to-face with Jan, establish what happened, and insist that he expressed this section in his own words, or by means of a bibliographically referenced quotation identified as such by quotation marks;

b you would be alerted to the possibility of other instances of plagiarism – for that is what it is – and if you found further examples insist on a rewrite, pointing out that had he submitted the

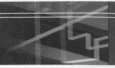

CASE EXAMPLE 13.1   Language and style (cont.)

work, he may have been failed, and certainly dealt with according to the university's disciplinary procedures.

Section 3.2 outlines the issue, and Section 7.1 the referencing conventions by which plagiarism can be avoided. There are of course more heinous forms of plagiarism, where someone whose English is entirely competent nevertheless steals ideas from another author, to pretend he or she knows more than he or she does. In the present case, it is very understandable if a person who knows what he or she wants to say, beautifully and perfectly in their own language, becomes frustrated enough to take someone else's wording. But it is still stealing, not borrowing, and needs to be discouraged.

Project Guide

If you have been following the activities suggested at the end of each chapter, you will probably have anticipated some of the activities suggested below.

1 Plan the production of your dissertation document in advance

a Assuming that you have been writing as you go along, make arrangements in good time for a clean printout of your chapters, and for the binding of your dissertation, first checking how many copies will be required.

b Leave sufficient time for the essential additional materials: contents pages, lists of tables and figures, and appendix material.

2 Structure the dissertation

a Choose one of the structures suggested in Section 13.2 and re-read Section 3.4.

b If your project is an empirical one, make your own drawing of Figure 3.1 or 3.2, filling in the different parts of the relevant shape with the chapter and section headings of your dissertation. In the case of a purely library-based project, make your own drawing of Figure 3.3 and do likewise.

c Alternatively, sketch out a system of headings, sub-headings and sub-sub-headings for each chapter. Don't use it as a straightjacket, but do check your material periodically to ensure that your reader can recognize a clear structure.

d Experiment with the Outline command of the VIEW menu of your word-processing software and if you feel comfortable with it, use this as another alternative.

e Lastly, make an appointment with your tutor to discuss how it's shaping up, and to check that it follows the structure which you agreed.

3 Meet your reader's needs and expectations

a As you finish each chapter, run your spelling checker over it prior to printout.

b Read it over to find errors that your spelling checker missed.

c Print out a section once it's complete. Now pick up the section you printed out immediately before this one and read through it. If you lose the thread of the argument between sections, or you find that you're losing sight of the main point because of the details, stop, and ask yourself what you can do to put things right. The answer will frequently be to write a bulleted summary, a table, or a figure at the end of the first of the two sections, or to provide a linking paragraph at the start of the second section.

d While you're at it, check whether the language you're reading is indeed non-sexist, non-racist, and unlikely to cause offence to people with disabilities.

References

Boyer, R., Charron, E., Jurgens, U. and Tolliday. S., (eds.) (1998) *Between Imitation and Innovation: the transfer and hybridization of productive models in the international automobile industry*, Oxford: Oxford University Press.

Bryson, W. (2004) *Bryson's Dictionary of Troublesome Words: a Writer's Guide to Getting it Right*, London: Broadway Books.

Czarniawska, B. and Joerges, B. (1996) 'Travels of ideas', in Czarniawska B. and Sevon, G., (eds.) *Translating Organizational Change,* Berlin: De Gruyter.

Edwards, T. and Ferner, A. (2004) 'Multinationals, reverse diffusion and national business systems', *Management International Review*, 51, Special Issue and Contemporary Issues in Multinational Structure and Strategy.

Levitt, B. and March, J. G. (1988) 'Organizational Learning', *Annual Review of Sociology,* 14: 319–340.

Mohr, L. B. (1969) 'Determinants of innovation In organizations', *American Political Science Review,* 63: 111–126.

Ortiz, L. (1998) 'Union response to teamwork: the case of Opel Spain', *Industrial Relations Journal*, 21: 9: 42–57.

Orwell, G. (1957) *Politics and the English language*, Harmondsworth: Penguin.

Phillips, M. (1994) 'The strange death of liberal England', *Spectator*, 273: 9–12.

Rogers, E. M. (1995) *Diffusion of Innovations,* Glencoe Ill.: The Free Press.

Saunders, M., Lewis, P. and Thornhill, A. (2003) *Research Methods for Business Students*, London: Prentice Hall.

Strunk, J. W. and White, E. B. (1972) *The Elements of Style*, London: Allyn and Bacon.

Szulanski, G. (1996) 'Exploring internal stickiness: impediments to the transfer of best practice within the firm', *Strategic Management Journal*, 17 (Winter Special Issue): 27–43.

Turk, C. and Kirkman, J. (1989) *Effective Writing*, London: E & FN Spon.

Watson, G. (1987) *Writing a Thesis: a Guide to Long Essays and Dissertations*, London: Longman.

Glossary

A list of definitions of key ideas, terms and techniques, referenced to the page on which the definition first appears. The list deals largely with issues of methodology, and is useful at all stages of your project. It is particularly helpful if you care about the precision of the language you will use in your project report.

Academic rigour Procedures which ensure a scholarly approach to your findings. The more rigorous you are, the higher the grade you'll receive [222].

Alternative For the purposes of this book, a string of words which expresses a potential answer to a question [296], and see *item* and *response*.

Analytic framework a set of ideas used to make sense of a situation being studied, and provide guidelines on what needs to be attended to if the situation is to be understood. Examples are Maslow's Hierarchy, 'Trompenaars' seven dimensions of cultural difference, Porter's five Forces [120]

Area A broad field of scholarly endeavour an academic discipline, business function, or course title [33].

Aspect A more detailed facet of a Field, q.v., which provides you with the topic of your project [33].

Census The measurement of a complete population, rather than a sample; worth considering in in-company work [208].

Citation index A listing, by author, of everyone who has referred to that author's publications since they appeared. Very useful when you want to see what happened to an idea which you are reading about for your literature review [176].

Concept An abstract idea or general notion which forms a constituent of the taught content of the curriculum [6].

Conceptual analysis an account of the main ideas, relevant to your

dissertation, drawn from other people's work, which compares, contrasts, and builds an argument stating what you must do to answer your research question. Drawing on pre-existing analytic frameworks *(q.v)* or providing its own, it is what makes the difference between a merely descriptive literature review and an argument which states a case *c.f.* evidence and argument [120].

Construct A particular way in which an individual expresses the meaning he or she intends [336].

Constructivism a form of interpretivism *(q.v.)* which asserts that knowledge is developed by active construction and invention rather than (as in the case of positivism, *q.v.*), through discovery [116].

Content analysis A technique used to categorize the answers to open-ended questions, so that the meanings expressed in the data can be classified, coded, and tabulated [229].

Controlled variables The variables which would get in the way of a causal explanation of the relationship between independent and dependent variable, and whose effects you try to eliminate. The impossibility of doing so without distorting what you are doing is frequently the reason for avoiding experimental methods in project work [238].

Core texts books and articles which are central to the field in which you are doing your research. You know that your literature review is progressing when you find yourself becoming confident that you know the main ones in and around your topic [173].

Critical analysis The approach you use in order to convince the reader of your dissertation, consisting of conceptual analysis *(q.v.)* and evidence and argument *(q.v.)* [120].

Data Specific findings and results, which may or may not be meaningful [177] *c.f. information.*

Dependent variable The variable which forms the focus of your observations, and which you hope will express the effects of your activity in manipulating the independent variable, *q.v.* [238].

Design A particular approach to the collection of data, which combines validity of findings with economy of effort [196]. For example, examining contrasting modes of operation [200]; time-sampling [200]; Before-After [200].

Effectiveness Has to do with constraints on the applicability of technically acceptable recommendations [40].

Efficiency Has to do with technical possibility and feasibility [40].

Empathizer A role in project work in which you offer your services as a sympathetic problem-solver [145].

Empirical data The result of new observations, made in order to check out your assertions [109].

Epistemology The study of what counts as knowledge, and of what you need to do to prove something [109].

Evidence and argument An account of the main findings from your own empirical work. Following the rules provided by the particular research *method (q.v.)* adopted, it turns a set of data into information which is used, together with the *conceptual analysis (q.v.),* to state your case. [122].

Experiment An arrangement for testing a hypothesis in terms of the association, or the causal relationship, between two or more variables, in which the influence of extraneous variables is controlled [112].

Expert A role in project work in which you utilize coercive power arising from

your specialist knowledge or techniques [144].

Facilitation Posing a series of questions which stimulate, maintain, and direct the flow of discussion in a focus group [284].

Field A component of an Area *q.v.*, being a sub-discipline, theme within a business function, or some issue dealt with by a course [33].

Field experiment Also known as a 'natural experiment' or 'found experiment', being a situation in which events occur in such a way that at least two levels of an independent variable happen to be available, and an appropriate dependent variable suggests itself [238].

Flash-card A card on which the alternative answers to a question in a fully structured questionnaire are printed, to assist the respondent in remembering the options available to him or her [323].

Fully structured technique A technique in which the content and sequence of questions, and the form of answers, have been determined in advance *c.f. semi-structured technique* [295].

Generality One of the attributes of a good research question is when it has relevance beyond the situation and setting in which the date that addresses the question is collected [56].

Grounded theory not a theory as such, but a process of analytic induction by which beliefs are generated from the ground up using an *interpretivist (q.v.)* approach, for eventual testing by *hypothetico-deductive (q.v.)* procedures [121].

Hermeneutic technique One way of determining the meaning and significance of an utterance, written statement, or event by interpreting the symbols in which these are expressed. Depends crucially on the understanding of the context, and plausible to the extent that consistency with an appropriate conceptual background, and triangulation with other techniques, are explicitly demonstrated [227].

Hypothesis The formal statement of a deduction that if a theory is true, then a relationship can be found between at least two variables [111].

Hypothetico-deductive method A set of procedures in which a hypothesis is deduced from a theory and expressed in terms of a relationship between one or more variables, each operationally defined. Measurements are made in order to test the hypothesis and verify the theory [111].

Illustrative quotation An attractive and interesting way of stating and substantiating your main findings, requiring careful presentation [275]; *c.f. narrative account* and *tabular presentation*.

Independent variable The variable you regard as possibly the cause of the effect being observed, and which you set out to control directly; in project work, this is rarely possible without distorting data or information [238].

Information Data expressed in such a way that they remove uncertainty and create meaning [177]; *c.f., data*.

Interpretivism A somewhat loose term standing for several more specific ones (such as phenomenology, constructivism, constructionism) all of which share the assumption that knowledge is the result of people's attempts to make sense of what is going on around them, and that this is an active process far removed from the supposed neutrality asserted by positivist approaches (*q.v.*) [116].

Item For the purposes of this book, a string of words by which you elicit data from a respondent [296] and see *alternative* and *response*.

Key terms or keywords. Word and short phrases which describe important issues or themes mentioned in a journal article, normally listed just after the abstract, and used in literature searching [173].

Measurement The making of observations using standard units and/or a standard scheme [111].

Mentor Someone who's already completed the level of course which you're studying, and done a project as part of it [30].

Method A systematic and orderly approach towards the collection of data so that information can be obtained from those data [220]; *c.f., technique*.

Methodology The analysis of, and rationale for, the particular method used in a project [224].

Narrative account A very common way of presenting the findings of business/management projects, by blending empirical information with reasoned argument in connected prose; the key to success is the quality of the reasoning [274]; compare with *tabular presentation* and *illustrative quotation*, *q.v.*

Negative case analysis An inductive technique used to guide data-collection in a way that continually adjusts the explanation supported by those data until the explanation admits of no exceptions and can be accepted as plausible [274].

Negotiator A role in project work in which you handle the task of problem definition and resolution in cooperation with the people you're studying. More likely to be successful than either the expert or the empathizer roles [145].

Non-parametric test A statistical test for all numeric data in which few assumptions are made about the shape of the distribution, or the equality of variance, of the data themselves [Table 9.5, 242].

Non-probability sampling A variety of techniques for drawing a sample in such a way that findings will require inference, judgement and interpretation before being applied to the population; often the only, or most sensible, thing to do in the circumstances [202].

Novelty One of the attributes of a good research question is that it is original, likely to produce new findings, ideas, or techniques [56].

Ontology The study of the nature of being or, in more immediate terms, of what counts as an event worth noticing [109].

Ontological position Your stance about

that part of reality which is involved in your particular investigation. Is this a 'people' issue or a 'management' issue? Is it about efficiency or effectiveness?; is it about 'the bottom line' or is it about the values that underlie corporate social responsibility? [106].

Open-ended technique A technique in which respondents are asked to answer your questions in their own words [257].

Operational definition A careful statement of what you need to measure in order to observe two variables varying [111].

Operational description A description of an observable event, particularly useful in labelling the different positions on a rating scale [346].

Parametric test A statistical test, strictly speaking only for interval and ratio numeric data, in which the distribution is assumed to be normal and the variance of data equal; in survey practice, ratings can sometimes be treated as having interval data properties, but rankings, being ordinal data, shouldn't [Table 9.5, 242].

Paraphrase a note which reproduces an argument in about the same length while reflecting your own emphases and expression (most usefully cast in a form which links the material to other ideas which you plan to use) [94].

Phenomenological An adjective applied to a non-positivist approach to the study of people, at work and elsewhere an appropriate alternative to positivist approaches for most in-company projects; used similarly to 'interpretivist' and 'constructivist', q.v. [116].

Pilot work An essential stage of work, during which you identify and resolve doubts about the content, structure, and design of the questions you intend to ask your respondents, by conducting a trial on a small subgroup [250].

Plagiarism 'Copying' from someone else's work; a crime which, if intentional and proven, is terminal [56].

Population A complete set of people, occurrences or objects from which a sample will be drawn [202].

Positivism The philosophical assumptions which underlie hypothetico-deductive method, which assert that this method is the only rational way of knowing things; that the purpose of theory is application; that truth can always be distinguished from untruth; and that truth can be discerned either by deduction or by empirical support and by no other means. Highly misleading when taken as a model for all in-company project work, though it may apply to some [110] c.f., interpretivism.

Précis a note which summarizes an argument in briefer form while staying faithful to the source's assumptions and mode of expression [94].

Primary data Data that you have collected yourself [59]; see also secondary data.

Probability sampling A variety of techniques which attempt to ensure that a sample is representative of the population in such a way that findings can be directly generalized to the population [202].

Projective technique An elicitation technique used in semi-structured interviewing (particularly in market research) in which the answer to an apparently unrelated and neutral question is interpreted as indicative of the respondent's feelings or motives. To be used with caution [268].

Provenance Origin and background. In the context of a dissertation, a table showing on which Areas (q.v.), Fields (q.v.) and Aspects (q.v.) a given topic relies. A very useful technique for identifying the various concepts, ideas, techniques and authors on which your topic will be drawing [32].

Psychological significance In contrast to statistical significance, a statement of the confidence with which you are prepared to accept that a set of results are meaningful and relevant; a property of the design (q.v.) of your investigation [313].

Qualitative analysis A set of techniques which takes people's experiences and their verbal expression seriously, while checking their value, meaningfulness and applicability when generalizing conclusions [274].

Quantitative analysis A set of techniques in which the frequency of occurrence of responses is counted. Very powerful when applicable, the results need cross-checking, and are often the result of the ease, rather than relevance, with which the chosen technique has been applied [224].

Rational thinking An endeavour in which the rules of logic and common-sense apply [110].

Reading questions a set of questions which you should tackle and answer for yourself before you begin reading a journal article or a book. This enables you to read in a structured and purposeful way. The questions are listed in [178].

Reliability of measurement The precision of measurement, such that the same result would be obtained on re-measurement assuming the situation had not changed. Takes priority over *validity*, q.v., since it sets limits to validity as assessed [111].

Research question The precise question that you ask in doing your research, as distinct from the general idea you first had about what you wanted to study. The research question determines your research *design*, q.v. [38].

Response For the purposes of this book, the utterance or action a respondent makes to indicate his/her views in reply to a question [296] and see *item* and *alternative*.

Response rate the proportion of the sample who actually return your questionnaires or agree to be interviewed. This is always smaller than the intended sample size [210].

Role A set of expectations of the behaviour felt to be appropriate for a person in any social position (e.g. 'researcher'; 'investigator'; 'competitor'; 'supplicant'). How you understand people's expectations and how you perform the role will make a difference to your success [131].

Sample A set of people, occurrences or objects chosen from a larger population

in order to represent that population to a greater or lesser extent [202].

Sampling frame A list, often divided into subgroups, of a population, used in order to draw a sample and to keep track of its representativeness [202].

Secondary data Data you use to support the argument in your dissertation, which have been gathered by someone other than yourself [59]; and see also *primary data*.

Semi-structured technique A technique in which the content and sequence of questions is not fully specified in advance [257].

Sponsor the organization on whose premises you are carrying out your research; a senior manager from within that organization (sometimes your own line manager) who has a special interest in supporting your project [10].

Stakeholder analysis A description of the people to whom particular issues matter, together with the reasons, both personal and systemic, for why they matter. Very useful as a technique in case study method [233].

Statistical significance A statement of the confidence with which you are prepared to accept that the results in a sample reflect the realities in a population. Offering exact precision of your chances of making a mistake, but not necessarily the same as psychological significance *q.v.* [313].

Synopsis a note which summarizes briefly, but in your own words; needs substantial reworking and expansion before using the material in your project document [94].

Tabular presentation A common way of presenting survey results, in which tables of frequencies and proportions of answers to your questions are accompanied by verbal statements of the information contained in each table [318]; *c.f., narrative account* and *illustrative quotation*.

Taxonomy A classification scheme. A simple one is used in Section 2.3 to help clarify your thinking about your research topic [32].

Technique A step-by-step procedure for

doing something. Used in a specialist sense in Chapter 9, where the procedure relates to the gathering and analysis of data [6].

Testing Drawing conclusions about a hypothesis [111].

Theory Generally, a belief expressed in words or through action. In hypothetico-deductive method, a formally expressed general statement which has the potential to explain things [111].

Triangulation The use of one method or technique to cross-check the results of another. Very useful in all cases, and essential in qualitative work [225].

Validity of measurement The accuracy of measurement, such that the process or event you intended to measure, is indeed properly measured [111].

Verification The drawing of implications from empirical conclusions to theory [111].

Subject index

References to tables are in bold.

Index of first-named authors